Liberty for All

Liberty for All

Reclaiming Individual
Privacy in a New Era
of Public Morality

Elizabeth Price Foley

Yale University Press

New Haven and London

Published with assistance from the Mary Cady Tew Memorial Fund.

Set in Adobe Garamond by The Composing Room of Michigan, Inc.
Printed in the United States of America.

Library of Congress Cataloging-in-Publication Data

Foley, Elizabeth Price.
    Liberty for all : reclaiming individual privacy in a new era of public morality /
Elizabeth Price Foley.
       p.   cm.
    Includes bibliographical references and index.
    ISBN-13: 978-0-300-10983-2 (cloth : alk. paper)
    ISBN-10: 0-300-10983-0 (cloth : alk. paper)
    1. Privacy, Right of—United States.   2. Constitutional law—United States.
3. Law and ethics. I. Title.
KF1262.F65 2006
342.7308′58—dc22

                                          2006010502

A catalogue record for this book is available from the British Library.

The paper in this book meets the guidelines for permanence and durability of the Committee on Production Guidelines for Book Longevity of the Council on Library Resources.

10 9 8 7 6 5 4 3 2 1

With love and appreciation to my mother, Diana McKinnon Price,
and the fond memory of my father, Edgar Jack Price III (1928–2004)

O! liberty—thou greatest good—thou fairest property—
with thee I wish to live—with thee I wish to die!
Pardon me if I drop a tear on the peril to which she is exposed:
I cannot, sir, see these brightest of jewels tarnished!
A jewel worth ten thousand worlds!
And shall we part with it so soon? O! no.
—*Samuel Nason, Speech Before the Massachusetts
Ratifying Convention, Feb. 1, 1788*

Contents

Preface

The constitution and laws of a State are rarely attacked from the front; it is against secret and gradual attacks that a Nation must chiefly guard. Sudden resolutions strike men's imaginations; their history is written, and their secret sources made known; but changes are overlooked when they come about insensibly by a series of steps which are scarcely noted. One would do a great service to Nations by showing from history how many States have thus changed their whole nature and lost their original constitution.
—*Emmerich de Vattel,* The Law of Nations or the Principles of Natural Law, 1758

I began thinking about this book more than a decade ago, after I had begun the intellectual journey into the realm of constitutional law under the tutelage of one of my favorite law professors, Jerry Phillips (who sadly passed away while I was writing this book). I remember sitting in Professor Phillips's classroom, being both alarmed and amazed by inconsistencies between the text of the Constitution and its interpretation by the U.S. Supreme Court. Although I had always considered myself politically liberal (having served several years on Capitol Hill as health policy advisor to two decidedly left-leaning Democrats) and supportive of most aspects of the modern liberal welfare state, I harbored a seed of originalism, in the sense that I believed that the words of the Constitution and the meaning ascribed to those words by the Framers provided the guideposts to legitimate constitutional interpretation and could not be undone by causes du jour.

My originalist position solidified in the ensuing years, through a clerkship with Judge Carolyn King on the U.S. Court of Appeals for the Fifth Circuit, an LL.M. at Harvard Law School, and as a professor of law. With new knowledge came fresh insights—and I did not like what I saw. The Supreme Court's case law was drifting further from the original constitutional design: from the history and purpose of the Constitution and Bill of Rights. Although I can understand the pragmatic and political considerations that have driven the Court's departures from text and original meaning—including the notion that it's "too late to go back now"—I have not accepted that these considerations should trump, allowing the Constitution to be effectively amended *sub silentio.*

One of the most ironic things about the Court's interpretive trajectory is that it is so often employed in the name of liberalism and hailed by self-confessed liberals as normatively desirable. The phenomenon of amendment-through-interpretation undercuts the necessity for vigorous public political involvement, allowing "we the people" to sit passively and eat our chicken nuggets while other, more zealous ideologues discuss and debate the issues of the day. If the Supreme Court can simply "amend" the Constitution through its decisions, the people need not be politically engaged—no doubt a welcome relief to many overburdened Americans.

The problem with this course is that American government is no longer functioning as it was designed to function. If there is a problem with the Constitution—in the sense that it will not allow us to reach the results the people want—the modern response is to let the Supreme Court fix it; no need to resort to the cumbersome super-majoritarian amendment processes of Article V. We the people do not need to get involved; we can let the pros handle the dirty work of advocating our interests before the Supreme Court, and we can trust the Supreme Court to get it right.

This court-induced popular political lethargy is obviously not a good way to run a republican railroad, so to speak. In order to fulfill its potential, representative democracy requires constant interest, knowledge, and activism by ordinary people, not just hired-gun lobbyists and zealous members of special interest groups. As Thomas Jefferson put it back in 1787, "Lethargy [is] the forerunner of death to the public liberty."

Many liberals seem to have concluded that amendment-through-interpretation is a net societal good, since it has generally allowed desired changes to occur. For example, the Court's infamous "switch in time that saved nine" during the New Deal is hailed by liberals as a positive transformative moment because the Court's interpretive turnabout permitted various legislative acts—presumably endorsed by the citizenry—to go into effect. The important thing, to the liberals, is that the Court reached the right results, even if the analytical path by which those results were reached is fraught with intellectual thorns that are hazardous, in the long term, to both the legitimacy of the written constitution and the preservation of individual liberty itself. Liberal endorsement of amendment-through-interpretation implicitly has legitimated the idea that ends, not means, matter most. Liberals often claim that their theory of malleability is merely subscribing to the philosophy of a "living Constitution," which sounds wonderful when contrasted to the theoretical opposite—until one realizes that, in its hard liberal form, a living Constitution means one whose most important constitutional provisions rest on a foundation of sand.

Let me be clear: I believe constitutional interpretation should focus on text and its original meaning. But many words in the Constitution are sufficiently broad that their interpretation by succeeding generations can grow and adapt to new understandings and technology. In this sense, the Constitution is (and was intended to be) a living document, setting forth foundational principles, alterable only by the super-majoritarian process of Article V, but often employing language broad enough to allow these principles to meet the changing needs of society.

The necessary focus on contemporary issues, nevertheless, should not provide carte blanche to ignore the Constitution and its foundational principles. The Framers have given us wonderful words and principles that cannot be ignored or wished away. With this understanding of originalism in mind, I would agree with Thomas Jefferson's bifurcation of fixed principles versus evolving manners and notions: "Time indeed changes manners and notions, and so far we must expect institutions to bend to them. But time produces also corruption of principles, and against this it is the duty of good citizens to be ever on the watch, and if the gangrene is to prevail at last, let the day be kept off as long as possible."

If liberals may ignore inconvenient constitutional text and its meaning then ipso facto the conservatives may do the same when given the chance. Indeed, conservatives have done so on many occasions, ignoring key constitutional language protective of individual liberty when it has been convenient to do so.

While conservatives more often pay lip service to the importance of constitutional text and original intent than do their liberal counterparts, they, too, are guilty of adopting the win-at-all-costs approach to constitutional interpretation: start with the answer and work backwards, eruditely rationalizing the desired outcome, even if it is at odds with the text and its original meaning. They try to cover their ideological bias in the wrapping of judicial restraint, asserting that activist judges should not second-guess the will of the legislatures, even though the text and meaning of the Constitution suggests that the Framers did not intend to adopt the British system of Parliamentary supremacy. Instead, as this book will demonstrate, the Framers envisioned a blended system of majoritarian rule within certain limited boundaries.

The radical conservative's disdain for the most important liberty-protecting language of the Constitution is both obvious and sad. Underneath the emotionally charged rhetoric about activist judges inventing rights is an undeniable and deep-seated paternalism, a sense of superiority, and a dislike and distrust of others who do not think and act the same way. There is, in short, a desire to control society, shape it in a conventional mold, and stamp out individuality (and hence, equality and diversity), not through education and persuasion, but through coercion.

The loser in this ideological game is the American people, whose immunities against government—in other words, their liberty—have been stolen away in gradual degrees. The silent majority passively looks on, failing to push any particular ideological agenda of their own. These quiet Americans deeply respect the principles of individualism, diversity, and equality upon which this country was founded and believe that the law and its interpretation should further these principles in an objective, unbiased manner. But there is a high price to pay for silence and inaction, as American constitutional law has become one of the primary weapons in the battle for ideological domination from both the far left and far right. The old adage "live and let live"—and thus the morality of American law—has been lost, resulting in harm to all.

The problem, of course, is that radical ideology sells. It is much sexier to be an ideologue than an idealist. Stridently pushing a political ideology can propel adherents into the spotlight and reward them with our attention. Yet few would dispute that this law-is-politics ideology is driving Americans farther apart rather than bringing them closer together. As American society becomes increasingly diverse, this drive for ideological domination in law will fuel the flames of division.

This book is for the idealist, not the ideologue. Although the thesis presented will undoubtedly require that Americans swallow a strong dose of toleration—a bitter medicine in some instances—it is a medicine I believe the Framers intended us to take so that America, a melting pot of society, could live up to its potential. I will argue that there is a morality of American law, embodied in the Constitution, that transcends ideology—indeed, was designed by the Framers for that very purpose: to protect individual liberty (the highest expression of equality) and promote social harmony. So if anyone asks, "What is the relationship of morality to law in the United States?" I hope future generations will answer, "American law is based on a secular morality designed to maximize individual liberty."

I am aware that, in many respects, this book may raise more questions than it answers. No book offering a comprehensive theory of American law can answer all of the intriguing questions that will inevitably arise upon careful examination. Nonetheless, I will consider the book a success if it generates additional questions that, in turn, stimulate refinements to our understanding of and appreciation for individual liberty within a constitutional regime of government.

I also am aware that the position this book espouses is bound to be controversial, to segments of both the ideological right and left. But I wanted to explore the pragmatic implications of a constitutional theory grounded in original meaning—a starting point that, as an originalist, I find normatively desirable and wholly plausible. What would the world look like, in other words, if we adhered to the Framers' understanding of government? I realize that many other theories of American constitutional law have numerous passionate votaries. My point here is not to debate these theorists by spending countless pages comparing and contrasting my theory with theirs. Rather, I hope to offer an alternative theory of constitutional law that will resonate with most Americans and end the political rancor that is stifling our country.

I suppose it would be correct to say that I have developed libertarian leanings in the context of constitutional theory, but only because, after extensive study of American constitutional law and history, I have concluded that "liberty for all" was meant to be the pre-eminent value underlying American law. If this is deemed ideological (undoubtedly it will by those who think that all constitutional theory is inherently ideological), it at least has the distinct advantage, over liberalism or conservatism, of being truly tolerant of all points of view— something I think America needs more of these days.

Acknowledgments

This book is the end product of many presentations and writings in the field of constitutional law. Portions of Chapters 6 (Reproduction) and 7 (Medical Liberty) are loosely based on prior articles that appeared in the *Arizona Law Review* and the *Albany Law Review,* and I am grateful for those journals' permission to reproduce.

I am eternally grateful to my editor, Michael O'Malley, who adroitly shepherded me through the process of publishing my first book. Sincere thanks are also owed to a corps of energetic research assistants, including Alex Alvarez, Sheila Janati, Brenda Kuhns, and Peter Wizenberg, as well as the ideas, comments, and suggestions of Tom Baker, Randy Barnett, Brannon Denning, Michael Lawrence, Matthew Mirow, Glenn Reynolds, and Howard Wasserman. Thanks also to Dean Leonard Strickman, who provided institutional support that helped make this book possible.

I am particularly indebted to Randy Barnett, whose ground-breaking work on the Ninth Amendment inspired me in law school. His recent books, *The Structure of Liberty: Justice and the Rule of Law* (2000) and *Restoring the Lost Constitution: The Presumption of Liberty* (2003), have begun a substantial new movement in originalist constitutional scholarship to which I hope this book is an important contribution. Special appreciation is also owed to Dean Evan Caminker, library Director Margaret Leary, IT Director Rosa Peters, and librarian Sandra Zeff of the University of Michigan Law School, for extending various important professional courtesies to me while I was researching this book during the past several summers.

Last but not least, I am grateful for the love and support of my husband, Patrick Foley, who was endowed by the Creator with a keen editorial eye and unusual dose of patience, and my little one, Kathleen Elizabeth Glee Foley, who reminds me to laugh and look at butterflies.

Chapter 1 Introduction:

A Nation of Laws, Not Men

Our peculiar security is in the possession of a written Constitution. Let us
not make it a blank paper by construction.
—*Letter from Thomas Jefferson to Wilson Nicholas, 1803*

A middle-aged, married father of two is diagnosed with testicular cancer. The cancer spreads through his body, inflicting intense pain. He
undergoes radiation and chemotherapy, which causes severe nausea
and appetite loss. Numerous prescriptions prove ineffective or produce intolerable side effects. As a last-ditch effort, the man smokes
marijuana and finds that it relieves his pain and stimulates his appetite. He begins cultivating marijuana at his home for medical use.
Federal officers seize the marijuana and arrest him for drug possession.
Although the state where the man lives allows the use of marijuana for
medical purposes, the federal government considers it a felony. If convicted, he faces many years in prison and the loss of his rights to vote
and possess a gun.

An American meets the love of her life while vacationing in Ireland.
She returns to the United States and her new love follows her, obtain-

ing a temporary work visa. When the work visa expires, the couple decides that they would like to marry, which would enable them to stay together in the United States. Unfortunately, they live in a state that has enacted a state constitutional amendment prohibiting same-sex marriage. If they are to remain together, they must leave the United States.

In situations such as these, which should trump: individual privacy or public morality? Should an individual be at liberty to act in a manner that does not harm[1] others, even if doing so is offensive to many? May the public, acting through its elected representatives, enact laws restricting individual liberty, based solely on the majority's belief that the act is offensive or immoral? In this book, I will attempt to answer these questions.

Specifically, I will document and discuss the significance of two foundational principles embodied in the U.S. Constitution: limited government and residual individual sovereignty. I will explore how these twin foundational presumptions evince a morality of American law itself, a set of higher values by which to gauge the legitimacy of ordinary laws.[2] Subordinate to the Constitution are ordinary laws, enacted by a legislative majority, that tell citizens what specific actions are punishable. These ordinary laws often reflect "public morality"—i.e., the passions, prejudices, and moral beliefs of a portion of the citizenry. But are they legitimate exercises of governmental power? Should we restrain our neighbor's liberty because she engages in an activity we consider icky, gross, or just plain wrong? This book will argue that the answer is no because public morality–based laws are immoral exercises of governmental power, inconsistent with the morality of American law.

Unfortunately, popular understanding of and appreciation for the morality of American law has vanished into thin air. There is a pervasive popular amnesia regarding the twin foundational constitutional principles of limited government and residual individual sovereignty.[3] Indeed, modern constitutional jurisprudence turns the original constitutional structure on its head, placing the burden on citizens to convince the courts that laws restricting liberty are "irrational"—a heavy burden indeed—rather than requiring the government to articulate the need for restricting individual liberty.[4]

Narrow judicial interpretation of several important liberty-protecting constitutional phrases combined with a steadily expanding interpretation of government powers has fundamentally altered the original Constitution sub silentio.[5] Even the Supreme Court's acknowledgment in 1965 of a "right to privacy"[6] is mischievously narrow, suggesting that citizens have a right only to engage in certain activities in private places. The so-called right to privacy is thereby confined behind closed doors, protecting only a small subset of individual liberty.

The American public has embraced the right to privacy as the source of its most precious liberties, yet most are unaware that employing the shibboleth "privacy" instead of "liberty" inherently narrows individual rights rather than expands them. I will therefore use the more apt word "liberty" to describe the right of individuals to act without illegitimate governmental restraint.

The slow, steady, and silent subversion of the Constitution has been a revolution that Americans appear to have slept through, unaware that the blessings of liberty bestowed upon them by the founding generation were being eroded. Over-burdened Americans with inadequate knowledge of constitutional history have been unable to gauge how far their governments have drifted from the original design. The result of the silent constitutional revolution is a labyrinth of laws regulating virtually every aspect of behavior, limiting what citizens can say, read, see, consume, and do.[7]

One need only peruse the 36,000-plus pages of the United States Code, the corresponding 210-plus volumes of the Code of Federal Regulations, the over 75,000 pages of the Federal Register, and the innumerable pages of informal agency opinions and guidance documents to appreciate the magnitude of the problem and reach of the law. Federal laws, of course, are merely the tip of the legal iceberg. Hundreds of thousands of pages of state and local laws and regulations, the minutiae of which is mind-boggling, restrict individual liberty under pain of fine or imprisonment. There are current laws prohibiting the wearing of hats in public places such as theaters or courtrooms; catching fish with one's bare hands or from a bridge; carrying a slingshot; selling or possessing dyed baby chicks or rabbits; using "indecent" language on the phone or in a park; displaying a deformed animal; spitting on the sidewalk; teaching others about polygamy; having a garage sale for more than two days a year; fortune telling; keeping more than two cats in a yard; serving alcohol within one mile of a religious camp meeting; being drunk in your own house if it annoys others; or working, playing cards, or buying merchandise on Sunday.[8]

In addition to the cornucopia of picayune laws, there are larger, more substantial intrusions on individual liberty. A shocking number of laws restrict basic personal decisions such as whom one may marry; whether, with whom, and in what manner one may have sex; whether and with whom one may cohabit; whether one may read or view sexually explicit materials; whether or when one may avoid or terminate pregnancy; what types of medical care and providers one may access; whether and under what circumstances one may refuse medical treatment; and whether, how, or to what extent one may become intoxicated.

As the breadth and complexity of law grows, individual liberty declines. The loss of liberty is a direct result of the uncontrolled power of the majority, acting through its legislative representatives. Legislators win or lose elections based on their perceived receptivity to the majority's desires, with the result that legislatures are in a constant state of activity, enacting, repealing, and refining laws.

The exponential growth of laws is an ineluctable by-product of disregarding the morality of American law. Growing legislative power and its inherent exercise in the name of majoritarian whims have slowly eroded the principles of limited government and residual individual sovereignty and created the very omnipotent government the founding generation spilled its blood to resist. The net result is that America has become a nation of too many laws, virtually unchecked by judicial oversight, with precious few pockets of individual liberty. Although the founding generation certainly envisioned that the United States would become a "nation of laws, not men,"[9] this laudable goal has been taken much too far. We have, unfortunately, become a nation of "laws, not liberty."[10]

The amnesia regarding the morality of American law and the resulting growth of law itself has created an intractable conflict between public morality and individual privacy. This conflict is increasingly evident in litigation involving issues such as abortion, same-sex marriage, assisted suicide, and medical marijuana. Exit polling from the 2004 presidential election confirms the importance of the conflict in the minds of many Americans: voters reported "moral values" as the most important issue on their minds, surpassing the economy, terrorism, the war in Iraq, health care, taxes, and education.[11]

Although it is difficult to discern exactly what these voters had in mind when they expressed concern about "moral values," it seems fair to say that they feel America is experiencing a general moral decline. The perceived attack on moral values is unrelenting and ubiquitous, emanating from music, video games, television, and movies that glorify violence, flaunt sexuality, and shun courtesy and respect for authority, as well as from a plethora of social changes that challenge traditional understandings of right and wrong. Many Americans feel powerless to protect themselves or their children from these socio-demographic changes or from the insidious influence of a pop culture run amok.[12]

The tendency of human beings, when they feel their values are besieged, is to fight back using all of their available power—in America, influence with elected representatives—to prohibit the activities they deem morally objectionable. In this environment, judicial decisions in favor of individual liberty over public morality prove particularly controversial. They appear to add insult to injury, exacerbating the decline of moral values and providing legal sanctuary to activities many Americans consider distasteful and deeply offensive.[13] Indeed, recent polls indicate that a large majority of Americans blame the current state of moral decline on the judiciary, agreeing with the statement, "Judicial activism . . . seems to have reached a crisis. Judges routinely overrule the will of the people, invent new rights, and ignore traditional morality."[14]

In the present social and political environment, it is difficult for anyone—judge, scholar, or neighbor—to advocate for more, rather than less, liberty. In the passion of the moment, it is difficult to stop and consider whether, in the long run, the cure being proposed is worse than the disease. If the cure requires a modification or temporary suspension of constitutional values, so be it. The ends justify the means.

But even Americans who are deeply concerned about moral values should take a deep breath before demanding that government stamp out morally offensive activity. Americans routinely decry the perceived intolerance of other societies—radical segments of Islam, for example—yet they rarely stop to consider whether their own zeal to legislatively coerce moral values is the same ugly beast wrapped in an American flag. American history is replete with tragic examples of legislatively enforced intolerance fueled by majoritarian passion or frustration. Witch hunts, Jim Crow laws, Prohibition, Japanese internment, and McCarthyism were all driven by deeply felt fears about people and activities perceived as dangerous to the public's moral values. We must restrain the liberty of morally deficient individuals, the argument goes, in order to prevent their pestilence from spreading throughout society.

The current judicial response to public morality–based laws is to presume them constitutional. The American judiciary has erected a stilted and apologetic approach to judicial review, throwing its hands up and declaring that the United States is a representative democracy wherein the "majority rules." If the legislature enacts a public morality–based law and there is no specific constitutional language prohibiting such a law, the only remedy for those restrained by the law lies with the political process.[15] Judges should not read too much, according to current orthodox theory, into constitutional language such as "due process," "privileges or immunities," or "[other] rights . . . retained by the people" because doing so will allow judges to sit as a super-legislature over the people and invalidate democratically enacted laws by an inherently undemocratic, appointed-for-life judiciary.[16] Citizens unhappy with public morality–

based laws should complain to their elected representatives and lobby for legislative (or constitutional) change. If individuals want to be able to marry another individual of the same sex, smoke pot, purchase sex toys, or keep more than two cats, they should simply plead their case to their elected officials and hope for the best.

The problem with this logic is that it presupposes far too much about the proper scope of legislative power under American law. It assumes that legislative power is plenary in the absence of some specifically enumerated limitation to the contrary rather than assuming the opposite—in other words, that citizens retain all power (sovereignty) unless they have expressly and specifically ceded their power to the government.

Presuming plenary legislative power in the absence of a specific limitation to the contrary literally turns the constitutional structure on its head, dishonoring both twin foundational principles of limited government and residual individual sovereignty. The orthodox "majority rules" position is utterly incompatible with the morality of American law. As Friedrich Hayek once put it, "If it is to survive, democracy must recognize that it is not the fountainhead of justice and that it needs to acknowledge a conception of justice which does not necessarily manifest itself in the popular view on every particular issue."[17] While the majority may indeed rule on many issues, there is a large sphere of residual individual sovereignty intentionally placed beyond its grasp.

In addition to these basic theoretical reasons for discarding current legal orthodoxy, there are pragmatic reasons to rethink it as well. A rigid reliance on the "majority rules" position exacerbates cultural tensions inherent in a heterogeneous society. Legislatively enacted preferences of the majority may appear heavy-handed, culturally insensitive, or motivated by prejudice, generating alienation between the affected minority and the majority. It should come as no surprise that over time, entrenchment of the majority rules philosophy has bred resentment against government. Americans from all walks of life, particularly racial and ethnic minorities and younger generations,[18] feel disenfranchised and disengaged from their own government.[19] As Professor Lani Guinier aptly observed, the consistent failure of representative democracy to grant an equal voice to members of a minority group makes them feel like perpetual losers in a game they can never win, creating a "lack [of] incentive to respect laws passed by the majority over their opposition."[20]

Restoring the morality of American law would help strike the proper balance between public morality and individual privacy, which in turn would help reduce these societal ills. But restoring the morality of American law would require a sustained and conscious effort—a difficult task for a politically disengaged citizenry grown accustomed to monolithic government and voluminous liberty-disregarding laws.[21] Yet this sort of sustained effort to return to the foundational American legal principles of individuality, equality, and liberty is precisely what is needed in a heterogeneous society.

Recognizing and restoring the morality of American law would reduce the open hostility between public morality and individual privacy, provide an objective analytical structure for resolving such conflicts, and create more consistent results across cases. This, in turn, would enhance the legitimacy of government itself. If America is not yet lost, it does appear to be wandering aimlessly, ignoring the principles designed to keep us on track. If this country is to find itself again, this book suggests that we will need to take out our Constitution, dust if off, and regain proper respect for the morality of American law that it reveals.[22]

Chapter 2 The Morality
of American Law

We hold these Truths to be self-evident, that all Men are created equal,
that they are endowed by their Creator with certain inalienable Rights,
that among these are Life, Liberty, and the Pursuit of Happiness—That to
secure these Rights, Governments are instituted among Men, deriving
their just Powers from the Consent of the Governed. . . .
—*Declaration of Independence*

There is a morality underlying American law itself that is designed to
minimize conflicts between individual privacy and public morality. If
we want to strike a balance between these competing forces, we must
disinter the structure of this morality. This chapter will examine the
Framers' understanding of the legitimate purpose of government
which, in turn, will illuminate their understanding of the legitimate
scope of governmental power. Once the proper boundaries of government power are identified, we can then discern what lies beyond those
boundaries—that is, the scope of individual liberty. If we can grasp
the original meaning of these two concepts—limited government and
residual individual liberty—we can understand the morality of American law.

FOUNDATIONAL PRINCIPLES: LIMITED GOVERNMENT AND RESIDUAL POPULAR SOVEREIGNTY

The American Revolution did not merely break the colonies' formal ties with Great Britain; it transformed the definition of government itself. Those who came to the New World rejected the British model of a *Leviathan*[1] government in which various "privileges" to exercise individual liberty were forcibly extracted from an omnipotent monarch. In its place, they substituted a remarkable new model of government in which the people themselves were sovereign, relinquishing only those portions of their sovereignty as were necessary to effectuate the limited purposes of government, and retaining the great residuum for themselves. This radical new political philosophy was announced in the Constitution's Preamble: "We the People of the United States, in Order to form a more perfect Union, establish Justice, insure domestic Tranquility, provide for the common defence [sic], promote the general Welfare, and secure the Blessings of Liberty to ourselves and our Posterity, do ordain and establish this Constitution for the United States of America."[2] In these words, the people of the fledgling states joined together, proclaiming their belief that government existed for the people, not vice-versa, and that its purpose was to protect them from harm, make their lives more prosperous, and guard their liberty. Under this new view of government, individual liberty was no longer a privilege wrested from an all-powerful monarch but an inalienable human right.[3]

The newly formed federal government, however, was not the exclusive repository of this political philosophy. Numerous revolutionary-era state constitutions reflected it as well. The Maryland Constitution of 1776, for example, declared in its first article that "all government of right originates from the people, is founded in compact only, and instituted solely for the good of the whole."[4] The revolutionary constitutions of Delaware, Georgia, Massachusetts, New Jersey, New York, North Carolina, Pennsylvania, Vermont, and Virginia similarly proclaimed that sovereignty resided in the people themselves—a concept that became known as "popular" sovereignty.[5]

Popular sovereignty was not just a political phrase bandied about to mollify the masses. Although some Framers privately may have been less than enamored of the concept, it was nonetheless passionately professed to the American public and deeply embedded into the fiber of the Constitution. It was the primary tool by which the government could be kept within its limited boundaries and likewise ensured that a small group of wealthy aristocrats could not oppress the majority, as had historically occurred in Great Britain. To effectuate popular sovereignty, individuals were given the right to elect representatives who were empowered to enact laws.[6] In this sense, popular sovereignty is a collective concept: a majority of citizens (or, more accurately, a majority of those voting) would keep their representatives in line by wielding the power of the franchise.[7]

But popular sovereignty is not an unidimensional collective concept. It has a more subtle, but equally important, individual dimension. Constitutional scholars assume that the Framers viewed popular sovereignty as encompassing only a collective right of the majority to control government through elections.[8] This collective dimension of popular sovereignty, thought undoubtedly important, was but one side of the coin. Popular sovereignty was also understood to include the right of individuals to control their own lives, shape their own destinies, and experience liberty at its most personal level. This individual dimension of popular sovereignty was reflected in the enumeration of specific individual rights within the Constitution.

The trickling down of popular sovereignty to the individual level was essential to protect individual liberty from erosion. Threats to liberty could emanate just as easily from majoritarian passions and prejudices as elected representatives who ignored their constituents' desires. James Madison acknowledged the majoritarian threat to liberty in a letter to Thomas Jefferson in 1788: "Wherever the real power in Government lies, there is the danger of oppression. In our government the real power lies in the majority of the Community, and the invasion of private rights is chiefly to be apprehended, not from acts of Government contrary to the sense of its constituents, but from acts in which the Government is the mere instrument of the major number of the constituents. This is a truth of great importance, but not yet sufficiently attended to . . . ."[9]

Jefferson agreed with Madison that collective popular sovereignty was likely to prove oppressive to individual liberty if left unchecked: "Of liberty I would say that, in the whole plentitude of its extent, it is unobstructed action according to our will. But rightful liberty is unobstructed action according to our will within the limits drawn around us by the equal rights of others. I do not add 'within the limits of the law,' because law is often but the tyrant's will, and always so when it violates the rights of an individual."[10]

The Framers understood that republican government posed an inherent triple threat to individual liberty, each aspect of which necessitated a different constitutional response: (1) the possibility that elected representatives would ignore the desires of the majority; (2) the possibility that elected representatives would exceed the limits of defined governmental power; and (3) the possibility that the majority would enact laws that denied or disparaged inalienable individual rights. The first—ignoring constituents' desires—was controlled exclusively by collective popular sovereignty through the power to vote unresponsive officials out of office. The second threat—exceeding legitimate powers—also could be corrected by collective popular sovereignty, but it was feared that, over time, meaningful limits on governmental power would be gradually, perhaps imperceptibly, eroded.[11] If the citizenry became apathetic or forgetful regarding the limits on governmental power, the checking function served by elections would lose its effectiveness. Another check was needed, not only to help guard against the slow expansion of governmental power, but also to protect against the third threat to liberty—the innate majoritarian tendency to deny or disparage the rights of the minority. For this, neutral principles of individual liberty for all, unalterable by mere majorities, were needed.

It was the desire to deal with these threats to individual liberty that sparked the demand for a bill of rights. Federalists claimed that a bill of rights was unnecessary because the national government, being limited in its powers, lacked any legitimate authority to infringe upon individual rights.[12] Federalists accordingly argued that a bill of rights might prove antithetical to individual liberty, since the enumeration of some individual rights could imply that others did not exist.[13] The fear was that the enumeration of rights might be construed, over time, as establishing the only meaningful limits on government power when, in fact, the Framers intended the opposite: a government limited to specific purposes, surrounded by a large realm of residual individual sovereignty. The Federalists ultimately conceded the necessity of a bill of rights to assuage the concerns of the Anti-Federalists, who did not trust the national government to stay within its defined limits and feared that the judiciary would acquiesce to an expansion of governmental power by construing amorphous power-granting constitutional language broadly.[14]

The Bill of Rights thus erects a constitutional fence around governmental power by cordoning off areas of individual liberty that are immune from governmental intrusion. Although the Federalists and Anti-Federalists disagreed about the necessity of a bill of rights, they both agreed that there were limits to the legitimate exercise of governmental power and, ipso facto, zones of individual liberty beyond the reach of governmental power. Indeed, even ardent Federalist Alexander Hamilton acknowledged, in *Federalist No. 78,* the need for meaningful and enforceable limits on governmental power in order to protect individual liberty: "This independence of the judges is equally requisite to guard the Constitution and the rights of individuals from the effects of those ill humors [by]which the arts of designing men . . . occasion dangerous innovations in the government, and serious oppression of the minor party in the community. . . . [I]t is not to be inferred . . . that the representatives of the people, whenever a momentary inclination happens to lay hold of a majority of their constituents incompatible with the provisions in the existing Constitution, would, on that account, be justifiable [sic] in a violation of those provisions . . . . Until the people have, by some solemn and authoritative act, annulled or changed the established form, it is binding upon themselves collectively, as well as individually . . . . [N]o man can be sure that he may not be tomorrow the victim of a spirit of injustice, by which he may be a gainer today."[15]

The Anti-Federalists were even more insistent on protecting against majoritarian passions to protect residual individual rights. The Anti-Federalist writing as "A Maryland Farmer," for example, proclaimed, "If . . . there is no bill of rights in the United States—how can [a citizen] take advantage of a natural right founded in reason, could he plead it and produce Locke, Sydney, or Montesquieu as authority? . . . The truth is, that the rights of individuals are frequently opposed to the apparent interests of the majority—For this reason the greater the portion of political freedom in a form of government the greater the necessity of a bill of rights—often the natural rights of an individual are opposed to the presumed interests or heated passions of a large majority of [ ] democratic government; if these rights are not clearly and expressly ascertained, the individual must be lost. . . . [T]he tyranny of the legislative is most to be dreaded."[16]

The tyranny of the legislative branch was witnessed first-hand by American colonists, who were subjected to numerous acts of Parliament that were considered violative of individual liberty.[17] The Framers understood that all citizens may find themselves among the minority on some issue, necessitating meaningful, enforceable limits to ensure that exercises of collective popular sovereignty did not infringe upon the realm of residual individual rights. As Richard Henry Lee expressed it, "[T]he good people of the U. States in their late generous contest, contended for free government in the fullest, clearest, and strongest sense. They had no idea of being brought under despotic rule under the notion of 'Strong government,' or in the form of *elective despotism.* Chains being still Chains, whether made of gold or iron. The corrupting nature of power, and its insatiable appetite for increase, hath proved the necessity, and procured the adoption of the strongest and most express declarations of that *Residuum* of natural rights, which is not intended to be given up to

Society; and which indeed is not necessary to be given for any good social purpose."[18]

The oppressive power inherent in representative democracy was tempered by two distinct mechanisms: limited governmental power and explicit recognition of individual rights. The two concepts were complementary, providing a double security for the blessings of liberty. Even if the limits on government power were eventually eroded, there would still be legally enforceable protection for liberty through an express reservation of individual rights retained by the people.

The people's desire to retain a realm of individual sovereignty was memorialized in eight specific amendments (one through eight) and two residual amendments (nine and ten), each of which served as potent reminders of the twin foundations of American law, limited governmental power and residual individual sovereignty.

RESIDUAL INDIVIDUAL SOVEREIGNTY
UNDER STATE GOVERNMENTS

The normal starting point in any discussion of individual rights and their existence vis-à-vis the states is whether the federal Bill of Rights was made applicable to the states by enactment of the Fourteenth Amendment. I will postpone this standard incorporation inquiry for now, though I will address it later and explain why I think it cannot be avoided.

I prefer to postpone the incorporation debate because I believe it is based on an unfortunately myopic view of American law that compartmentalizes and separates federal law from state law. Although the United States is a federalist system in which there is meaningful delineation between the federal and state governments, it is often overlooked that the United States and the states comprising it were the product of the same ideas, the same political philosophy, and the same generation of founders. The Framers did not wear one philosophical hat when it came to their national government and another when it came to their state governments. Their view of government as a whole was shaped by their experience as colonists, their assessment of the strengths and weaknesses of British and other antecedent forms of government, and an animating desire to build a better mouse trap.

The Federalists and Anti-Federalists vehemently debated which powers properly belonged to the federal government and which properly belonged to the states, but it was a debate about precisely how to divide the governmental pie, not the parameters of the pie itself.[19] The Framers had a clear concept of the legitimate scope of government power in toto and the formation of a national government focused merely on which level of government—federal or state—should exercise these legitimate powers.

There is ample evidence that the founding generation embraced the concept of residual individual sovereignty—and hence, limited government—with equal vigor at both the state and federal levels. That the people in their capacity as state citizens still retained a large degree of individual sovereignty is evident in both the text and the meaning of the Ninth and Tenth Amendments.

The Ninth and Tenth Amendments

The Constitution conferred upon the federal government a very specific laundry list of powers. For example, congressional powers are neatly enumerated in Article I, section eight, giving Congress power to regulate commerce, borrow and coin money, establish uniform bankruptcy and naturalization laws, etc. Once the Constitution delineated the scope of the new federal government's powers, what powers were left to the states? This was a question of great concern to the states, who feared their powers would diminish through an expansive interpretation of federal powers combined with the force of the Supremacy Clause, which declares that the "Constitution, and Laws of the United States . . . shall be the supreme Law of the Land . . . any Thing in the Constitution or Laws of any State to the Contrary notwithstanding."[20]

To quell these fears, the Framers provided within the Bill of Rights two important constitutional bookmarks, ensuring both that states would continue to possess a realm of residual power and that individuals would enjoy a zone of immunity from the exercise of those powers, thus retaining residual rights. This is the message of the Ninth and Tenth Amendments. The Ninth Amendment declared, "The enumeration in the Constitution of certain rights shall not be construed to deny or disparage others retained by the people."[21] The Tenth Amendment declared, "The powers not delegated to the United States by the Constitution, nor prohibited by it to the States, are reserved to the States respectively, or to the people."[22] It is clear from the Ninth Amendment that the Framers understood that the citizens possessed a greater realm of individual sovereignty than could be specifically listed in the first eight amendments. It also is clear from the Tenth Amendment that the powers not granted to the United States were "reserved to the States" and that a subset of these residual powers were understood as reserved "to the people." Taking the Ninth and Tenth Amendments together, the following principles of American law emerge:

(1) the federal government's powers are limited to those enumerated in the constitutional text;

(2) if a power is not granted to the federal government, it is reserved to the states or to the people; and therefore

(3) there are necessarily certain rights reserved to the people that neither federal nor state government can take away.

The principal idea of American law at both the state and the federal level, therefore, is that the people are sovereign and that any powers not ceded to government (whether federal or state) remain in the possession of individual citizens.[23] There is thus a strong presumption in favor of individual liberty that may be rebutted if the government can establish a clearly defined power to act. The default position, in other words, is that "the claimant of governmental power must show title to it" and, if not, individual liberty prevails.[24]

The Legitimate Scope of Government Power

In order to ascertain the extent of residual individual sovereignty, it is necessary to examine the legitimate reach of governmental power. If we know how far government may legitimately reach, we will necessarily know what lies beyond its grasp.

If there is one thing that the terrorist attacks of 9/11 and the devastation of Hurricane Katrina have demonstrated, it is that the American people, of whatever political stripe, agree on one important thing about governmental power: it can and should be used to protect citizens from harm. Beyond this, Americans are deeply divided, particularly as to whether government may restrain individual liberty simply because its exercise offends public morality.

Agreement on the issue of using governmental power to protect us from harm is not surprising because it is deeply ingrained in the American political understanding. The dominant political philosophy of the founding generation recognized that the purpose of government is to protect and enhance the life, liberty, and property (LLP) of its citizens.[25] The historical record is replete with declarations by the Framers—Federalist and Anti-Federalist alike—that the purpose of government, whether federal or state, was to protect its citizens' LLP.[26]

This philosophy was not limited to the new federal government but applied to the states as well, as revealed in the words of James Madison, who recognized in *Federalist No. 45* that, in reserving certain unenumerated powers "to the States respectively, or to the people," the Tenth Amendment he authored inherently assumed that the residual powers of the states would extend to enhancing and protecting its citizens' LLP and no further: "The powers delegated by the proposed Constitution to the federal government are few and defined. Those which are to remain in the State governments are numerous and indefinite. The former will be exercised principally on external objects, as war, peace, negotiation and foreign commerce; with which last the power of taxation will, for the most part, be connected. *The powers reserved to the several States will extend to all the objects which, in the ordinary course of affairs, concern the lives, liberties and properties of the people, and the internal order, improvement and prosperity of the State.*"[27]

In this remarkable passage, Madison assumes that, though the states will have many more powers than those given to the federal government, their powers legitimately may be addressed only to the LLP of the citizenry, and only when such exercise of power will further or improve internal order or prosperity. Madison elaborated his philosophy further in 1792 when, writing in the widely circulated *National Gazette,* he declared, "In its larger and juster meaning, [property] embraces every thing to which a man may attach a value and have a right; and which leaves to every man the like advantage. . . . *Government is instituted to protect property of every sort; as well that which lies in the various rights of individuals, as that which the term particularly expresses. This being the end of government, that alone is a just government, which impartially secures to every man, whatever is his own.*"[28] Madison's essay broadly defines property to include individual liberty as well as tangible property,[29] and significantly asserts that government—of whatever kind—is legitimately formed to "protect property of every sort."

But the Framers' statements and the Tenth Amendment are not the only evidence that the legitimate purpose of government was to enhance and protect the LLP of citizens. Numerous state constitutions of the revolutionary era made explicit proclamations to this effect. The preamble to the Vermont constitution, for example, declared that "all government ought to be instituted and supported, for the security and protection of the community, as such, and to enable the individuals who compose it, to enjoy their natural rights. . . ." [30] It defined these "natural rights" that government was formed to protect as "enjoying and defending life and liberty; acquiring, possessing and protecting property, and pursuing and obtaining happiness and safety."[31] Similar declarations were made by the people in the constitutions of Delaware, Massachusetts, New York, Pennsylvania, and Virginia.[32] The depth and importance of this philosophy at the state level is reinforced by the statements of several states that, while ratifying the original Constitution, prefaced their ratification with language declaring that the purpose of *all* governments was to protect the LLP of their citizens.[33]

THE POLICE POWER

Prior to the ratification of the Constitution and Bill of Rights, the incipient American states struggled with defining the reach of their powers. There was a natural desire to differentiate themselves from the British model of plenary parliamentary power, yet there was not yet any model upon which to fashion the evolving and unique vision of limited government and residual individual sovereignty. Many early laws therefore not surprisingly seem to violate either or both of these principles, causing many legal scholars to conclude that these incipient American states did not genuinely embrace them.

But these early laws—adopted at a time when states were colonies of the British empire—are reflective of British norms in governing, not American. The American vision of government was sui generis, driven and sold to the American public by men well versed in Enlightenment political philosophy, and its ultimate realization—ratification of the Constitution and Bill of Rights—marked the first moment in time in which the foundational principles unique to American law could be tested.

And tested they have been. The foundational principles of American government—limited government and residual individual sovereignty—have been tested over and over again, and ultimately discarded and forgotten. Although these principles were embedded in the text of the Constitution itself—most notably evident in the Ninth and Tenth Amendments—they have proven both controversial and difficult to enforce. Why this is so is perhaps merely a reflection of human nature: those in power prefer to employ their power in a way that furthers their own political ends. The inherent human tendency—a tendency of which the Framers were well aware—is to expand power once held and to use it a way that is popular with the majority of one's constituents.[34] Given this nature, it should come as no surprise that the idealistic, perhaps even naive, foundational principles of limited government and residual individual sovereignty have never been fully realized at either the federal or the state level.

The idealistic political philosophy of American government applied not only to the newly created federal government, but also to the states, whose role had been reconceptualized within a federal constitutional framework. As discussed above, revolutionary-era state constitutions provided early glimpses of the new

American political philosophy, declaring that citizens ceded their natural sovereignty to government for the limited purpose of improving and protecting citizens' LLP. Despite these clear declarations, the residual power remaining with the states after ratification of the Constitution and Bill of Rights has been interpreted as plenary, as though the final phrase of the Tenth Amendment ("or to the people") or the entire text of the Ninth Amendment did not exist.

The vehicle for state assumption of plenary residual power has been the so-called police power. One of the fascinating aspects of the police power is that it did not really exist, as a distinct concept, until the mid-1800s at the earliest.[35] Since the phrase was coined, its basic meaning has slowly mutated, from a relatively limited concept of regulating rights and protecting citizens, to a virtually plenary legislative power over citizens.[36] Why this has happened is a complex story, worthy of a book of its own. For present purposes, suffice it to say that a variety of political, economic, and social forces have contributed to the broadened meaning of police power. My task here is not to explain, justify, or document those forces, but merely to show what the states' internal power of police most likely meant in the late 1700s, at the time of the ratification of the Constitution and Bill of Rights.[37]

The power of policing the internal affairs of a state inherently suggests that there is some need to get the police involved. And generally speaking, there is no need to summon the police unless an individual has harmed or is threatening harm to another (a topic that will be more elaborately discussed in the next chapter). This was the understanding of state power up until at least the mid-1800s.

If one parses the statements of prominent legal scholars, courts, and statesmen from the ratification of the early constitutions up until the mid-1800s, a general understanding of a state's power of internal police emerges: state governments may regulate any activity that harms or threatens to harm the LLP of other citizens, granting states the ability to enforce the fundamental maxim *sic utere tuo ut alienum non laedas*.[38] The further one gets from the ratification of the Constitution and Bill of Rights, however, the broader the understanding of police power becomes.

There were unfortunately very few comprehensive American legal treatises for many decades after ratification of the Constitution and Bill of Rights. American lawyers and courts relied very heavily on English legal treatises such as Blackstone's *Commentaries* for many years, for the simple reason that American constitutional law and philosophy were both new and novel, necessitating the education of a new generation of lawyers who could properly espouse the new constitutional philosophy. Because of this early reliance on British legal texts, it is not unusual to find state courts and legal scholars embracing a broad Blackstonian conception of offenses "against the public police and oeconomy [sic]" which he defined as "the due regulation and domestic order of the kingdom: whereby the individuals of the state, like members of a well-governed family, are bound to conform their behaviour to the rules of propriety, good neighbourhood, and good manners; and to be decent, industrious, and inoffensive in their respective stations."[39]

Yet there is also a glimmer of recognition in the first wave of American legal texts that the American conception of government was not so broad. One of the first prominent American legal scholars, John Bouvier, authored the most widely circulated American law dictionary of the 1800s as well as a comprehensive 1851 American law treatise, *Institutes of American Law,* in which he describes a system of law in which civil or criminal punishment may be imposed upon those who inflict "injuries and wrongs" upon others, which he defines as "a violation of a right" to life, liberty, or property.[40]

Another prominent early American legal scholar, Thomas Cooley, penned the influential *A Treatise on the Constitutional Limitations Which Rest Upon the Legislative Power of the States of the American Union,* which simultaneously embraces the Blackstonian conception of] police power, yet clearly modifies it to fit the unique American legal system: "The police of a State, in a comprehensive sense, embraces its system of internal regulation, by which it is sought not only to preserve the public order and prevent offences against the State, but also to establish for the intercourse of citizen with citizen those rules of good manners and good neighborhood which are calculated to prevent a conflict of rights, and to insure to each the uninterrupted enjoyment of his own, so far as is reasonably consistent with a like enjoyment of rights by others."[41]

Notice that Cooley's mention of "rules of good manners and good neighborhood" is virtually identical to the language used by Blackstone. Yet notice also that, unlike Blackstone, Cooley places an important qualification on such rules. Specifically, he asserts that "rules of good manners and good neighborhood" must be "calculated to prevent a conflict of rights . . . to insure to each the uninterrupted enjoyment of his own." With this important qualification, Cooley's conception of state police power is not a plenary power to control individual behavior, but instead a very limited power to limit individual behavior only when necessary to "prevent a conflict of rights" in which one person's liberty impedes the enjoyment of another's.

Thus, although Cooley's discussion of state police power seems at first blush to adopt a broad Blackstonian view, upon further inspection it does not. He posits two distinct exercises of state police power that are legitimate, both of which are consistent with the principles of limited government and residual individual sovereignty inherent in the morality of American law: laws restraining individual liberty in order to preserve order; and laws restraining individual liberty in order to prevent the individual from interrupting the enjoyment of others' LLP. The first category addresses harms inflicted by one citizen against an innocent citizen (e.g., theft). The second category addresses the classic conflict of rights between citizens, wherein Ann's enjoyment of her LLP conflicts with Betty's. Cooley recognizes that in such situations, the law legitimately may mediate the dispute between Ann and Betty so that they are not tempted to breach the peace and take the law into their own hands. In both of Cooley's categories, the common theme is one of a police power limited to carrying out the purpose of government itself—that is, preventing and remedying harm to citizens' LLP.

Another influential early American law treatise, Christopher Tiedeman's *Treatise on the Limitations of the Police Power,* agreed with Cooley's understanding of state police power, asserting: "It is to be observed, therefore, that the police power of the government, as understood in the constitutional law of the United States, is simply the power of government to establish provisions for the enforcement of the common as well as civil-law maxim, *sic utere tuo, ut alienum non laedas.* . . . Any law which goes beyond that principle, which undertakes to abolish rights, the exercise of which does not involve an infringement of the rights of others, or to limit the exercise of rights beyond what is necessary to provide for the public welfare and the general security, cannot be included in the police power of the government. It is a governmental usurpation, and violates the principles of abstract justice, as they have been developed under our republican institutions."[42] Similarly, W. P. Prentice's 1894 treatise devoted exclusively to the subject of police powers is entitled *Police Powers Arising Under the Law of Overruling Necessity,* which, as its title suggests, explains that concept of police power originated in the law of necessity—specifically, a need for government to intervene in the affairs of its citizens in order to prevent the spread of fire, pestilence, or other imminent harm.[43] Even as late as 1907, Willis Reid Bierly's book surveyed available case law and declared that "[t]he police power has been defined to be devoted to the protection of the lives, health and property of citizens and the maintenance of good order. . . . But laws cannot prohibit that which is harmless in itself, under pretense of police regulations."[44]

This limited conception of state police power also crops up in early-to-mid-eighteenth-century court decisions, though as with early American legal treatises, this period is equally replete with court decisions embracing the broader

Blackstonian vision. For example, in 1851 the Supreme Judicial Court of Massachusetts described the police power this way: "We think it is a settled principle, growing out of the nature of well ordered civil society, that every holder of property, however absolute and unqualified may be his title, holds it under the implied liability that his use of it may be so regulated, that it shall not be injurious to the equal enjoyment of others having an equal right to the enjoyment of their property, nor injurious to the rights of the community. . . . *Rights of property, like all other social and conventional rights, are subject to such reasonable limitations in their enjoyment, as shall prevent them from being injurious. . . . The power we allude to is . . . the police power. . . .*"[45]

Similarly, in 1854 the Vermont Supreme Court, *in Thorpe v. Rutland and Burlington Railroad Company,* defined the legitimate scope of the police power as follows: "This police power of the state extends to the protection of the lives, limbs, health, comfort, and quiet of all persons, and the protection of all property within the state. According to the maxim, *Sic utere tuo ut alienum non laedas,* which being of universal application, it must of course, be within the range of legislative action to define the mode and manner in which every one may so use his own as not to injure others."[46] A few years later, in 1859, the Maine Supreme Court asserted:

> With the Legislature, the maxim of the law, "salus populi suprema lex," should not be disregarded. It is the great principle on which the statutes for the security of the people is based. It is the foundation of criminal law, in all governments of civilized countries, and other laws conducive to safety and consequent happiness of the people. This power has always been exercised by government, and its existence cannot be reasonably denied. How far the provisions of the Legislature can extend, is always submitted to its discretion, provided its Acts do not go beyond the great principle of securing the public safety—and its duty, to provide for this public safety, within well defined limits and with discretion, is imperative. . . . All laws, for the protection of the lives, limbs, health and quiet of persons, and the security of all property within the State, fall within this general power of the government.[47]

The U.S. Supreme Court's early police power jurisprudence—generally involving an allegation that a state exercise of police power was a regulation of commerce (and hence, properly within the exclusive power of the federal government)—likewise contains glimpses of a limited rather than plenary police power. For example, in its 1877 decision in *Munn v. Illinois,* the Supreme Court cited the Vermont Supreme Court's decision in *Thorpe* with approval, declaring:

When the people of the United Colonies separated from Great Britain, they changed the form, but not the substance, of their government. They retained for the purposes of government all the powers of the British Parliament, and through their State constitutions, or other forms of social compact, undertook to give practical effect to such as they *deemed necessary for the common good and the security of life and property.* All the powers which they retained they committed to their respective States, unless in express terms or by implication reserved to themselves. Subsequently, when it was found necessary to establish a national government for national purposes, a part of the powers of the States and of the people of the States was granted to the United States and the people of the United States. This grant operated as a further limitation upon the powers of the States, so that now the governments of the States possess all the powers of the Parliament of England, except such as have been delegated to the United States or reserved by the people. The reservations by the people are shown in the prohibitions of the constitutions.

When one becomes a member of society, he necessarily parts with some rights or privileges which, as an individual not affected by his relations to others, he might retain. 'A body politic,' as aptly defined in the preamble of the Constitution of Massachusetts, 'is a social compact by which the whole people covenants with each citizen, and each citizen with the whole people, that all shall be governed by certain laws for the common good.' *This does not confer power upon the whole people to control rights which are purely and exclusively private, Thorpe v. R. & B. Railroad Co., but it does authorize the establishment of laws requiring each citizen to so conduct himself, and so use his own property, as not unnecessarily to injure another. This is the very essence of government, and has found expression in the maxim sic utere tuo ut alienum non laedas. From this source come the police powers. . . .*[48]

The Supreme Court employed similar reasoning the following year in *Railroad v. Husen,* in which the Court described the police power as follows:

[T]he police powers of a State justifies the adoption of precautionary measures against social evils. Under it a State may legislate to prevent the spread of crime, or pauperism, or disturbance of the peace. It may exclude from its limits convicts, paupers, idiots, and lunatics, and persons likely to become a public charge, as well as persons afflicted by contagious or infectious diseases . . . a right founded . . . in the sacred law of self-defence. The same principle, it may also be conceded, would justify the exclusion of property dangerous to the property of citizens of the State; for example, animals having contagious or infectious diseases. *All these exertions of power are in immediate connection with the protection of persons and property against noxious acts of other persons, or such a use of property as is injurious to the property of others. They are self-defensive.*[49]

In *Husen,* the Supreme Court clearly viewed the state's police power as limited to protecting the LLP of citizens. While one may certainly debate the correctness of some of the Court's conclusions (e.g., that lunatics and idiots harm others), its analytical foundation was undeniably a reflection of the unique American principles of limited government and residual individual sovereignty.

These select cases echo an early understanding of the limitations and purposes of American law that was all too quickly forgotten, for reasons we will now explore.

THE RELATIONSHIP BETWEEN FEDERAL
LIBERTIES AND STATE GOVERNMENTS

Current legal orthodoxy accepts that the Framers did not intend to apply the federal Bill of Rights to the states, yet the language of those amendments—other than the First Amendment and a portion of the Seventh Amendment[50]—is sufficiently broad to require allegiance by the states, particularly in light of the Supremacy Clause.[51] The orthodox view has been developed for pragmatic purposes, but it has spawned troubling intellectual inconsistencies and significant limitations on the ability of the courts to honor the twin foundational principles of limited government and residual individual sovereignty.

Early Case Law

Despite the current assumption that the federal Bill of Rights originally did not apply to the states, early state case law often assumed the opposite. Several state supreme courts believed that the federal Bill of Rights *was* applicable to the states for several decades after ratification. In 1820, for example, the New York Supreme Court of Judicature (at the time, the highest court in New York) was asked to determine whether the Double Jeopardy Clause of the Fifth Amendment applied to a state defendant:

> The defendant's counsel rely, principally, on the 5th article of the Amendment to the Constitution of U. S., which contains this provision: "Nor shall any person be subject for the same offense to be twice put in jeopardy of life or limb." It has been urged by the prisoner's counsel that this constitutional provision operates upon state courts *proprio vigore*. This has been denied on the other side. I do not consider it material whether this provision be considered as extending to the State tribunals or not; the principle is a sound and fundamental one of the common law, that no man shall be twice put in jeopardy of life and limb for the same offense. *I am, however, inclined to the opinion that the article in question does extend to all judicial tribunals in the U. S., whether constituted by the Congress of the U. S. or the states individually. The provision is general in its nature and unrestricted in its terms; and the 6th article of the Constitu-*

tion declares that the Constitution shall be the supreme law of the land; and the judges in every state shall be bound thereby, anything in the Constitution or laws of any state to the contrary notwithstanding. These general and comprehensive expressions extend the provisions of the Constitution of the U. S. to every article which is not confined, by the subject matter, to the national government and is equally applicable to the states. Be this as it may, the principle is undeniable that no person can be twice put in jeopardy of life and limb for the same offense.[52]

Although the court's belief that the Double Jeopardy Clause of the Fifth Amendment was applicable to the states is dicta, it provides an important snapshot into the minds of high-ranking state judges, revealing that, in the early years following ratification of the federal Bill of Rights, it was plausible to conclude, based on the plain language, that many of the provisions applied to the state and federal governments equally. A similar conclusion was reached by the Mississippi Supreme Court in 1823: "The defendant's counsel relied much upon the 5th Article of the amendment to the constitution of the United States, which contains the following provision: 'nor shall any person be subject for the same offence, to be twice put in jeopardy of life or limb.' I must confess, this amendment to the constitution of the United States, created the only doubt I have ever entertained upon this important question. It was properly admitted in argument, that this provision of the constitution was binding in the United States, as well as the state courts of the Union, for I take it, it has never been questioned, but that the constitution of the United States is the paramount law of the land, any law usage or custom of the several states to the contrary notwithstanding."[53] Similarly, the Missouri Supreme Court in 1832 unequivocally applied both the Indictment and Due Process Clauses of the Fifth Amendment:

> My first answer to this inquiry is, that by the 5th article of the amended constitution of the U. S., it is declared that "no person shall be held to answer for a capital or otherwise infamous crime, unless on a presentment or indictment of a grand jury, except in certain cases therein mentioned. This declaration of the constitution of the U. S., I understand to be the supreme law of the land. It therefore follows, that whenever the offense is made capital by law, and where the crime is infamous, the Legislature cannot authorize any other mode of proceeding, than by indictment or presentment. This throws a shield around the citizen to a great extent. What would be the true meaning of the words, infamous crimes, I will not now enquire, because I conceive breaches of the peace are not of that character. . . .
>
> I am aware that in the 5th article of the amendment to the Constitution of the U.S., this language is used (to-wit): that no person shall be deprived of life, liberty, or

property, without due process of law. This due process of law I understand is to be such as the law may have provided. It surely cannot mean in this instance an indictment or presentment, because the same article, in the first point thereof, points out the cases in which an indictment or presentment must be used, which cases are where the crime is capital or otherwise infamous. I understand that in this case and in all others, except those excepted therein, where the judgment would be against life, liberty, or property, the process must in all respects be legal process, such as is provided for by the law. [54]

The Supreme Court of New Jersey reached the same conclusion, applying the Fifth Amendment's Indictment Clause to state court proceedings.[55]

These early state decisions grappling with the new federal Bill of Rights appear to be in accord with early Supreme Court decisions. As William Crosskey has demonstrated, early post-ratification decisions of the Supreme Court appear to have assumed that at least some portions of the federal Bill of Rights were directly applicable to the states.[56] In *Bank of Columbia v. Okely*,[57] for example, the Court was asked to determine the constitutionality of a summary procedure to collect on an unpaid bank note. The plaintiff contended that the summary procedure violated both the Seventh Amendment and a similar provision in the Maryland constitution. The procedure was explicitly allowed by a Maryland statute and Congress had passed an act adopting the "laws of the state of Maryland, as they now exist" as the laws for the District of Columbia. The Court refused to view the act of Congress as a "re-enactment" of the laws of Maryland pursuant to Congress' exclusive power of legislation over the District.[58] The question, therefore, was whether the summary procedure law of Maryland, as a law of Maryland (not as a "re-enacted" D.C. law), was constitutional.[59]

The *Bank of Columbia* Court unanimously concluded that Maryland's summary procedure law, as a law of Maryland, was valid:

> By making the note negotiable at the bank of Columbia, the debtor chose his own jurisdiction; in consideration of the credit given him, he voluntarily relinquished his claims to the ordinary administration of justice . . . . That this view of the subject is giving full effect to the seventh amendment of the constitution, is not only deducible from the general intent, but from the express wording of the article referred to. Had the terms been, that "the *trial* by jury shall be preserved," it might have been contended, that they were imperative, and could not be dispensed with. But the words are, that the *right* of trial by jury shall be preserved, which places it on the foot of a *lex pro se introducta,* and the benefit of it may therefore be relinquished.[60]

The Court went on to conclude that the summary procedure law of Maryland, as a law of Maryland, was also valid under the Maryland constitution.[61] The Court does not hang its analytical hat solely on the Seventh Amendment, yet it is clear that the Court feels it necessary to address the validity of the Maryland law under the Seventh Amendment and indeed tackles that broader claim first. The *Bank of Columbia* Court thus concluded that the Maryland law, as a law of Maryland, was valid under the Seventh Amendment as well as the Maryland constitution. It is therefore reasonable to surmise that the Supreme Court of 1819 unanimously thought it not only plausible but probable that the Seventh Amendment applied to the states.

It is also interesting to note that several prominent members of the Thirty-Ninth Congress who debated the Fourteenth Amendment articulated their view that the privileges and immunities bestowed by the federal Bill of Rights were already applicable to the states. This was undoubtedly the view held by the Fourteenth Amendment's author, John Bingham.[62] It also appears to have been the view of Republican Robert Hale of New York, who objected to Representative Bingham's original draft of the Fourteenth Amendment[63] on grounds that it gave Congress the power to enact legislation affecting the life, liberty, and property of state citizens—a power Hale viewed as belonging exclusively to the states.[64] Hale believed that the federal Bill of Rights was fully applicable to both state and federal governments and enforceable by the courts, and there was thus no need to enlarge congressional power in the name of protecting the rights of United States citizens (particularly, the newly emancipated slaves):

> Now, what are these amendments to the Constitution, numbered from one to ten . . . ? What is the nature and object of these articles? They do not contain, from beginning to end, a grant of power anywhere. On the contrary, they are all restrictions of power. They constitute the bill of rights, a bill of rights for the protection of the citizen, and *defining and limiting the power of Federal and State legislation. They are not matters upon which legislation can be based. . . . Throughout they are prohibitions against legislation. Throughout they provide safeguards to be enforced by the courts, and not to be exercised by the Legislature.*[65]

Bingham challenged Hale by demanding that he "point to a single decision" of the federal or state courts in which a "party aggrieved in his person within a State"—e.g., a slave or freed slave—was acknowledged to enjoy the privileges and immunities of the federal Bill of Rights "or whether the nation has not been dumb in the presence of the organic act of a State which declares eight hundred thousand natural-born citizens of the United States shall be denied the right to prosecute a suit in their courts, either for the vindication of a right or the redress of the wrong? Where is the decision? I want an answer."[66] Hale replied: "I have not be able to prepare a brief for this argument, and therefore cannot refer the gentleman to any case. . . . I do not know of a case where it has ever been decided that the United States Constitution is sufficient for the protection of the liberties of the citizen. But still I have, somehow or other, gone along with the impression that there is that sort of protection thrown over us in some way, whether with or without the sanction of a judicial decision that we are so protected. Of course, I may be entirely mistaken in all this, but I have somehow had that impression."[67]

Representative Eldridge of Wisconsin, who apparently held similar views to Hale, then asked Bingham if he "has found or heard of a case in which the Constitution of the United States has been pronounced to be *insufficient* [to protect the rights of citizens]?"[68] Bingham responded the following day by citing *Barron v. Baltimore*[69] to Hale and his congressional colleagues—the Supreme Court case which declared, with virtually no explanation or discussion, that the federal Bill of Rights did not apply to the States. Bingham's citation to *Barron* thereafter went unchallenged.

Barron v. Baltimore

The case that Representative Bingham used to illustrate the need for the Fourteenth Amendment—*Barron v. Baltimore*[70]—oddly does not discuss any of the early cases acknowledging the textual breadth of the federal Bill of Rights and applying them to the states. *Barron,* which was decided in 1833, is a terse opinion by Chief Justice John Marshall, in which he declared that the Fifth Amendment's Takings Clause[71] did not apply to the states.

Although the holding of *Barron* was technically limited to the Takings Clause, Marshall's dicta was much broader, asserting that the entire federal Bill of Rights did not apply to the states because "[t]hese amendments contain no expression indicating an intention to apply them to the state governments. This court cannot so apply them."[72] But even after the Supreme Court decided *Barron,* there was a period of several decades in which several state supreme courts ignored Marshall's broad dicta and continued to apply various provisions of the federal Bill of Rights.

The Supreme Court of Georgia, for example, concluded in several remarkable post-*Barron* cases that the Bill of Rights was fully binding upon the states. In 1846 the Georgia high court concluded that the Second Amendment's right to keep and bear arms was directly applicable to the states, since the language of the amendment did not refer specifically to the national government only and the right seemed sufficiently important to apply with equal force to the states:

> [D]oes it follow that because the people refused to delegate to the general government the power to take from them the right to keep and bear arms that they designed to rest it in the State governments? Is it a right reserved to the States or to themselves? Is it not an unalienable right, which lies at the bottom of every free government? We do not believe that, because the people withheld this arbitrary power of disfranchisement from Congress, they ever intended to confer it on the local legislatures. This is a right too dear to be confided to a republican legislature.
>
> Questions under some of these amendments, it is true, can only arise under the laws and Constitution of the United States. But there are other provisions in them, which were never intended to be thus restricted, but were designed for the benefit of every citizen of the Union in all courts and in all places; and the people of the several States, in ratifying them in their respective State conventions, have virtually adopted them as beacon-lights to guide and control the action of their own legislatures, as well as that of Congress.[73]

A few years later, in *Campbell v. State*,[74] the Georgia Supreme Court became even more adamant in its insistence that the state was not free to legislate in a manner contrary to a provision of the federal Bill of Rights. The *Campbell* Court began by declaring that "[t]he principles embodied in these [federal Bill of Rights] amendments, for better securing the lives, liberties, and property of the people, were declared to be the 'birthright' of our ancestors, several centuries previous to the establishment of our government."[75] The question, therefore, was whether the state of Georgia, by virtue of its "reserved powers" under the Tenth Amendment, could violate these "birthrights" of Georgia citizens: "And the question to be decided now is, not whether these amendments were intended to operate as a restriction upon the government of the United States, but whether it is competent for a State Legislature, by virtue of its inherent powers, to pass an Act directly impairing the great principles of protection to person and property, embraced in these amendments? That the power to pass any law infringing on these principles is taken from the Federal Government, no one denies. But is it a part of the reserved rights of a State to do this?"[76] The court concluded that the answer was no because "let it be constantly be borne in mind, that notwithstanding we may have different governments, a nation within a nation, imperium in imperio, we have but one people; and that the same people which, divided into separate communities, constitute the respective State governments, comprise in the aggregate, the United States Government; and that it is in vain to shield them from a blow aimed by the Federal arm, if they are liable to be prostrated by one dealt with equal fatality by their own."[77] The court thus reveals a view perfectly consonant with the morality of American law. Specifically, the *Campbell* court clearly acknowledges that: (1) the federal Bill of Rights evinces "great principles" regarding the legitimate purpose of government; (2) those principles are "protection to person and property"; and (3) that neither the federal nor the state governments may exceed those legitimate purposes. This is even more clearly revealed in the following passage:

> When it can be demonstrated that an individual or a government has the right to do wrong, contrary to the old adage, that one person's rights cannot be another person's wrongs, then, and not before, will it be yielded that it is a part and parcel of the original jurisdiction of the State governments, reserved to them in the distribution of power under the Constitution, to enact laws, to deprive the citizen of the right to keep and bear arms; to quarter soldiers in time of peace, in any house, without the consent of the owner; to subject the people to unreasonable search and seizure, in their persons, houses, papers and effects; to hold a person to answer for a capital, or otherwise infamous crime, without presentment or indictment, to be twice put in jeopardy of life or limb for the same offence; to compel him, in a criminal case, to be a witness against himself; to deprive him of life, liberty or property, without due course of law; to take private property for public use, without just compensation; to deprive the accused in all criminal trials, of the right to a speedy and public trial, by an impartial Jury; to be informed of the nature and cause of the accusation; to be confronted with the witnesses against him; to have compulsory process for obtaining witnesses in his favor, and to have the assistance of counsel for his defence; to enact laws requiring excessive bail, imposing oppressive and ruinous fines, and inflicting cruel and unusual punishments!
>
> From such State rights, good Lord deliver us! I utterly repudiate them from the creed of my political faith!
>
> It was not because it was supposed that legislation over the subjects here enumerated might be better and more safely entrusted to the State governments, that it was prohibited to Congress. It was to declare to the world the fixed and unalterable determination of our people, that these invaluable rights which had been established at so great a cost of blood and treasure, should never be disturbed by any government. . . .
>
> One of the reasons set forth in the preamble to these amendments, for their adoption was, that it would "extend thereby, the ground of public confidence in the government, and thus best secure the beneficent ends of its institution." What confidence will be reposed in a State government, whose legislation should be characterized by acts which disgrace the most tyrannical epoch of the British monarchy? A free people would instantly and indignantly reject it and its authors. . . . [78]

The court was apparently well aware that its view of the federal Bill of Rights would anger those who ardently clung to the idea of "states' rights," particularly in an era of secessionist zeal. Yet the court bravely rejected the conceptualization of "states' rights" as being supreme to individual rights, stating, "While this Court yields to none in its devotion to State rights, and would be the first to resist all attempts at Federal usurpation, it feels itself called on by the blood of the many martyrs, who nobly died to maintain the great principles of civil liberty contained in these amendments—our American Magna Carta—to stand by, support and defend the rights which they guarantee, against all encroachments, whether proceeding from the National or State governments."[79] The court was also cognizant that the question of the applicability of the federal Bill of Rights to the states was still, even after *Barron,* subject to debate: "Other precedents are cited to sustain the proposition, that none of these amendments extend to the State governments, but were intended for Congress and the United States Courts. I will not stop to examine these cases, or to array the conflicting opinions of Courts and Jurists, equally eminent, on the other side. The question, I am aware, is still regarded as an unsettled one; but in this country, the weight of authority will be found in favor of the doctrine, that governments are not clothed with absolute and despotic power. . . ."[80]

The *Campbell* court was even prescient enough to acknowledge that its opinion would be attacked as imposing a subjective "natural law" limitation on the powers of the legislature, yet responded in a rather remarkable, originalist way:

> [O]ne of the strongest arguments against Judicial interposition in such cases is, that apart from a written Constitution , our ideas of natural justice are vague and uncertain, regulated by no fixed standard; the ablest and best men differing widely upon this, as well as all other subjects.
>
> But as to questions arising under these amendments, there is nothing indefinite. The people of the several States, by adopting these amendments, have defined accurately and recorded permanently their opinion, as to the great principles which they embrace; and to make them more emphatic and enduring, have had them incorporated into the Constitution of the Union—the permanent law of the land. Admit, therefore, that the Legislature of a State may be absolute and without control over all other subjects, where its authority is not restrained by the Constitution of the State or of the United States; *still, viewing these amendments as we do, as intended to establish justice—to secure the blessings of liberty—to protect person and property from violence; and that these were the very purposes for which this government was established, we hold that they constitute a limit to all legislative power, Federal or State, beyond which it cannot go; that these vital truths lie at the foundation of our free, republican institutions; that without this security for personal liberty and private property, our social compact could not exist.* No Court should ever presume that it was the design of the people to entrust their representatives with the power to take away or impair these securities.

Such an assumption would be against all reason. The very genius, nature and spirit of our institutions amount to a prohibition of such acts of legislation, and will overrule and forbid them.[81]

Taking the *Campbell* opinion as a whole, it is abundantly clear that the Georgia Supreme Court viewed the federal Bill of Rights' textual protections for individual life, liberty, and property to be declarative of the legitimate purpose of government. These constitutional protections provided the demarcation between legitimate and illegitimate exercises of governmental power—whether federal or state—by carving out a large zone of immunity from governmental action. There is in *Campbell* a clear exposition of the morality of American law and an equally clear defiance of the *Barron* doctrine. Several other state supreme courts similarly either assumed or concluded, post-*Barron,* that various provisions of the federal Bill of Rights were binding upon their states.[82]

Yet despite the state courts' misgivings about the breadth of *Barron*'s dicta, it is now accepted as legal gospel. The *Barron* Court's rationale, however, is deserving of criticism and its outcome warrants reconsideration. Let us consider Chief Justice Marshall's brief analysis:

Had the people of the several states, or any of them, required changes in their constitutions; had they required additional safeguards to liberty from the apprehended encroachments of their particular governments: the remedy was in their own hands, and would have been applied by themselves. . . . The unwieldy and cumbrous machinery of procuring a recommendation from two-thirds of congress, and the assent of three-fourths of their sister states [as required by Article V], could never have occurred to any human being as a mode of doing what might be effected by the state itself. Had the framers of these amendments intended them to be limitations on the powers of the state governments, they would have imitated the framers of the original constitution, and have expressed that intention. . . . But it is universally understood, it is a part of the history of the day, that the great revolution which established the constitution of the Unite States, was not effected without immense opposition. . . . These [Bill of Rights] amendments demanded security against the apprehended encroachments of the general government—not against those of the local governments. . . . These amendments contain no expression indicating an intention to apply them to the state governments. This court cannot so apply them.[83]

Notice that Marshall's conclusion is predicated on three propositions. First, the people within the respective states would never have relinquished their cherished rights to the "unwieldy and cumbrous" amendment process of Article V. Second, the Anti-Federalists' opposition to the Constitution was based upon fears that the federal government would usurp the citizens' inalienable rights. And third, the ten amendments within the Bill of Rights "contain no expression" indicating an intent to apply to the states.

Marshall's analysis is deficient on all three counts. First, Marshall failed to realize that the "unwieldy and cumbrous" amendment process of Article V actually served to better secure the citizens' inalienable rights, not render them more insecure. By making the Constitution difficult to amend, Article V's processes were designed to preserve the Constitution's meaningful limits on governmental power as well as the large zone of residual individual sovereignty delineated in the Bill of Rights. Moreover, in making this argument Marshall—ironically the author of *Marbury v. Madison*—does not acknowledge that, under American law, citizens who believed that their government (whether federal or state) exceeded its constitutionally granted power were entitled to relief through the mechanism of judicial review. There was, in other words, no need to resort to the "cumbrous and unwieldy machinery" of Article V in instances where the government exceeded its powers. All that was necessary was to file a lawsuit and obtain relief from the appropriate court.

Marshall's second argument—that the Bill of Rights was designed to quell Anti-Federalists' fear about the federal government—is of course a correct characterization. But simply because the Anti-Federalists were most afraid of the newly formed federal government does not mean that they were not equally interested in preserving individual liberty against *all* government, whether federal or state. The Anti-Federalist focus on the federal government was understandable given that the federal government was the new entity being created. The Anti-Federalists' concerns regarding the new federal government were subsequently addressed by the Bill of Rights, a document that employed broad language protective of individual liberty—indeed, much broader protection than was contained in most state constitutions of the day.

Finally, Marshall's last argument—that the Bill of Rights "contain no expression" of an intent to apply to the states is worthless illogic. He is correct that, other than the First Amendment and the Reexamination Clause of the Seventh Amendment, the Bill of Rights does not expressly declare that the liberties contained therein operate to limit state power. But by the same token, the Bill does not state that the individual liberties recognized therein were intended *not* to limit state power, either. The simple fact is that the plain language of most of the Bill of Rights declares liberty *simpliciter.* Accepting the plain language, combined with the undeniable import of the Supremacy Clause, leads to the conclusion that, whether or not it was widely realized, the federal Bill of

Rights granted individuals within the United States broad immunity against tyrannous exercises of governmental power, whether federal or state.

The unfortunate result in *Barron* gave the Supreme Court's first official blessing to the southern states' continuation of slavery. After all, if the *Barron* Court had reached the opposite result and concluded that the federal Bill of Rights was binding upon the state legislatures, how could the slave states, particularly state judiciaries, continue to countenance slavery? If "the people" enjoyed inalienable rights such as keeping and bearing arms, due process, speedy and impartial jury trials, and security against unreasonable searches and seizures, how could state judges—sworn to uphold the Constitution[84]—continue to ignore the claims of slaves or freed slaves who had been denied these inalienable rights? They could not. The result in *Barron,* therefore, pragmatically was designed to keep the Union intact.

The second blessing for the continuation of slavery was conferred in 1856 in the *Dred Scott* case, in which the Court again attempted to avoid civil war by declaring that slaves were not "citizens" entitled to enjoy the privileges and immunities conferred by Article IV of the Constitution.[85] In both *Barron* and *Dred Scott,* the Court emasculated the federal Bill of Rights and granted states carte blanche to continue disregarding the inalienable liberties expressly granted to all people within the United States. These decisions—in a classic ends-justify-the-means rationalization—rendered the liberty of all citizens, black and white alike, vulnerable to majoritarian legislative whims, and significantly undermined the original foundational principles of limited government and residual individual sovereignty.

THE INEFFECTIVENESS OF STATE BILLS OF RIGHTS

Barron and *Dred Scott* made it impossible for slaves or freed slaves to seek legal relief. Because the Court had definitively foreclosed any federal constitutional relief for the human rights abuses suffered by slaves and freed slaves, their only potential source of legal relief was state bills of rights. And while it was theoretically possible to find state constitutional provisions supportive of the claims of slaves and freed slaves, the social and political context in which these claims were presented to the state courts made relief pragmatically impossible.

Why would state courts be reluctant to invalidate legislative acts that violated state constitutional guarantees? First, several hundred years of history and legal training had ingrained this reluctance into the collective judicial brain.[86]

When the fledgling American states declared their independence in 1776, the custom and practice of their common law ancestors was to leave primary enforcement of individual rights to the legislative, not judicial, branch. In Great Britain, individual rights had been forcibly extracted as "privileges" granted by the monarch after bloodshed and rebellion.[87] Magna Carta, for example, was forcibly wrested from King John in the thirteenth century by rebellious barons.[88] The English courts were not entrusted with protecting these hard-won privileges because the courts were appointed and controlled by the king and designed to protect the king's interests.[89] Instead, it was the Parliament, particularly the House of Commons, that was entrusted with the power to represent the interests of citizens and protect their privileges against usurpation.[90] Parliamentary power was plenary, sufficient even to alter the Magna Carta if it wished.[91] Given this historical backdrop, the relatively immature American state courts did not have much precedent for enforcing their states' bills of rights against legislative or executive disparagement. State legislatures initially were assumed to have the same powers as those of the British Parliament, and state courts accordingly hesitated to invalidate state legislation.

State judicial reluctance to enforce declarations of individual rights against usurpation was also exacerbated by racial animosity toward blacks, in the context both of the continuation of slavery and the desire to restrict the liberty of freed slaves. This animosity may have motivated parsimonious interpretation of state constitutional provisions, which delineated broad individual rights. For example, the Virginia Declaration of Rights of 1776 declared in its first article that "all men are by nature equally free and independent and have certain inherent rights, of which, when they enter into a state of society, they cannot, by any compact, deprive or divest their posterity, namely, the enjoyment of life and liberty, with the means of acquiring and possessing property, and pursuing and obtaining happiness and safety."[92] Yet nowhere in the Virginia Declaration of Rights is there an acknowledgment of slavery or how its existence can be reconciled with such rights. Similarly, the North Carolina Constitution of 1776 limited some of its declared rights to "freem[e]n"—presumably either white or black—while others lacked such limiting language.[93] Incongruous text in the constitutions of Georgia and Maryland posed similar interpretive problems by broadly declaring rights for all persons, yet elsewhere granting rights only to freemen or white persons.[94]

State constitutions that made delineations between white and black persons or freemen and slaves thus made it exceedingly difficult for state courts to sanction existing legal discrimination without substantially ignoring or reinterpreting plain constitutional language that granted rights without regard to racial distinctions. Honoring state constitutional text thus would have required courts to apply many rights equally to both white and black—a result that was clearly unacceptable to southern society. Moreover, the broad dicta in *Barron v. Baltimore* and several provisions of the U.S. Constitution that sanctioned the continuation of slavery[95] sent a rather strong signal to state judges that they were under no obligation to enforce the federal Bill of Rights, either—at least not yet.

THE CIVIL WAR AND THE FOURTEENTH AMENDMENT

The enactment of the Civil War Amendments presented a clear opportunity to return to the original constitutional balance and apply the foundational principles of limited government and residual individual sovereignty to the states. The ratification of the Fourteenth Amendment marked a significant turning point in American constitutional law, providing strong ammunition for applying the Bill of Rights directly to the states. Specifically, the Fourteenth Amendment contained a clause which declares, "No state shall make or enforce any law which shall abridge the privileges or immunities of citizens of the United States."[96] It seems patently obvious that, in declaring that states may not abridge the "privileges or immunities of citizens of the United States," the Fourteenth Amendment was referring to the most important privileges or immunities enjoyed by U.S. citizens—namely, those set forth in the federal Bill of Rights.[97]

Shockingly, however, the Supreme Court, in the *Slaughterhouse Cases*,[98] declined to honor the amendment's plain language and its history. It determined that the "privileges or immunities of citizens of the United States" referred only to privileges or immunities that "owe their existence to the Federal government, its National character, its Constitution, or its laws."[99] The *Slaughterhouse* majority attempted to elucidate some of these uniquely "national" privileges and immunities that states were forbidden from abridging by the Fourteenth Amendment, providing a short laundry list that included: accessing the federal government and transacting business with it, accessing national seaports, demanding federal protection of one's life, liberty, or property when on the high seas or abroad, petitioning for redress of grievances by the federal government, petitioning for a writ of habeas corpus.[100]

The stunning interrelationship between *Barron* and *Slaughterhouse* is never discussed. The *Barron* Court concluded that the Bill of Rights, by its nature an enumeration of privileges and immunities granted to citizens, applied only to the federal government. These privileges and immunities enumerated in the Bill of Rights were, in other words, specifically *national* in character, belonging to every citizen of the United States and enforceable against the federal sovereign. *Slaughterhouse* then strangely concluded that the Fourteenth Amendment's reference to "privileges or immunities of citizens of the United States" did not refer to the Bill of Rights, despite the fact that *Barron* had characterized the Bill of Rights as a list of privileges and immunities belonging to all United States citizens.

The only possible way to justify the result in *Slaughterhouse* is to conclude that the Bill of Rights, characterized by the Supreme Court as a list of privileges and immunities belonging to U.S. citizens qua U.S. citizens, was not what the American people had in mind when they ratified an amendment which declared, "No State shall make or enforce any law which shall abridge the privileges or immunities of citizens of the United States." Instead, we are asked to believe that the people, when ratifying the Fourteenth Amendment, were not trying to force the southern states to bestow these privileges and immunities upon all citizens regardless of color, but merely trying to stop states from limiting citizens' access to the federal government and its navigable waters.

So we must once again ask ourselves: Why has this happened? What caused the United States Supreme Court to contort the Constitution in such an unjust and unsupportable manner? Once again, the ineluctable answer is slavery. Although slavery had been officially abolished by the Thirteenth Amendment, the former slave states were far from accepting African-Americans as equal citizens. The enactment of Jim Crow laws beginning in the Reconstruction era were designed to keep the white and black races separate and unequal—and in fact did so for at least another hundred years.[101] If either *Slaughterhouse* Court had interpreted the Privileges or Immunities Clause of the Fourteenth Amendment as making the federal Bill of Rights applicable to the states, the southern states could not have continued to enact legislation that denied the Bill's liberties to African-Americans. And if the former slave states had been forced by the Court to grant equal liberty to African-Americans, the tenuously reconstructed Union might have collapsed.

THE EXTENT OF INCORPORATION

The Supreme Court was pragmatically aware of its role in maintaining the Union and thus proceeded slowly in applying the federal Bill of Rights to the states. It has preferred to adopt a so-called selective incorporation approach, whereby the Court determines, on a case-by-case basis, whether certain provisions of the Bill of Rights are binding on the states.[102] The Court has reached this result through its interpretation of the Fourteenth Amendment's Due Process Clause, even though the Privileges and Immunities Clause was much better suited to the task.

Strikingly, the Court's selective incorporation approach to the Bill of Rights via the Due Process Clause has been careful to limit eligibility for incorporation to the first eight amendments of the Bill of Rights, specifically excluding the Ninth and Tenth Amendments.[103] Exclusion of the Tenth Amendment from the selective incorporation approach is understandable, given that the Tenth Amendment refers explicitly to the states, reserving to them (or to the people, assuming the people have not ceded the power in question to their state governments) "the powers not delegated to the United States by the Constitution. . . ."[104] There is no need to decide whether the Tenth Amendment was intended to apply to the states, since it is expressly designed to protect them (or their citizens, as the case may be) from the national encroachment. Incorporation is simply inapposite.

But as to the Ninth Amendment, the Court's casual assumption—without any explanation—that it is ineligible for incorporation is puzzling. If one accepts the orthodox view pronounced by Robert Bork and others that the Ninth Amendment is a constitutional "inkblot" devoid of substantive meaning,[105] there is no great loss in the Court's ineligibility assumption, since it would pragmatically accomplish nothing to incorporate nothing. On the other hand, if the Ninth Amendment is both important and meaningful (as I think it is), declaring the Ninth Amendment ineligible for incorporation (particularly without proffering a reason why) is deeply troubling.

Nothing in the text of either the Ninth or Fourteenth Amendments would suggest that the Ninth Amendment is peculiarly ineligible for application to the states. Indeed, unlike many of the other provisions of the Bill of Rights, such as the First and Seventh Amendments, which refer explicitly to the national government only, the Ninth Amendment simply declares that there are "rights" that are "retained by the people," despite the enumeration in the Constitution of other specific rights. The Ninth Amendment, by its plain language, is thus not limited to the federal government.

Beyond this textual issue, however, there is a deeper spiritual problem with excluding the Ninth Amendment from selective incorporation eligibility: its exclusion violates the explicit language of the Ninth Amendment itself. The

Ninth Amendment declares that "the enumeration in the Constitution of certain rights shall not be construed to deny or disparage others retained by the people."[106] Yet the Supreme Court's selective incorporation approach, by excluding the Ninth Amendment from incorporation eligibility under the Due Process Clause, is doing exactly that: it is construing an enumerated right—due process—in such a way as to deny or disparage the unenumerated rights retained by the people, something the Framers explicitly declared inappropriate.

Some might argue that excluding the Ninth Amendment from incorporation eligibility is essentially harmless, since the Court's substantive due process jurisprudence has effectively filled the gap by becoming the vehicle for protecting unenumerated rights that the Ninth Amendment was designed to protect.[107] True, substantive due process provides a vehicle for recognizing and protecting unenumerated individual rights. Yet—to carry through with the vehicular metaphor—it is a clunky and unreliable jalopy for transporting something so precious as residual individual sovereignty. The Court's substantive due process jurisprudence has generally required both that the right being asserted be "carefully described," but also that it be "objectively, deeply rooted in this Nation's history and tradition" and "implicit in the concept of ordered liberty" such that "neither liberty nor justice would exist if [it] were sacrificed."[108]

The Court's present-day substantive due process jurisprudence imposes a highly technical formula that affords little opportunity to accommodate new societal conditions and challenges. It erects barriers to liberty that are nowhere mentioned in the constitutional text and thereby invites an incredible degree of subjective navel-gazing to determine what liberties are deeply rooted, implicit in the concept of ordered liberty, and essential to liberty. All of these Court-created prerequisites are designed to be virtually impenetrable locks that individual citizens must pick before the door of liberty can swing open. There is no presumption of liberty here; quite the contrary. Much as in the British parliamentary system, legislative power is virtually absolute.

The rights-retaining language of the Ninth Amendment, combined with the similar powers-retaining language of the Tenth Amendment, would—if taken seriously—alter the current presumption in favor of legislative power over individuals. It would fulfill its intended function of reminding all branches of government that there are limits to the legitimate exercise of governmental power (protecting/enhancing LLP) and that these limits exist to effectuate the true meaning of individual equality through the mechanism of residual individual sovereignty.[109] The Ninth and Tenth Amendments, in other words, are the quintessential embodiment of the morality of American law.

The Court, however, has consciously chosen to pursue the oxymoronic substantive due process route in its half-hearted role as protector of individual liberty. Its substantive liberty jurisprudence has been erratic, uneven, and oftentimes illogical, yet it has slowly succeeded in applying much of the federal Bill of Rights to the states. This, in turn, has exacerbated the privacy-morality tension in American law. As states have become increasingly obliged to abide by the federal Bill of Rights, state laws grounded in public morality have been accused of infringing upon those rights.[110] The evolving incorporation of the federal Bill of Rights has thus begun to both cause and reveal, in an increasing number of cases, a seemingly intractable tension between public morality and individual privacy.

CONCLUSION

As I have attempted to describe and demonstrate, there is an underlying morality to American law that distinguishes it from British and all other antecedent legal systems. American law itself is thus firmly grounded in morality, but it is a very different type of morality than that to which most people commonly refer when they speak of morality. The colloquial understanding of morality refers to the beliefs, passions, and prejudices of the citizenry, which are often grounded in theology. This type of morality, which I term "public morality," often motivates the enactment of ordinary laws. It is this type of morality, moreover, that clashes so predictably and routinely with individual liberty.

One critical and common mistake is to assume that a law based on public morality reflects a community-wide moral consensus. It would be more accurate to conclude that public morality–based legislation reflects a political consensus on a moral issue among a majority of elected representatives. Given the high profile and passion associated with public morality–based legislation, it seems too ambitious to conclude that a law with such a basis necessarily reflects the moral preferences of a present majority of citizens or even a past majority of citizens at the time the law was enacted. A public morality–based law thus may reflect instead a passionate but vocal minority's moral beliefs as interpreted by a majority of legislators at a certain point in time.

But even assuming an ordinary law based on public morality accurately reflects the extant majority's moral beliefs, the hierarchy of American law demands that such ordinary laws conform to a higher morality than mere majoritarian preferences. The higher morality to which I refer is the morality of law itself. The morality of law is not based upon any particular set of religious or political beliefs. Its foundational principles (limited government and residual individual sovereignty) are intended to benefit all citizens, regardless of age, gender, sexual orientation, and religious or political affiliation. It is a timeless, secular morality that reflects the Framers' beliefs about the right and wrong purposes of government.

If there is indeed a morality of law animating the American legal system, how can this morality be implemented in a pragmatic sense? The next chapter will examine this question in detail, attempting to find a workable standard, consonant with the morality of American law, that can be used by legislators and judges when faced with a clash between public morality and individual liberty.

Chapter 3 Being Sovereign:
The Harm Principle

The fate of sovereignty has been similar to that of the Nile. Always magnif-
icent, always interesting to mankind, it has become alternately their blessing and their curse. Its origin has often been attempted to be traced. . . .
Lately, the inquiry has been recommenced with a different spirit, and in a
new direction; and although the discovery of nothing very astonishing,
yet the discovery of something very useful and true, has been the result.
The dread and redoubtable sovereign, when traced to his ultimate and
genuine source, has been found, as he ought to have been found, in the
free and independent man.
—James Wilson, Introductory Lecture of the Study of Law
in the United States, 1790

If there is an underlying morality of American law that defines the
limits of governmental power (protecting LLP) and concomitantly
values residual individual sovereignty, the question remains: How do
we apply this morality, pragmatically? How can recognizing and understanding this morality of American law help legislators and judges
determine whether ordinary legislation is a legitimate exercise of governmental power? How can we take this macro-theory and make it
work on a micro level?

WHAT DOES IT MEAN
TO BE SOVEREIGN?

If one of the foundational principles of American law—at both the state and federal level—is residual individual sovereignty, what does this mean? If the people are sovereign, not merely in a collective but also an individual capacity, what meaning does this have for constitutional analysis?

To declare that someone possessed sovereignty at the time of the founding generation was to declare that the individual possessed an autonomy from control by others. One of the most influential Framers, James Wilson, recognized this fascinating result: "The law of nations is the law of sovereigns. In free states, such as ours, the sovereign or supreme power resides in the people. In free states, therefore, such as ours, the law of nations is the law of the people. . . . But when I say that, in free states, the law of nations is the law of the people; I mean not that it is a law made by the people, or by virtue of their delegated authority. . . . I mean that it [the law of nations] . . . is indispensably binding upon the people, in whom the sovereign power resides. . . . How vast—how important—how interesting these truths! They announce to a free people how exalted their rights. . . ."[1] Wilson's statement reflects his understanding that the "law of nations" was binding not merely upon the United States as a nation, but also upon the individual people of the United States, "in whom the sovereign power resides." He believed that if this basic principle was properly understood, it would "announce to a free people how exalted their rights."

So what did Wilson understand that he knew others would fail to understand? He understood the implications of applying the law of nations to the people of the United States, who were themselves sovereign.

At the time of the founding, various writings on the law of nations—the precursor to modern-day international law—acknowledged that to be sovereign was to possess the power to pursue one's own desires, free from the control or intermeddling of other sovereigns.[2] Yet even sovereigns were constrained by one overarching principle: they owed other sovereigns a duty to refrain from inflicting injury unless in self-defense.[3] As co-equals, therefore, sovereigns were obligated under the law of nations to treat each other with respect and avoid being aggressive or injurious to each other; short of this basic prescription, however, a sovereign was accountable to none but itself.

If the morality of American law considers individual citizens to be sovereign in all areas not expressly ceded to government, this suggests that individuals, as sovereigns, are obligated to refrain from injuring other sovereigns (individuals). It further suggests that it would be a moral exercise of governmental power to prevent or punish acts injurious to others. The reasonable conclusion is that there is a harm principle at work in American law or, more specifically, that the morality of American law inherently incorporates a harm principle. As the next section will demonstrate, the existence of a harm principle underlying American law is significantly reinforced upon consideration of the purpose of government.

PROTECTING LIFE, LIBERTY, AND PROPERTY (LLP)

If, as discussed in the previous chapter, the purpose of government is to protect the lives, liberty, and property (LLP) of its citizens, it seems reasonable to conclude that government acts legitimately when it fulfills this purpose and illegitimately when it does not. If this is the case, then it suggests that exercises of governmental power beyond these limited purposes (protecting citizens' LLP) are illegitimate and unnecessarily intrusive upon residual individual sovereignty. This leads to the conclusion that government may act to restrain individual liberty only when the individual has harmed or threatened harm to another individual's LLP.

As a preliminary matter, it should be acknowledged that the harm principle has been criticized as inadequate to the task of providing a cohesive theory for defining the legitimate boundaries of law. The two chief criticisms are: (1) the harm principle's inability to define legitimately proscribable harm in any meaningful way;[4] and (2) its inability to appreciate the society-improving function of majoritarian morality.[5] One of the fascinating aspects of these two criticisms is that they are diametrically opposed: the former laments that harm is so amorphous and broad that it could open the door to excessive restrictions on individual liberty, while the latter laments that harm is so rigid and narrow that it will impede sufficient governmental control.

The first criticism was articulated in the thoughtful work of Joel Feinberg, who asserted that Mill's harm principle "is too vague to be of any potential use at all. . . . Without [ ] further specifications, the harm principle may be taken to invite state interference without limit, for virtually every kind of human conduct can affect the interests of others for better and worse to *some* degree, and thus would properly be the state's business."[6] The latter criticism is exemplified by Patrick Devlin, who asserts that embracing a harm principle will narrow governmental power, depriving society of the authority to preventing moral decline: "[w]hat Mill demands is that we must tolerate what we know to be evil and what no one asserts to be good. He does not ask that in particular cases we should extend tolerance out of pity; he demands that we should cede it for ever as a right. . . . Why do ninety of us have to grant this license to the other ten or, it would be truer to say, ninety-nine to the other one?"[7] I will deal with these criticisms in greater detail when I offer a workable definition of harm. For now, suffice it to say that the criticism of the harm principle as both too broad and too narrow suggests that its critics on both the ideological right and left find it inadequate to suit their particular agendas—an outcome that in turn suggests that it can offer an appropriate and ideologically neutral guidepost for defining the reach of governmental power.

Despite its modern controversy, the harm principle was widely embraced, in one form or another, at the time of the American Revolution. Its most forceful proponent—though, as we will see, certainly not the first[8]—has been post-revolutionary philosopher John Stuart Mill, whose essay *On Liberty* has provoked considerable and continuing debate. Mill's basic premise is that "the only purpose for which power can be rightfully exercised over any member of a civilized community, against his will, is to prevent harm to others. His own good, either physical or moral, is not a sufficient warrant. . . . Over himself, over his own body and mind, the individual is sovereign."[9]

Though Mill receives much of the credit for articulating the harm principle, his work built upon the dominant political philosophy of the eighteenth century. Indeed, virtually every major political philosopher of the eighteenth century appears to have embraced some version of a harm principle as the defining limit of governmental power. The most prominent and influential political philosopher of the founding era was John Locke, whose *Second Treatise of Government* proclaimed that the purpose of government was serve as an umpire to adjudicate harms inflicted upon the life, liberty, or property of citizens.[10] Another prominent revolutionary philosopher, Algernon Sidney, concurred:

> I am not afraid to say, that naturally and properly a man is the judg[e] of his own concernments. No one is or can be depriv'd of this privilege, unless by his own consent, and for the good of that Society into which he enters. . . . If I find my self afflicted with hunger, thirst, weariness, cold, heat, or sickness, 'tis a folly to tell me, I ought not to seek meat, drink, rest, shelter, refreshment, or physick [sic], because I must not be the judge of my own case. The like may be said in relation to my house, land, or estate; *I may do what I please with them, if I bring no damage upon others. But I must not set fire to my house, by which my Neighbour's house may be burnt. . . . My Land is*

not simply my own, but upon condition that I shall not thereby bring damage upon the Publick [sic], by which I am protected in the peaceable enjoyment and innocent use of what I possess. . . . I cannot reasonably expect to be defended from wrong, unles [sic] I oblige my self to do none. . . . But without prejudice to the Society into which I enter, I may and do retain to my self the Liberty of doing what I please in all things relating particularly to my self, or in which I am to seek my own convenience.[11]

Notice that Sidney presupposes an autonomy to employ one's own life, liberty, and property in a way most conducive to individual happiness, yet recognizes a legitimate governmental power to restrict such autonomy if it harms the lives, liberty, or property of others. In a similar vein, Jeremy Bentham's *Principles of Legislation* posited that "the greatest possible latitude should be left to individuals, in all cases in which they can injure none but themselves, for they are the best judges of their own interests. . . . The power of the law need interfere only to prevent them from injuring each other."[12] Richard Price, writing his *Observations on the Nature of Civil Liberty*, published in 1776, stated the harm principle thus: "Government is an institution for the benefit of the people governed. . . . *A free state, at the same time that it is free itself, makes all its members free by excluding licentiousness, and guarding their persons and property and good name against insult. It is the end of all just government, at the same time that it secures the liberty of the public against foreign injury, to secure the liberty of the individual against private injury.* I do not, therefore, think it strictly just to say, that it belongs to the nature of government to entrench on private liberty. It ought never to do this, except as far as the exercise of private liberty encroaches on the liberties of others."[13] Although Price acknowledges that government legitimately may "exclud[e] licentiousness," he does so in a context that unmistakably suggests that licentiousness should be defined as an exercise of liberty that results "private injury," thereby "encroach[ing] on the liberties of others."

Numerous other prominent political philosophers prior to and contemporaneous with the American Revolution, such as Thomas Paine,[14] Edmund Burke[15] Lord John Somers,[16] Burlamaqui,[17] David Hume,[18] Lord Kames,[19] DeLolme,[20] Beccaria,[21] Grotius,[22] Montesquieu,[23] Samuel Von Pufendorf[24] and John Warr,[25] articulated the view that the purpose of government was to secure the citizenry by providing a neutral and peaceful means of punishing acts that harmed the life, liberty, or property of others.

Even assuming that the dominant political philosophy of the founding generation accepted some form of a harm principle as the animating factor of law, one must still be convinced that this philosophy spilled over to the Framers themselves. The historical evidence is abundant in this regard. James Wilson, a

Federalist member of the Continental Congress, delegate to the federal constitutional convention, and one of the first Justices of the Supreme Court, bluntly proclaimed the harm principle: "[Nature] has endowed [man] with intellectual and active powers; she has furnished him with a natural impulse to exercise his powers for his own happiness, and the happiness of those, for whom he entertains such tender affections. If all this be true, the undeniable consequence is, that *he has a right to exert those powers for the accomplishment of these purposes, in such a manner, and upon such objects, as his inclination and judgment shall direct; provided he does no injury to others. . . .*"[26]

Wilson more pointedly declared in his famed lectures on law, "Suppose . . . that one has done neither a wrong nor an injury to any individual, yet if he has committed something which the law has prohibited, it is a crime, which demands reparation, because the right of the superiour [the government] is violated, and because an injury is offered to the dignity of his [the government's] character. How naturally one mistake leads to another! A law which prohibits what is neither a wrong nor an injury to any one! What name does it deserve? . . . The doctrine, that a crime may be committed against the publick [sic], without an injury being done to an individual, is as little consonant to the history, as it is to the principles of criminal jurisprudence."[27] The necessary prerequisite of an injury to fellow citizens perceived by Wilson was not limited to criminal law. Wilson recognized that civil law was also predicated on injury to a fellow citizen—what he termed a "wrong" rather than an "injury"—so that all laws, whether civil or criminal, required for their legitimacy an antecedent infliction of harm to a fellow citizen.[28] Similarly, Federalist John Dickinson, in *The Letters of Fabius,* urged ratification of the proposed Constitution with the following appeal to his fellow citizens:

> Each individual then must contribute such a share of his rights, as is necessary for attaining that security that is essential to freedom; and he is bound to make this contribution by the law of his nature, which prompts him to a participated happiness; . . . therefore, he must submit his will, in what concerns all, to the will of all, that is of the whole society. What does he lose by this submission? The power of doing injuries to others—and the dread of suffering injuries from them. What does he gain by it? The aid of those associated with him, for his relief from the incommodities of mental or bodily weakness—the pleasure for which his heart is formed—of doing good—protection against injuries—a capacity of enjoying his undelegated rights to the best advantage—a repeal of his fears—and tranquility of mind—or, in other words, that perfect liberty better described in the Holy Scriptures, than any where else, in these expressions—"When every man shall sit under his vine, and under his

fig-tree, and none shall make him afraid." . . . [C]onfederation should promote the happiness of individuals, or it does not answer the intended purpose.[29]

Fabius thus assumes that, although individuals cede some of their natural liberty when joining together to form a government, they do so only in order to make their lives better, more secure, and happier overall. The natural liberty that citizens lose when forming government, in Fabius's words, is the "power of doing injury to others—and the dread of suffering injuries from them." Citizens relinquish their liberty to hurt others at whim or in retaliation and gain in return governmental protection from external harm.

John Jay—one of the three authors of the *Federalist Papers*—likewise proclaimed that the "order [in society] consists in every man *moving in his own sphere,* doing the duties incumbent upon him, and *not going out of the circle of his own rights and powers to meddle with or officiously supervise those of others.*"[30] Jay's statement suggests that he conceptualized individual liberty broadly, encompassing actions within an individual's "own sphere," which Jay defined as actions that did not "meddle with or officiously supervise" the rights of others. This conceptualization of liberty is consistent with the dominant political philosophy, implicitly incorporating a notion of harm as demarcating the division between individual liberty and governmental power.

Madison's *Federalist No. 54* similarly revealed that he believed "[g]overnment is instituted no less *for protection of the property than of the persons of individuals,*" an implicit reference to a harm principle defining the reach of legitimate governmental power.[31] Madison's embrace of a harm principle was even more evident in a 1792 essay he wrote about property in the *National Gazette,* in which he proclaimed that "[g]overnment is instituted to protect property of every sort; as well that which lies in the various rights of individuals, as that which the term particularly expresses. *This being the end of government, that alone is a just government, which impartially secures to every man, whatever is his own.*"[32] Many other Federalists, including John Hancock,[33] James Iredell,[34] Fisher Ames,[35] Alexander Hamilton,[36] and Elbridge Gerry[37] made similar declarations evincing knowledge of and support for the idea that government was instituted for the purpose of protecting citizens' LLP from harm.

The Federalists' approval of the harm principle was shared by the Anti-Federalists, who were even more ardent in their belief that governmental power should restrain individual liberty only when needed to prevent harm to others. Thomas Jefferson asserted the need explicitly to protect freedom of conscience on the basis that "[t]he legitimate powers of government extend only to such acts as are *injurious to others*. But it does me *no injury* for my neighbor to say there are twenty Gods, or no God. *It neither picks my pocket nor breaks my leg.* If it be said, his testimony in a court of justice cannot be relied on, reject it then, and be the stigma on him."[38] Similarly, in his presidential inaugural speech in 1801, Jefferson declared, "[Providence] delights in the happiness of man here and his greater happiness hereafter; with all these blessings, what more is necessary to make us a happy and a prosperous people? Still one thing more, fellow citizens—*a wise and frugal government which shall restrain men from injuring one another, shall leave them otherwise free to regulate their own pursuits of industry and improvement. . . . This is the sum of good government,* and this is necessary to close the circle of our felicities."[39] Indeed, by the early nineteenth century, Jefferson had become angered by what he perceived to be the failure of the American legislative branch to adhere to the harm principle and restrain the exercise of its powers: "Our legislators are not sufficiently apprised of the rightful limits of their power; that their true office is to declare and enforce only our natural rights and duties and to take none of them from us. *No man has a natural right to commit aggression on the equal rights of another, and this is all from which the laws ought to restrain him; every man is under the natural duty of contributing to the necessities of the society, and this is all the laws should enforce on him. . . .*"[40]

Other vocal and prominent Anti-Federalists such as Centinel,[41] the Impartial Examiner,[42] Brutus,[43] James Winthrop,[44] James Warren,[45] Mercy Otis Warren,[46] and George Clinton[47] indicated an acceptance of a harm principle. The historical record thus reveals that, whether Federalist or Anti-Federalist, the founding generation acknowledged a harm principle as defining the legitimate boundary of governmental power, thereby preserving a broad residual realm of individual liberty.

DEFINING HARM TO LLP

How does a government prevent harm to the life, liberty, and property (LLP) of its citizens? It does so by enacting laws and providing a system of justice for the resolution of disputes in which either an individual citizen's or the collective society's LLP has been deprived. Some deprivations of LLP are deemed criminal acts because, although the harm has been suffered by a particular individual, society has found the harm sufficiently malicious or severe that the action potentially warrants a loss of liberty by the wrongdoer. Other deprivations of LLP are deemed civil violations because the injury inflicted is viewed as less malicious or severe and thus warrants not a loss of liberty, but the loss of property by the wrongdoer. The line between criminal and civil law has been debated extensively elsewhere and will not be reexamined here. The important thing for present purposes is that under either criminal or civil law, there has been an act by a wrongdoer that has deprived another individual of LLP.

An act that deprives an individual (or society) of LLP is thus within the legitimate cognizance of American law, whether civil or criminal, and sanctions may be levied upon the actor who causes such deprivation. Yet this begs the more important question: What constitutes a deprivation of LLP that is properly cognizable by the law? Can a person or society be considered deprived of LLP if the deprivation has been self-inflicted? Likewise, would an act that harms the moral sensibility of an individual or of a significant segment of society be considered a deprivation of LLP? In other words, how do you know if there has been a deprivation of LLP?

Unfortunately, neither the Framers nor the influential political philosophers of the era offered much guidance as to how, precisely, to define harm. And it has been the inherent difficulty in defining harm that has spawned the most ardent criticism of the harm principle's utility. The definition of harm I offer below, therefore, is derived from the historical understanding of the legitimate purpose of government as protecting the life, liberty, and property of citizens, which creates three categories of harm to define and consider: (1) harm to life; (2) harm to liberty; and (3) harm to property.

What does it mean to harm another person's life? A common-sense definition would include acts that cause or reasonably threaten to cause physical injury of the body, such as bruises, cuts, broken bones or, of course, death. Much of criminal law (and a good deal of tort law as well) is aimed at remedying these sorts of life harms, including laws proscribing assault, battery, rape, and murder. This definition of life harm tracks substantially Blackstone's common law definition of "the right of personal security," thus providing a plausible and appropriate historical context.[48]

An individual's liberty may be harmed by an act that causes or reasonably threatens to cause a loss of physical locomotion or bodily control. Laws prohibiting kidnaping and false arrest are classic examples. Once again, this definition of liberty harm offered is consistent with historical references. Thomas Jefferson, for example, asserted that harm to personal liberty would consist of action that denied a citizen's right to "mov[e] and us[e] [his body] at his own will."[49] Blackstone's *Commentaries* similarly defined personal liberty as "the power of loco-motion, of changing situation, or removing one's person to whatsoever place one's own inclination may direct; without imprisonment or restraint, unless by due course of law."[50] Blackstone's definition, by allowing restraint or imprisonment when afforded "due course of law," was incorporated into the Due Process Clauses of the Fifth and Fourteenth Amendments. It is also reflected in the reverence afforded the writ of habeas corpus, which was incorporated into the Constitution in Article I, section nine.[51] And finally, the Supreme Court's recognition of a constitutionally protected "right to travel" necessarily implies that either governmental or private interference with individual locomotion is illegitimate.[52]

The third category of harm that may be restrained by government is harm to property. Harm to property occurs when an act causes or reasonably threatens to cause a loss of value, possession, or peaceful enjoyment to the owner of one of the four types of property recognized and valued by the Framers: real, personal, intellectual, or reputational.[53] Examples of such laws include prohibitions against larceny, embezzlement, trespassing, copyright infringement, and defamation. That property was one of the most important rights valued by the Framers is evident in numerous constitutional provisions, including the Fifth Amendment Takings Clause, the Fourth Amendment Search and Seizure Clause, the Contracts Clause of Article I, and the Due Process Clauses.[54] And again, the legitimacy of governmentally imposed punishment for property harms is echoed in Blackstone's *Commentaries,* which devoted an entire volume to the topic.[55]

Excluding Emotional Harm

Acts that result in emotional or psychological harm—including such things as pain and suffering—are not, according to the definition of LLP harms proffered above, acts that result in legally cognizable harm.[56] Thus, when an individual commits adultery, it reasonably can be expected to harm the adulterer's spouse emotionally, though not a loss of life, liberty, or property.[57] Similarly, when one slanders a merchant by accusing him of failing to deliver goods as promised, such a comment, if untruthful, reasonably can be expected to result in demonstrable reputational (property) harm[58] to the merchant. Conversely, if one merely expresses the opinion that the merchant is a jerk, the comment, though perhaps emotionally harmful, cannot reasonably be expected to result in demonstrable reputational (property) harm.

This is not meant to suggest that emotional harm is not sincerely felt or somehow insignificant. It is meant to suggest, however, that emotional harm, because of its subjectivity and ubiquity, should not be considered a proper subject for the law. There are simply too many actions that potentially can result in emotional harm to others, and the existence of emotional harm is too variable to be either reasonably measurable or predictable. If citizens could be jailed, fined, or sued for any action that is emotionally hurtful or offensive to others, there would be very few areas of individual liberty indeed. Living in a pluralistic society demands that adults develop a certain thickness of skin toward offensive acts, though this does not prevent us from attempting to avoid them, voicing our objections, or attempting to educate or persuade others to cease.

Some will undoubtedly point out that pain and suffering are widely recognized as legitimate bases for recovery under principles of tort law. This is certainly true, though recovery for these kinds of emotional damages is increasingly facing restriction under various tort reform laws.[59] Someone might try to hypothesize a situation in which Y subjects Z to a series of painful electrical shocks against Z's will and query whether the law legitimately may provide a remedy.[60] My response is that under such circumstances, Z's liberty interest has been harmed since Z has been held against his will during the duration of the electric shock treatment. Moreover, Z's life interest has also likely been harmed, since he may have experienced some bruising or cuts as a result of Y's attempt to restrain Z. These life and liberty interests are the proper subject of legal remedies, though Z's subjective allegations of pain and suffering are not.

Others will undoubtedly complain that excluding emotional harm would render illegitimate the torts of intentional or negligent infliction of emotional distress. This is accurate but not lamentable. These torts are new creations in American law, with their origins in the post–New Deal era, and stand as the only instances in which the American legal system allows recovery for purely emotional harm.[61] The inconsistent and seemingly unjust application of these torts, their potential to chill free speech, and their simultaneously aggressive and frivolous use in contexts such as divorce and employment litigation have prompted extensive academic criticism.[62] Their demise is accordingly long overdue.

Whatever the current acceptance of purely emotional damages, their recognition is not harmonious with the harm principle espoused here. Although we may have great empathy for a victim who suffers emotional distress as a result of the harmful act of another, pain and suffering are incapable of objective verification or measurement, and attempting to compensate for such emotional harms contributes to the unfortunate perception that civil judgments, particularly those rendered by so-called runaway juries, are out of control. There is ample latitude for adequate and objective compensation for victims of harm without resorting to the standard-less and ultimately futile effort to compensate for emotional suffering. If A's actions render B disabled for life, B will be permitted to recover significant damages for the harm to his life, including recovery for things such as medical expenses and lost future earnings. He will, in this sense, be made as whole as the law can reasonably provide. If the defendant's harmful acts were sufficiently callous, the law of punitive damages additionally may be applied to deter the defendant (and others in his position) from inflicting similar harm in the future. In a sense, punitive damages are little more than a means-based tax imposed on those who have demonstrated, through particularly callous conduct, a high threat of harm to others. The tax is intended to prevent future harm to the LLP of others, and punitive damages are therefore a legitimate exercise of governmental power consonant with the morality of American law.

Excluding Societal Harm

The reader will likely note that the definition of harm I have proffered is limited to demonstrable harm or threatened harm to individuals, not to society as a whole. This does not mean, however, that societal interests are never a legitimate basis for restricting individual liberty. The legitimacy of societal interests as a basis for restricting individual liberty depends on the basis for concluding that societal interests exist.

Perhaps the best place to start is with a hypothetical. Ten people form a small community on an island. One of the ten discovers an intoxicating substance and begins consuming it, to the point of intoxication, on a daily basis. In his intoxicated state, he does not harm others physically or disturb their quiet enjoyment of the island. The other nine refrain from consuming the intoxicant, believing it is debauchery and evil.[63]

Assuming the nine offended citizens cannot banish or exile their fellow citizen, what are the offended nine to do? As Patrick Devlin puts it, "must they in the name of freedom leave the [one] at large, relying on the strength of their own virtue to resist contamination and in time to convert the vicious?"[64] Does the potential for contamination and the moral weakness of the nine justify restraining the liberty of the one to consume the intoxicant? Devlin and others argue that the answer is yes—restrictions on individual liberty are "good for the individual who is being punished" and "good [for] those who might be led into evil by example or temptation."[65]

Devlin's response is both unabashedly paternalistic and majoritarian. His theory of liberty makes no room for the minority, who, although competent adults, are told "it's for your own good" even though their actions do nothing more than offend the sensibilities and test the moral convictions of the majority. Such a view of liberty is deeply antithetical to the concept of individual equality (and hence, individual sovereignty) because it reincarnates the conception of plenary legislative power—which may be very well and fine under the morality of British law, but which is utterly incompatible with the morality of American law.

Yet there are some instances in which societal interests legitimately may trump individual liberty. "Aha!" some may now proclaim, "the list of exceptions begins." Actually, no. There is a specific textual reason why some societal interests may trump individual sovereignty. The Constitution is a proclamation of the legitimate interests of government. Because the Constitution expressly grants certain powers to government, a citizen's liberty has been relinquished according to the extent of the power granted. A citizen is obligated to support the legitimate exercises of governmental power and may be punished when he fails to do so. For example, Article I, Section Eight of the Constitution grants the federal government power to lay and collect taxes. When the government decides to levy taxes, citizens have a corresponding duty to pay them, and failure to do so may result in a legitimate restriction on their liberty. A citizen's failure to pay taxes harms society's interests that have been explicitly declared in the Constitution. Similarly, Article III of the Constitution creates a federal judiciary to adjudicate specific types of cases. In order carry out the judicial function effectively, judges are appointed, juries are empaneled, and witnesses are called to the stand. If a citizen commits perjury or attempts to bribe a judge or witness, such acts harm society's explicitly declared interest in adjudicating specific types of disputes. A citizen thus is not at liberty to lie on the witness stand. Perjury is legitimately proscribable, not because lying is immoral, but because citizens have ceded a judicial power to the government and relinquished their liberty to the extent necessary to effectuate the judiciary's basic purpose of achieving justice.

These types of collective societal interests are legitimately cognizable (whereas normally they are not) because the people have explicitly acknowledged in the Constitution that these collective societal interests exist. The people, in ratifying the Constitution, consciously relinquished their individual sovereignty over these matters, and their liberty to act may be proscribed in order to effectuate the goals of these governmental powers. These kinds of explicitly pronounced collective societal interests are thus distinguishable from other alleged societal interests that sometimes motivate the enactment of ordinary laws. Although legislators often sincerely believe they are acting with societal interests in mind, mere majoritarian beliefs that X is in society's best interest simply cannot justify restrictions on individual sovereignty. Something more is required before government may restrict individual liberty in the absence of evidence that the act harms the LLP of others—an explicit declaration, within the constitutional text, of the existence of a collective societal interest. This ensures that individual liberty will not be eroded in the name of societal interests that are pretexts for discrimination, hatred, passion, or simply ignorance.

It is also important to recognize that society as a whole constantly benefits by laws that proscribe harm or threatened harm to the LLP of its individual members. If a law prohibits battery, for example, I can be expected to benefit from that law even if no one ever hits me. The deterrent effect of legal proscription benefits society as a whole. Similarly, society benefits from laws that prohibit threatened harm. If someone stores explosives in an unsafe manner, escapes prison, bribes a police officer, or refuses to obtain certain vaccinations, there may be no resulting harm to any one particular individual, but such acts pose a reasonable threat of harm to others if they are not proscribed. The building may later explode, the prisoner may commit new crimes, the police officer may fail to protect the innocent, and the neighbors may become infected. Laws aimed at preventing reasonably threatened harms are thus legitimate exercises of governmental power that benefit society as a whole. The same logic justifies the enactment of environmental laws. Polluting the environment may not always demonstrably harm any particular individual, but it can reasonably be expected to do so if unchecked. Individuals who drink polluted water or breathe polluted air may become ill or nearby property owners' land values may decline, all of which constitute cognizable LLP harms.[66]

Competing Sovereignty

Though collective societal interests are not a legitimate basis for restricting individual liberty, there is another, more subtle dimension to societal interests than just majoritarian desires to restrain fellow citizens. In particular, there are many situations in which one person's exercise of individual sovereignty clashes head-on with another's. In such instances of competing sovereignty, whose sovereignty should prevail? To what extent may the law interfere with these competing sovereignties?

A few examples will set the stage. Suppose Arthur wants to play Metallica loudly at 2 a.m. but Betty next door wishes to sleep. Perhaps Andrew wants to peep into Barbara's window to see her undress but Barbara does not desire onlookers. Or what if Amanda and Bob want to have sex in a public park, but Carol and Dick want to enjoy their picnic without this distraction. In situations where individuals' sovereignty is at odds, the law must first determine whether any of the individuals' acts may be fairly characterized as harmful to others.

The law of nuisance operates on this principle and is the primary vehicle by which competing individual sovereignties are adjudicated.[67] Consistent with the harm principle advocated here, the law of nuisance requires proof of injury or harm to another's property.[68] Thus, Arthur's love for Metallica and Andrew's desire to peep at naked ladies clearly diminishes the ability of Betty and Barbara to peacefully enjoy their own property and thus constitutes a harm to their LLP. Similarly, Amanda and Bob's passion, if expressed in a public park, reduces the enjoyment (and hence value) of that property by others such as Carol and Dick. Although Carol and Dick do not own the public park in the sense of possessing title, they have a share in the ownership of it as citizens and therefore an interest in both its value and quiet enjoyment.

The same logic goes, of course, for other common types of nuisances such as pig farms, slaughterhouses, smoke stacks, explosives storage, and the like. In each case, it is the actual or reasonably threatened harm to the LLP of others that justifies their classification as a nuisance and the resulting imposition of legal sanctions. Indeed, the common law of nuisance clearly hinged on the application of the maxim *sic utere tuo ut alienum non laedas*.[69]

A more complicated case is presented when John wishes to smoke a cigarette at a restaurant after dinner. If Mary at the next table objects, whose sovereignty should prevail? As an initial matter, it should be clear that Mary has no property interest in the privately owned restaurant. If John's liberty to smoke in the restaurant is going to be restricted, the most obvious source of the restriction would be the restaurant owner, who has authority to dictate whether patrons may smoke on his property. Assuming the restaurant owner does not mind patrons smoking, may the government mandate that the restaurant be smoke free? This is a question that has been debated in recent years.

The justification for anti-smoking ordinances is not harm to property, but harm to the life of others. Specifically, it was not until evidence surfaced regarding the potentially harmful effects of second-hand smoke that anti-smoking ordinances began to be enacted. The logic is that smoking in public involuntarily subjects non-smokers to potentially harmful second-hand smoke.[70] Assuming there is sufficient evidence to support a conclusion that second-hand smoke reasonably threatens harm to others, it is a legitimate exercise of governmental power to prohibit or regulate smoking in public. It should be kept in mind, however, that respect for the principles of limited government and residual individual sovereignty demands that there be an appropriate "fit" between the evidence of harm and the scope of the law. A law that banned smoking on public streets or in public parks, for example, would likely be overbroad, since there is no evidence that smoking in open air venues poses a reasonable threat of harm to others. A law that banned smoking in enclosed spaces such as restaurants or office buildings, by contrast, could provide an appropriate ends-means fit.

In nuisance situations, wherein one person's exercise of liberty threatens or harms another person's LLP, the government should strive always to regulate rather than prohibit. Reasonable "time, place, or manner" restrictions should therefore be the preferred approach to liberty conflicts between citizens, in order to best respect the principles of residual individual sovereignty and limited government. Much can be learned, therefore, from First Amendment jurisprudence, which employs the time, place, manner concept to resolve many disputes. Although the First Amendment uses perhaps the most absolute language of all individual rights in the Constitution—"Congress shall make no law"—the Supreme Court has never interpreted First Amendment rights to be absolute, allowing the imposition of reasonable time, place, or manner restrictions.[71] A similar approach in the context of other individual liberties thus would be both textually and contextually reasonable, and would honor the principles of limited government and residual individual sovereignty.

Excluding Self-Harm

Of the many Framers and philosophers who espoused the harm principle, few stopped to consider whether it would be a legitimate exercise of governmental power to restrain individuals from harming themselves. Of those who did give some cursory thought to the issue, some seem to have assumed that self-harm was not within the legitimate reach of governmental power,[72] while others assumed the contrary, though the discussion was often limited to the specific act of suicide.[73] Thomas Jefferson was unusual in his explicit reference to self-harm, declaring that "the care of every man's soul belongs to himself. [B]ut what if he neglect the care of it? [W]ell what if he neglect the care of his health or estate, which more nearly relate to the state. [W]ill the magistrate make a law that he shall not be poor or sik? [L]aws provide against injury from others; but not from ourselves. God himself will not save men against their wills."[74]

The early Supreme Court seems to have assumed that preventing self-harm was not a legitimate function of government. In the 1819 case of *Bank of Columbia v. Okely*[75] a debtor argued that a Maryland statute allowing summary procedures to collect on an unpaid bank note violated the federal and state guarantees to a civil jury trial. The Court's preliminary analysis of the constitutionality of the summary procedures statute queried, "What was the object of those restrictions [the right to civil jury trial]?" [76] The Court answered, "It could not have been to protect the citizen from his own acts, for it would have operated as a restraint upon his rights. It must have been against the acts of others."[77] The Court went on to conclude that because the debtor had voluntarily chosen to sign a note negotiable at a bank that was under the jurisdiction of the Maryland law (which allowed summary collection procedures), the debtor had knowingly relinquished his right to a civil jury trial for the collection of the unpaid debt.[78] The *Bank of Columbia* Court thus unanimously assumed that the right to a civil jury trial was not designed to "protect the citizen from his own acts"[79] because paternalistic protection against self-harm would constitute "a restraint upon his rights."[80] Rather, the right to a civil jury trial was designed to protect "against the acts of others."[81] The *Bank of Columbia* Court unflinchingly began its analysis, not only by acknowledging a harm principle, but by acknowledging that protection against self-inflicted harm was not a legitimate exercise of governmental power because it disregarded the principle of residual individual sovereignty.

Excluding self-harm is not only consistent with the morality of American law but crucial to its realization. There are innumerable acts that may cause or threaten to cause self-inflicted harm: excessive consumption of fatty food, bungee jumping, riding a bicycle without a helmet, attempting suicide, using intoxicating substances, and having sex without a condom, to name but a few. The defining characteristic of these activities is that the risk of harm is borne exclusively by the actor. Although society may condemn poor eating habits or snorting cocaine, these activities alone do not threaten the LLP of others.

There are, of course, some self-harming activities that may indeed pose a risk of harm to others' LLP and, because of this risk of external harm, are legitimately proscribable by law. A classic example is driving while intoxicated, which has been shown to pose a reasonable risk of harm to the lives and property of others. Individuals are therefore not at liberty to choose to drive while intoxicated, though they are at liberty to choose to drink, even past the point of intoxication.

One might argue that engaging in self-destructive or risky behaviors poses a risk of harm to others because, say, riding a motorcycle without a helmet may harm the cyclist, which, in turn, may harm fellow citizens' property, because they will pay for the cyclist's medical care, either directly (through government-sponsored health programs such as Medicare or Medicaid) or indirectly (through higher health insurance premiums). The response to this argument is that the chain of causation used to establish the harm to other individuals' property is too attenuated. It requires us to make several unreasonable, purely speculative inferences: (1) that the helmet-less cyclist will eventually fall and suffer physical harm to his head; (2) that the government (and hence, other individual taxpayers) will bear the cost of the cyclist's physical harm; or alternatively, (3) that the cyclist's care will be paid for by private insurance; and (4) that the private insurer will then raise premiums for all other beneficiaries, resulting in a cognizable property harm.

Inference (1) is reasonable, as far as it goes. Most people would agree that some cyclists who fail to don helmets will eventually fall and suffer head injuries that could have been ameliorated or prevented by the use of a helmet. But inference (2) is not reasonable since most Americans do not receive government-sponsored medical care, so generalized harm of this nature is too speculative.[82] Inference (3) is plausible, however, since the chances are good that the helmet-less cyclist's care will be paid for by private insurance. Inference (4) once again takes us beyond the bounds of reasonable inference, however, since whether or to what extent a private insurer will raise premiums is a complex matter dependent upon multiple variables unaffected by helmet-less cyclists' injuries, including the health of other members of the insured group; the amount of reserves on hand; the regulatory and political environment; competition in the marketplace; and the presence or effectiveness of cost management mechanisms such as selective provider contracts, utilization review, and beneficiary cost-sharing. There is simply no reasonable causal link between helmet-less riders and an increase in health care premiums and thus no reasonable threat to others' LLP.

In instances of self-inflicted harm, the wrongdoer and the victim are the same. If there is no harm or reasonably threatened harm to others, there is no legitimate basis for governmental intervention. If society wishes to deter individuals from engaging in risky, potentially self-destructive behavior, the legitimate way to accomplish this goal is to appeal to fellow citizens' reason and self-interest, persuasion which can be undertaken privately or with public dollars. Educational efforts aimed at preventing self-inflicted harm would respect the principles of limited government and residual individual sovereignty and likely yield more effective and meaningful results over the long term than heavy-handed governmental prohibitions.

Harm to Incompetents

The preceding discussion should make clear that the morality of American law suggests that, for adults, there should be a "presumption of liberty"[83] in favor of individuals and against governmental restraint, permitting restraint only when an exercise of individual liberty has harmed or can reasonably be expected to harm another's LLP. The burden should fall on the government to articulate the need for liberty-restraining laws, not on individuals to articulate the necessity of their liberty (as is the current practice). Such a shift in presumptions would more faithfully honor the morality of American law.

A shift in favor of liberty, however, would apply only to competent adults, who are in no need of paternalistic protection by the government. They are capable of making their own decisions and living with the consequences. But not all members of society possess such a presumptive right to autonomy. Minors and those adjudged *non compos mentis* legitimately are deserving of paternalistic protection by the state because they do not have (or, in the case of minors, do not yet have) the requisite capacity to make their own decisions.[84] For those citizens unable to exercise autonomous choice, the government legitimately may make decisions to protect their best interests. Because incompetent individuals' ability to self-govern (sovereignty) is impaired, government may protect them from harm, whether the risk of harm emanates from themselves or from others.

THE MORALITY OF LAW VERSUS
PUBLIC MORALITY

The circumference of the morality of American law is much narrower than that of public morality. Public morality, which is grounded in particular religious or cultural beliefs, concerns itself with many activities beyond those that harm or threaten harm to the life, liberty, or property of others. Public morality, for example, may condemn dancing or drinking alcohol and thus drive the legislature to enact prohibitory laws. But dancing and drinking alcohol do not per se harm or reasonably threaten harm to the LLP of others and, as such, prohibiting them would be an illegitimate exercise of governmental power. A law that prohibits driving while intoxicated, however, would be a legitimate exercise of government power, since impaired driving can reasonably be expected to result in harm to another person's LLP. The threat to others' LLP thus provides the legitimate basis for driving-while-intoxicated laws, not a belief that consumption of certain substances or intoxication itself is immoral.

Public morality also may mandate that individuals take certain affirmative actions, such as giving to charity, attending religious services, or telling the truth. The morality of American law, by contrast, would not tolerate a law mandating individual action other than that necessary to carry out the powers explicitly ceded to government. Beyond requiring citizens to support the exercise of explicitly ceded government powers (e.g., paying taxes), the morality of law does not demand affirmative acts from the citizenry. We cannot be forced to (or punished for failure to) bathe regularly or exercise three times a week. Even though our odor or obesity may be deeply offensive to others, it does not harm their LLP in any way. Similarly, if one fails to warn a blind man of an open manhole cover, the blind man will likely fall into the hole and hurt himself. But the harm to the blind man was not caused by the failure to warn because there was a necessary and independent cause—the open manhole cover—that created the risk in the first place. Failure to warn the blind man may be a disconcerting moral or ethical lapse, but it is not the cause of his harm and therefore not the legitimate subject of governmental punishment.

This causation logic also explains why the law legitimately may provide a civil remedy for negligence, which is often predicated on a failure to take certain actions deemed reasonable under the circumstances. For example, one may be negligent for failing to install a light in a dark parking lot or failing to restrain a vicious dog. The failure to take reasonable care under these circumstances creates a risk of harm to the LLP of others, and the law legitimately may punish those who create such risks when they subsequently result in harm to others. Similarly, the law legitimately cannot mandate truth-telling, yet it may punish fraud. If a person buys a home relying upon the seller's representation that the roof is new, the person may recover for fraud if he can prove that the seller lied and that the lie resulted in a loss of property—for example, the payment of a higher purchase price. The seller's fraud caused the purchaser to pay a price he would not otherwise have paid, constituting a cognizable LLP harm to the purchaser. The legitimate basis for a law prohibiting fraud is thus its deprivation of another's LLP, not a moral condemnation of lying per se.

The same reasoning applies to the keeping of promises. Although many consider it immoral to break a promise, if government legitimately could punish individuals merely because they broke a promise the jails would be crowded indeed. If Bill promises to call Nancy after their date and fails to do so, Nancy may be heartbroken, but her LLP has not been harmed. But if Bill offers to buy Nancy's television for $100, she accepts, and Bill subsequently fails to pay, the law of contracts legitimately provides a remedy. This is not because Bill broke his promise to Nancy but because Bill's promise was supported by consideration, an essential contractual element defined as a performance or return promise that is bargained for (and thus inherently valued).[85] Bill has not merely failed to keep a promise to Nancy but has failed to keep his *bargain* with her, and she has lost something valuable ($100) as a result. It is the presence of consideration that distinguishes unenforceable promises from enforceable contracts.[86] And it is the lost bargain—a harm to the property of the other contracting party—that legitimates the imposition of a civil remedy, not bare moral condemnation against breaking promises.[87]

THE PRESENT ROLE OF PUBLIC MORALITY
IN AMERICAN LAW

The ensuing chapters will examine and apply the morality of American law to specific important applications of governmental power that restrict individual liberty. But before doing this, we should pause to consider how American law currently conceptualizes the tension between individual privacy and public morality.

The basic question, "Is morality alone a sufficient basis for law?" has been excessively debated yet remains curiously unanswered, even after more than two hundred years of American legal development. The most significant case to present the question arose just a few years ago, when the U.S. Supreme Court, in *Lawrence v. Texas*,[88] was asked to determine whether a Texas law criminalizing adult homosexual sodomy was constitutional. The Court invalidated the law and strongly intimated (though did it not explicitly declare) that laws grounded solely in public morality were violative of individual liberty.

In reaching its decision, the *Lawrence* majority reversed a contrary decision of the Court only seventeen years earlier in *Bowers v. Hardwick*.[89] Five Justices in *Lawrence* based their decision on substantive due process, reasoning that the law infringed upon the liberty component of the Fourteenth Amendment.[90] A sixth Justice, Justice O'Connor, agreed that the law was unconstitutional, not because it violated substantive liberty, but because it violated the guarantee of equal protection under the law.[91]

O'Connor's concurrence highlights the intractability of the debate regarding the proper role of morality as a basis for law. On the one hand, she clearly believed that the promotion of morality is a legitimate basis for a law in the specific context of a substantive liberty challenge.[92] On the other hand, she also clearly believed that the promotion of morality was not legitimate basis for a law in the context of an equal protection challenge because she considered legislative classifications grounded solely in public morality as a pretext for discrimination.[93] Justice O'Connor thus concluded that "the State cannot single out one identifiable class of citizens for punishment that does not apply to everyone else, with moral disapproval as the only asserted state interest for the law."[94]

Justice O'Connor's concurrence in *Lawrence* posits an interesting constitutional conundrum: a state may legitimately restrict the liberty of everyone solely because of moral offense, yet it may not restrict the liberty of a certain class of citizens because of moral offense. Viewed this way, moral condemnation can be the basis of law only if it is applied universally. Thus, if the Texas law had prohibited sodomy for all—not just homosexuals—O'Connor presumably would have viewed this as a valid exercise of government power. The constitutional message discerned by Justice O'Connor was not a respect for residual individual liberty, but a respect for equal application of the law. The legislative power to restrict individual liberty is thus not only plenary, but can and should be exercised to restrict the liberty of all, not merely a subset of the citizenry.

Three dissenting Justices in *Lawrence*—Scalia, Rehnquist, and Thomas—agreed with Justice O'Connor that moral condemnation is a legitimate basis for restricting the liberty of all citizens. They reiterated the *Bowers* Court's earlier statement that "[t]he law is constantly based on notions of morality, and if all laws representing essentially moral choices are to be invalidated under the Due Process Clause, the courts will be very busy indeed."[95] The dissenters suggested that if moral disapproval was not a legitimate basis for restricting liberty, there would be a "massive disruption of the current social order,"[96] because "[s]tate laws against bigamy, same-sex marriage, adult incest, prostitution, masturbation, adultery, fornication, bestiality, and obscenity"[97] as well as laws prohibiting "prostitution, recreational use of heroin, and . . . working more than 60 hours per week in a bakery" would be unconstitutional.[98]

A close parsing of *Lawrence* thus reveals four votes for the notion that moral condemnation, alone, is a proper basis for legal proscription, at least so long as the proscription applies to all citizens equally. But what of the other five Justices—the ones who joined in the majority? What do they think about morality as a sole basis for law? The answer, unfortunately, is not entirely clear.

The *Lawrence* majority attacked the historical analysis in *Bowers,* asserting that the *Bowers* Court offered an inaccurate and incomplete portrayal of the history of anti-sodomy laws.[99] The *Lawrence* majority also appears to have based its decision, in part, on the broad scholarly criticism of *Bowers,*[100] on the lack of detrimental reliance induced by *Bowers,*[101] and on post-*Bowers* decisions such as *Planned Parenthood of Southeastern Pennsylvania v. Casey* and *Romer v. Evans.*[102]

The missing link in the *Lawrence* majority's opinion, however, is any clear reference to the role of morality as a basis for law. The Court intriguingly quotes from Justice Stevens's dissenting opinion in *Bowers,* in which he states, "Our prior cases make two propositions abundantly clear. *First, the fact that the governing majority in a State has traditionally viewed a particular practice as immoral is not a sufficient reason for upholding a law prohibiting the practice;* neither history nor tradition could save a law prohibiting miscegenation from constitutional attack. Second, individual decisions by married persons, concerning the intimacies of their physical relationship, even when not intended to produce offspring, are a form of 'liberty' protected by the Due Process Clause of the Fourteenth Amendment. Moreover, this protection extends to intimate choices by unmarried as well as married persons."[103] The *Lawrence* majority asserted that "Justice Stevens' analysis, in our view, should have been controlling in *Bowers* and should control here."[104] This undoubtedly suggests that the *Lawrence* majority believed that moral condemnation alone is an insufficient basis for restricting liberty, at least insofar as it relates to the "intimacies of [a] physical relationship."

But what of liberty beyond intimate physical association? May moral condemnation provide a legitimate basis for restricting liberty if the action is not necessarily intertwined with physical intimacy? For example, could a state criminalize wearing boots[105] or playing shuffle-board[106] if a majority believed it was immoral? What about other morality-based laws that restrict the form of intimate relationships, but not the physical aspects of those intimate relationships, such as laws banning same-sex marriage? The answer to these questions, even post-*Lawrence,* remains elusive.

Lawrence undoubtedly provides a glimmer of recognition for the morality of law this book espouses. Yet it is far from a ringing endorsement, revealing deep ideological conflict among the bench, bar, and lay population on the issue of the proper relationship between public morality and law. At best, *Lawrence* is a shiny green jurisprudential shoot that may grow and revive the morality of American law. At worst, *Lawrence* will be a lightning rod for those who believe that law and public morality are proper bedfellows and fear the consequences of a separation. Despite its analytical and rhetorical potential, *Lawrence* may thus be relegated to little more than an interesting blip on the jurisprudential radar screen, a *sui generis* oddity limited to its specific facts.

Whatever the eventual meaning of *Lawrence,* this much is clear: the theoretical debate about the proper balance between public morality and individual privacy is no longer merely theoretical. An avalanche of lawsuits, posing the question and citing *Lawrence* as authority, will be litigated and, eventually, an analytical framework will emerge. Although this book may raise as many questions as it answers (or more), my general thesis—advocating a return to and application of the morality of American law to resolve the privacy-morality conflict—will, I hope, advance the discourse. The remaining chapters will explore various types of public morality–based laws—including limits on marriage, sex, reproduction, medical choice, and the sale or use of various intoxicants—and examine whether (or to what extent) they are consistent with the morality of American law.

Chapter 4 Marriage

What greater thing is there for two human souls
than to feel that they are joined together to strengthen
each other in all labor, to minister to each other in all sorrow,
to share with each other in all gladness,
to be one with each other in the
silent unspoken memories?
—*George Eliot*

There is perhaps no clearer illustration of the tension between individual privacy and public morality than laws relating to marriage. There are numerous laws that limit when, how, and to whom one may be married. This chapter will demonstrate that many marriage laws are based solely on public morality and therefore are illegitimate restrictions on individual liberty. Yet some marriage laws may be consistent with the morality of American law because they are reasonably calculated to prevent harm to others. Before we can dissect the legitimate from illegitimate marriage laws, however, it is useful to explore what exactly "marriage" is.

CIVIL VERSUS RELIGIOUS MARRIAGE

Civil marriage, though it varies from state to state, is the recognition of an intimate relationship from which flows various legal benefits such as workplace and retirement benefits, surrogate decision-making authority, and adoption, evidentiary, property, and tort rights. Civil marriage also bestows various extra-legal benefits such as emotional and financial support, sexual intimacy, and assistance with child-rearing. In recent years, however, these extra-legal benefits have become realizable outside the context of civil marriage, as individuals increasingly opt for committed relationships without marriage.

Religious marriage, by contrast, is distinct from civil marriage since it may be conferred only by religious authorities and the benefits and responsibilities it bestows are spiritual, not legal. Religious marriage is thus restricted to unions that are harmonious with the particular theology recognizing the marriage. Religious authorities cannot grant a civil marriage license, and the grant or denial of a civil marriage license has no impact on religious marriage. There is, in this sense, a meaningful separation of church and state.

The line between church and state gets substantially fuzzier when one examines the legal limitations imposed on marriage. Until relatively recently, marriage was considered to be a religious institution with which the government interfered very little. Whom one could marry, when one could marry, and how one should conduct one's self during marriage were defined by God's laws (as interpreted by the relevant religious authorities). The only role for secular law was to enforce marriage covenants as a private contract between families, in which the betrothed couple exchanged specific property rights.[1] It was not until the passage of Lord Hardwicke's Marriage Act in 1753 that English civil courts obtained jurisdiction to enforce secular marriage laws.[2] Secular marriage—the idea that marriage was a state-sanctioned rather than church-sanctioned institution—is a relatively new phenomenon.

The secularization of marriage in England was designed to bring a sense of uniformity and clarity to marriage that did not depend upon reference to one's religious affiliations. All marriages, to be legally recognized, were required to conform to statutory requirements and were a matter of public record. These goals were accomplished, though perhaps not without a price. Uniform laws regarding marriage infused marriage with a rigidity, a secular orthodoxy, about what constitutes marriage. What was once a matter of private morality between individual and church became a matter of public legality between individual and state.

THE NATURE OF CIVIL MARRIAGE

While civil marriage is a relatively recent legal phenomenon, its use as an exclusive means of conferring various social and legal benefits has rendered it both pragmatically and emotionally significant. Legal entanglement in marriage is extensive and perhaps pragmatically irreversible. But it is nonetheless important to ask ourselves: What liberty do individuals have to choose a spouse? Are laws restricting or encouraging marriage legitimate exercises of governmental power?

The Right to Marry

The Supreme Court has declared marriage to be a "fundamental" right,[3] suggesting that under either an equal protection or a substantive due process challenge, legal restrictions on an individual's liberty to marry should be presumptively unconstitutional. Unfortunately, the Supreme Court's marriage jurisprudence has not been so analytically tidy.

In *Loving v. Virginia,* the Court invalidated a Virginia law that deemed interracial marriage a felony,[4] depriving individuals of a "freedom to marry," which was "long recognized as one of the vital personal rights essential to the orderly pursuit of happiness by free men."[5] Because the Virginia statute drew race-based distinctions, the *Loving* Court presumed the law unconstitutional and concluded that the racial animus underlying the statute rendered it violative of both the Equal Protection and Due Process Clauses.[6]

Later, in *Zablocki v. Redhail,* the Supreme Court further elucidated the contours of marital liberty, invalidating a Wisconsin law that prohibited marriage to those who had fallen behind in child support payments or who could not convince the court that existing children would not become public charges if the marriage took place.[7] The *Zablocki* Court confirmed that the liberty to marry "is part of the fundamental 'right of privacy' implicit in the Fourteenth Amendment's Due Process Clause."[8] The Court's emphasis on the "fundamental" nature of marriage suggested that it would presume the unconstitutionality of any state law restricting marriage, yet the majority in *Zablocki* explicitly rejected this suggestion, asserting that states were free to regulate "the incidents of or prerequisites for marriage" so long as they "do not significantly interfere with decisions to enter into the marital relationship[.]"[9] Because the Wisconsin statute did indeed "significantly interfere" with indigent persons' decision to enter into marriage, the Court presumed its unconstitutionality and concluded that the statute was not narrowly tailored to effectuate the state's proffered objectives.[10]

The salient question, post-*Zablocki,* is whether a law regulating marriage is properly classified as merely regulating the "incidents or prerequisites for marriage" or whether it "significantly interferes" with a "decision to enter into" marriage. The former is, under the dicta of *Zablocki,* presumptively within the state's police power; the latter presumptively is not.[11] The difficulty, as Justice Powell's concurrence pointed out, is that the *Zablocki* majority provides no guidance as to how to differentiate these two categories.[12] Indeed, the Court's attempt to distinguish between permissible regulation of the "incidents or prerequisites" of marriage versus "substantial interference" with the "decision to enter into" marriage may sound eerily similar to civil procedure scholars, who recall an analogously frustrating attempt by the Court to draw a principled distinction between "procedural" and "substantive" law in its *Erie* jurisprudence.[13] At some level of abstraction, all procedural rules can have substantive effect and similarly, the "incidents and prerequisites" of marriage can undoubtedly have a significant impact on a person's decision to marry.

At what principled point, therefore, can the Court distinguish between laws that merely regulate the incidents/prerequisites of marriage and those that affect the decision to enter into marriage? Laws prohibiting incest or same-sex marriage, for example, could be viewed as mere regulations of the prerequisites of marriage, yet they undoubtedly impact the decision to enter into marriage by denying marriage to certain persons altogether. The diaphanous nature of these phrases suggests that doctrinal clarity or consistency across cases cannot be achieved within the existing analytical framework.

A Positive or Negative Right?

Pursuant to *Loving* and *Zablocki,* we know astonishingly little about the constitutional parameters of marriage. We do know that individuals enjoy a right to marry under the "liberty" interest of substantive due process; and that laws restricting marriage based upon race violate the Equal Protection Clause. We do not know how far this liberty to marry extends, what level of scrutiny should be applied in a particular case, or whether laws restricting marriage based on classifications other than race (e.g., sexual orientation) would violate equal protection. As odd as it may sound, we do not yet know whether the liberty to marry confers an affirmative right to obtain a state-sanctioned civil marriage, or whether it merely grants individuals a liberty to marry without undue interference from the government.

Although this may seem like hair splitting, it is a question of some importance. And it is evident from Justice Stewart's concurrence in *Zablocki* that the

Justices have at least momentarily pondered the distinction between a negative and affirmative right to marry. Justice Stewart said that he did "not agree with the Court that there is a 'right to marry' in the constitutional sense. That right (or more accurately, that privilege) is, under our federal system, defined and limited by state law."[14] Viewed as a privilege defined by the state for which certain individuals receive governmental benefits, marriage becomes something that states may not only "significantly interfere" with but could "in any circumstances absolutely prohibit," including prohibiting incestuous and polygamous marriages, marriages by minors, and marriage by those with venereal disease.[15] Justice Stewart's conception of marriage as a privilege means that, once bestowed, the status is subject to state control and could be deemed unconstitutional only if deemed fundamentally unfair[16] or violative of equal protection.

Aside from Justice Stewart's conception of civil marriage as a privilege akin to the receipt of welfare benefits, the Court has not addressed whether the right to marry is a positive or negative right. But the context of those decisions suggests that the right to marry is, like all other individual liberties, a negative right to be free from undue governmental restraint. In both *Loving* and *Zablocki,* the Court invalidated the state laws in question because they substantially interfered with an individual's "decision to enter into" marriage. Because substantial interference with an individual's marital choice is the heart of the Court's marriage jurisprudence, the liberty to marry is an autonomy-based liberty, grounded in principles of individual sovereignty. The Court's marriage jurisprudence therefore does not conceptualize the right to marry as an affirmative entitlement to a state-sanctioned marriage. Rather, the right to marry is best conceptualized as a negative right—that is, a right to be free from illegitimate governmental restrictions—a view that is harmonious with the morality of American law.

Viewed as a negative right, marital decisions fall within the realm of residual individual sovereignty, and laws restricting marriage are therefore subject to the same harm principle that animates the rest of American law. Moreover, marriage as a negative right means that states are free to abolish civil marriage—a course of action recently touted by some as a preferable alternative to extending marriage to same-sex couples.[17]

If indeed the right to marry is a negative right—that is, a type of liberty as opposed to an affirmative entitlement to state-sanctioned marriage—we must next explore whether the various laws regulating marriage are legitimate exercise of governmental power. Are these laws designed to prevent harm to the LLP of others?

As a preliminary matter, we should deal with the most commonly espoused global justifications for marriage laws. These global justifications attempt to convince us that marriage restrictions are consonant with the morality of American law because they are designed to prevent harm. For instance, it is sometimes argued that marriage restrictions are designed to protect prospective spouses by prohibiting unwise, immoral, or socially condemned choices. This argument is little more than self-harm paternalism, a form of public morality wrapped in the pretext of preventing adults from suffering moral harm or social ostracism. Under the morality of American law, this sort of paternalism is an immoral basis for restricting individual liberty because competent adults are presumptively free to make their own choices, even bad ones, so long as they do not harm the LLP of others.

Similarly, supporters of current marriage restrictions suggest that they are designed to protect the property interests of citizens. Admittedly, marriage may enhance individual citizens' prosperity by allowing spouses to combine incomes, share expenses, and reap the economic benefits bestowed by employers and state and federal governments. Yet how does restricting marriage help citizens reap these financial advantages? In fact, marriage restrictions accomplish the opposite: by limiting whom one can marry, we limits individuals' ability to live in a way that is economically advantageous. In this sense, marriage restrictions tend to harm the property interests of individual citizens, not protect them.

Other than these rather specious global attempts to justify marriage restrictions, is there any evidence that specific marriage restrictions actually do prevent harm to the LLP of other citizens? The harm-based justifications for marriage restrictions vary from law to law, and therefore we will proceed to examine specific marriage laws and discern whether the they are reasonably designed to prevent harms to the LLP of others.

COHABITATION

One of the striking oddities of American law is that, in some states,[18] marriage is the exclusive means to lawful cohabitation with a lover, which means that shacking up is criminal if the roommates have sex.[19] In some states, it is even a special crime to cohabit with a former spouse after divorce.[20] This is likely news to millions of adults, as there are more than five million unmarried partner households[21] and significantly more adults have cohabited at some point in their lives.[22] In states that have anti-cohabitation statutes, lovers who wish to live together, whether as a trial-run for marriage, for mutual convenience, or simply because they do not wish to marry, risk both criminal prosecution and equally pernicious secondary effects. Many courts, for example, consider cohabitation to be a relevant factor in determining an award of child custody.[23] Overt discrimination in housing,[24] employment,[25] and membership in private organizations[26] is lawful. Similarly, cohabitation may adversely affect a parolee's ability to relocate. A recent case involved a young woman who relocated from New York to North Carolina to be near to family. Although she was on probation for welfare fraud in New York, she was permitted to leave under the assumption that North Carolina would supervise her probation. Upon checking in with her North Carolina probation officer, the woman was informed that the state would not supervise her probation because she was violating North Carolina's anti-cohabitation law by living with the father of her two-year-old child.[27] North Carolina gave the woman three lawful choices: get married; move to another state that accepts cohabitation; or live separately from the father of her child.[28]

The only rationales offered for anti-cohabitation laws are: (1) it is immoral for anyone other than married persons to have sex; and (2) forbidding cohabitation furthers the institution of marriage by encouraging unmarried persons to marry. Preliminarily, we should question the moral nature of the result in the North Carolina case mentioned above, which effectively required the parents of a toddler to separate. But even assuming a community considers this result to be morally just, public morality cannot justify restricting an individual's liberty to choose a domestic companion, which is surely is one of the most intimate choices one can make. And if it were legitimate for a legislature to restrict liberty in order to "encourage marriage," the results would be astounding. For example, what if a legislature decided to prohibit adults from dating more than one person simultaneously because they believed players are less likely to marry? This may be a rational conclusion, but is it just? Could women be prohibited from wearing glasses while on a date pursuant to Dorothy Parker's oft-repeated admonition, "men seldom make passes at girls who wear glasses"?

There simply is no identifiable—much less demonstrable—harm to the LLP of others posed by one's choice of domestic partner. If individual sovereignty is respected as an animating principle of American law, laws prohibiting cohabitation are clearly immoral exercises of governmental power.

SAME-SEX MARRIAGE

Challenging the One Man,
One Woman Tradition

There is perhaps no more controversial subject in America today than same-sex marriage. Ideologically, culturally, and generationally, Americans are deeply divided as to whether they think same-sex marriage should be permitted by law. The debate currently taking place in early twenty-first-century America regarding the legal status of same-sex unions is remarkable considering that same-sex marriage was, until very recently, considered an oxymoron.

The historic American definition of marriage as restricted to one man and one woman[29] reflects Judeo-Christian attitudes, the genesis of which is likely the biblical command in Leviticus that "[t]hou shalt not lie with mankind, as with womankind."[30] In recent years, however, the one man, one woman norm has come under legal attack.

The first serious challenge to traditional marriage came in 1993, when the Hawaii Supreme Court ruled that restricting marriage to members of the opposite sex would be presumed to violate the state constitutional guarantee of equality unless the state could demonstrate a compelling interest in maintaining the traditional definition.[31] In response, the citizens of Hawaii amended their constitution to allow the legislature to restrict marriage to opposite-sex couples,[32] which the legislature promptly did.[33]

In response to the Hawaii case, Congress in 1996 enacted the Defense of Marriage Act (DOMA), which permits states to refuse legal recognition to the statutes or judicial decisions of other states that recognize same-sex marriages.[34] DOMA appears to reflect extant public morality: recent polls indicate that a solid majority of Americans oppose legal recognition of same-sex marriage.[35] Given public opposition to same-sex marriage, it is not surprising that most American states followed the congressional lead and enacted DOMA-inspired statutory or state constitutional bans on same-sex marriage.[36]

The enactment of DOMA-inspired bans on same-sex marriage, combined with the Supreme Court's decision in *Lawrence v. Texas,*[37] has unleashed a new wave of litigation challenging the traditional definition of marriage. Although the *Lawrence* Court repeatedly intimated that laws prohibiting same-sex marriage may be constitutional,[38] the decision's broad emphasis on individual autonomy has created new hope among supporters of same-sex marriage.[39] The lower courts that have considered the issue, post-*Lawrence,* have been deeply split on the federal constitutional issues presented,[40] and most of them have consciously avoided those issues by resting their decisions solely on state constitutional provisions.[41] At present, only one state, Massachusetts, permits same-sex couples to enter into a civil "marriage."[42]

Same-sex couples legally wed in Massachusetts will undoubtedly face discrimination by states that refuse to grant Full Faith and Credit[43] to their marriages. The salient legal question, therefore, is whether DOMA itself can withstand constitutional scrutiny, a question about which both courts and legal scholars have divided.[44] The future of same-sex marriage is also clouded by the prospect of a constitutional amendment—the Federal Marriage Amendment (FMA)—which would, if successfully ratified by two-thirds of both houses of Congress and three-quarters of the state legislatures, limit marriage in all states to one man and one woman.[45] The momentum for a federal constitutional amendment banning same-sex marriage appears to have abated, at least for the moment, most likely because Americans have a deep-seated respect for the Constitution and are loath to tinker with it unless absolutely necessary.[46] Americans are willing to wait and see what develops in the courts before deciding whether a constitutional amendment is needed. If a critical mass of state courts begins to agree with Massachusetts that prohibiting same-sex marriage is unconstitutional, it seems likely that the majority's disapproval of same-sex marriage and the perception that activist judges are thwarting democratically expressed desires will rekindle interest in a federal constitutional amendment.[47]

Applying the Morality of American Law to Same-Sex Marriage

One of the fundamental maxims of our constitutional government is that the citizenry, as possessors of residual individual sovereignty, are free to cede some of their residual liberty to the government if they deem it necessary. Relinquishment of a portion of residual individual sovereignty, however, must be accomplished, under our constitutional government, pursuant to the supermajoritarian procedures established in Article V. The Framers made it purposefully difficult for the citizens to amend the Constitution in order to maintain the delicate balance between government and individual citizen that they had achieved. But if the hurdles of Article V are overcome, the Constitution, as amended, is binding upon all. Thus, if the American public mobilizes and ratifies a constitutional amendment prohibiting the legal recognition of same-sex marriage, this amendment would be entitled to respect and enforcement.

In the absence of such a federal constitutional ban on same-sex marriage, however, we must ask ourselves: Is limiting marriage to opposite-sex couples consonant with the morality of American law? More specifically, is it reasonable to conclude that same-sex marriage would result in harm to the lives, liberty, or property of others?

Pursuant to *Lawrence,* the Court characterized its earlier abortion jurisprudence as "confirm[ing] that our laws and tradition afford constitutional protection to personal decisions relating to marriage, procreation, contraception, family relationships, child rearing, and education."[48] The Court concluded that "[p]ersons in a homosexual relationship may seek autonomy for these purposes, just as heterosexual persons do."[49] The *Lawrence* Court's analysis implies that marriage is one component of a constitutionally protected zone of residual individual sovereignty.

Yet the *Lawrence* Court was assiduous to avoid tipping its hand on the constitutionality of bans on same-sex marriage, declaring that the case did "not involve whether the government must give formal recognition to any relationship that homosexual persons seek to enter."[50] Indeed, the *Lawrence* Court strained to limit its decision to sexual, not marital, autonomy, noting that anti-sodomy statutes "touch[] upon the most private human conduct, sexual behavior, and in the most private of places, the home."[51] The majority concluded that "as a general rule" laws should not attempt to "define the meaning of the [personal] relationship or to set its boundaries *absent injury to a person or abuse of an institution the law protects.*"[52] If indeed this is a general rule that would be applied in future cases, the *Lawrence* decision suggests that there is some sort of harm principle guiding the Court.

Legal restrictions on the definitions or boundaries of intimate relationships thus would be valid only if the Court is convinced that the restriction is necessary to prevent "injury to a person" or "an abuse of an institution the law protects." The former—injury to a person—is perfectly consonant with the morality of American law. The second—abuse of an institution the law protects—is murkier. Presumably, the *Lawrence* Court was implicitly referring to the institution of marriage and possibly also the institution of family. What other institutions might fall within the *Lawrence* Court's version of the harm principle is unclear. But the salient question, in a legal challenge to a ban on same-sex marriage based on *Lawrence,* is whether restricting marriage to heterosexual couples prevents injury to other persons (e.g., children) or the institutions of marriage or family.

Opponents of same-sex marriage argue that those relationships are immoral and that, as a restriction on immoral behavior, laws limiting marriage to opposite-sex couples are within the police power of the states. But the *Lawrence* decision—consistent with the morality of American law—rejected the notion that morality alone was a legitimate basis for restricting individual liberty. If banning same-sex marriage is a legitimate exercise of governmental power, it must be because the Court is convinced that limiting marriage to heterosexuals is a reasonable measure to prevent harm to others or important institutions. Let us proceed to examine the bases for these possible harms.

ENCOURAGING PROCREATION

One of the arguments most frequently espoused in support of limiting marriage to opposite-sex couples is that doing so will encourage procreation.[53] This argument is based on a historical assumption with deep theological roots that the dominant purpose for marriage is procreation.[54] Spouses in the Christian tradition owe each other a conjugal debt, described as a "mutual exchange by a man and wife of their bodies for perpetual use in the procreation and nurture of children."[55]

The Christian expectation of sex between spouses is evident in various marriage laws, such as those that render marriages voidable if consummation is impossible.[56] Likewise, laws prohibiting extramarital sex (adultery) and premarital sex (fornication) reflect the Christian view that sex is moral only if undertaken within the context of marriage. Early court decisions echoed this assumed link between marriage, sex, and procreation. A typical example is a 1926 opinion from the Court of Appeals of New York, which denied financial support to a woman seeking legal separation from her husband because she had withheld sexual "services" from him:

> [T]he refusal of husband or wife without any adequate excuse to have ordinary marriage relations with the other party to the contract strikes at the basic obligations springing from the marriage contract when viewed from the standpoint of the State and of society at large. However much this relationship may be debased at times it nevertheless is the foundation upon which must rest the perpetuation of society and civilization. If it is not to be maintained we have the alternatives either of no children or of illegitimate children, and the State abhors either result. The mere fact that the law provides that physical incapacity for sexual relationship shall be ground for annulling a marriage is of itself a sufficient indication of the public policy that such relationship shall exist with the result and for the purpose of begetting offspring.[57]

The historical link between sex, children, and marriage is a by-product not only of religious beliefs, but also of a complex set of social, financial, medical, and emotional circumstances. Until recently, reliable contraception was neither theologically accepted nor widely available, rendering sex outside marriage a risky proposition, both socially and financially, particularly for women.[58] If an individual wanted to have sex, marriage provided the only safe context. Once a couple was married, children were not only inevitable but also desirable, for both emotional and financial reasons. Children maximized opportunity for wealth by providing additional help around the house, shop, or farm, as well as providing a source of support for the parents in old age. In short, the deep linkage between marriage and procreation is both a theological and pragmatic inevitability: Children were a desirable commodity obtainable and feasible only within the context of marriage.

If these religious, financial, and social pressures were removed, there would of course be no need to view sex, children, and marriage as necessarily linked. Indeed, these contextual circumstances linking marriage and procreation have been slowly eroding. Contraception and abortion are now readily available. Many married women are financially capable of supporting themselves and their children. The social stigma attached to single parenthood has essentially disappeared. Children are no longer viewed as financial assets but financial burdens, creating a strong incentive toward fewer children. The availability of adoption and artificial reproductive technologies such as artificial insemination and in vitro fertilization have expanded parental possibilities to single persons and same-sex couples in ways unimaginable only a few decades ago. All of these factors suggest that marriage has been transformed from a relationship centered on procreation into a relationship centered on emotional intimacy, with children purely optional.

The modern marriage is no longer a baby-making institution but an intimate companionate relationship benefiting spouses emotionally, financially, and physically. Modern law implicitly acknowledges this revised view of marriage by various means. For example, individuals are allowed to marry without declaring any intention to have children. Indeed, many modern marriages are formed wherein neither partner harbors any intent to procreate at all.[59] Likewise, individuals who are rendered infertile either through disease or simply advanced age are not barred from marriage, though the chance of their procreating is remote or even nonexistent.

PROTECTING CHILDREN

Another common justification for limiting marriage to opposite-sex partners is that doing so will encourage long-term stable relationships that benefit children.[60] In other words, marriage is designed to foster relationships that will create traditional families comprised of two committed parents and their offspring—a family structure that is beneficial to the welfare of children.

As a preliminary matter, it is obvious that restricting marriage to opposite-sex couples appears to have had little, if any, tendency to confine children within traditional families headed by two opposite-sex parents. Divorce and out-of-wedlock births are ubiquitous, creating an increasing number of non-traditional families of infinite varieties. Over one-third of lesbian couples and almost one-quarter of gay male couples are raising children.[61] Many children today are born into households governed by individuals of the same sex, or where the head of household is homosexual.[62] Same-sex couples are more likely than married opposite-sex couples to adopt children, particularly children with disabilities.[63] Laws that permit homosexual couples to adopt, retain custody of children after divorce, and access artificial reproductive technologies all suggest that the homosexual orientation of a parent or parents is not itself a detriment to the well-being of children. These laws are tantamount to a confession that there is no demonstrable harm to children from the mere fact that one or both parents is gay. If this is indeed the case, laws prohibiting same-sex marriage in such jurisdictions cannot be justified on grounds of protecting children; the justification sweeps too broadly, making assumptions about the fitness of homosexual parents belied by legislation that assumes otherwise.

PROTECTING THE INSTITUTION OF MARRIAGE

One argument in support of retaining traditional marriage is that prohibiting homosexual marriage may encourage homosexuals to enter into heterosexual relationships and, hence, marriage. If gay people cannot marry each other, the argument goes, they may turn to straight relationships as the next best alternative. There is, of course, no data to support this hypothesis. But is it a rational conclusion nonetheless? A recent U.S. District Court opinion concluded that it was, asserting that it was "at least debatable that prohibiting same-sex marriage will make it more likely people will enter into opposite sex unions."[64] The District Court, of course, was applying the highly deferential rationality review standard, which requires courts to uphold legislation if an issue is "at least debatable." But of course everything is debatable, particularly on issues of public morality. The existence of differing opinions, however, does not necessarily imply that all opinions are rational.

Does anyone seriously believe that homosexuals who cannot marry other homosexuals will give up homosexuality and live the straight life? Is it not more rational to conclude that homosexuals will simply opt to live together, without the benefit of civil marriage? Moreover, even assuming arguendo that some homosexuals would be encouraged to enter into heterosexual marriage, is it logical to conclude that such marriages will be stable? Are dishonest, second-best marriages a net positive for society?

Another argument put forth by opponents of same-sex marriage is that expanding marriage dilutes its value. If marriage is broadened to include same-sex couples, the argument goes, the increased population of married persons will dilute the value of marriage. As a preliminary matter, it should be noted that only about 2 percent of the American population ever engages in acts of homosexuality.[65] Even if every single homosexual in America got married, the percentage of married couples who were of the same gender would be exceedingly low. The potential for "dilution" of marriage by same-sex couples is accordingly de minimis.

More importantly, however, the dilution argument presupposes many things about same-sex couples that do not appear to be based on evidence. If there is a public perception today that same-sex couples do not possess the same level of commitment or family values as their heterosexual counterparts, this may, in part, be due to the chicken-and-egg phenomenon: Are same-sex couples perceived as less committed because they are not permitted to marry? Or are same-sex couples somehow inherently less committed to each other? Similarly, are same-sex couples perceived as less committed to family values because it is more difficult for them to have children and adopt? Or are same-sex couples somehow inherently less committed to family values?

The reduced incidence of parenthood in same-sex couples likely contributes to the perception that same-sex couples lack the same level of commitment and family values as opposite-sex couples. But the limited data available from the Census Bureau suggests that same-sex couples who are raising children are quite stable, with over 40 percent in relationships that have lasted five years or more.[66] This statistic reveals that homosexual couples with children are significantly more stable than unmarried heterosexual couples, only 20 percent of whom have been together five years or longer.[67] Similarly, a recent study conducted by researchers at the University of Vermont of 400 same-sex civil unions granted by Vermont revealed that, on average, those couples had been in a committed relationship for eleven to twelve years.[68]

Similar devaluation arguments were made with regard to interracial marriage and are still sometimes made with regard to inter-religious marriages. In *Loving v. Virginia* the anti-miscegenation statute was titled "An Act to Preserve

Racial Integrity" and was designed to prevent the alleged devaluation of the white race.[69] Although the *Loving* Court explicitly declined to address whether preserving racial integrity was a legitimate state interest,[70] the Supreme Court today would presumably reject any racial devaluation argument as thinly disguised discriminatory animus. The assertion that same-sex marriage prohibitions are necessary to prevent the devaluation of marriage is eerily similar. Assuming the state has a legitimate interest in preserving the integrity of marriage, barring same-sex couples from marriage is little more than a pretext for discriminatory animus that, apart from validating the animus, does nothing to further the goal of preserving marriage.[71]

ADULTERY

Defining Adultery

The Bible reveals as God's seventh commandment, "Thou shalt not commit adultery,"[72] a sin that was punishable by death.[73] Strangely, however, the Bible contains numerous casual references to the existence of concubines and the children of concubines.[74] The New Testament defined adultery much more broadly, with Jesus proclaiming that "whosoever looketh on a woman to lust after her, hath committed adultery with her already in his heart."[75] Jesus also announced that any man who married a divorced woman committed adultery.[76]

Reconciliation of the apparent contradiction between the prohibition on adultery and the existence of adulterous relationships in the Bible is possible if one assumes that adultery was defined narrowly to include only sexual relations between a man and another man's wife, an act which was considered tantamount to the theft of the married man's property. The sexist, male-centered definition of adultery thus permitted married men to have affairs with unmarried women because it did not involve stealing another man's property.[77] It also acknowledged an unavoidable biological fact: A married man who has sex with an unmarried woman does not create a risk that a child will be born and deceptively passed off as intra-marital offspring. This type of marital fraud is possible only in the context of a married woman who commits adultery.

Given this sexist biblical backdrop, it is not surprising that common law defined adultery as sexual intercourse by a man, married or single, with a married woman not his wife.[78] But English criminal courts did not assume jurisdiction over adultery. Instead, adultery was left to the ecclesiastical courts and civil courts, the latter of which recognized a tort action called "criminal conversation" that permitted a husband to recover monetary damages against a man who seduced his wife.[79]

American states, by contrast, did not have ecclesiastical courts and therefore gave criminal courts jurisdiction over adultery as a public offense. American civil courts were given jurisdiction to adjudicate criminal conversation. Under early American law, American women who committed adultery could be summarily divorced (and left without alimony), imprisoned, or even sentenced to death, and their paramours could be sued in tort.[80]

The male-oriented property roots of adultery lingered for many years. Because cheating husbands were not considered to be harming their wives' property (since wives had no independent right to property), women were not permitted to divorce a philandering husband until the early 1920s.[81] Surprisingly, these antediluvian property roots of adultery are still evident in some current laws. Michigan, for example, criminalizes adultery committed by either married men or women, but its treatment of the paramour is decidedly sexist, criminalizing only the behavior of an unmarried man who has sex a married woman, not an unmarried woman who has sex with a married man.[82] Minnesota is even more overtly sexist, deeming as adulterous sex outside marriage by married women but not married men.[83] In all, twenty-four American states still prohibit adultery,[84] four of which classify it as a felony offense punishable by over a year in prison.[85] The vast majority of states criminalize the conduct of both married and unmarried participants,[86] with a handful of states punishing only married adulterers, not unmarried persons who have sex with married persons.[87]

Punishing Adultery

Recent studies indicate that approximately 15 to 18 percent of persons who have ever been married have had sex with someone other than their spouse while married.[88] Despite the relatively common nature of adultery, there are few prosecutions in those states that still retain adultery statutes. Yet it would be incorrect to characterize adultery statutes as moribund, since prosecutions still occasionally occur. In a recent well-publicized case in Virginia, the town attorney for a small town was prosecuted for adultery, pleaded guilty, paid a $125 fine and court costs, and was forced to resign his job, a position he had held for over thirty years.[89] In another recent publicized case, a Special District Attorney in New York initiated a prosecution for adultery against a police officer who admitted to having an extramarital affair with an unmarried woman.[90] In a recent child custody dispute in North Carolina, a trial judge ordered the issuance of an arrest warrant against a woman and her boyfriend, who were living together and raising the woman's two daughters.[91] The judge granted temporary custody of the daughters to their father, stating that he was "appalled" by the adultery which was "detrimental to the welfare of [the] children."[92] In Wisconsin, a woman was recently prosecuted for felony adultery and agreed to serve 40 hours of community service and attend two months of parental counseling in exchange for having the charges dropped.[93]

In addition to the potential for criminal prosecution, adultery statutes create secondary effects that can be equally pernicious. The Alabama constitution, for example, disqualifies individuals convicted of adultery from both registering to vote and voting.[94] Military personnel are routinely disciplined for adultery.[95] Police officers or other government employees can (and with some regularity do) lose their jobs[96] and fail to get promoted[97] for committing adultery. Judges may be disciplined for adulterous affairs.[98] Spouses who commit adultery may lose entitlement to alimony.[99] Parents who commit adultery may lose custody of their children.[100] Aliens may be involuntarily deported or denied naturalization for failure to establish "good moral character" if they commit adultery.[101] And the threat of adultery prosecution is sometimes used as leverage in plea bargaining, forcing a defendant to accept a harsher sentence than he otherwise would.[102]

Despite the highly selective nature of criminal adultery prosecutions and the wide range of adverse secondary effects that flow from retaining sanctions, lawsuits challenging the constitutionality of adultery laws have uniformly failed. For instance, in 1983 the Supreme Judicial Court of Massachusetts refused to overturn a jury conviction of a woman charged with adultery after police officers observed her having intercourse in the back of a van.[103] The court unanimously rejected the woman's assertion that the adultery law violated her constitutional right to privacy, even though the court conceded that the sex was both consensual and private.[104] The court stated that criminalizing adultery was a legitimate exercise of the state's police power that promoted the legitimate interest in preserving the institution of marriage.[105]

In addition to criminal sanctions, adultery may result in tort liability. The common law tort of criminal conversation still exists in a handful of states, though the vast majority of states have abolished it either by statute or by judicial decree.[106] Courts that have abolished criminal conversation have stated various reasons, including the fact that it allows a plaintiff in an unhappy marriage to receive a windfall when the spouse is unfaithful;[107] it may be motivated by greed or revenge;[108] it imposes liability upon only one of two persons who have participated in a consensual act;[109] and it is based on an antediluvian sense of morality.[110]

The gradual abolition of criminal conversation over the past few decades is an odd contrast to the relatively steadfast maintenance of adultery as a crime. Many of the justifications for abolishing criminal conversation also apply to adultery. For example, several states' adultery laws permit charges to be brought only if the injured spouse complains. Certainly in these jurisdictions, revenge is an inherent element of adultery, just as it is in criminal conversation.[111] Even in states where spousal complaint is not required, criminal prosecution ultimately may be initiated due to the exertion of pressure by the injured spouse upon the prosecutor.[112] In addition, in those jurisdictions that impose criminal liability only upon the married party who commits adultery, the law punishes only one of two parties to a consensual act. And if modern reality and mores justify abolishing the tort of criminal conversation, why do they not also justify abolishing the crime of adultery? An action that is not bad enough to warrant civil liability should not, ipso facto, be bad enough to warrant criminal liability.

Applying the Morality of American Law to Adultery

Adultery laws are often justified by claiming that they are designed to preserve marriages. Pursuant to *Lawrence,* states should not set the boundaries of an intimate relationship "absent injury to a person or abuse of an institution the law protects."[113] The first possibility—injury to a person—is compatible with the morality of American law. The second possibility—abuse of an institution the law protects—is not. Despite the fact that *Lawrence* offers great potential to reclaim the morality of American law, this disjunct between the two is rather significant. The morality of American law does not recognize preventing abuse to "an institution the law protects" as a legitimate exercise of governmental power. Why not? Because it would be exceedingly difficult to discern what these institutions are and, more importantly, defining what constitutes an abuse of these institutions inherently involves reference to subjective moral values.

Presumably, the *Lawrence* Court's reference to "an institution the law protects" meant marriage, since the *Lawrence* decision created questions about the validity of bans on same-sex marriage. But presumably law also protects the institution of family in various meaningful ways, so we should add family to the list of protected institutions. The law also protects various other institutions, such as business associations, which are essentially artificial persons.[114] What other institutions may be protected by *Lawrence* are not immediately clear.

But beyond this basic definitional difficulty, how does one know when one of these institutions has been abused? Institutions are not like people. They cannot be cut or bruised. They cannot have their locomotion restrained. How would a court know, for example, whether recognizing same-sex marriage would constitute an abuse of the institution of marriage? Similarly, for present purposes, is adultery an abuse of the institution of marriage? The chief difficulty with allowing abuse of institutions as a legitimate basis for restricting liberty is that the perceived abuse may be little more than non-conformance with majoritarian morality. How does one know whether an institution such as marriage is being abused without considering how the practice at issue alters or affects the traditionally accepted conception of that institution? And if any material deviation from the traditionally accepted conception of an institution is tantamount to "abuse" of that institution, then "abuse of an institution" is little more than a thinly veiled reference to public morality. Allowing "abuse of an institution the law protects" to serve as a legitimate basis for restricting individual liberty thus creates a backdoor opportunity for public morality to trump individual liberty—a result that is intolerable under the morality of American law.

But let us assume, for the sake of argument, that it is legitimate for the government to protect certain institutions *qua* institutions, as opposed to merely protecting the individuals within those institutions. We must further assume that these institutions can be harmed, not in the classic sense embraced by the morality of American law, but in the sense that certain actions taken by individuals tend to discourage or dissolve these institutions. Thus, we arrive at the present question: Do laws prohibiting adultery protect the institution of marriage?

Undoubtedly there are many divorces in which one or both of the spouses has committed adultery. But did the adultery—the act of sex with another—actually cause the demise of the marriage? Imagine a Orwellian world in which the government had the ability to swoop down and stop all acts of adultery, thereby eradicating sex outside marriage. In this brave new world, adultery is impossible but no-fault divorce is still readily available. Would the divorce rate really decline? Would a married person who had identified a willing paramour choose to remain in his marriage, unable to consummate his lust? Or would he opt for divorce instead, since the government's foreclosure of his extra-marital affair has created a pressure to divorce that would not exist if he could have his cake and eat it too? And if he would opt to remain married, is it reasonable to conclude that the marriage would really last? Or should we conclude that such a marriage would eventually collapse due to incompatibility, immaturity, or whatever other issues caused the wanderlust in the first place?

There are no clear answers to these questions. Reasonable minds may disagree on the effect that adultery laws have on stabilizing marriages. The truth is that divorce occurs for many reasons, and very few, if any, divorces are caused solely by the sexual act of adultery. Adultery is often but a symptom of an independent marriage-threatening illness such as boredom, emotional distance, incompatibility, or immaturity—none of which can be eradicated by governmental coercion. There is no real evidence that adultery laws help keep marriages intact.

If adultery does not cause the demise of marriages, perhaps adultery laws may be justified not by reference to protecting some abstract institution, but by reference to protecting the individuals within the marriage itself. As we have already discussed in Chapter 3, emotional harm is not a cognizable harm under the morality of American law. Adultery laws therefore cannot be legitimated merely because cheating on one's spouse often causes emotional distress to the faithful spouse.

Some might argue, however, that adultery laws are legitimate because adultery harms the faithful spouse's reputation—and thus constitutes a type of cognizable property harm. Yet it does not seem reasonable to conclude that an adulterous spouse harms the reputation of the faithful spouse. If anything, an individual who commits adultery harms his or her own reputation, a self-inflicted harm not cognizable under the morality of American law. The reputation of a faithful spouse should remain good, if not improve, after the public becomes aware of the adultery. Along the same lines, some might argue that adultery laws are designed to protect the property interests of the faithful spouse by preventing divorce, which causes dilution of property assets by separating them among the spouses. But again, there is no meaningful evidence that adultery actually causes divorce and, even if it did, the separation and concomitant dilution of assets necessitated by divorce is an inevitable consequence of divorce that cannot be alleviated by any means other than prohibiting divorce itself. To the extent that adultery is deemed by a court to be a contributing factor in a divorce—i.e., a "fault"-based divorce—the court may indeed take this into account in determining an equitable division of assets.[115]

POLYGAMY

The American preference for monogamous marriage is inherited from an evolved Judeo-Christian notion of a one man, one woman ideal. I refer to it as an evolved Judeo-Christian notion because the Old Testament is replete with multiple simultaneous marriages, which appeared to echo the patriarchal structure of marriage prevalent in the region at the time. The New Testament, by contrast, prohibits multiple marriages for either men or women, classifying any marriage that takes place while a previous spouse is alive as "adultery."[116]

It should thus come as little surprise that English common law prohibited polygamy, classifying it as a felony, with any subsequent civil marriage being considered void ab initio.[117] American states inherited the English common law model of monogamous marriage, and today every state (as well as the District of Columbia) except Hawaii criminalizes multiple marriages.[118] The overwhelming majority of these consider polygamy to be a felony.[119] Notably, within the minority of states that classify polygamy as a misdemeanor, there does not appear to be any increase in the prevalence of polygamous marriages, suggesting that, for most Americans, monogamous marriage results more from cultural preference than the threat of legal sanctions.[120]

Communes: The Oneida
and Hippy Experiments

Bans on polygamy have faced numerous legal challenges, though none have succeeded. One noteworthy challenge was raised by the Oneida Community of New York, which practiced what it termed "complex marriage," a form of group marriage whereby adult members considered themselves married to all other adult members of the group, with no exclusive sexual relationships permitted.[121] The Oneida Community's practices were based upon a passage from the New Testament in which Jesus explains how individuals with multiple spouses (married after the death of previous spouses) will relate in the afterlife: "The children of this world marry, and are given in marriage: But they which shall be accounted worthy to obtain that world, and the resurrection from the dead, neither marry, nor are given in marriage: Neither can they die any more: for they are equal unto the angels; and are the children of God, being the children of the resurrection."[122] From this passage, the founder of the Oneida Community, John Humphrey Noyes, concluded that because there would be no marriage in the afterlife, marriage was not considered by God to constitute the highest or purest form of relationship between man and woman.[123] Noyes and his followers condemned monogamous marriage as "egotism for two," an awkward social and legal construct that encouraged jealousy, unnaturally restricted sexual appetites, and isolated the married couple into a distinct family, removed from the larger community.[124]

The Oneida Community's practices did not constitute polygamy, since the members of the community did not obtain civil marriages. Their practices might have constituted other offenses such as fornication or cohabitation, yet no prosecution for such offenses ever ensued.[125] The demise of the Oneida Community's complex marriage experiment was due not to prosecution or social disapproval, but instead, the community—some 250 to 300 persons—changed its ways voluntarily and eventually allowed its members to enter into exclusive marriages.[126]

Similar experiments in group relationships surfaced in the 1960s, when communes of hippies experimented with alternative social structures. As with the Oneida Community, the failure of hippies to obtain a civil marriage meant that prosecution for polygamy was not possible. Various other laws were invoked in an attempt to disband these communes, including prosecutions for disorderly conduct, lewd and lascivious behavior, keeping a disorderly or bawdy house, and zoning laws.[127]

In one well-known case, *Palo Alto Tenants Union v. Morgan*[28] a federal trial court rejected the claims of commune members, who asserted that city officials were violating their constitutional rights by enforcing zoning ordinances that limited certain areas of the city to "single families," defined as "one person living alone, or two or more persons related by blood, marriage, or legal adoption, or a group not exceeding four persons living as a single housekeeping unit."[129] The trial court presumed the law was constitutional because the court did not believe it infringed any "fundamental" right.[130] The court believed that communal living groups, unlike traditional families, lacked characteristics worthy of triggering First Amendment free association protection because the individuals within such groups lacked biological links and were comprised of fluctuating, voluntary members. Emotional intimacy within the group was not sufficient to warrant constitutional protection because "this is true of members of many groups."[131] The court concluded that "[t]he right to form such groups may be constitutionally protected, but the right to insist that these groups live under the same roof, in any part of the city they choose, is not."[132]

The court's conclusion put the statutory cart before the constitutional horse. If the *Palo Alto Tenants Union* court believed that the communal group was constitutionally entitled to exist, an ordinance restricting their ability to live together would undoubtedly infringe their right to associate which, in turn, should have required the invocation of a presumption of unconstitutionality. The court instead concluded that even if the ordinance substantially burdened the group's ability to freely associate, deference was owed to the city's belief that the law was needed to preserve the integrity of the traditional family, reduce noise and traffic problems, and preserve the economic value of surrounding homes.[133]

The weak analytical structure of *Palo Alto Tenants Union* was subsequently extended by the Supreme Court in *Belle Terre v. Boraas,*[134] a case challenging the constitutionality of a similar zoning ordinance. Specifically, the ordinance restricted certain areas to traditional families related by blood or marriage or, alternatively, to no more than two persons unrelated by blood or marriage. The litigation was initiated by the owners of a house and six unrelated college students who occupied the house as tenants. They asserted that the ordinance infringed their constitutional rights to privacy, due process, equal protection, and free association. The Court rejected these arguments, concluding that the ordinance did not implicate any "fundamental" rights that would require a presumption of unconstitutionality.[135] The Court thus inquired only whether the ordinance was rational, concluding:

> A quiet place where yards are wide, people few, and motor vehicles restricted are legitimate guidelines in a land-use project addressed to family needs. . . . The police power is not confined to the elimination of filth, stench, and unhealthy places. It is ample to lay out zones where family values, youth values, and the blessings of quiet seclusion and clean air make the area a sanctuary for people.

The *Belle Terre* rationale is too sweeping, allowing state governments to restrict citizens' liberty to choose something as fundamental as a living companion, simply because the citizens' choices would be antithetical to "family values" or "youth values." In other words, if a majority of citizens do not approve of a fellow citizen's living arrangements, they can effectively banish the fellow citizen from the community or relegate him to a community-approved ghetto. If there had been evidence in *Belle Terre* that the unrelated students had harmed the property interests of neighbors (the "blessings of quiet seclusion," to use the words of the Court) by depriving them of the peaceful enjoyment of their own property—for example, by having loud parties until the wee hours of the morning—this would indeed be a legitimate basis for governmental action. Similarly, if there had been evidence that the unrelated students had harmed the property interests of neighbors by burning old tires or setting off stink bombs ("the blessings of . . . clean air," to use the words of the Court), this, too, would provide a legitimate basis for governmental action. But short of these sorts of demonstrable LLP harms, the students should not have been forced to leave their home simply because the neighbors found their living arrangement offensive.

Indeed, legal restrictions on living arrangements, though ubiquitous, are relatively ineffective at accomplishing their public morality—based goals. The majority's desire to stamp out non-traditional living arrangements, reflected in the Oneida and zoning cases, is woefully ineffective, even when such offensive relationships are carried out in an open and notorious manner. Such laws do not discourage persons from forming non-traditional families; rather, they accomplish only geographic segregation—the creation of alternative family ghettos—for non-traditional families deemed offensive to the majority. In the absence of demonstrable harm to neighbors' LLP, such overbroad laws restricting an individual's sovereign choice of living companions is fundamentally antithetical to the morality of American law and its underlying respect for the equality of individuals.[136]

The Mormons

A more serious threat to monogamous marriage came in the form of the so-called "Mormon Question" of the mid-nineteenth century.[137] The Mormon Church's association with polygamy began in 1843, when church founder Joseph Smith, issued his "Revelation on Celestial Marriage." In this revelation, Smith proclaimed that the biblical example of Abraham permitted men to take additional wives, provided the existing wives consented, and that all such polygamous marriages would be eternally blessed.[138] Mormon doctrine established polygamy as a higher form of marriage, which eventually became an important part of religious exercise for believers. These practices caused the Mormons to be ostracized from their communities and led to Smith's murder by an angry Illinois mob in 1844, after which the Mormons, under the new leadership of Brigham Young, moved westward, seeking a place where they could constitute the majority and exercise their religious beliefs free of majoritarian oppression.[139]

The political dominance of the Mormons in the Utah territory disturbed many Americans. The Mormon "question" generated intense debate and a wave of anti-polygamy literature that fascinated eastern Americans with lurid tales of women and lustful polygamous husbands.[140] Polygamy was painted as harmful to women and children and a dangerous mixing of church and state, violating the spirit, if not the letter, of the Establishment Clause.[141] In 1862, Congress finally responded to anti-polygamy sentiment by enacting the Morrill Act, which prohibited polygamy within any territory of the United States.[142]

REYNOLDS V. SIMS

The Mormons objected to federal interference with the practice of polygamy on grounds that it infringed their First Amendment free exercise rights. After many years of non-enforcement of the Morrill Act due to evidentiary difficulties,[143] in 1875 a grand jury indicted George Reynolds for violating the act by being married to two women at the same time.[144] The case, *Reynolds v. Sims,* made its way to the Supreme Court, which rejected the Mormons' argument that polygamy was a protected form of religious exercise:

> Suppose one believed that human sacrifices were a necessary part of religious worship, would it be seriously contended that the civil government under which he lived could not interfere to prevent a sacrifice? Or if a wife religiously believed it was her duty to burn herself upon the funeral pile of her dead husband, would it be beyond the power of the civil government to prevent her carrying her belief into practice?[145]

Notice how the *Reynolds* Court's hypotheticals assume the existence of some sort of harm. Human sacrifices are obviously harmful to the individual sacrificed. The woman who burns herself on her husband's funeral pile obviously inflicts harm upon herself. If the Court is suggesting in these hypotheticals that a harm principle motivated its decision, it must have assumed that polygamy was harmful to the LLP of others—presumably women or children, though it did not explicitly say so. In any event, it is possible to interpret *Reynolds* as consistent with the morality of American law, although the Court's failure to discuss any evidence of polygamy's tendency to harm others is inexcusable. If the *Reynolds* Court had consciously and appropriately applied the morality of American law to the case, the government would have borne the burden of convincing the Court that such harm to others either occurred or was reasonably threatened. Moreover, if the Court had understood the morality of American law, one of its hypothetical cases—the wife burning herself at her husband's funeral pile—would have been inapposite, since the morality of American law does not permit the government to use its power to prevent self-harm inflicted by competent adults. If the grieving wife could be adjudged temporarily incompetent due to her distraught mental state, the morality of American law would permit the government to protect her against self-harm. Short of this, however, it would not be a legitimate exercise of governmental power to restrain her from harming herself.[146]

EMPLOYMENT DIVISION V. SMITH: THE PEYOTE CASE

Although *Reynolds* was decided over one hundred years ago, it is still good law. The Supreme Court's 1990 decision in *Employment Division, Department of Human Resources v. Smith*[147] reinforces *Reynolds* and suggests that any future challenges to anti-polygamy laws based upon the Free Exercise Clause are doomed to fail. Specifically, in *Smith,* the Court upheld a law prohibiting the use of peyote as a controlled substance, despite the fact that, as applied to the Native American church, it significantly interfered with religious worship.

The remarkable aspect of *Smith* is that a five-Justice majority refused to presume the law unconstitutional in the context of clash between public morality (condemnation of peyote use) and an explicitly protected constitutional right (free exercise of religion). This refusal meant that the affected citizens, in order to enjoy their constitutional liberty of free exercise, were required to prove to the Court that the peyote law was beyond all rationality—a virtually insurmountable burden that is arrogantly antithetical to the principles of limited government and residual individual sovereignty.

Smith thus transformed the Free Exercise Clause—a clause aimed at protecting exercises of one's religion, no matter how unpopular or offensive to public morality—into a Free Belief Clause that offers constitutional shelter only to those religious exercises deemed inoffensive to the majoritarian morality. Pragmatically, minority religions are now told that they may obtain meaningful protection for their religious exercise only from the legislature,[148] even though the *Smith* Court conceded that "leaving accommodation to the political process will place at a relative disadvantage those religious practices that are not widely engaged in[,]" a result it deemed an "unavoidable consequence of democratic government."[149]

The *Smith* decision is patently at odds with the morality of American law. If the *Smith* Court had honored the morality of American law, it would have placed the burden of persuasion upon the government to demonstrate that banning the use of peyote by Native Americans was needed to prevent harm to the LLP of others. This appears to have been the analytical framework implicitly embraced by Justices Brennan, Marshall, and Blackmun, who agreed that the burden of persuasion should rest with the government (as did Justice O'Connor in a separate concurrence) and concluded that the government had not satisfied its burden because there was no evidence that the religious use of peyote caused enough harm to qualify as a compelling government interest.[150]

Smith's impact on anti-polygamy laws is clear. Since anti-polygamy laws are facially neutral and applicable to all citizens, *Smith* suggests that they will enjoy a presumption of constitutionality when faced with a free exercise challenge. A recent decision of the Utah Supreme Court, *Utah v. Green*,[151] confirms this impression. In *Green*, the defendant, a Mormon, had sexual relationships with nine women over twenty-six years, fathering a total of twenty-five children.[152] At the time a bigamy prosecution was initiated against Green, he was living on a family compound with six women and numerous children, all of whom bore his name.[153]

Green was aware of the Utah law against polygamy and entered into only one licensed marriage at a time. He legally married four of his "wives," though he was careful to obtain a divorce prior to entering into another licensed marriage.[154] Because Green had meticulously divorced each wife before obtaining a new one, he reasonably believed that his living arrangements were legal. At the time of his prosecution for bigamy, Green had divorced his most recent wife and he was not, in fact, married to anyone.

Shortly after the prosecution was initiated, prosecutors convinced the trial court to recognize the existence of a common law marriage between Green and another woman with whom he was living.[155] When the court agreed, Green's common law marriage rendered his cohabitation with the other women criminal polygamy.

The Utah Supreme Court rejected Green's free exercise claim, noting that the U.S. Supreme Court's decision in *Reynolds* was still binding precedent.[156] The Utah Supreme Court concluded that *Smith* required only that the state articulate a rational basis for the law, which was satisfied because the law was rationally designed to protect the institution of marriage, prevent the perpetration of marriage fraud, and protect vulnerable children from exploitation and abuse.[157] Unfortunately, these supposedly rational bases for upholding the law were not supported by any evidence that polygamy was, in fact, a threat to marriage, a tool for fraud, or harmful to children. Instead, pursuant to the orthodox presumption of constitutionality, these bald assertions by the state were assumed to be true and, unless the citizen proved that they were not true (i.e., proof of a negative), the law against polygamy was held to be constitutional.

Applying the Morality of American Law
to Polygamy

What if the courts in *Reynolds* or *Green* had acknowledged and applied the morality of American law? Would the defendants' living arrangements have been held beyond the reach of governmental power? This is somewhat difficult to predict, since there is was—and still is—little evidence available regarding the potential for harm to others posed by polygamy. Polygamy has been practiced only rarely in the United States, and there is little evidence regarding its effects on marriage and children or its potential to perpetuate fraud. Although polygamy has been practiced extensively in other societies, those societies have very different cultural roles and expectations regarding women and children, making it difficult to determine whether their experiences with polygamy would translate into American society.

Many people assert that polygamy harms the women involved or results in the sexual or other physical abuse of children, yet what evidence is there to support these claims? These types of harms were relied upon to uphold the conviction in *Green,* for example, even though the Utah Supreme Court could cite to no evidence to support these assumptions other than a student note in a secondary law journal.

If we can free our minds of the "polygamy is bad" mindset with which most of us have been raised, we can critically examine the reasons why we find it so offensive. One of the most common objections to polygamy is that it is harmful to children. Why it is harmful is seldom articulated with much clarity, however. It seems reasonable to conclude that one effect of recognizing polygamy would be a greater number of children born within the context of a marriage, since marriage would be more widely available, particularly to women.[158] This would provide a net benefit, not harm, to children, since they would be less likely to have an absent father. In addition, by enlarging the family itself, polygamy could presumably increase the likelihood that an adult family member would be present to supervise and care for the children, lessening the need for non-family babysitters and the phenomenon of latch-key children. On the other hand, because polygamy generally increases the number of children born to any one father (since polygyny is more common than polyandry), the children will generally receive reduced benefits, such as time and financial support, on a per-child basis compared to what they would receive if they were born into an intact traditional family.[159] Yet allowing polygamy provides a legal release for some promiscuity, channeling more sexuality into marriage, and perhaps

lessening the perceived need for divorce—all of which tend to benefit any resulting children. In this sense, a child born of a polygamous marriage may
spend less time with his father because he has a large family, but he may spend
more with his family overall, and more time with his father than if he were born
of a monogamous marriage that ended in divorce.

One of the more specific accusations levied at polygamy is that parents in
plural marriage are more likely to abuse their children than parents in monogamous marriage. There is, however, no evidence indicating that this accusation
is true. Moreover, it must be remembered that if a parent in a plural marriage
abuses his or her children, the law legitimately may impose a penalty for such
harmful behavior, just as it does for instances of abuse by monogamous parents.
The existence of plural marriage does not make it more difficult to protect
abused children—if anything, it may occasionally make prosecution easier by
expanding the number of potential witnesses who can verify the existence of
abuse.

Another common justification articulated for prohibiting polygamy is the
widespread belief that polygamy victimizes women. Yet this belief, if examined
closely, is undoubtedly grounded in a paternalistic view of women as weak and
unable to protect themselves—a view that is deeply at odds with the morality
of American law and its foundational respect for the equality of competent
adults.

Suppose a man decides that he wants to enter into plural marriage and take a
second wife. The first wife has two choices: divorce her husband or remain in a
plural marriage. If she chooses to divorce her husband, she would be entitled to
the same financial support as she would if the husband had never sought plural
marriage. If she chooses to remain in a plural marriage, the law should presume
that she is a competent adult who has voluntarily decided that the benefits of a
plural marriage outweigh the burdens. She remains free to reevaluate her personal cost-benefit analysis at any time and seek a divorce if she comes to view
the burdens of plural marriage to be greater than the benefits. This is the presumption of liberty to which all competent adults are entitled—a presumption
that respects women as autonomous individuals capable of making their own
choices.

It should also be remembered that if a woman agrees to be in a plural marriage that subsequently turns abusive, she is still free to divorce the husband
and seek protection from and remedies for any abuse the husband has inflicted.
A woman's options in an abusive plural marriage are thus exactly the same as in
an abusive monogamous marriage, no more, no less. Although it is undoubt-

edly sometimes difficult to leave an abusive spouse, the existence of a plural marriage does not make this decision any more difficult.

Short of abuse, however, some people fear that allowing polygamy will result in relegating women to manipulative, oppressive, and paternalistic environments. For example, a group called Tapestry Against Polygamy, whose membership includes former wives of plural marriage, opposes polygamy on this basis.[160] It is easy to empathize with individuals who have fled abusive polygamous relationships. Yet they are a testament to the fact that women in such abusive relationships have the ability to walk away. The group's stated position, moreover, reveals how emotional opposition to polygamy leads to illogical arguments. The group states that it does not advocate aggressive enforcement against all polygamists; rather, polygamy should remain criminal so that polygamists accused of other crimes can receive harsher net sentences and so that "a man [will] think twice about marrying his 13 year-old niece."[161]

These rationalizations are unpersuasive. Retaining a law to ratchet up sentences for other crimes is both unfair and discriminatory. If an individual harms others, he should be punished and the punishment should reflect the severity of the crime actually committed. If existing sentences are too lenient, they should be enhanced not by trumping up other crimes to fill the void but by having an open debate about sentence proportionality. And if anti-polygamy activists wish to retain polygamy as a crime to deter grown men from marrying thirteen-year-old girls, they are wrestling a straw man. State laws already establish nonage—the age below which persons are presumed incapable of consenting to marriage—and this age is generally well above the age of thirteen. In Utah, for example, the minimum age for marriage (either male or female) is eighteen, though sixteen- and seventeen-year-olds may marry with parental permission and fifteen-year-olds may marry with parental permission and a court determination that the marriage is both voluntary and in the fifteen-year-old's bests interests.[162] If opposition to polygamy is based on the fear of coercing minors into marriage, the enactment and enforcement of nonage laws would prevent such coercion, whether it occurs in the context of polygamous or monogamous marriage.

If polygamy sometimes results in abusive relationships, this does not mean that it is appropriate for the government to ban polygamy. A shocking number of monogamous relationships are abusive, yet surely this unfortunate fact would not justify government prohibition of marriage or other relationships. As with abusive lovers and spouses in monogamous relationships, there are laws appropriately aimed at punishing harmful conduct without the need for wholesale condemnation of an entire class of relationships. And although polygamous relationships may be manipulative, paternalistic, or oppressive, these adjectives likewise attach to some monogamous relationships, not to mention employment relationships, friendships, and cults, yet none of these is deemed illegal. It is not the institution of polygamy but individuals who must bear the responsibility for creating physically or emotionally abusive relationships.[163]

In the absence of better evidence, therefore, it appears that both *Reynolds* and *Green* are contrary to the morality of American law. Absent evidence that polygamy reasonably threatens harm to others, competent adults should be free, pursuant to the principle of residual individual sovereignty, to choose the person or persons to whom they wish to be married. The Supreme Court's decision in *Lawrence,* through the invocation of a harm principle[164] and reliance on concepts of autonomy, dignity, and intimacy,[165] suggests that although anti-polygamy laws do not violate the myopic view of free exercise announced in *Smith,* they may nonetheless be unconstitutional deprivations of individual liberty.

If intimate choices to enter into relationships with others are the heart of the liberty protected by the Fourteenth Amendment, what could be a more intimate choice than the decision to marry? Entering into marriage with more than one person does not diminish the intimacy of the decision any more than having multiple children diminishes the intimacy of the family. The suggestion in *Lawrence* is that attempts by government to "define the meaning" of intimate relationships or to "set its boundaries" are permissible only to prevent "injury to a person or abuse of an institution the law protects."[166] The constitutionality of anti-polygamy laws, therefore, once again boils down to evidence of actual or reasonably threatened harm, not merely majoritarian abhorrence of the practice or speculation that polygamy results in such harm.

It should be noted that the harm principle espoused in *Lawrence,* by recognizing harm to "an institution the law protects,"[167] is broader than the one discussed in Chapter 3, which recognizes only harm to other individuals. Presumably this obscure reference, though it does not explicitly say so, is squarely aimed at marriage and family, since there are not many other institutions the law protects. But assuming arguendo that the Court is employing a duly modified harm principle (i.e., one that incorporates the protection of institutions protected by law), the Court must be convinced that anti-polygamy laws indeed harm marriage or the family. Although many people undoubtedly feel that polygamy is immoral or weird or just a bad idea, how does polygamy actually harm the institutions of marriage or family?

Opponents of same-sex marriage put forth similar arguments, asserting that the legal recognition of same-sex marriage would somehow devalue the institution of marriage itself. But it is not clear how expanding the availability of marriage dilutes its value. If anything, expanding marital possibilities for adults would seem to enhance the institution of marriage by recognizing the values it represents—love, commitment, emotional and physical intimacy. If these values are good and if they are the heart of marriage, why should it matter what specific shape the marriage takes? Moreover, if marital possibilities were expanded, many people who otherwise might remain single could experience the love, commitment, and intimacy of marriage.

The primary reason for opposition to polygamy is that it is difficult for many to envision marriage as anything other than a monogamous one man, one woman relationship. This notion is deeply ingrained in our culture, which has been deeply influenced by New Testament norms. While there is nothing wrong with having an opinion based upon one's culture or religion, there is something wrong with imposing this opinion upon others in a pluralistic society founded upon individual liberty. Opposition to polygamy is simply intolerance wrapped in the thin foil of concern for women or children, a concern which can be adequately addressed when harm to women or children occurs. Though many of us would not choose to enter into a polygamous marriage, the fact is that we, as Americans, should be at liberty to do so absent evidence that it reasonably threatens harm to others.

INCEST

Mention of the word incest immediately causes pained faces and horrific mental images of lecherous fathers seducing or assaulting innocent young daughters. The famous Greek myth of Oedipus, who killed his father and married his mother, also comes to mind, though parent-child incest is quite rare.[168] The Bible, in the book of Leviticus, proclaims that "[n]one of you shall approach to any that is near of kin to him, to uncover their nakedness"[169] and more specifically prohibits sexual relations with one's father, mother, step-mother, sister, half-sister, step-sister, granddaughter, aunt (by blood or by marriage), daughter-in-law, or sister-in-law.[170] Leviticus also prohibits having sex with a female lover's daughter or granddaughter,[171] or marrying an ex-wife's sister (until the ex-wife has died).[172]

Under English common law, incest was not criminal, but was instead considered a moral offense under the jurisdiction of the ecclesiastical courts.[173] An incestuous marriage, moreover, was not per se void, but merely voidable at the option of the parties; if the spouses chose to remain together, their marriage was "esteemed valid to all civil purposes."[174] It was not until 1935 that English statutory law finally deemed certain incestuous marriages to be void.[175]

American incest laws have generally been stricter than those in England, declaring marriages within prohibited degrees to be void ab initio as well as criminalizing incestuous sex between related persons. Every American state has an incest law, though the prohibited degrees of consanguinity or affinity and the sanctions that may be imposed vary considerably. All states, however, prohibit marriage or sexual relations between parents and children, brothers and sisters, uncles and nieces, and aunts and nephews.

Marriages between cousins is more controversial, with a notable geographic division existing between northern and southern states, the latter being less restrictive than the former. Nonetheless, cousin marriages in the United States are not unusual, and include many famous examples, including Edgar Allan Poe, Albert Einstein, Franklin Delano Roosevelt, and Jerry Lee Lewis, all of whom married their cousins. At present, 30 states severely restrict or prohibit first cousin marriage,[176] with only nineteen states and the District of Columbia allowing first cousin marriages without restriction.[177]

Applying the Morality of American Law to Incest

If the majority opinion in *Lawrence v. Texas* dictates that morality alone is an illegitimate basis for restrictions on liberty, or at least restrictions on intimate association, current American incest laws will undoubtedly face more significant legal challenge in the decades ahead. If public morality alone cannot justify incest laws, what can? Several possible harm-based justifications, consistent with the morality of American law, may exist to justify at least some prohibitions against incest.

Preventing Harm to Children

GENETIC DEFECTS

Perhaps the most common harm-based justification for banning incestuous relationships is the widespread belief that the potential offspring of such relationships would be more likely to suffer from genetic abnormalities—a "life" harm consonant with the morality of American law. Laws that permit cousins to marry if they undergo genetic counseling prior to marriage or produce evidence of sterility are evidence of this rationale.[178] Another possible legitimate basis for incest laws, articulated by anthropologist Margaret Mead, is that incest laws protect children by providing a healthy, affectionate, and non-sexual environment in which to live and grow.[179] Another anthropologist, Claude Lévi-Strauss, asserted that prohibiting incestuous sexual relations and marriage compels individuals to seek mates outside their family unit, expanding societal connections, tolerance, and understanding.[180]

Are any of these harm-based rationales sufficient to legitimate incest laws? Perhaps. With regard to the "genetic defects" rationale, the answer is probably "no." The most recent scientific data suggests that first cousins do not have a much greater chance than unrelated couples of having children with serious genetic defects.[181] This data suggests that marriage (or sex) between first cousins does not pose a reasonable threat of harm to offspring and accordingly, incest laws as applied to first cousins would be constitutionally infirm. Not only are the risks of genetic harm to offspring very low, but there is a significant under-inclusiveness problem here as well. Marriages with much higher probabilities of producing offspring with genetic defects are permitted without restraint, such as marriages by persons over age 40[182] or between those with recessive genes responsible for conditions such as Huntington's, Tay-Sachs, sickle cell anemia, and cystic fibrosis. The legislature's failure to prohibit marriages between such couples suggests that incest laws—at least as applied to first cousins—are based more on notions of morality or discrimination than on a desire to prevent harm to offspring.

ENSURING A NURTURING ENVIRONMENT

In the situation discussed above, incest laws were analyzed pursuant to the notion that incest posed a threat of harm to future persons. Since these future children are, well, future children—not present persons—the liberty of existing adults must be given conclusive weight. But once the offspring of an incestuous union are born, their lives, liberty, and property are entitled to the protection of the government—indeed, the government owes minors a much greater duty of protection than it does competent adults.

If an incest law were based on evidence that such laws protect children by enabling them to grow up without sexual pressure from adult relatives, the law would be a legitimate exercise of governmental power. Laws prohibiting incest between children and adult relatives are consonant with the morality of American law because of the legitimate paternalistic role the law assumes to protect children. Because children are emotionally immature and vulnerable in ways that adults are not, they are legally incapable of possessing the capacity to make decisions for themselves. A law aimed at preventing emotional or physical harm to children and to protect children from being victimized by their own immaturity is a legitimate exercise of governmental power.

Protecting the Institution of Family

Incest laws that prohibit marriage or sex between closely related adults obviously cannot be justified by reference to the compelling need to protect children. Adults are assumed by law to have the emotional capacity to make their own decisions and defend themselves emotionally. But laws that prohibit, for example, an adult father from marrying his adult daughter, or adult siblings from marrying, are more challenging analytically.

One of the most challenging applications involving adult-adult incest occurs when the consenting adults are not related by blood. The Uniform Marriage and Divorce Act (UMDA), for example, includes within its categories of incest all relationships "by the half or the whole blood or by adoption."[183] Suppose A is married to X and has a daughter named Amy. Further suppose that B is married to Y and has a son named Bill. If A and B subsequently marry each other, may Amy and Bill also marry? Assuming Amy and Bill are consenting adults, why should they be prohibited from marrying each other? There is no blood relationship between Amy and Bill and, indeed, they may never have lived in the same household.[184]

What are the justifications, other than public morality, for prohibiting marriages between closely related adults? Other than the potential genetic harm to offspring (which has already been discussed), the chief justification is the state's interest in promoting and protecting families. Banning incest is said to protect families by reducing intra-family rivalry, jealousy, and tension.[185] As an initial matter, there may be situations, such as when adoptive siblings wish to marry, in which all families members actually support the proposed marriage.[186] Denial of a marriage license under such circumstances would tend to cause family tension rather than family harmony. In addition, as discussed in Chapter 3, it is inherently difficult to measure emotional harms such as rivalry, jealousy, or tension, and concomitantly difficult to determine whether banning adult-adult incest actually reduces these emotional harms. Perhaps more significantly, there are numerous acts that create rivalry, jealousy, and tension within families that are not proscribed by law. Could a state, in the name of "protecting the family," prohibit adult siblings from competing in the same sport or practicing the same profession simply because it could create intra-family rivalry, jealousy, and tension? Similarly, would it be legitimate to prohibit fathers from giving expensive presents to their adult daughters because doing so might create rivalry, jealousy, and tension between mother and daughter? The intuitive answer to these questions is "no," and it suggests that promoting intra-family harmony is not a legitimate basis for restricting the marital liberty of related adults.

If we cannot ban adult-adult incest merely to promote intra-family peace and harmony, should we be concerned? Is there a reason to believe that adhering to the morality of American law will lead to the disintegration of American families? No. The real reason why incest is not widespread has nothing to do with legal prohibition and everything to do with the repulsion most Americans are psychologically and perhaps even biologically predisposed to feel. The ostracism resulting from incestuous relationships, as well as the emotional fallout within the family itself, is sufficient to encourage the overwhelming majority of Americans to self-regulate against such relationships. Moreover, research suggests that the Freudian theory of innate incestuousness (the famous "Oedipus complex") is wrong. There appears to be a natural aversion to incest that is created by close emotional bonding with family members.[187] Indeed, as Jean-Pierre Vernant cogently observed, Oedipus had no Oedipus complex, since he did not fall in love with Merope, the woman who raised him and whom he believed to be his biological mother.[188] Instead, Oedipus fell in love with his biological mother, Jocasta, for whom he had no maternal attachment because she was absent during his childhood. This suggests that emotional bonding during childhood, not necessarily biology, is responsible for establishing psycho-social incest avoidance. The familial bond hypothesis is reinforced by studies of children raised side by side on Israeli kibbutzim, who rarely marry or engage in sexual intercourse.[189] Similarly, studies of Taiwanese simpua marriages, in which brides-to-be are raised from infancy in the home of the future groom, reveal that the betrothed couple often fails to consummate the marriage due to sexual revulsion.[190] Nature, it seems, is a strong deterrent to incest between individuals raised in the same household.

On the other hand, there do appear to be some cultures that do not share the general aversion against incest, and therefore members of such cultural groups might be expected to engage in such relationships if not legally prohibited. For example, individuals from the Middle East, Africa, or Asia sometimes prefer to marry relatives such as cousins rather than strangers.[191] Indeed, in some parts of the world, 20 to 60 percent of marriages are between individuals who are closely related biologically.[192] But generally speaking these intra-family marriages involve family members who were not raised within the same household.

Instead, they are often marriages of distant cousins who know little about each other prior to their arranged marriage. In this situation, the close emotional bond that serves as a natural incest repellant is lacking.

For the vast majority of Americans nature alone will suffice to deter the most morally offensive incestuous relations between adults. As for relations between adult relatives who have not grown up in the same household or small community, nature may not dissuade their union, but there is no legitimate basis under the morality of American law for prohibiting their relationship.

Chapter 5 Sex

Love is the answer, but while you are waiting for the answer, sex raises
some pretty good questions.
—*Woody Allen*

THE RIGHT TO HAVE SEX

An adult American's right to participate in consensual sex is contin-
gent upon a laundry list of restrictions that hinge upon whether the
individual is single or married, heterosexual or homosexual, whether
the sex is obtained free or purchased, and the type of sex in which the
individual wishes to engage. This jumble of factors makes no principled constitutional sense and, as applied to competent adults, is inconsistent with the morality of American law.

Pre-*Lawrence* Sex Jurisprudence

In 1965 the Supreme Court announced, in *Griswold v. Connecticut*,
the existence of a constitutional "right to privacy," which encom-
passed the right of married persons to use contraceptives.[1] *Griswold*

implied the existence of sexual liberty, at least for married persons, since those who use contraceptives are necessarily engaging in recreational (i.e., non-procreative) sex.

Four years later, in *Stanley v. Georgia,* the Court announced that adults have a First Amendment right to possess obscene matter in the privacy of their homes.[2] The right to possess obscenity implied a liberty to engage in private sexual gratification (at least in the autologous sense) as a result of viewing the materials, although the *Stanley* Court did not explicitly say so. More significantly, in 1972 the Supreme Court, in *Eisenstadt v. Baird,*[3] held that the right to use contraceptives identified in *Griswold* extended to unmarried adults, implying that all adults, married or unmarried, enjoyed the liberty to engage in recreational sex.

The *Eisenstadt* Court invalidated a Massachusetts law that prohibited the distribution or sale of certain contraceptives to single persons. Pursuant to this law, married persons could obtain contraceptives either to protect against venereal disease or to prevent pregnancy, although the latter purpose—pregnancy prevention—required a physician's prescription. Single persons could also obtain contraceptives without a physician's prescription if their purpose was to protect against venereal disease. But unlike married persons, single persons could not lawfully obtain contraceptives to prevent pregnancy, even with a physician's prescription.

The Massachusetts law made condoms widely available to married and unmarried persons alike, since they helped prevent sexually transmitted diseases, while other contraceptives—such as diaphragms, IUDs, and the controversial, wildly popular new birth control pill—were available only to married persons with a doctor's prescription. The State of Massachusetts defended the law on grounds that it protected the public health and morals. The law helped protect health, it was claimed, by restricting distribution of allegedly risky birth control methods only to married persons under close physician supervision.[4] The law allegedly improved public morals by discouraging fornication and adultery, since single persons could not access the most effective contraceptives.[5]

The Supreme Court concluded that the law violated equal protection because the law irrationally discriminated between married and unmarried persons.[6] If certain contraceptives were potentially harmful, the Court reasoned, the risk was equal to married and unmarried alike, and could be addressed by requiring any patient wishing to use such contraceptives to obtain a physician's prescription.[7] The state's desire to prevent adultery was not advanced by the law since adulterous married persons could freely obtain contraceptives and share them with their paramours.[8] Similarly, the state's desire to prevent fornication was not rationally promoted because single persons could readily and lawfully obtain contraceptives such as condoms.[9]

Eisenstadt's equal protection holding left open the possibility that a law banning all commerce in contraceptives—that is, distribution or sale but not use—might pass constitutional muster. After all, *Griswold* had involved a law penalizing the *use* of contraceptives by married persons, and the *Griswold* Court had been meticulously careful about distinguishing between use versus commercial distribution or sale, declaring, "The present case . . . concerns a law which, in forbidding the use of contraceptives rather than regulating their manufacture or sale, seeks to achieve its goals by means having a maximum destructive impact upon [the marital] relationship. . . . Would we allow the police to search the sacred precincts of marital bedrooms for telltale signs of the use of contraceptives? The very idea is repulsive to the notions of privacy surrounding the marital relationship."[10] By criminalizing use, the Connecticut statute conjured up visions of police bursting into bedrooms to catch couples in the act—an unpalatable intrusion into the most intimate realm of marriage.

Griswold's privacy rationale implied that a law banning the commercial sale or distribution of contraceptives would be perfectly constitutional, since it would not necessitate intrusion into the marital bedchamber. The basic idea of *Griswold* was that married couples have a right to close the bedroom door and do as they please without government interference. But this did not necessarily give third parties a right to sell sexual aids to be used by married couples behind closed doors. Government could make it extremely hard for couples to access sexual aids, but once obtained, it could not prohibit their use without invading marital privacy.

This interpretation of *Griswold* and *Eisenstadt,* however, was finally rejected by the Court's 1977 decision in *Carey v. Population Services International,*[11] a case involving a New York law that banned the distribution of any contraceptives—including condoms—by anyone other than a licensed pharmacist.[12] New York defended the law by asserting that neither *Griswold* nor *Eisenstadt* granted constitutional protection for the sale or distribution of contraceptives.[13] The Court concluded that in light of its abortion decisions such as *Roe v. Wade,* the constitutional right involved in *Griswold* and its progeny is best characterized as "individual autonomy in matters of childbearing."[14] Not only do individuals have sovereignty to use contraceptives, they have a concomitant sovereignty to purchase them as well, because access to contraception—like abortion—is essential to exercising individual autonomy over the decision to bear or beget a child.[15] Laws restricting an individual's liberty regarding childbearing decisions are therefore presumptively unconstitutional unless the government can demonstrate a compelling need for the restriction.[16]

It was finally clear, post-*Carey*, that individuals enjoyed individual sovereignty over childbearing choices—whether relating to contraception or pregnancy termination. But this left unanswered an even larger question: Can the government interfere with sexual choices not related to childbearing? For example, can the government place limits on whom one may lawfully have sex with (e.g., adultery, fornication, prostitution)? Can it limit the sale of recreational sex aids (e.g., adult films, sex toys)? Can it limit any type of sex that is not procreative in nature (e.g., oral sex, anal sex, bestiality)? The great unresolved question, in other words, is whether individuals are sovereign with regard to their own sex lives, or merely with regard to the decision whether to become a parent. Is there a constitutional liberty to sex qua sex?

Lawrence v. Texas

Lawrence v. Texas, decided in the summer of 2003, answered the question with an unsatisfying maybe. The *Lawrence* Court invalidated a Texas law that criminalized sodomy (i.e., anal or oral sex) between individuals of the same gender. As discussed in previous chapters, there is language in *Lawrence* that both explicitly condemns public morality as the sole basis for law[17] and embraces a harm principle, at least with regard to laws infringing upon intimate relations.[18]

Remarkably, the *Lawrence* Court appears to have jettisoned traditional tiers of judicial scrutiny, invoking neither strict scrutiny, intermediate scrutiny, nor rationality review.[19] Instead, the Court began with a consideration of the scope of substantive liberty, concluded that it included private sexual conduct, and further concluded that the Texas anti-sodomy law unjustifiably restricted homosexuals' sexual liberty. In this sense, *Lawrence*'s analytical framework begins with a presumption of individual liberty and shifts the burden onto the government to establish the reasonableness of the restriction on liberty.

This modified analytical framework does not neatly fit within any of the orthodox tiers of judicial scrutiny, and its revolutionary potential lies in the shift of the burden of persuasion onto the government. Though the *Lawrence* Court did not go so far as to require Texas to establish a compelling need for the anti-sodomy statute—the traditional burden placed upon the government pursuant to strict scrutiny—the Court did seem to require Texas to establish a reasonable basis for the law, other than discriminatory animus or public morality. Viewed this way, *Lawrence* adopts rationality review, yet places the burden of persuasion upon the government rather than the individual. This subtle but important burden shift, if carried into future cases, will result in a victory for individual liberty in close cases. By requiring the government to offer reasonable justifications for restricting individual liberty, the Court's new analytical framework holds the potential to transform constitutional jurisprudence in a way that honors the principles of limited government and residual individual sovereignty.

And yet neither courts nor academics have interpreted *Lawrence* as the opening salvo in a constitutional transformation (or perhaps more accurately, reawakening) in favor of individual liberty. Perhaps the reason for this is that, although the decision is grounded in the liberty component of substantive due process and backed by strong autonomy language,[20] the Court's invocation of autonomy is made in the context of assuring an equality of rights between heterosexuals and homosexuals.[21] The Court intimated that it chose to invalidate the law on substantive due process rather than equal protection grounds to ensure an end to governmentally endorsed discrimination against homosexuals. The majority explicitly acknowledged that it did not want to leave open the possibility that Texas would simply reenact the law to prohibit all sodomy (whether heterosexual or homosexual)[22] because the Court believed that such a generally applicable ban on sodomy would still stigmatize all sexual activity between homosexuals.

The Court's emphasis on protecting homosexuals from the stigmatizing effects of anti-sodomy laws suggests that the decision may have limited utility for analyzing the validity of other generally applicable sex laws that do not create stigmatization or discrimination against identifiable classes. In this sense, the right to have sex recognized in *Lawrence* may be analogous to the right to free exercise of religion recognized in *Smith*—i.e., it may be extinguished by a law that prohibits the practice for everyone.

If the post-*Lawrence* Court limits sexual liberty as it has free exercise, generally applicable sex laws would enjoy a presumption of constitutionality. We will therefore proceed to examine the major categories of current sex laws and analyze their validity, with reference to both the analytical framework of *Lawrence* and the morality of American law.

WHY REGULATE SEX?

As an initial matter, we should ponder: Why is sex between consenting adults in private any of the law's business? The genesis of most sex laws is undoubtedly public morality—specifically, a Christian belief that the proper purpose of sex is procreation, and that procreation may morally take place only within the confines of marriage.[23] Under this view, sex is for procreation and procreation is for marriage. This deep linkage between sex, marriage, and procreation has permeated American sex law.

Indeed, lurking behind virtually all sex laws is the belief that sex is moral only when entered into as a baby-making, procreative enterprise. But the human sex drive is fueled by much more than a desire to create offspring, including equally powerful urges for physical pleasure and emotional intimacy.[24] The orthodox linkage of sex with procreation confuses cause with effect: the effect of heterosexual sex is often procreation, but procreation is not the cause of sex. The documented existence of homosexual behavior in over 450 animal species suggests that sexuality often is, biologically speaking, motivated by something other than a desire to procreate.[25]

This multi-dimensional view of sex was acknowledged by the Supreme Court in *Lawrence,* which described sex as "but one element in a personal bond that is more enduring."[26] Even a one-night stand (which the sexual act involved in *Lawrence* apparently was)[27] is granted constitutional protection, not because of its procreative potential, but because it is an intimate association that may blossom into a more lasting emotional bond.

The conceptualization of sex as integral to individual fulfillment and autonomy is consistent with common sense. Recent studies have confirmed that, similar to marriage and parenthood,[28] there is a strong positive correlation between sex and happiness; for both genders, those who have more frequent sex have higher self-reported levels of happiness.[29] If sex is integral to the "pursuit of happiness,"[30] does it not seem logical that sex should be entitled to the same degree of constitutional protection as other types of intimate, happiness-affecting decisions such as marriage and procreation?[31] If so, this suggests that laws restricting sexual liberty should be presumptively unconstitutional—the opposite of current law—unless the government can convince the court that the law is needed to prevent harm to the LLP of others.

So the salient question becomes: What harm is there in sex? Over fifty years ago, the American Law Institute (ALI) recommended that all consensual private sexual relations between adults be beyond the reach of criminal law, reasoning that "no harm to the secular interests of the community is involved in atypical sex practice in private between consenting adult partners" and "there is the fundamental question of the protection to which every individual is entitled against state interference in his personal affairs when he is not hurting others."[32] Implicit in the ALI's recommendation was the belief that acts contrary to public morality do not "hurt [] others" in a legally cognizable sense. Although an act that is contrary to public morality will, by definition, offend others, mere offense to public morality should not provide the basis for governmental restraint of liberty. The ALI was correct, and its recommendations are consistent with the morality of American law. With this framework in mind, we will now explore in greater detail the various types of sex laws that currently exist and the harms they are purportedly designed to address.

FORNICATION AND STATUTORY RAPE

The most obvious category of laws rendered defunct by *Lawrence* are those concerning fornication—at least insofar as these laws prohibit sexual relations between unmarried adults.[33] At present, nine American states still criminalize fornication,[34] yet the autonomy-based rationale of *Lawrence* undoubtedly renders these laws unconstitutional as applied to sex between consenting adults in private.

This hypothesis is confirmed by a unanimous post-*Lawrence* decision rendered by the Virginia Supreme Court in *Martin v. Ziherl*.[35] The plaintiff in *Ziherl* sued her lover under various tort theories after learning that he had infected her with the herpes virus. The defense asserted that there was no cognizable claim because the herpes infection resulted from the plaintiff's own criminal act of fornication. The plaintiff countered that Virginia's fornication statute was no longer constitutional after *Lawrence*, and the defendant tried to save the statute as a police power measure designed to promote "public health" and "encourag[e] that children be born into a family consisting of a married couple."[36]

These police power justifications were accepted by the trial court, but the Virginia Supreme Court concluded that they were insufficient per se in light of *Lawrence*.[37] The court quoted the *Lawrence* Court's statement that "[t]he Texas statute furthers no legitimate state interest which can justify its intrusion into the personal and private life of the individual"[38] and determined therefrom that *Lawrence* "sweeps within it all manner of states' interests and finds them insufficient when measured against the intrusion upon a person's liberty interest when that interest is exercised in the form of private, consensual sexual conduct between adults."[39] Thus, although prohibiting fornication may indeed encourage some persons to marry or lessen the spread of sexually transmitted diseases, these purposes were deemed by *Ziherl* to be insufficiently weighty to overcome the fornication statute's substantial restriction on individual autonomy.[40]

The *Ziherl* court may have read too much into *Lawrence,* however. It is far from clear that *Lawrence* establishes a per se rule whereby no governmental purposes can ever be weighty enough to outweigh an adult's autonomy to engage in private consensual sex. Presumably, the Court would uphold some restrictions on the sexual autonomy of consenting adults post-*Lawrence.*[41] In this context, therefore, we should examine the bases, other than public morality, that might underlie the continued existence and enforcement of fornication laws.

The most likely justification is public health. States might argue that fornication laws protect lives by deterring promiscuous sex which, in turn, deters the spread of sexually transmitted diseases (STDs).[42] It is true, after all, that less frequent sex with fewer sexual partners reduces the incidence of STDs. Arguably, then, forcibly limiting adults' consensual sexual encounters to sex within marriage helps protect them from harm.

Yet there is something amiss with this rationale. No one, for example, would seriously argue that pursuant to the goal of protecting public health the government could prohibit individuals from having sex with more than, say, three partners over a lifetime or mandate the use of condoms for sex between unmarried persons. Such laws would undoubtedly reduce the incidence of STDs, yet they clearly come at too high a cost to individual liberty.

One of the analytical deficiencies with linking consensual sex and the spread of STDs is that it assumes the existence of a causal relationship that is, in fact, quite remote. While STDs are by definition spread by sexual contact, most sexual contact does not involve exposure to STDs. Having sex does not per se result in the transmission of an STD, and even sex with someone infected with an STD does not necessarily spread infection. Only a relatively small subset of sexual contact threatens or results in STD harm, distinguishing sex from other harmful acts such as murder, attempted murder, battery, or attempted battery, which, by definition, always harm or threaten to harm others. If the goal of fornication laws is to reduce the spread of STDs, they are vastly overbroad, banning all sex outside marriage when a relatively small percentage of sexual encounters poses any risk of physical harm.

Another significant deficiency with attempting to justify fornication laws on public health grounds is that it requires us to ignore the consensual nature of the sexual encounter. Unmarried adults are presumably aware that they face some risk of contracting an STD if they have unprotected sex. It is therefore incumbent upon them to take simple steps such as asking questions and engaging in safe sex practices. Engaging in unprotected sex with a partner is analogous to bungee jumping and rock climbing: exhilarating, yet risky. But we likely would all agree that government cannot ban bungee jumping simply because it involves some degree of risk. And if potentially risky, non-intimate recreational activities such as bungee jumping are beyond the realm of governmental prohibition, it necessarily follows that potentially risky, intimate recreational activities such as sex should be as well.

Even if one accepts that a universal ban on non-marital sex is an illegitimate exercise of governmental power, there may be times when specific instances of consensual sex may trigger legitimate governmental power to punish. For example, if an individual knows that she has an STD and has sex without revealing the STD to her partner, any resulting physical harm would provide a legitimate basis for the imposition of penalties. Under such circumstances, the knowing concealment of an STD would be a material omission akin to fraud, and the material omission creates a reasonable threat of physical harm to the unwitting partner. The harm that is threatened or that actually results may be conceptualized, respectively, as either harm to the partner's liberty—i.e., deprivation of their ability to choose what to do with their body—or a harm to the partner's life. Other than this relatively narrow exception, however, prohibiting fornication by adults on the basis of protecting public health is unsupportable.

But what about minors? Are fornication laws, as applied solely to minors, still constitutional? The *Lawrence* Court intimated that sex involving minors would involve a different constitutional equation.[43] The Virginia Supreme Court's decision in *Ziherl* likewise thought that it was "important to note" that the "case d[id] not involve minors."[44] The constitutional protection granted to consensual sex between minors therefore remains fundamentally unresolved.

Consensual sex between minors implicates not only fornication laws (because minors are generally not married), but also statutory rape laws, which impose much harsher sentences upon conviction. Every state has a law that establishes the minimum age for consenting to sex, and these laws have evolved considerably over the years. At the beginning of the nineteenth century, the common age for sexual consent was ten years.[45] A majority of states currently establish the minimum consent age at sixteen,[46] although there is considerable variation from state to state. A significant number of states establish the age of consent at seventeen or eighteen,[47] and one state, Hawaii, establishes it at age fourteen.[48] Establishing sixteen as the age of consent for sex appears to be pragmatically useful, since the median age at first intercourse is presently about sixteen and a half years old.[49]

Present statutory rape laws generally protect either male or female minors[50] and often vary punishment according to the age of the victim, the age of the perpetrator, and the difference in age between the two, with increased penalties for acts committed by an individual substantially older than the victim.[51] The adoption of age-differential statutory rape laws reflects a conscious attempt to acknowledge reality by exempting consensual sex between teenagers who are close in age. Despite these efforts at reform, however, there are still nine states that criminalize consensual sex between an eighteen-year-old male and his sixteen-year-old girlfriend.[52]

One of the quandaries posed by the interrelationship between fornication and statutory rape laws is whether a minor who reaches the age of consent should be immune from prosecution for fornication, a separate crime which has no age requirement. In the abstract, statutory rape laws and fornication laws are designed to serve very different purposes. Statutory rape is designed to protect immature minors from the predatory sexual pressure of more mature individuals. Fornication, by contrast, is designed to prevent individuals, of any age, from engaging in sex outside marriage. Statutory rape therefore serves a legitimate purpose of protecting minors from harm, but fornication serves only to impose one segment of society's morality upon the rest.

Logic and fairness suggest that a minor who has reached the age of consent for purposes of statutory rape should not then face a backdoor prosecution for fornication. Yet such prosecutions have been attempted, as illustrated by a recent case rendered by the Georgia Supreme Court. In *In re J.M.*,[53] a sixteen-year-old boy was prosecuted for fornication for having consensual sex with his sixteen-year-old girlfriend in her bedroom. Because Georgia's statutory rape law established sixteen as the age at which a person can grant consent to sex,[54] the court concluded that "the only . . . rationale for the fornication statute is to enable the State to regulate the private, sexual conduct of persons who the legislature has determined are capable of consenting to that conduct, and that is an insufficient state interest to overcome Georgia's constitutional protections of privacy."[55]

The Georgia Supreme Court's analysis is undoubtedly correct. Once a state has established an age at which an individual is deemed capable of consenting to sex, the individual's sexual partners should not thereafter face criminal prosecution simply because there is another, antediluvian statute that criminalizes premarital sex based solely on notions of public morality. Once government has deemed an individual to be an adult for purposes of consenting to sex— even if they are not considered adults for other purposes—the individual should enjoy sovereignty to make decisions about sexual activity free from governmental paternalism.

PORNOGRAPHY AND OBSCENITY

At the time of the founding, legal proscription against the possession or sale of sexually explicit materials was virtually unknown, though such materials were widely available. The colony of Massachusetts enacted a general obscenity statute in 1711, but there were no recorded prosecutions until the infamous "Fanny Hill" case of 1821.[56] Indeed, despite their ubiquity today, obscenity statutes were uncommon in the United States until the late nineteenth century.[57]

As a preliminary matter, it is important to recognize the legal difference between pornography and obscenity. Although most Americans undoubtedly equate the two, the former—pornography—is a much broader, colloquial term encompassing any type of erotic material. The latter—obscenity—is a precise legal term, referring to material that lacks First Amendment protection because it "appeals to the prurient interest," portrays sex in a "patently offensive way" and lacks any serious scientific, literary, artistic, or political value.[58]

The line separating constitutionally protected pornography[59] from unprotected obscenity is a thin and wavering line, often leading to inconsistent, confusing, and even absurd results. Moreover, although obscenity itself supposedly falls outside the ambit of the First Amendment entirely, the Supreme Court in *Stanley v. Georgia*,[60] has drawn yet another wavy line, extending First Amendment protection to obscene materials if possessed in the privacy of the home.[61] But the right to consume obscenity has been limited to the facts presented in *Stanley*—that is, adults are insulated from governmental prosecution only when possessing obscenity in their residences. There is no corresponding constitutional right to sell, distribute, or transport obscene materials.[62]

The *Stanley* exception protecting private use of obscene materials is startlingly similar to the Court's early contraceptive jurisprudence that initially protected the private use of contraceptives, yet not the commercial sale or distribution thereof. The Court ultimately abandoned the use-versus-commerce distinction for contraceptives, but it strangely still clings to it in the context of other sex laws, including obscenity. Under current law, individuals are free to possess and enjoy obscenity to their heart's content, so long as it occurs in the privacy of their home,[63] yet there is no corresponding right to sell or distribute obscenity for use and enjoyment by others. If you can find a black market source for obscenity (increasingly easy in the Internet age), the law will leave you alone to enjoy it. But the person who provides those obscene materials to you risks many years in prison.

The logic behind the use-commerce distinction for obscenity is a belief that the private use of obscenity cannot possibly harm anyone else, whereas commerce in obscenity could. In *Stanley*, for example, Georgia attempted to justify its prosecution of Stanley by claiming that "exposure to obscene materials may lead to deviant sexual behavior or crimes of sexual violence."[64] The Court responded that there was "little empirical basis" for these assertions and thus "the State may no more prohibit mere possession of obscene matter on the ground that it may lead to antisocial conduct than it may prohibit possession of chemistry books on the ground that they may lead to the manufacture of homemade spirits."[65]

The *Stanley* Court's conclusion that there is insufficient evidence to link pornography to anti-social harmful behavior such as violence against women has been confirmed in the ensuing decades. Studies conducted since *Stanley* generally have concluded that viewing sexually explicit films and pictures does not contribute to negative attitudes toward women, acceptance of rape myths, or other attitudinal changes that might indicate an increased propensity toward actual violence against women.[66] More significantly, the one major study which indicated that "massive exposure" to nonviolent pornography may result in negative attitudes toward women concluded that there was no corresponding increase in levels of actual aggression, as repeated exposure appeared to result in habituation and a correspondingly lower level of excited response, including aggression.[67]

Research suggests that exposure to violence of any sort, sexual or nonsexual, leads to desensitization to violence generally, including violence against women.[68] This, in turn, may create a less empathetic and responsive society. In this sense, repeated exposure to graphic violence in slasher films or violent lyrics in gangsta rap, both of which often contain misogynist themes, is equally to blame for negative attitudes toward women.[69] It is, in other words, still very much a man's world, and there are numerous manifestations of a male desire to dominate women, of which erotic films and magazines comprise but a small subset.

If media portrayal of violence generally desensitizes individuals to violence and makes us less empathetic to pain suffered by others, these emotional alterations do not provide a legitimate basis for governmental restriction of individual liberty. Although this is undoubtedly hard for many Americans to accept, it is important to realize that such desensitization or loss of empathy does not itself harm or reasonably threaten harm to others' life, liberty, or property. Exposure to violence generally may result in a certain degree of emotional numbing, but it does not increase aggressive behavior. The evidence suggests that when we are exposed to violence, we are initially shocked, but the shock quickly wears off and we tune it out, responding with less emotional intensity. But we do not respond to repeated exposure to violence (whether pornographic or otherwise) with aggression. In short, repeated exposure to violence appears to lessen our emotional reaction to violence.

Although emotional desensitization to violence is undoubtedly unfortunate, it is crucial to accept that emotional states and mind control generally are not the legitimate business of government. There are innumerable activities that may negatively alter emotional states, yet none are within the proper sphere of governmental control. Crudely dumping a lover may negatively affect the lover's emotional well-being. Wealth makes some individuals less sensitive to needs of the poor. Education may render some individuals intolerant of the ignorant. Religion may create intolerance of individuals with different religious beliefs or lifestyles considered to be immoral. But none of these negative emotional effects—each a form of desensitization—provides a legitimate basis for governmental action. If they did, thought-controlling Big Brother government would be a frightening reality rather than entertaining fiction.

The best remedy for potentially desensitizing material or activity is education and the adoption by each individual of a private set of values. If individuals are aware that certain activities may have negative emotional effects, they can make an informed decision to take appropriate steps to mitigate or avoid those effects. But the bottom line is that, pursuant to the morality of American law, competent adults remain sovereign to make these important decisions for themselves, free of governmental coercion.

If there is no evidence of a causal link between viewing obscenity and harm to others, why should selling or distributing obscenity to the public be presumed harmful and hence subject to governmental prohibition? Is there any evidence that purchasing an obscene magazine at a bookstore or viewing an obscene film at a theater somehow causes harm whereas viewing the same magazine or film at home does not? The answer, of course, is that there is no such evidence. If private consumption of obscenity by adults is harmless, commercial transactions of obscenity with adults are likewise harmless.

Indeed, this was the conclusion reached in 1970 by the congressionally chartered Commission on Obscenity and Pornography. It recommended "that federal, state and local laws prohibiting the sale, exhibition, or distribution of sexual materials to consenting adults should be repealed"[70] because "[e]xtensive empirical investigation, both by the Commission and by others, provides no evidence that exposure to or use of explicit sexual materials play a significant role in the causation of social or individual harms such as crime, delinquency, sexual or nonsexual deviancy or severe emotional disturbances."[71]

Some argue that commerce in obscenity presents risks of harm that are not present with mere private consumption. For example, the public sale or distribution of obscenity may expose minors to obscene material. Of course, minors may similarly be exposed to obscene material when it is being viewed in the home by an adult. Yet the possibility of exposure to minors did not stop the Supreme Court in *Stanley* from protecting the adult's right to view obscenity at home. The Court presumably would sanction the protection of minors from exposure to obscenity in the home through prosecution for offenses such as contributing to the delinquency of a minor or child abuse. In this way, adults are at liberty to view obscenity in the home but not at liberty to expose children to material that may prove developmentally harmful. And although there is no evidence linking exposure to obscenity to harms to children, the ethical prohibitions on using children in obscenity experiments will prevent such evidence from being gathered. It is therefore prudent, in exercising its parens patriae power, that the government err on the side of caution—a power it legitimately does not possess when dealing with adults.[72] The morality of American law acknowledges the protection of children as a legitimate function of law, and therefore reasonable time, place, or manner restrictions—not total prohibitions on commerce in obscenity—would be a legitimate way to balance the need to protect minors with the residual individual sovereignty of adults.[73]

Others may contend that commerce in obscenity, unlike private consumption, poses a risk of offense to adults who do not wish to be exposed to obscenity. Embedded within this argument are two distinct ideas: (1) that adults should not be forced to consume obscenity if they do not wish to; and (2) that the existence of commerce in obscenity is per se offensive within a community, even if no adults are forced to actually consume obscenity. The first argument is a legitimate harm-based rationale for law; the latter is not.

If an adult is unwittingly exposed to obscenity—that is, she is effectively forced to consume it without being given a reasonable opportunity to look away—she has effectively been denied her liberty to choose for herself whether to consume obscenity. In this sense, unwitting exposure to obscenity constitutes a liberty harm cognizable under the morality of American law. Governments legitimately may enact laws designed to prevent this kind of harm, while at the same time permitting other adults, who do want to consume obscenity, to exercise their own sovereign choice. If, for example, an individual wishes to sell obscene material to adults over the Internet, it would be reasonable for government to require the merchant to post various warnings or employ other reasonable means for avoiding forced consumption of obscenity.[74] Reasonable time, place, or manner regulations can balance the competing sovereignties of adults and minimize the risk of liberty harm through forced consumption.

Another plausible argument for regulating commerce in obscenity is that it reasonably threatens harm to the property of those who live nearby. The morality of American law clearly acknowledges that a demonstrable loss of property value is an LLP harm sufficient to trigger governmental action. Assuming the government can demonstrate a causal relationship between commerce in obscenity and harm to nearby property, the governmental remedy for this harm must bear a logical relationship to the harm. A total ban on commerce in obscenity would be an excessive use of governmental power if the protection of property values could be achieved by less drastic means, such as enforcing existing noise restrictions or establishing zoning regulations to separate obscenity establishments from residential neighborhoods.[75]

Finally, some may argue that permitting commerce in obscenity is immoral and will accelerate the moral decline of America.[76] Under both *Lawrence v. Texas* and the morality of American law, however, a mere belief that a particular activity is immoral cannot justify governmental restrictions on individual liberty. Indeed, a recent decision by a federal trial court in *United States v. Extreme Associates, Inc.*[77] confirms the possibility that obscenity laws grounded solely in public morality may be invalid post-*Lawrence*.

The defendants in *Extreme Associates* operated a subscription-only Web site that posted sexually explicit pictures and video clips and were charged with violating federal obscenity statutes after a U.S. postal inspector provided a credit card number, became a subscriber, and downloaded various video clips. The defendant-distributors moved to dismiss the charges on grounds that the laws infringed upon the rights of liberty and privacy recognized in *Lawrence* and *Stanley.*

The government in *Extreme Associates* asserted that *Lawrence* did not create a new fundamental right and therefore the federal obscenity law should be subjected only to rationality review. Moreover, because the federal ban on obscenity was designed to further the government's legitimate interests in protecting minors from exposure and protecting unwitting adults from involuntary consumption, the government contended that the law satisfied the basic test of rationality.[78]

The federal trial court rejected the government's arguments, concluding that the issue was not whether there is a fundamental right to distribute obscenity, but whether the federal ban on distributing obscenity unduly burdened the fundamental right of individuals to consume obscene materials in private, as recognized in *Stanley*.[79] Because the right recognized in *Stanley* was explicitly labeled "fundamental,"[80] the *Extreme Associates* court reasoned that laws burdening the individual's right privately to consume obscenity are unconstitutional unless the government can demonstrate they are narrowly tailored to further a compelling governmental interest.[81]

Applying this strict scrutiny, the *Extreme Associates* court concluded that a total ban on obscenity was not narrowly tailored to further the government's interests in protecting minors or unwitting adults. Both goals could be—and indeed were—accomplished by the use of less restrictive measures such as credit card prepayments, computer filtering software, and age restrictions on pornography consumption. To the extent that the federal obscenity law was designed merely to enforce public morality, the court in *Extreme Associates* noted repeatedly that *Lawrence* had declared public morality alone to be an illegitimate basis for law.[82]

The *Extreme Associates* decision was bound to be controversial, if for no other reason than it upsets the status quo and forces us to rethink the true basis for obscenity laws. Decisions rendered after *Extreme Associates* indicate that a desire to maintain the status quo is strong and that other courts will be reticent to go so far.[83] Indeed, in late 2005, the U.S. Court of Appeals for the Third Circuit reversed the District Court's decision in *Extreme Associates*.[84] In so doing, the Third Circuit invoked the Supreme Court's admonition in earlier cases that "if a precedent of this Court has direct application in a case, yet appears to rest on reasons rejected in some other line of decisions, the Court of Appeals should follow the case which directly controls, leaving to this Court the prerogative of overruling its own decisions."[85] The Third Circuit reasoned that the Supreme Court's obscenity jurisprudence left no doubt that the commercial distribution of obscenity was without constitutional protection and "[t]he fact that [the Supreme Court's obscenity] analysis has never been applied within the precise scenario outlined by the District Court—i.e., use of the talismanic phrase 'substantive due process' in the context of a vendor proceeding under derivative standing on behalf of a consumer's right to privately possess obscene material—does not negate the binding precedential value of the Supreme Court cases employing that [obscenity] analysis. The Court's analysis need not be so specific in order to limit a district court's prerogative to overturn an entire category of federal statutes, even as applied to particular defendants, based on speculation about a later decision [*Lawrence v. Texas*] that fails even to mention those statutes."[86] The court was "satisfied" that *Lawrence v. Texas* did not implicitly overrule the Supreme Court's obscenity jurisprudence and that "[t]he possibility that *Lawrence* has 'somehow weakened the precedential value' of [the obscenity cases] is irrelevant . . . ."[87]

Despite its controversial nature, the District Court in *Extreme Associates* undoubtedly reached the right result. There is no reason to invoke the coercive power of government to prohibit the commercial distribution of obscenity, since there is no evidence, as recognized in *Stanley*, that the private consumption of obscenity results in harm to others. If there is a fundamental constitutional right to consume obscenity, there must be a corresponding fundamental right to provide it. Laws which interfere with a citizen's ability to access materials that he has a fundamental right to consume should therefore be presumptively unconstitutional, permissible only if necessary to prevent harm to others. A total prohibition on the sale or distribution of obscene materials to adults, however, sweeps much too broadly, significantly interfering with the fundamental rights of adults in a way that is unnecessary and disrespectful of residual individual sovereignty.[88]

More fundamentally, the Third Circuit's opinion in *Extreme Associates* reveals that lower courts are balking at giving full effect to *Lawrence's* condemnation of public morality as a legitimate basis for law, treating it as amusing dicta or temporary judicial insanity that should be ignored rather than embraced as a fundamental limitation on governmental power. There is a continuing, deep-seated judicial reticence to come to terms with a simple truth: If, in the name of public morality, individuals may be jailed for engaging in behavior deemed morally offensive to others or hazardous to their own souls, there is no such thing in America as private morality, individuality, equality, or liberty.

SEX TOYS

One of the most interesting recent developments in the area of individual liberty has been the regulation of sex toys such as vibrators, dildos, artificial vaginas, and an astonishing array of others. Despite their relatively widespread use and increased social acceptance, there are many states that still criminalize the commercial sale or distribution of sex toys, often classifying them as "obscene devices."[89] Similar to early laws regulating contraceptives and current laws regulating obscenity, states have opted to draw a line between use and commerce, permitting the former yet prohibiting the latter. As with current obscenity law, an adult may use and enjoy a sex toy once obtained, but there is no corresponding ability to sell or distribute sex toys to willing adults.[90]

The Supreme Courts of Colorado, Kansas, and Louisiana have invalidated their obscene devices law as infringing upon federal constitutional privacy, but remarkably have done so only because the statutes broadly criminalized the sale of sex toys to all persons, including those who use them for therapeutic reasons.[91] These courts have emphasized that sex toys are widely prescribed by therapists and physicians for sexual dysfunction, particularly for the treatment of anorgasmic women.[92] The odd result is that courts seem much more comfortable condemning prohibitions on the sale of sex toys on grounds of protecting their medical or therapeutic use, rather than simply acknowledging that healthy adults should be at liberty to use them as part of their private sexual activity. A similar attitude is echoed in federal Medicaid law, which mandates payment for erectile-dysfunction (ED) prescription drugs such as Viagra in those states that opt to include some degree of prescription drug coverage.[93] Ironically, current law allows states to ban the sale of recreational vibrators yet requires them to pay for drugs that induce erections.

Both vibrators and ED drugs are designed and marketed as aids to improve sexual pleasure. So why is the former proscribable by law but not the latter? One could surmise that the disparate treatment evinces some form of sexism, on the assumption that the most widely used sex toys are those that enhance sexual pleasure for women. But this is too simplistic an explanation. The truth is that both Medicaid payment for ED drugs and laws regulating the sale of sex toys share the common theme of medical necessity: Medicaid pays for Viagra and courts sometimes protect a liberty to sell sex toys because they are both integral components of medical therapy for those suffering from sexual dysfunction. Sex toys and sex drugs are legally acceptable, it seems, when used to help individuals achieve a normal sex life.

No one would deny that individuals should have a right to access effective medical therapies (a topic explored in Chapter 7). But why are sex toys not similarly accepted when they are used to enhance the sexual pleasure of adults who do not suffer from sexual dysfunction? Why is it easier for courts to declare that an anorgasmic woman should be at liberty to use a vibrator rather than one who simply wishes to make climax easier or more intense? The end result—orgasm—is the same in either case, and there is no harm to anyone in either scenario. If adult Americans have sexual liberty, particularly post-*Lawrence,* should not this liberty necessarily include the right to buy and use sex toys to heighten their sexual pleasure?

Moreover, it is important to question why sexual devices are generally placed in the same legal category of obscenity as adult magazines, videos, and sex shows. After all, one of the primary justifications for restricting obscene magazines, videos, and sex shows is their alleged negative psychological and physical effects, such as encouraging sex crimes, discouraging marriage, and devaluing women. Yet none of these effects is generally associated with vibrators, dildos, or other sex toys. No one seriously asserts that vibrators or dildos encourage sex crimes. Likewise, statistical data indicates that sex toys are generally purchased by individuals in relationships, often marriage.[94] There is zero evidence that couples who use sex toys are discouraged from marriage or that the use of sex toys hurts marriage. To the contrary, research indicates that better sex leads to greater happiness, and sex toys are specifically designed to enhance sexual pleasure.[95]

Similarly, there is no evidence that sex toys devalue women. Many sex toys are designed to enhance and encourage orgasm in women, many of whom are unable to achieve climax through coitus.[96] As historian Rachel Maines has shown, various types of mechanical, hydriatic, and electrical vibrators were developed as a means of providing more efficient therapy for women diagnosed as suffering from hysteria.[97] Hysteria, commonly diagnosed until the mid-twentieth century, was a condition variously ascribed to sexual dysfunction, deprivation, or dissatisfaction which was treated, until the advent of vibrators, by the manual stimulation to climax of a woman's genitalia by a midwife or physician.[98] Once electrical vibrators were invented in the 1880s, they were widely marketed directly to women as an aid to health and relaxation, even by such a staid American corporation as Sears and Roebuck.[99]

Today, the majority of adult American women admit using sex toys and deriving greater sexual satisfaction from their use than from manual stimulation or coitus.[100] Vibrators are widely available in big box retail stores, marketed as massagers. Sex toys are now so popular with women that many companies sell them exclusively to women at home in Tupperware-style parties.[101] So why do so many American states criminalize commerce in sex toys that apparently produce nothing but sexual satisfaction, particularly for women? And why is it permissible to sell a massager at Wal-Mart but not a vibrator at an adult novelty store?

The answer, in the words of the U.S. Eleventh Circuit Court of Appeals, is that "commerce in the pursuit of orgasms by artificial means for their own sake is detrimental to the health and morality of the State." The Eleventh Circuit's justification for banning the commerce in sex toys was pronounced not in 1904, but 2004. Specifically, in *Williams v. Attorney General of Alabama,*[12] the Eleventh Circuit was asked to consider the constitutionality of an Alabama law that criminalized the sale or distribution of "any device designed or marketed as useful primarily for the stimulation of human genital organs."[103] The plaintiffs were owners of adult novelty stores, distributors of sex toys, and individuals who used sex toys. They argued that the Alabama law placed a substantial burden on married individuals' autonomy to engage in private, consensual sexual activity.[104]

The plaintiffs' argument was directly analogous to the argument accepted by the Supreme Court in *Carey v. Population Services International*[105]—namely, that by limiting who may sell or distribute a certain product (in *Carey,* contraceptives), a state limits individuals' access to those materials, thereby placing a substantial burden on the individual's constitutional right to use the product.[106] The difference between contraceptives and sex toys, however, is that the Supreme Court has explicitly acknowledged that individuals have a constitutional liberty to use the former but not the latter. Yet what about the liberty of an adult to engage in private consensual sex that was recognized by the Court in *Lawrence v. Texas?* Does not the liberty of adults to engage in private consensual sex imply that they have a concomitant right to use sexual aids?

According to the Eleventh Circuit in *Williams,* the answer is no. *Williams* was decided after *Lawrence,* yet the Eleventh Circuit upheld the ban on sex toys. The court concluded that *Lawrence* did not recognize a fundamental right to private sexual intimacy and therefore the Alabama law was presumptively constitutional, and would be overturned only if the plaintiffs could prove it was irrational.[107] The Eleventh Circuit also, in a footnote, implied that *Lawrence* was inapposite because "[t]here is nothing 'private' or 'consensual' about the advertising and sale of a dildo. And such advertising and sale is just as likely to be exhibited to children as to 'consenting adults.'"[108]

Perhaps most significantly, the Eleventh Circuit in *Williams,* much like the Texas federal trial court in a recent obscenity case,[109] refused to accept the *Lawrence* Court's condemnation of public morality as a sole basis for law. Instead it preferred to cling to the broadened version of the police power invoked to justify the results in pre-*Lawrence* obscenity jurisprudence. It asserted that "the Supreme Court has noted on repeated occasions that laws can be based on moral judgments. . . . In addition, our own recent precedent has unequivocally affirmed the furtherance of public morality as a legitimate state interest."[110] The "own recent precedent" to which the Eleventh Circuit referred was its first opinion in the *Williams* case, decided prior to *Lawrence* in 2001, in which the court invoked the orthodox mantra that "safeguarding of public morality has long been an established part of the States' plenary police power to legislate."[111]

The Eleventh Circuit's stubbornness in *Williams* is apparent. It ignored the Supreme Court's unequivocal instruction in *Lawrence* to disregard public morality as a legitimate basis for law. And in so doing, it provides yet another example of the modern orthodox conception of plenary legislative power. Under this orthodoxy, legislatures are free to do as they wish, restricting individual liberty on the mere premise that it offends the morality of others. The only possible saving grace for individual liberty is lodged in the Court's parsimonious substantive due process jurisprudence, which imposes virtually insurmountable obstacles to claims of individual liberty, presuming all liberty restrictions constitutional unless the individual citizen can carry the burden of convincing the court that the act in question is deeply rooted in American history and tradition and "implicit in the concept of ordered liberty, such that neither liberty nor justice would exist" without it.[112]

This was the precise analytical framework employed by the *Williams* court to reject an asserted liberty to distribute sex toys to consenting adults, despite the fact that the Supreme Court in *Lawrence* recognized the right of adults to engage in consensual private sex, the fact that there was no demonstrable harm flowing from their sale, and the fact that there was no evidence that children or unwitting adults were exposed to such items. The Eleventh Circuit reasoned that the liberty to use or distribute sex toys was not "deeply rooted" because there was no history of American statutes explicitly permitting their use or distribution. It concluded that "nothing in [the Supreme Court's prior substantive due process jurisprudence] indicates that an absence of historical *prohibition* is tantamount, for purposes of fundamental-rights analysis, to an historical record of *protection* under the law."[113]

The Eleventh Circuit's view is fundamentally antithetical to the conception of individual liberty. After all, the essence of liberty is an absence of historical prohibition—a right to be left alone, free from governmental coercion. By requiring individual citizens to prove the existence of "an historical record of protection"—i.e., affirmative statutory acknowledgment of a right to live one's life as one pleases, so long as it does not harm others—the Eleventh Circuit demonstrates a lack of understanding of (or refusal to acknowledge) the very meaning of individual liberty. The *Williams* decision exemplifies all that is wrong with modern liberty jurisprudence. It confines the realm of residual individual sovereignty to a narrow subset of actions that are, in the court's opinion, deeply rooted in history and implicit in the concept of liberty, phrases which are inherently subjective and vulnerable to political manipulation.

The Eleventh Circuit's insistence in *Williams* on the existence of a plenary legislative police power in the absence of a historical record of affirmative protection for individual liberty starkly illustrates the stinginess of modern constitutional liberty—and how very far we have drifted from the foundational principles of limited government and residual individual sovereignty. The Eleventh Circuit defended its position by invoking the orthodox counter-majoritarian cry, "Once elevated to constitutional status, a right is effectively removed from the hands of the people and placed into the guardianship of unelected judges. We are particularly mindful of this fact in the delicate area of morals legislation. One of the virtues of the democratic process is that, unlike the judicial process, it need not take matters to their logical conclusion. If the people of Alabama in time decide that a prohibition on sex toys is misguided, or ineffective, or just plain silly, they can repeal the law and be finished with the matter."[114]

Implicit in this statement is the old majority-rules idea of plenary legislative power. If a majority of legislators want to ban sex toys because they think they are icky, weird, offensive, or immoral, they are free to do so. Those individuals who wish to purchase and use sex toys are out of luck, unless they can convince their legislators to repeal the law. As the Framers of this country well understood, there is no meaningful liberty under a government with this sort of omnipotent legislature; the foundational principles of limited government and residual individual sovereignty are shattered.

PROSTITUTION

Prostitution—the so-called oldest profession—has existed in every recorded civilization. Unless and until the sexual drive is suppressed completely, there will always be commerce in sex. Respect for the twin principles of limited government and residual individual sovereignty, combined with the sheer fruitlessness of attempts at eradication, led early American states and localities to allow prostitution to take place, provided it was kept out of obvious public view. It was not until the zeal of Progressive social reform captured the American psyche in the early twentieth century that targeted prostitution laws began to appear.[115] Since the Progressive era, however, legal prohibition has been the norm. Today, forty-nine states prohibit all prostitution. The State of Nevada stands alone in legalizing prostitution within certain counties.[116]

Despite its prevalence in movies, music, and the news, having sex with a prostitute is uncommon. Recent national studies indicate that approximately 2 percent of women have ever received payment for oral, anal, or vaginal sex.[117] The corresponding numbers of men who report having paid for sex within the last year are similarly small:[118] 0.3 percent of men in rural areas and 2.0 percent of men in the twelve largest American cities.[119] Factors that have a positive correlation to the likelihood of ever having sex with a prostitute include lower income, serving in the military, infrequent church attendance, being divorced or separated, living in a metropolitan area, and being black.[120] There is also a strong correlation between self-reported marital unhappiness and the use of prostitutes within the previous year.[121]

Criminal arrests and prosecutions for prostitution-related offenses in the United States overwhelmingly focus on the prostitute, not his or her customer.[122] Because the vast majority of prostitutes are female, this means that the brunt of the effects of criminalization—arrest record, fines, incarceration—are borne by women and their families, including many children. In a handful of major cities there has been a recent effort to institute "john schools" that focus attention at the demand side of the equation, by educating johns about the causes and effects of prostitution.[123] But these efforts at lessening the demand are very limited, and the vast bulk of dollars spent to enforce prostitution-related laws are spent on supply-side efforts to round up, restrain, and prosecute the prostitutes themselves.

Numerous constitutional objections to prostitution laws have been litigated, most of which have centered upon the Supreme Court's privacy jurisprudence first articulated in *Griswold v. Connecticut.*[124] Although these challenges have uniformly failed, the *Lawrence* decision will undoubtedly spawn a new round of constitutional challenges.[125] The *Lawrence* majority explicitly noted that its decision did not raise the issue of sex-for-hire,[126] thereby intimating that it might view prostitution differently from consensual sex that lacks the commercial exchange element. Justice Scalia's dissent in *Lawrence,* however, predicted the majority's opinion would undermine governmental ability to criminalize many types of sexual activity, including prostitution.[127] Scalia's concerns about the future validity of prostitution laws post-*Lawrence* may be warranted. The *Lawrence* Court's conception of sex as an integral component of individual autonomy and its condemnation of public morality as the sole basis for law fairly implies that many applications of prostitution laws impermissibly infringe upon the liberty of adults to engage in private consensual sex. *Lawrence*'s repeated emphasis on private, consensual sexual activity, however, suggests that prohibiting streetwalking—the most prevalent and public manifestation of prostitution—may be considered by the Court to be an acceptable exercise of governmental power, provided there is a purpose underlying such prohibitions other than public morality.

So what are the justifications for criminalizing prostitution? Public morality is undoubtedly one justification, since prostitution is purely recreational sex, which is traditionally condemned by many Christian denominations. Beyond public morality, however, are there any other legitimate reasons to ban prostitution? Proffered justifications have included protecting marriage and family, protecting women from exploitation and physical abuse, protecting minors, protecting adults from unwanted propositions, and preventing the spread of sexually transmitted diseases (STDs).

Under the morality of American law, all of these justifications, other than protecting the institutions of marriage and family, are legitimate harm-based rationales designed to protect the LLP of citizens. As stated before, institutions such as marriage and family are not property interests cognizable of protection under the morality of American law, since the definition of these institutions is an artificial legal construct inherently based on public morality. If one honors the twin foundational principles of limited government and residual individual sovereignty, one cannot accept that an artificially constructed institution defined by notions of public morality may legitimately trump individual liberty to enter into other, non-conforming intimate relationships, provided those relationships do not result in harm to the LLP of others.

It should be pointed out, however, that even assuming arguendo that protecting the institutions of marriage and family is a legitimate governmental goal, laws prohibiting prostitution have little, if any, positive relationship to these goals. The majority of men who employ a prostitute are not married,[128] and there is no evidence that their access to prostitutes keeps them from entering into marriage if and when they are able to do so. If the goal of prostitution laws is to protect marriage and family, the legitimate scope of governmental power would be commensurate to effectuating this goal, prohibiting only the employment of a prostitute by married men.

Moreover, as stated in Chapter 4's discussion of adultery, there is a debatable question as to whether sex outside marriage—whether in the form of gratuitous adultery or non-gratuitous prostitution—causes harm to marriage. Although there are undoubtedly many instances of divorce in which a spouse has committed adultery or visited a prostitute, it is too simplistic to assume that extramarital sex is the cause of the divorce rather than innumerable other social, emotional, and financial factors. In the specific case of prostitution, evidence suggests that married men turn to prostitutes because they are unable to obtain sexual satisfaction from their wives, either because their wives are unable or unwilling to perform specific sexual acts, or because they simply prefer having sex with a wide variety of sexual partners.[129] Much like gratuitous extra-marital affairs, the availability of prostitution may serve as an outlet for sexual urges and thereby encourage marriage and reduce pressure for divorce.

More importantly, there is no evidence that prostitution itself results in harm to the life, liberty, or property of others. The physical abuse of prostitutes is a distinct life harm that is legitimately proscribed by numerous non-prostitution-related offenses such as battery. If protecting prostitutes from physical abuse is the goal, criminalization of prostitution is perhaps the worst conceivable way to effectuate this goal, since the criminal nature of the prostitute's work makes it exceedingly difficult for her to seek legal recourse in the event of physical abuse. Similarly, if protecting minors from exploitation is the goal, the law may undoubtedly prohibit prostitution by or solicitation of minors as part of its parens patriae power without unnecessarily infringing upon the liberty of adults.

Perhaps the best argument for prohibiting prostitution is the goal of reducing the incidence of STDs. When contracted, STDs constitute a life harm that is cognizable under the morality of American law. But is it reasonable to ban all prostitution in an effort to reduce the incidence of STDs? Most sexual encounters do not involve a risk of contracting an STD, but concededly the risk of contracting STDs is higher when one of the partners is a prostitute because the prostitute has been exposed to many unknown partners. Precisely how much higher the risk is unclear, however, and undoubtedly varies according to the type of sexual practices engaged in and the prevalence of condom usage. Several studies, for example, suggest that the use of prophylactics by prostitutes is very high, resulting in a lower incidence of STD transmission in commercial sex than non-commercial sex.[130] Moreover, the most common activity sought by a john is oral sex, not vaginal sex, and the risk of contracting an STD though oral sex is very remote.[131] This would suggest that pursuant to the goal of preventing the spread of STDs, the government may have some power to regulate vaginal intercourse with a prostitute, but not the more popular, less risky types of sexual activity such as oral sex and manual manipulation.

Moreover, the goal of preventing the spread of STDs through vaginal intercourse could be more reasonably achieved by regulations such as requiring the use of condoms and regular health examinations of prostitutes. Such steps have been taken in the context of legalized prostitution in Nevada and have proven successful in preventing the spread of STDs. Nevada's approach is to impose a high degree of regulation, including various time, place, and manner restrictions on brothels and prostitutes, in exchange for legalization.[132] Most significantly, Nevada's prostitution law requires each prostitute to have a card issued by the state that certifies that she is free of STDs. Weekly examinations by a licensed physician are required, in addition to monthly blood tests to determine whether the prostitute is infected with HIV or syphilis.[133] Condom use is likewise mandated by state law.[134] These requirements appear to be reasonably related to the legitimate goal of preventing harm posed by STDs and offer an alternative to total prohibition that is respectful of the twin principles of limited government and residual individual sovereignty.

"DEVIANT" SEX

The variation in the types of human sexual behavior is enormous. Not only are people heterosexual, homosexual, bisexual, and transsexual, but a small portion of the human population also appears to enjoy or even prefer what is commonly referred to as deviant sex, such as sex with animals (bestiality), dead bodies (necrophilia), or children (pedophilia), or sex involving the infliction or receipt of pain (sado-masochism) or human excretion. Other more prevalent, but less morally troubling sexual turn-ons include high-heeled shoes, sexually explicit language, money, power, fast cars, and tight jeans.

What among this catalog of sexual idiosyncrasies is legitimately proscribable by government? The extant legal orthodoxy says that any sexual practices that are offensive to the morals of a majority of legislators are proscribable and hence there is no real analysis to be conducted, just deference to the plenary power of the legislature. The morality of American law, however, requires that to assess the legitimacy of laws, we must analyze whether the practices proscribed—in this case, unusual sexual propensities—harm or reasonably threaten harm to the LLP of others. We shall now examine the most prevalent categories of deviant sex regulated by American states and determine whether they are consistent with the morality of American law.

Pedophilia

It bears repeating that the morality of American law recognizes that minors are incompetent to make their own decisions and may therefore be protected from sexual pressure or aggression by adults. As part of its parens patriae power, the government may legitimately restrict the liberty of both adults and minors to protect children, not just from traditional LLP harms, but also from emotional or psychological harm, since children are not emotionally or psychologically mature. The government may therefore legitimately punish any adult who has or attempts sexual contact with a minor.

Bestiality

Bestiality—having sex with an animal—is prohibited in Leviticus, which classifies it as a sin punishable by death.[135] Early common law reflected the moral indignation evident in the Bible, and individuals convicted of bestiality could be executed.[136] Today, bestiality is still considered a separate crime in thirty-three American states, though it is generally considered only a misdemeanor.[137] Several additional states have laws prohibiting cruelty against animals that employ sufficiently broad language to include sexual acts with an animal.[138] In all states, photographs or films that portray bestiality are considered obscene and those who sell or distribute such materials are therefore without First Amendment protection.

In applying the morality of American law to bestiality, we must first recognize that, under American law, animals are considered the property of human beings, albeit a special class of property with a life of its own. As such, if the animal involved belongs to someone other than the perpetrator and the sexual contact is without the consent of the owner, the act of bestiality harms the property interest of the owner. Bestiality laws under these circumstances undoubtedly are a legitimate exercise of governmental power designed to protect the LLP of the animal owner.

On the other hand, if the animal owner is the perpetrator or the animal owner grants permission to the perpetrator, we cannot fairly characterize the bestiality as a property harm to the owner. Yet forcing sex on an animal undoubtedly threatens harm to the animal, which lacks the ability to consent or protect itself from physical harm. In such situations, the animals are analogous to children in the sense that they are unable to protect themselves from the sexual aggression of adults. Both bestiality laws and statutory rape laws are designed to prevent sexual aggression against those legally incapable of consenting to sex. Government may act as the protector of the animal in situations where such protection is deemed necessary, as is the case with generic animal cruelty laws, and laws prohibiting bestiality are therefore an appropriate exercise of governmental power, consistent with the morality of American law.

Necrophilia

Necrophilia—sexual contact with a dead human body—is prohibited in twenty-three American states and is generally considered a felony.[139] As an initial matter, it should be recognized that any contact, sexual or otherwise, with a dead human body is not, by definition, harmful to the deceased, who is no longer a legally cognizable person. If necrophilia statutes are a legitimate exercise of governmental power, therefore, they must punish harm or reasonably threatened harm to the LLP of individuals other than the deceased.

The most obvious individuals protected by necrophilia statutes are family members of the deceased. Indeed, the Model Penal Code and many necrophilia statutes acknowledge this by incorporating a standard that requires that the contact with the deceased outrage ordinary family sensibilities.[140] The salient question, therefore, is whether these family members suffer a cognizable LLP harm, or merely an emotional harm?

If the deceased's body is considered a form of property belonging to the deceased's family, touching the body without the family's consent would harm the family members' LLP interests. There are, however, some situations in which the analysis would not be so tidy. First, not all deceased individuals have surviving family members or, if they do, the survivors may not be interested in what happens to the deceased's remains. In such situations, the property interest in the deceased's remains should revert to the state. Second, there may be rare situations in which necrophilia is committed by a family member of the deceased. In such a case, other family members' property interests may have been harmed, providing a basis for legitimate governmental interference.

In addition, an individual should be permitted to designate someone as the official caretaker of his/her remains, either in a will or in a separate document, much as with durable health care powers of attorney or living wills. To make matters simpler, state law could simply state that, in the absence of an explicit designation of a caretaker for remains, the executor of the individual's will would be so designated by default. If the individual did not have a will, the state could enact a specific consent statute, setting forth a hierarchy of default caretakers, or simply cross-reference existing consent statutes that exist for purposes of surrogate health care decision-making.

Sado-Masochism

The practice of sadistic or masochistic sex is not prohibited by any American state. At first blush, this may seem odd since undoubtedly many Americans find sado-masochistic sex (S&M) to be immoral. If public morality condemns S&M, why are there no laws prohibiting it? Why has S&M escaped legal proscription while other sexual practices deemed to be deviant pursuant to public morality, such as sodomy and bestiality, have been legally condemned? The answer likely lies in the fact that, unlike other types of deviant sex such as bestiality, necrophilia, or pedophilia, S&M involves sex between consenting adults.

But the absence of direct prohibition of S&M does not mean that S&M has completely escaped the wrath of public morality, as the sale or distribution of materials depicting S&M is often included within a state's definition of obscene materials.[141] Pursuant to *Stanley v. Georgia*,[142] individuals have a constitutionally protected liberty to possess S&M materials in the privacy of their own home, but as with other obscene materials, individuals are not at liberty to sell or distribute such materials to willing adult buyers. The illogic of the use-versus-sale distinction was discussed in detail in the preceding section on pornography and obscenity and applies with full force here as well.

Chapter 6 Reproduction

Making the decision to have a child—it's momentous. It is to decide forever to have your heart go walking outside your body.
—*author Elizabeth Stone*

THE RIGHT *NOT* TO REPRODUCE

The Supreme Court's contraceptive and abortion cases have made it clear that Americans have a right not to reproduce. This negative right to avoid reproduction has been extended to the married and unmarried alike and even to minors.[1]

As an initial matter, it is important to understand the close, often indistinguishable, relationship between contraception and abortion. Contraception, as the name suggests, prevents conception by keeping sperm and egg apart, often through the imposition of a physical barrier. Diaphragms, condoms, and the withdrawal method, for example, all operate on this simple premise. But not all contraceptive methods prevent sperm and egg from uniting. Notably, the birth control pill works either by suppressing ovulation entirely, by thickening cervical mucous to retard sperm motility, or by irritating the uterine lining to prevent implantation of a fertilized egg.[2] In the latter instance—preventing implantation—the pill essentially acts as a chemical abortifacient by creating a uterine environment that is hostile to the embryo.

The modern "mini-pills" widely prescribed today lack estrogen and contain only progestin, a synthetic form of progesterone. Women taking mini-pills are thus more likely to ovulate, become pregnant, and experience a chemical abortion, though they are rarely, if ever, aware of it.[3] Popular modern birth control methods such as Depo-Provera and Norplant work in a similar fashion.[4] Another commonly used birth control method, the intrauterine device (IUD), is believed to work either by interfering with the mobility of sperm and egg or by causing an inflammation of the uterine lining which prevents successful implantation of a fertilized egg.[5]

The truth, though it is rarely openly acknowledged, is that many of the most popular birth control methods sometimes work by preventing implantation of a fertilized egg. Because a fertilized egg is, by definition, an early-stage embryo, birth control methods may act as abortifacients by making it impossible for the embryo to survive. The recent furor over the so-called morning after pill is thus remarkably out of proportion when its action is compared to other birth control methods.[6] The morning after pill is an emergency contraceptive that is taken shortly after a woman has engaged in unprotected sex. The woman takes a relatively high dose of birth control pills over a short period of time, and the pills work essentially the same way as ordinary birth control pills, either by preventing ovulation from occurring, by delaying ovulation, or by sufficiently irritating the uterine lining so as to prevent implantation of the fertilized egg.

Another similar product, the controversial "abortion pill," RU-486 (mifepristone), is an artificial steroid that blocks production of progesterone, the hormone that helps prepare the uterine wall for nourishing the embryo. By interfering with progesterone, RU-486 tricks the woman's body into thinking that it is no longer pregnant, allowing menstruation to occur, and resulting in the passage of the embryo.[7]

The ardent characterization of the morning after pill and RU-486 as chemical abortifacients by right-to-life groups is therefore accurate, yet also odd, since many popular birth control methods work in the same or very similar ways but are not similarly morally condemned. If preventing or interfering with the implantation of a fertilized egg is considered abortion, then we must realize that most birth control methods, including traditional birth control pills, birth control patches and implants, and copper IUDs all potentially work by causing the abortion of an early embryo. Those who believe that life begins at conception should therefore direct their moral ire to all of these birth control methods, not merely surgical abortion, the morning after pill, and RU-486.

If American law incorporated the view that life begins at conception, all of these birth control methods that potentially involve the destruction of an early embryo would have to be banned, not just surgical abortion. There simply is no principled way to say, on the one hand, that surgical abortion should be prohibited because it destroys an embryo, while simultaneously tolerating the use of drugs or devices that also potentially destroy an embryo. If destroying an embryo is tantamount to murder, the means chosen to effectuate the murder should not matter.

Realistically, it is difficult to characterize the use of all birth control methods that may destroy an early embryo as murder. Such methods are extensively used, extremely reliable, and presumably morally accepted by the millions of Americans who use them. Rather than condemning any method that may terminate development of an early-stage embryo, the Supreme Court has instead acknowledged that individuals are at liberty to choose whether to become a parent, including choosing whether to use abortion or contraception, at least up to a certain point. Specifically, the Court has adopted an analytical framework that allows legal recognition of personhood beginning at the point of fetal viability, the moment when the developing fetus has a realistic chance of survival outside the mother's womb.[8] Prior to viability, the Court had concluded that government lacks sufficiently strong interests to trump the liberty interests of the mother, who by definition is an existing person. After viability, there are two competing, potentially independent persons, each of which is entitled to governmental protection and respect. Post-viability, modern abortion jurisprudence recognizes that the government's interest in protecting the potentially independent life of the fetus is sufficiently strong to allow some infringement of the mother's liberty.

Drawing the legal line at the point of fetal viability reflects a political and pragmatic compromise between those who believe that life begins at conception and those who believe that life begins at birth. Somewhere along this spectrum of human development, the law must identify where life begins in order to interpret and apply a panoply of laws that hinge upon personhood, including various torts, crimes, contracts, and constitutional provisions. Although the point of viability is not entirely precise, there is scientific consensus that it occurs at approximately twenty-three to twenty-four weeks' gestation.[9] Viability recognizes that until there is a realistic chance of survival outside the mother's womb, a potential life is just that—merely potential. Personhood, with all of its rights and responsibilities, is extended to those who have a reasonable potential for independent existence. Once this potential has been fulfilled, the person remains a person under the law, entitled to equal legal status and respect, regardless of the person's physical or mental capacities.

Prior to the point of viability, American law treats potential life as a unique type of property whose disposition is controlled by the intentions and rights of the progenitors.[10] To some, classifying potential human life as a form of property is immoral because it fails to adopt the view that life begins at conception. To others, recognizing any degree of governmental interest in potential human life is an immoral exercise of governmental power because it fails to adopt the view that life begins at birth. The Supreme Court's decision to draw the line at viability therefore satisfies neither of these polar extremes and adopts a morally neutral and pragmatic position.

The Court's viability demarcation is both consistent with and necessary under the morality of American law. It implements a secular moralism that mandates governmental respect for differing views by limiting governmental power over our lives and carving out a large zone of residual individual sovereignty. It allows individuals to practice their own private morality, but prohibits them from transforming it into governmentally imposed public morality.

Because there is no legally cognizable person prior to viability, there can be no legally cognizable LLP harm. This should come as a relief to every woman, regardless of her religious beliefs. If a pre-viability embryo could be considered a legal person, government would be justified in exercising its power to protect the pre-viable embryo from harm. It would be legitimate, for example, for government to prohibit all women from engaging in any activities deemed by the legislature to be potentially risky to a pre-viable embryo (or even potential future embryo) such as smoking, drinking alcohol, jet skiing, horseback riding, working in a physical or stressful occupation, or eating too much junk food. If government legitimately has power to protect potential lives based merely on a remote possibility, women would be little more than hostages to their own potential offspring and vessels for the unborn, whose liberty could be restrained at the whim of the legislature. Modern abortion jurisprudence, with its emphasis on fetal viability, is a secular, scientifically sound, and pragmatically useful way to balance potentially competing individual sovereignties that is consistent with the morality of American law.

THE POSITIVE RIGHT TO REPRODUCE

Although it is clear that individuals have a right to avoid reproduction, we do not yet know to what extent this negative reproductive right includes a positive component—i.e., whether there is also an affirmative right to have a child of one's own. The lower courts have agreed that there is no constitutional right to adopt a child, since adoption is a privilege bestowed by statute.[11]

Beyond adoption, there are many open questions. Do Americans have a constitutionally protected liberty to bear or beget biologically related offspring? If so, does this liberty include only the right to have children by sexual intercourse, or does it more broadly include the use of artificial reproductive technologies (ARTs)? If it includes the use of ARTs, does it also include the use of asexual ARTs such as cloning? This chapter will attempt to answer these questions.

Involuntary Sterilization

In 1941, in *Skinner v. Oklahoma,* the Supreme Court acknowledged a fundamental right to reproduce, suggesting that any law restricting an individual's reproductive liberty should be presumptively unconstitutional.[12] The *Skinner* case challenged an Oklahoma law that required involuntary sterilization of anyone convicted of two or more felonies involving moral turpitude.[13] The law reflected early twentieth-century acceptance of eugenics, a form of social Darwinism that advocated improving the human race by weeding out genetically undesirable individuals.

The widespread enactment of involuntary sterilization laws presented the first opportunity for American courts to consider whether individuals have a liberty to reproduce. The Supreme Court in *Skinner* strongly intimated that such a liberty existed, though in strict terms the Court concluded only that the law violated the Equal Protection Clause because it irrationally classified some felonies as crimes of moral turpitude while similar ones were not so classified.[14]

Because the *Skinner* Court did not declare mandatory sterilization per se unconstitutional, it signaled that such laws might be permissible if rationally and uniformly applied to specific classes of individuals. Most notably, *Skinner* left untouched the Court's earlier decision in *Buck v. Bell,* in which Justice Oliver Wendell Holmes upheld a Virginia law permitting involuntary sterilization of the feeble minded.[15] The failure of the *Skinner* Court to overrule *Buck* implied that mandatory sterilization is constitutionally acceptable, at least in the context of the mentally disabled, and consequently many states still have such statutes in effect.[16]

While involuntary sterilization of the mentally disabled is still widely accepted, modern statutes and court opinions differ in tone from their early twentieth-century predecessors in one significant sense: they appear, at least on the surface, to be less concerned with eugenics and more concerned with the welfare of the mentally disabled. Early eugenics-based sterilization laws were justified on grounds that procreation by mentally disabled persons would likely result in socially or mentally defective offspring, a public welfare harm that was could be remedied by an exercise of the police power. Holmes's majority opinion in *Buck,* for example, reasoned that Virginia's authority to sterilize mentally disabled individuals derived from its police power to protect public welfare, declaring: "[T]he public welfare may call upon the best citizens for their lives. It would be strange if it could not call upon those who already sap the strength of the State for these lesser sacrifices . . . in order to prevent our being swamped with incompetence. It is better for all the world, if instead of waiting to execute degenerate offspring for crime, or to let them starve for their imbecility, society can prevent those who are manifestly unfit from continuing their kind. The principle that sustains compulsory vaccination is broad enough to cover cutting the fallopian tubes. . . . Three generations of imbeciles are enough."[17]

Today's involuntary sterilization laws, by contrast, generally (though not always) focus not on public welfare interests, but on whether sterilization is in the best interests of the mentally disabled individual.[18] Yet even in those states that consider the individual's best interests, there are still decisions that explicitly or implicitly rely on the rationale employed in *Buck:* namely, the police power to protect public welfare. For example, in 1976 the Supreme Court of North Carolina, in *In re Sterilization of Moore,* rejected arguments that the mandatory sterilization of mentally disabled individuals violated the due process, equal protection, or cruel and unusual punishment guarantees of the Bill of Rights.[19] In denying the substantive liberty arguments, the court acknowledged that the state possessed a plenary police power to protect the public welfare which included the power to protect the welfare of the mentally disabled person, the life of the unborn child, and the people of North Carolina as a whole.[20]

This first welfare interest—the welfare of the mentally disabled person—is inherent in the parens patriae power of the state. This second welfare interest—the life of the unborn child—is similarly part of the parens patriae power, but only after the unborn has reached the point of viability outside the womb, as recognized in the Supreme Court's abortion jurisprudence.[21]

The third welfare interest identified by the North Carolina Supreme Court (as well as Justice Holmes in *Buck*)—the collective interest of the people—is deeply antithetical to individual liberty. The North Carolina Supreme Court declared that "[t]he people of North Carolina [ ] have a [public welfare] right to prevent the procreation of children who will become a burden on the State."[22] The court cited an earlier decision of the Nebraska Supreme Court with approval which declared, "Measured by its injurious effect on society, the state may limit a class of citizens in its right to bear or beget children with an inherited tendency to mental deficiency, including feeblemindedness, idiocy, or imbecility. It is the function of the Legislature, and its duty as well, to enact appropriate legislation to protect the public and preserve the race from the known effects of the procreation of mentally deficient children by the mentally deficient."[23] The North Carolina Supreme Court also bolstered its conclusion by citing *Buck,* interpreting it as holding that "the welfare of all citizens should take precedence over the rights of individuals to procreate."[24]

If governmental power to sterilize individuals is grounded in the state's police power to protect public welfare, it conveys an unlimited and undefined paternalistic power to decide what is best for public welfare—the very sort of Leviathan government that American colonists rebelled against. If legislatures may sterilize citizens in the name of public welfare, they may also implement more extreme eugenic measures. The Nazis' Eugenic Sterilization Law, for example, mandated sterilization of all Germans who exhibited what were thought to be genetic abnormalities antithetical to the advancement of German society, including physical deformities, mental illness, and blindness.[25] If the American police power encompasses the power to involuntarily sterilize the mentally disabled in the name of public welfare, there necessarily is also a power, perhaps even a duty, to sterilize all others considered to be socially undesirable.[26] And if sterilization may be carried out under the guise of improving public welfare, so may extermination, since it would accomplish the desired societal improvement much faster and more efficiently than mere sterilization.

In short, a power to legislate for public welfare gives the majority of the legislature discretionary power to judge what steps should be taken to improve public welfare, and the courts, under current orthodox legal thinking, must defer to this discretionary legislative determination. Such a police power is breathtaking in scope, virtually unchecked by meaningful judicial oversight, and fundamentally at odds with the foundational principles of limited government and residual individual sovereignty.

This does not mean, however, that state governments lack legitimate power to order involuntary sterilization of some citizens. While this power cannot and should not be grounded in a plenary and subjective legislative power to decide what is in the interests of public welfare, it can and should be grounded in the parens patriae power. The parens patriae power, by definition, is invoked only when an individual has been deemed incompetent to make her own decisions. Grounding sterilization power in the parens patriae power, therefore, has the immediate advantage of severely limiting the exercise of this power to those who have been formally adjudicated as incompetent by a court. The judicial determination of incompetence provides a check against unreasonable or irrational exercises of legislative power, requiring an adversarial hearing prior to effectuating legislatively sanctioned sterilization. Moreover, if the power to sterilize lies in the parens patriae power, by definition it can be exercised only against the incompetent, thus preventing sterilization of those who are physically disabled, diseased, socially inept, criminal, or from certain racial or ethnic backgrounds.

In legal terms, an incompetent individual is functionally equivalent to a child, and the government legitimately may act to protect them, both from their own immaturity and incompetence and from abuse from others. In such instances, a guardian may be appointed to provide for and protect the ward's best interests. When the government exercises its parens patriae power, therefore, the government is doing what government was designed to do, and which government does best: protecting the life, liberty, and property of its citizens—specifically, its most vulnerable citizens.[27] Pursuant to the parens patriae power, government legitimately has power to order involuntary sterilization if a court determines that it is truly in the best interests of the incompetent.[28] As with all other cases involving restrictions of individual liberty, the burden of persuasion should rest with the government to convince the court that the best interests standard has been satisfied.

Artificial Reproductive Technologies

No appellate court in this country has yet definitively decided whether the fundamental right to reproduce includes the right to use artificial reproductive technologies (ARTs) such as artificial insemination (AI), in vitro fertilization (IVF), surrogacy, or even cloning. A few cases have reached the issue in dicta, concluding that reproductive liberty includes the use of ARTs.

One such case, *Lifchez v. Hartigan*,[29] was brought by a class of physician-plaintiffs specializing in reproductive endocrinology and fertility counseling who sought a declaration that the Illinois fetal anti-experimentation statute was unconstitutional.[30] The court agreed that the statute was unconstitutionally vague because a physician could not be sure whether the law prohibited the use of certain artificial reproductive technologies and procedures such as in vitro fertilization.[31] The vagueness of the statute was evinced by its legislative history, which revealed that the bill's sponsor intended to allow IVF only "as it is presently performed and permitted" and disallow future research or alteration of IVF techniques.[32] Because of the uncertain legality of new or altered IVF techniques, the court concluded that the law "impermissibly restricts a woman's fundamental right of privacy, in particular, her right to make reproductive choices free of governmental interference with those choices."[33] The court opined that "[i]t takes no great leap of logic to see that within the cluster of constitutionally protected choices that includes the right to have access to contraceptives, there must be included within that cluster the right to submit to a medical procedure that may bring about, rather than prevent, pregnancy."[34]

The *Lifchez* dicta suggests that the Supreme Court's case law that protects the right of competent individuals to use contraceptives, obtain pre-viability abortions, and avoid involuntary sterilization is illustrative of a broad right to reproductive autonomy which is perhaps best defined as a liberty to "be free from unwarranted governmental intrusion into matters so fundamentally affecting a person as the decision whether to bear or beget a child."[35] Conceptualized in this manner, the *Lifchez* court unequivocally suggests that reproductive autonomy includes the liberty to use available ARTs.

Another interesting case, the famous "Baby M" case rendered by the New Jersey Supreme Court in 1988, likewise contains useful dicta supporting the inference that the right to reproduce includes the use of ARTs.[36] In this case, Stern entered into a surrogacy contract with Whitehead, whereby Stern would provide semen to artificially inseminate Whitehead. Pursuant to the contract, Stern was given exclusive legal custody of any resulting child and Whitehead agreed to take all steps necessary to terminate her maternal rights to the child.[37] After the baby was born, however, Whitehead refused to give up the baby, and Stern sued to enforce the contract.[38]

Stern and Whitehead both asserted that their state and federal constitutional rights would be violated if not granted custody of Baby M, Stern basing his argument on the right to reproduce, Whitehead on the right to companionship of her child.[39] The New Jersey Supreme Court explicitly acknowledged that both of these asserted rights existed and that they were both fundamental.[40] The court described Stern's asserted right to reproduce as "the right to have natural children, whether through sexual intercourse or artificial insemination."[41] In so stating, the New Jersey Supreme Court clearly indicated that the fundamental right to reproduce includes the right to use AI. Indeed, because the court defined the right as "the right to have natural children," this implicitly suggests that it encompasses the use of other ARTs such as IVF and perhaps even cloning. Because Baby M had been conceived by AI and subsequently born, the court concluded that Stern had not been deprived of his fundamental right to reproduce.[42]

An interesting area in which the right to reproduce has arisen is prisoner cases. For example, in *Goodwin v. Turner,* a federal prisoner asserted that the Bureau of Prisons' denial of his request to provide semen to his wife for artificial insemination violated his constitutional right to procreate.[43] The trial court denied his habeas corpus petition, concluding that the right to reproduce did not survive incarceration.[44] The Eighth Circuit Court of Appeals affirmed, asserting that "[e]ven assuming, without deciding, that the exercise of Goodwin's right to procreate is not fundamentally inconsistent with his status as a prisoner, the restriction imposed by the Bureau is reasonably related to achieving its legitimate penological interest."[45] The Eighth Circuit in *Goodwin* thus assumed that the refusal to allow Goodwin to undertake AI with his wife violated his constitutional right to reproduce, yet upheld the refusal because it was reasonably related to a legitimate penological interest—the standard articulated by the Supreme Court for assessing the constitutionality of prison regulations generally.[46]

A recent similar case, *Gerber v. Hickman,* was decided by the en banc Ninth Circuit Court of Appeals.[47] Similar to Goodwin, Gerber was a prisoner who claimed that the prison's refusal to allow him to provide semen to his wife for AI violated his constitutional right to reproduce. Like the Eighth Circuit in *Goodwin,* the Ninth Circuit in *Gerber* ruled against the prisoner and upheld the right of the prison to deny access to AI. Yet the Ninth Circuit's reasoning was different from the Eighth Circuit's because it explicitly declared that the right to reproduce was "fundamentally inconsistent" with incarceration.[48] The majority explained that their "conclusion that the right to procreate is inconsistent with incarceration is not dependent on the science of artificial insemination, or on how easy or difficult it is to accomplish. Rather, it is a conclusion that stems from the nature and goals of the correctional system, including isolating prisoners, deterring crime, punishing offenders, and providing rehabilitation."[49]

The interesting thing about both *Goodwin* and *Gerber* is that, despite their disagreement as to the analytical framework that should be employed, they both assumed ab initio that denying access to AI constituted interference with the prisoners' constitutional right to procreate. Despite the fact that the pris-

oners' claims ultimately failed, neither court questioned the premise that restricting access to ARTs infringed upon the prisoners' right to reproduce. The
prisoner cases reinforce the impression that, at least among lower American
courts, the right to reproduce includes the right to use ARTs such as AI and
IVF.

Asexual Artificial Reproductive Technologies

Even assuming that there is a constitutional liberty to reproduce by sexual
ARTs such as AI or IVF, the question remains as to whether the liberty extends
to include the use of asexual ARTs such as cloning, parthenogenesis, or androgenesis.[50]

As an initial matter, we should consider why anyone would even want a liberty to reproduce asexually. Why not simply make babies the old-fashioned
way or, if that is not possible, utilize sexual ARTs that are widely available, such
as AI or IVF? There is a widespread perception that reproductive cloning could
be attractive only to lunatics or ego-maniacs desirous of making headlines or
breeding for nefarious purposes.

But this popular perception is myopic. Reproductive cloning could offer certain advantages to infertile couples that are not available with existing ARTs.
For example, couples who use IVF, gamete intrafallopian transfer (GIFT) or
zygote intrafallopian transfer (ZIFT)[51] might opt to clone the embryos created
to avoid the necessity of future invasive, painful, and expensive egg retrievals
from the mother. Likewise, reproductive cloning would allow infertile couples
to avoid the risks inherent with using donated sperm or eggs from an unknown
donor. Cloning would not only allow infertile couples to avoid this physiological risk but would offer a psychological benefit as well, since the parents would
be assured that their child's biological link is undiluted by the genes of someone
outside the marriage or relationship. The ability to avoid the risks associated
with donated sperm or eggs may be a particularly attractive benefit to homosexual couples, since homosexuals who wish to conceive a biologically related
child currently must use donated sperm or eggs and perhaps even a surrogate
mother, forcing them to assume the associated financial, physiological, and
psychological risks. In addition, reproductive cloning has the added benefit of
allowing some individuals to reproduce without the risk of passing on certain
genetic diseases to their children, such as sickle cell anemia, Tay-Sachs, Down
syndrome, or Huntington's disease.

Despite these potential benefits, many ethicists and legal scholars insist that
asexual reproduction is qualitatively different from sexual reproduction and

should be afforded little or no constitutional protection.[52] The gist of this objection is that cloning, precisely because it is asexual, should be treated differently, even though the end goal is the same: the birth of a child. Opponents of cloning assert that an individual's right to reproduce should depend upon the means employed, not the ends sought to be achieved.

The emptiness of this objection should be apparent. It begs the important question: Why should a difference in the means employed matter? Why should the law care, in other words, how our children are conceived? If the law does not care what sexual position we assume when we conceive or whether conception is accomplished with a turkey baster or in a petri dish, why should it care if we conceive through the use of asexual reproductive technologies such as cloning?

The one functional difference between sexual and asexual reproduction is that the former requires the presence of both sperm and egg, and the latter requires only one, generally only an egg.

So why is the conception of a child without the use of sperm so objectionable? A legal construct that allows reproduction by sexual intercourse or by the artificial sexual union of sperm and egg (e.g., IVF) but not by cloning or parthenogenesis smacks of sexism, or more precisely, sperm-ism. How could the law justify allowing all means of reproduction except those that do not require sperm? Is there something magical about sperm that gives lawmakers comfort, other than the fact that most of them have it?

Although the Framers never envisioned the possibility of reproduction without the use of sperm, do we really believe they would allow government to deny citizens the liberty to have a biologically related child simply because the means employed did not involve its use? Should the ability of an individual to fulfill the dream of raising and loving his or her own child hinge upon the presence or absence of this one substance?

To give the opponents of reproductive cloning credit, their arguments do not assert that sperm is a mandatory reproductive substance, yet this is undeniably the pragmatic effect. Rather than focusing on the absence of sperm, opponents of reproductive cloning focus instead on the perceived ill effects that allegedly flow from its absence. Generally speaking, their harm-based objections can be placed into one of two categories: (1) fears that asexual reproduction may have a negative impact on the institutions of marriage and family and the sanctity of life; and (2) fears that asexual reproduction might pose an unacceptable risk of harm to the developing embryo or gestational mother. Under the morality of American law and the definition of harm offered in this book, the latter are harm-based rationales, but the former are not. As such, the non-harm based rationales—harm to the institutions of marriage or family and the sanctity of human life—will not be discussed in detail here, as they have already been analyzed and found deficient in preceding chapters.[53]

The harm-based rationales for opposing reproductive cloning are of two types: (1) harm to the unborn child; and (2) harm to the gestational mother. Both types of risks are of course purely speculative at this juncture since there have been no reported attempts at reproductive cloning in humans. If there is any reasonable threat of harm involved in reproductive cloning, therefore, it must be evident in the data available from other animal species in which reproductive cloning has been successfully performed, such as cattle, sheep, and mice.

Several harm-based arguments articulated in opposition to reproductive cloning have already been effectively debunked by the accumulation of data. For example, one of the most popular myths is that cloning will result in a reduced life span, a myth that gained tremendous momentum upon the death of Dolly the sheep.[54] This fear is based on evidence that the ends of chromosomes—called telomeres—present in somatic cells become shorter with age, which may result in altered production of proteins from genes near the end of these shortened chromosomes.[55] If a thirty-five-year-old man donates one of his cells to conceive a child by cloning, it was feared that the child would start life with the shortened telomeres and hence be prematurely old.

The premature aging hypothesis has not been supported by available data. Several studies have now demonstrated that the offspring of cloning have normal telomere lengths.[56] Indeed, one study involving cows indicated that cows conceived by cloning had significantly longer than normal telomeres, leading the study's author to surmise that there is a "real possibility" that animals conceived by cloning might live up to 50 percent longer than animals conceived in more traditional ways.[57] Other initial harm-based concerns with reproductive cloning have also proved unfounded, such as the possibility of greater mutations from the use of adult cells, the risk of X-chromosome inactivation, and the possibility of growth deficiency due to conflict between the mitochondria of the cell donor and egg donor.[58]

The two remaining serious possible sources of risk created by reproductive cloning are reprogramming and imprinting failures.[59] Reprogramming refers to a phenomenon in which the nucleus of the donor cell, such as one scraped from the cheek or arm, resets itself to prepare for the laborious process of division and embryonic growth.[60] Because the donor cell is an adult, differentiated cell—i.e., one that has become specialized to be a cheek or skin cell—it must somehow be coaxed into reverting to a totipotent stage in which it effectively becomes immature again, able to develop into the myriad types of cells that make up the human body.

The reprogramming difficulty potentially posed by cloning is that once inserted into an empty egg, the donor cell begins to divide very rapidly, which may leave insufficient time for appropriate reprogramming to take place.[61] If reprogramming is not completed, it is surmised that the resulting embryo may develop in a haphazard or inappropriate way, creating deformities. Although there has been much speculation on the issue, there is currently little evidence that cloning causes reprogramming errors, that reprogramming errors result in physical or mental abnormality, or that such reprogramming errors are irremediable.[62]

Another risk potentially posed by reproductive cloning is a genetic imprinting failure. Imprinting refers to the process by which some specific genes are inherited either from the mother or father, but not both.[63] In sexual reproduction, the combination of sperm and egg causes the mother's imprinted genes to compete with the father's imprinted genes, which usually results in a harmonious balance between the two. An imprinting failure occurs when the competition is won by one or the other, resulting in inheritance of only the mother's or the father's imprinted genes. Because cloning does not involve the combination of sperm and egg, there is a heightened chance that the embryo created asexually would have an imprinting failure, which could result in abnormalities. For example, studies of mouse embryos that inherited imprints exclusively from their mother or father revealed that the mice exhibited abnormalities in fetal size, placental size, and fetal death.[64] Similarly, in human embryos, it has been established that the inactivation of maternal or paternal markers by spontaneous mutation can result in an imprinting failure that manifests itself in the development of several specific genetic disorders.[65]

There is very little evidence that would suggest that cloning itself causes imprinting failure or that imprinting failure necessarily results in abnormality. While imprinting failures have been observed in animal cloning experiments, the cause is often attributable to the culture medium itself, rather than cloning. Differences in the chemicals or other substances used as culture medium have been directly linked to imprinting failures, leading researchers in one recent report to declare, "It is remarkable that the U.S. Food and Drug Administration regulates tissue-culture media for human ex vivo use only for toxicity and sterility and does not consider the effect of varying media on pregnancy outcome or birth defects."[66]

If the culture medium or process itself is to blame for most instances of imprinting failure, the risk of resulting abnormalities would be the same in reproductive cloning as with other ARTs, since they both require and use essentially the same in vitro culture medium and process. Indeed, studies have recently begun to confirm this possibility, indicating that children conceived by ARTs are more likely to suffer epigenetic abnormalities caused by imprinting failures.[67] For example, the medical community recently has begun to consider whether there is a causal link between conception via intracytoplasmic sperm injection (ICSI)[68] and Angelman syndrome, a neurological disorder marked by developmental delay, inability to speak, inappropriate laughter, and seizures.[69] Moreover, in the last several years, evidence has emerged that children conceived by ARTs are three to six times more likely to have Beckwith-Wiedemann syndrome (BWS), a genetic disease that results in abdominal wall and placental defects, increased tumor incidence, and most significantly, prenatal overgrowth resulting in large offspring.[70] These comparatively high rates of BWS in children conceived by ARTs are "probably underestimated, as specific questions regarding ART have only been asked systematically in the past [few] year[s]."[71]

The increased incidence of BWS is particularly intriguing because of widespread fears that human reproductive cloning will result in large offspring syndrome (LOS), which has been observed in several cloned animal species. The association of ARTs with Beckwith-Wiedemann syndrome thus suggests that, to the extent that cloning may pose a risk of LOS, the risk is inherent in all ART processes that involve the use of in vitro culture and is not unique to cloning. In addition, it should be noted that imprinting failures such as LOS that have been observed in cloned animals are not necessarily translatable into humans due to imprinting differences in species. LOS, for example, is likely to occur less often in humans than other animals because an important gene that regulates fetal growth, insulin-like growth factor II (IGF2R), is not imprinted in humans and not susceptible to imprinting failure.[72]

The bottom line is that cloning may pose some risks of harm to the developing embryo and correspondingly perhaps also to the gestational mother as well. But it should be remembered that all procreative attempts are inherently risky, particularly those that employ ARTs. Babies conceived via ARTs are approximately twice as likely to be born with a birth defect.[73] And 60–70 percent of embryos conceived the old-fashioned way are never born.[74] Fifteen percent of all pregnancies end naturally through miscarriage.[75] Many early-stage embryos fail to thrive and are reabsorbed by the body, often because they are severely deformed, and the woman may never even know that she was pregnant.[76]

One way to assess the potential risk of conception by cloning and conception by ARTs is to compare, to the extent possible, the relative so-called take-home-baby rate. There is no data available for artificial insemination, but federal law requires the U.S. Centers for Disease Control (CDC) to collect and disseminate voluntarily reported success rates for IVF clinics, and this may provide some baseline for comparison.[77]

The take-home-baby rate of IVF is quite low—indeed, much lower than is commonly understood. To fully understand and compare success rates of animal cloning experiments with human IVF, we must first understand the various ways in which ART success rates may be reported. There are essentially four ways to report ART success rates: (1) the number of live births expressed as a percentage of all ART attempts (a "per attempt" rate); (2) the number of live births expressed as a percentage of embryos produced (a "per embryos produced" rate) ; (3) the number of live births expressed as a percentage of all embryos transferred into the womb (a "per embryos transferred" rate); and (4) the number of live births expressed as a percentage of transfers attempted (a "per transfer" rate).

The success rates that result from these four different reporting methodologies are, by definition, highest for the fourth methodology—i.e., the "per transfer" rate—and lowest for the first methodology—i.e., the "number of attempts" rate. This is so because of the realities of ARTs. There are many attempts at ART, but only a subset of these attempts will result in successful fertilization and hence produce an embryo. Of the embryos produced by ART, only a subset will prove viable enough to transfer into a womb. Of all the embryos transferred into the womb (with multiple embryos per transfer being the norm), an even smaller subset will ultimately be born.

Expressed on a "per attempt" basis, therefore, ART success rates will be very low. Expressed on a "per embryos created" basis, the success rate will be higher. Expressed on a "per embryos transferred" basis, the success rate will be higher still. Expressed on a "per transfer" basis, the success rate will be highest of all.

So what is the take-home-baby rate of IVF? Using the highest possible success rate—i.e., the "per transfer" rate—the CDC reports the success of IVF using fresh embryos as approximately 35 percent.[78] For frozen embryos, the success rate is lower, approximately 25 percent.[79] In simple terms, a woman undergoing IVF has roughly a one-in-three chance of having a baby using fresh embryos, and a one-in-four chance using frozen embryos.

Yet in many ways these IVF success rates are misleading, particularly when they are used to compare the success of IVF to that of cloning. Specifically, the

IVF success rates, because they are generally reported on a "per transfer" basis, do not take into account the number of embryos used per transfer. According to the CDC, IVF procedures average three embryos per transfer,[80] since transferring multiple embryos increases the chance of obtaining clinical pregnancy. Of the three embryos transferred, usually only one survives to birth.[81] This means that in the vast majority of instances, three embryos are transferred, but only one is likely to survive to term, and even this one successful birth occurs only in approximately one-third of all transfer attempts.

Take a simple example. Say that an average IVF clinic performs 100 transfers involving 300 fresh embryos, reflecting the fact that each transfer averages three embryos. We could expect these 100 transfers would result in approximately thirty-five birth events. Of these thirty-five birth events, we could expect approximately twenty-two singleton babies, twenty-two twins (i.e., eleven pairs) and around four to seven babies that are triplets or greater.[82] The total number of babies that result from the transfer of 300 embryos would thus be approximately forty-eight to fifty-one babies, yielding a take-home-baby rate, on a "per embryos transferred" basis, of only 16–17 percent—far less than the widely publicized 35 percent per transfer rate touted by the fertility industry and CDC.

The use of higher "per transfer" success rates for IVF is misleading because the success rates reported for animal cloning experiments generally use the lower rate methodologies. For example, opponents of human reproductive cloning often cite statistics from the Dolly experiments, insinuating that because only one of the 277 cloning attempts resulted in a live birth, there were 276 out of 277 baby lambs that died—a "per attempt" success rate of only 0.0035 percent.[83] But the truth is that of the 277 successful egg-donor cell fusions, only twenty-nine were successfully stimulated to begin any cell division and hence properly classifiable as embryos at all.[84] These twenty-nine embryos were transferred to the uteruses of thirteen different ewes, only one of which resulted in a live birth.[85] If we use a "per embryos transferred" success rate, the take-home-baby rate for the Dolly experiments was one out of twenty-nine, or approximately 3.5 percent. If we use a "per transfer" success rate—the same rate used by the CDC for reporting IVF success—the take-home-baby-rate was one out of thirteen, or approximately 7.7 percent.

Indeed, one of the frustrating oddities of trying to compare take-home-baby rates for IVF versus cloning is that because IVF success rates are reported using the inherently higher "per transfer" rate, comparing IVF success rates to cloning success rates is often a comparison of apples to oranges, since the rates are based on entirely different data. For example, a 2002 report on cloning by the National Academy of Sciences (NAS) compiled a useful table comparing the success rates for various animal cloning experiments, but included only the lower "per embryos transferred" success rate.[86]

The NAS report revealed a remarkable variation in "per embryos transferred" success rates. Not only were there significant differences in the success rates of individual species (with cattle and goats generally experiencing the highest success), but there were also significant differences according to the type of donor cell used and from researcher to researcher. Among sheep cloning experiments, for example, the "per embryos transferred" success rate varied from a low of 2.3 percent to a high of 17.5 percent. The higher rate (17.5 percent) is slightly higher than the "per embryos transferred" success rate of an average IVF clinic. Experiments in cattle likewise revealed wildly varying "per embryos transferred" success rates, with several experiments yielding less than5 percent live births, while several others yielded more than 20 percent live births.[87]

Regardless of whether cloning can yield success rates that are comparable with other ARTs, the important legal question is whether, assuming cloning presents some risks, those risks are legitimately cognizable by law. In other words, even assuming arguendo that all of the risks to result from human reproductive cloning are true, are these risks the proper subject of legal prohibition? To answer this question, it is crucial to realize that potential harms to the unborn are not generally cognizable under current law.

If reproductive cloning presents risks to the unborn, these risks are created at the moment the cloning technique is employed or very shortly thereafter. As such, the risks potentially posed by cloning are imposed upon an egg, a donor cell, and—if the cloning technique is initially successful—a tiny clump of cells called a morula. After about five days of growth in a petri dish, the morula becomes a more defined clump of cells called a blastocyst, which can then be transferred into a womb. If the blastocyst successfully implants itself into the womb, it may ultimately develop into a fetus and may survive to term and be born. Cloning-associated risks, such as reprogramming or imprinting errors, are incurred at a very early developmental stage, perhaps prior to the beginning of any cell division, and certainly well before the point of viability.[88] This is significant because current law, as evidenced by the Supreme Court's abortion jurisprudence, draws the line of demarcation between potential life and life at viability.[89]

Because there is no constitutionally cognizable life prior to viability, current law would consider the risks potentially posed by human cloning techniques to be risks incurred by, at most, a potential life. Although one might argue that a potential life is entitled to a greater degree of respect than ordinary property, nonetheless this argument presupposes that potential life is a type of property, whose owners generally are the biological progenitors.[90] Illustratively, American law recognizes that embryos created by the IVF process may be used, discarded, donated for research, or frozen indefinitely at the option of individuals recognized by statute or contract to have dispositional authority.[91]

The ineluctable conclusion is that a pre-viability potential life is not a life, it is not a constitutionally cognizable person, and it cannot suffer legally cognizable harms in the same manner as persons. This conclusion is reinforced by various statutes that recognize feticide as a distinct crime. When feticide statutes attach criminal liability only after fetus is "quick"—the common law terminology essentially synonymous with viability—the harm inflicted is a life harm inflicted against a legally cognizable person, consistent with the Supreme Court's abortion jurisprudence.[92] By contrast, when feticide statutes attach criminal liability prior to the point of viability, the harm inflicted is a property harm inflicted against the embryo's progenitors, consistent with lower courts' frozen embryo jurisprudence.[93]

Finally, it has been argued that reproductive cloning should be prohibited because it poses too many risks to the gestational mother. The speciousness of this argument is apparent when one recognizes that pregnancy is an inherently risky undertaking, but one that women are permitted to undertake without limitation, including situations in which disease, physical deformities, genetic abnormalities, or mental conditions pose severe threats to the mother's wellbeing. No one would seriously suggest, for example, that women should be prohibited from giving birth just because it would present a risk to their health.

For example, if we are concerned that conception by cloning would create a higher than average risk of large offspring, does this mean that it would be a legitimate exercise of governmental power to prevent women from giving birth any time this risk is present? For example, would it be legitimate for government to forbid petite women from childbearing when the father is exceptionally large? Although bearing a large fetus is a realistic possibility and would undoubtedly pose some risk to the mother, should the law interfere in the woman's childbearing choice under such circumstances? Traditionally, the answer to this question has been no, presumably because the law presumes that the mother is a competent adult who is capable of making her own informed decision as to whether to continue a pregnancy under risky circumstances. This presumption is not only reflective of reality, but it also honors the foundational principles of limited government and residual individual sovereignty that animate American law.

If women are capable of making autonomous decisions to continue pregnancy in other potentially risky contexts, they are capable of making the same decision in the context of cloning. Although opponents of reproductive cloning attempt to disguise their moral condemnation in concern for the health of the mother, there are no other instances in American law when government has interfered in reproductive choice based upon such paternalistic concerns. If a paternalistic concern for the health of pregnant women is a legitimate basis for interfering in the liberty of women to reproduce, the slope will be slippery indeed, permitting virtually unlimited control over women's bodies in the name of protecting them from their own informed decisions.

As with other risky medical procedures, competent adult women who become pregnant as a result of cloning should be presumed to retain the individual sovereignty to make the decision as to whether to continue or terminate their pregnancy.

Chapter 7 Medical Care

No right is held more sacred, or is more carefully guarded, by the common law, than the right of every individual to the possession and control of his own person, free from all restraint or interference of others, unless by clear and unquestionable authority of law. As well said by Judge Cooley, "The right to one's person may be said to be a right of complete immunity: to be let alone."
—*U.S. Supreme Court,* Union Pacific Railway Co. v. Botsford *(1891)*

INFORMED CONSENT

A fundamental facet of residual individual sovereignty is sovereignty over one's own body, so long as exercising such sovereignty does not harm or reasonably threaten harm to the LLP of others. This bodily sovereignty—more commonly referred to as bodily autonomy—has been recognized by the common law for centuries, taking root in cases that treated the imposition of unwanted medical treatment as criminal battery or homicide.[1] Eventually a distinct negligence tort emerged, defined as the provision of medical care without the patient's fully informed consent.

Today, most instances of non-consensual medical care are of the tort variety rather than the criminal variety. This is because patients generally are aware that they are receiving medical care and have explicitly consented to it, yet their consent may be vitiated by the physician's failure to inform the patient of all material information relating to the care, constituting a form of negligence. Providing informed consent to patients has two primary benefits. First, it has a beneficent effect, improving the chances of successful treatment by reducing anxiety and confusion, increasing the chances of adherence to treatment, and facilitating communication between patient and provider.[2] Second and more important, informed consent respects individual autonomy by recognizing that competent adults are capable of making their own health care decisions and that their decisions are entitled to deference by providers.[3] Respecting patient autonomy, in turn, provides a check against nefarious motives of providers and a mechanism for implementing individualistic values regarding life and its quality.[4]

The informed consent doctrine's focus in recent years has been more on patient autonomy than beneficence, fueled by various factors including revelations of egregious experiments by Nazi doctors, surreptitious research by the government as well as private institutions,[5] and an explosion of medical technology that maintains life far beyond the point that many deem desirable. The doctrine of informed consent is an integral part of modern medicine, providing patients with the power to control their own bodies and destinies in the face of numerous competing interests. Pursuant to the doctrine, patients are recognized as having autonomy not merely to make their own medical choices, but to make bad choices, or even extremely risky choices.

Perhaps the most extreme example of patient autonomy is the acceptance and availability of clinical trials. Under federal law, drugs and medical devices may not be sold unless there is sufficient evidence to provide a reasonable assurance that the drug or device is both safe and effective for its intended use.[6] Generally, the reasonable assurance standard requires that the manufacturer of the drug or device conduct extensive testing on both animals and humans.[7] The testing conducted on humans, called clinical trials, depends entirely upon the enrollment of volunteers. Depending on the design and specific phase of the clinical trial, enrollees may or may not have the disease or condition for which the drug is being tested and may receive a placebo instead of actual treatment. The primary legal focus during a clinical trial is to ensure that all enrollees have given adequate informed consent.[8] The emphasis on informed consent within a clinical trial illustrates the breadth of patient autonomy and patients' inherent right to assume significant risks of harm.

Individuals may access novel and risky medical therapies in ways other than clinical trials. First, physicians often try out novel surgical procedures on patients outside the context of clinical trials. Indeed, most clinical innovation, particularly in the field of surgery, has been achieved this way, through a process of trial and error with individual patients, not clinical trials.[9] The latest technique for heart, eye, brain, or any other kind of surgery is thus generally conceived of by a surgeon, tried out on a willing patient and, if successful, spreads rapidly by word-of-mouth or publication in a journal. Physicians are unfettered in their ability to try novel procedures and techniques on their patients and will face legal sanction only ex post facto, if the patient is dissatisfied with the results and can establish that there was inadequate informed consent or that the use of the procedure was unreasonable under the circumstances.

Second, there is widespread off-label use of drugs and devices. Once a drug or device has been approved by the Food and Drug Administration (FDA) for condition X, a licensed physician may prescribe the drug or device for conditions other than X.[10] As with the use of novel therapies, a physician may face tort liability or licensure action as a result of off-label recommendations, but such liability will attach only if the off-label use is determined to be unreasonable under the circumstances.[11] Because off-label therapy necessarily involves the use of a drug or device which has not been proven safe and effective through the clinical trial process, it inherently involves a higher degree of risk. Despite this relatively high degree of risk, off-label therapy is commonplace, providing another strong indicator of the deep acceptance of patient autonomy to take medical risks.

Third, patients are granted autonomy to forgo traditional medical therapies and use dietary supplements or even home remedies, neither of which is required to be proven safe or effective, and both of which are widely used.[12] Dietary supplements, for example, are a twenty billion dollar per year business in the United States, largely because of the passage in 1994 of a federal law, the Dietary Supplement Health Education Act (DSHEA), which classified dietary supplements as food and stripped the FDA's power to classify dietary supplements as drugs.[13] The net effect is that dietary supplements, unlike drugs, do not have to undergo preclinical or clinical testing for safety or effectiveness prior to being sold to consumers. DSHEA creates a presumption that dietary supplements are safe and, as with adulterated food, the government bears the burden of affirmatively rebutting this presumption if it believes the dietary supplement poses a significant or unreasonable risk of illness or injury when taken as directed in the product's labeling.[14]

The FDA has attempted to carry its heavy statutory burden and halt the sale of a dietary supplement only once—its decision in 2004 to ban the sale of ephedra, a stimulant widely used in weight-loss and sports performance products.[15] Ephedra had been linked to at least eighty deaths nationwide, mostly involving heart attack or stroke, including the death of Baltimore Orioles pitcher Steve Bechler in 2003.[16]

In April 2005, a federal trial judge in Utah invalidated the FDA's ephedra ban.[17] The FDA's ban was challenged by manufacturers who sold ephedra supplements with labeling that recommended a daily dosage of less than 10 mg.[18] They argued that the FDA ban on all ephedra supplements violated DSHEA because: (1) the FDA had engaged in a risk-benefit analysis to determine that ephedra supplements posed an unreasonable risk of harm; and (2) the FDA had insufficient evidence to conclude that ephedra supplements were harmful at a daily dosage of 10 mg per day.

The court agreed with both arguments. Specifically, the court concluded that the FDA's use of a risk-benefit analysis violated DSHEA because, contrary to congressional intent, it required dietary supplement manufacturers to establish that a supplement offers a demonstrable benefit to users.[19] DSHEA was designed to shift the burden onto the FDA to prove a dietary supplement is injurious to health, and "the imposition of a risk-benefit analysis requires the producer of an EDS [ephedrine-alkaloid dietary supplement] to establish a benefit and alleviates the burden Congress placed squarely on the government to demonstrate the existence of a significant or unreasonable risk."[20] Even though the FDA had concluded that there were only temporary and modest benefits from taking ephedra which were outweighed by the risk of serious adverse health effects, the court deemed such balancing inappropriate because the only permissible consideration under DSHEA is whether the dietary supplement, when taken as directed on the labeling, poses a substantial or unreasonable risk of harm.

The court then considered whether the FDA had gathered enough evidence to prove, by a preponderance of the evidence, that the defendants' supplements—which recommended a daily dosage of 10 mg—posed an unreasonable risk of harm. Although many scientists had informed the FDA that they could not identify a safe recommended dosage for ephedra, the court concluded that "[a] negative inference is different from the affirmative proof required by [DSHEA]. The statute requires an affirmative demonstration of 'significant or unreasonable' risk at a particular dose level. . . . The statement that a safe level cannot be determined is simply not sufficient to meet the government's burden. To find otherwise would be to place the burden on the manufacturers of EDS to show that their recommended dosages are safe. This would be directly contrary to the statutory language placing the burden of proof on the government. . . ."[21]

Although many have lamented the outcome of this decision, it is undoubtedly a correct interpretation of DSHEA's language and congressional intent. The whole purpose of DSHEA was to treat dietary supplements as food and create a presumption that they are safe when used as directed—a presumption that, despite the fears and negative media attention given to some supplements, is respectful of individual sovereignty to make medical decisions, even those involving potential risk.

I am not suggesting that dietary supplements should be exempt from reasonable regulations to protect consumers from snake oil claims and other material misrepresentations that deprive them of their property (money). Nor am I suggesting that dietary supplements should be exempt from reasonable regulations to protect consumers from supplements that harm or reasonably threaten to harm lives. As with any ingested substance, including many foods, dietary supplements may pose a risk of harm. But as pointed out by the federal trial judge in the ephedra litigation, the burden should rest with the government to proffer evidence of actual or reasonably threatened harm before it can restrict competent adults' liberty to make their own decisions regarding what supplements to ingest.

Placing the burden on the government to demonstrate actual or reasonably threatened harm prior to exercising its power to restrict individual liberty is not as onerous as some might claim. Indeed, experience with the burden-shifting mechanism in DSHEA is illustrative. In recent years the FDA has warned consumers of serious risks associated with supplements containing ingredients such as kava, glyburide, comfrey, aristolochic acid, L-tryptophan, St. John's wort, and tiratricol.[22] But a quick Internet search confirms that each of these supplements remains widely available and legally sold, with few reported problems. This indicates that, despite claims to the contrary, a framework that begins with a presumption of individual liberty rather than governmental power is workable and suitably protective of citizens' safety; a presumption of governmental power to restrict citizens' access to supplements is both unnecessary to protect their LLP and disrespectful of their residual sovereignty to make their own decisions.[23] DSHEA thus represents one of those rare moments when the legislature has backed away from a presumption of power and instead given individuals room to decide for themselves. The net result is that DSHEA has opened up a world of alternative, relatively low-cost medical treatment options to Americans, proving that individuals are capable of heeding governmental warnings, adhering to recommended dosage limitations, and deciding whether or to what extent to ingest potentially hazardous substances.

The clinical trial process, widespread availability of off-label therapy, dietary supplements, and home remedies illustrate that Americans enjoy broad liberty to access drugs and devices that have not yet been proven safe and effective. But as the next section will show, there are some medical treatments for which there is evidence of both safety and efficacy, yet Americans are denied the liberty to use them, simply because those medical treatments are deemed offensive to public morality.

FORBIDDEN TREATMENTS

The government's power to require reasonable evidence of safety before permitting the sale of a drug or medical device is a legitimate exercise of its power to protect the lives of its citizens.[24] But a more complex question is raised with respect to the government's power to prohibit the sale of drugs or devices that satisfy this evidentiary standard. If there is reasonable evidence that a drug or device is both a safe and an effective treatment, does the government legitimately have the power to restrict or prohibit its use?

I would hope that the reader's answer to this question, at this late point in the book, would be no. Pursuant to the morality of American law, the primary purpose of government is to protect the lives, liberty, and property of citizens. Government may step outside this strictly protective role and act for the purpose of improving collective societal LLP interests, but only if these interests have been identified by the grant of explicit powers ceded to government in the relevant constitutional document. The citizens of the United States, for example, explicitly ceded to the federal government the power to regulate interstate commerce, and this specific grant of power (like all grants of power to government) was designed to enable the federal government not merely to protect, but to improve, the LLP of all Americans. The grant of an interstate commerce power vests the federal government with a power deemed desirable to further government's LLP-improving function.

The importance of understanding this analytical framework becomes apparent when one considers the legal controversy over medical marijuana. In recent years, there has been mounting evidence that cannabinoids, and in particular, delta-9-tetrahydrocannabinol (THC), are therapeutically beneficially for many conditions, most notably chronic pain, nausea, and weight loss. In 1999, the Institute of Medicine concluded that smoking marijuana had potential therapeutic benefit and recommended development of a rapid-onset delivery system for providing a safe and reliable means of delivering THC.[25]

A synthetic capsule version of THC, marketed under the name Marinol, is sold legally in the United States as a Schedule II prescription drug. Marinol has been approved by the FDA as a safe and effective treatment for nausea and vomiting associated with chemotherapy and anorexia for individuals who suffer from AIDS. Because Marinol is a synthetic form of THC, it does not require cultivation of marijuana plants, and this undoubtedly contributed to its ability to garner FDA approval.

Marinol has been legally available since 1985 and there has been no evidence of significant adverse effects or diversion to the recreational drug market. But Marinol remains only a modest success, primarily because large doses of it are needed to yield a sufficient amount for symptom relief, and such relief is slow in coming.[26] In comparison studies with inhaled and intravenous marijuana, oral THC such as Marinol resulted in the highest variation in individual response and the lowest bioavailability.[27] Not surprisingly, many patients who have used Marinol prefer to smoke marijuana, which provides faster, more predictable relief with fewer side effects.

Responding to growing evidence of the therapeutic benefits of marijuana, numerous states and localities in recent years have passed laws that permit the use of marijuana when recommended by a licensed physician.[28] But the federal government has refused to recognize the therapeutic benefits of marijuana by denying a petition to reschedule it, and it has taken the position that, despite state and local laws that allow use of medical marijuana, the cultivation or possession of any amount violates the federal Controlled Substances Act (CSA).[29] The government's position on the CSA and its relationship to medical marijuana was put to the test in *Gonzales v. Raich*,[30] a case involving two California women who used locally grown and cultivated marijuana, pursuant to their physicians' recommendation, to treat otherwise intractable pain, nausea, and anorexia.[31] The home of one of the women was searched by local sheriff's deputies and federal Drug Enforcement Administration (DEA) agents, who discovered six cannabis plants.[32]

Local law officials concluded that the cannabis plants were lawfully possessed pursuant to the California Compassionate Use Act, a law enacted by popular initiative that permits possession and use of limited quantities of marijuana for medical purposes, provided a physician's recommendation is obtained.[33] Federal officials disagreed, concluding that possession of any marijuana for any purpose was illegal under the CSA. The woman whose home was searched, together with another woman in similar circumstances, subsequently sought declaratory and injunctive relief prohibiting enforcement of the federal CSA against them.

The plaintiffs' lawsuit raised several constitutional objections against enforcement of the CSA: (1) the Due Process Clause of the Fifth Amendment; (2) the Ninth and Tenth Amendments; and (3) the Commerce Clause.[34] The first two arguments—due process and the Ninth and Tenth Amendments—were liberty-based objections to the use of federal power. The plaintiffs claimed a constitutional right to be left alone to use homemade remedies recommended by their physicians.[35] They asserted that the due process guarantee, as well as the reservation of rights and powers language of the Ninth and Tenth Amendments, was designed to protect individual liberty from illegitimate exercises of governmental power and necessarily incorporated the common law right to bodily autonomy, including the right to use substances that could prolong life and ameliorate pain.[36]

The plaintiffs' third argument was based not on residual individual sovereignty but the other foundational principle of American law—limited government power. Specifically, the plaintiffs asserted that Congress lacked power to regulate purely intrastate, non-economic activity. This argument did not assert that government lacked power to prohibit marijuana consumption and cultivation per se, but more narrowly that marijuana consumption and cultivation for personal medicinal use, sanctioned by state law, was not within the congressional power to "regulate Commerce . . . among the several States[.]"[37] The Ninth Circuit agreed with the plaintiffs and ruled that the CSA, as applied to the plaintiffs' particular conduct, was beyond the reach of federal power to regulate interstate commerce.[38]

The Supreme Court agreed to review the *Raich* decision and disagreed with the Ninth Circuit, holding that the CSA, as applied to the plaintiffs, was a valid exercise of the federal commerce power. Specifically, the *Raich* Court believed it was rational for Congress to conclude that cultivation and possession of locally grown marijuana for medicinal purposes would "substantially affect" the interstate market for illicit recreational marijuana.[39] In reaching this conclusion, the majority relied heavily on its 1942 decision in *Wickard v. Filburn*,[40] a case that has been routinely criticized as establishing the high water mark for Commerce Clause jurisprudence.[41]

In *Wickard,* the Supreme Court was asked to rule on the constitutionality of the Agricultural Adjustment Act (AAA), an important piece of New Deal legislation that sought to stabilize and increase wheat prices by limiting the volume of wheat produced for interstate and international commerce. Filburn, the plaintiff in *Wickard,* was a farmer who sowed more acreage than was permitted under the AAA, using the excess to feed his own family. He argued that the wheat grown for home consumption was not a proper subject of federal interstate commerce power. A unanimous Court in *Wickard* disagreed, reasoning that the aggregate volume of wheat grown for home consumption could undermine the effectiveness of the AAA, and was thus within the scope of federal interstate commerce power.[42]

Wickard's aggregation principle broadened federal power to regulate interstate commerce by allowing federal power to reach exclusively intrastate activity. So long as the intrastate activity is rationally viewed by Congress as having a substantial effect on interstate commerce, it falls within the grasp of federal power. This analytical framework does not require the government to prove that the intrastate activity actually has a substantial effect on interstate commerce. Instead, by invoking rationality review, the Court merely asks whether it would be "rational" for Congress to think that the activity in question has a substantial effect, even if the government offers no evidence whatsoever to demonstrate the effect.[43]

The *Raich* ruling confirmed the Supreme Court's continuing adherence to the aggregation principle and the application of highly deferential rationality review for exercises of federal power predicated on a claim that an activity substantially affects interstate commerce. By doing so, the *Raich* decision exemplifies all that is wrong with current constitutional jurisprudence. It starts with a presumption that a non-commercial intrastate activity, explicitly sanctioned by state law and within an area traditionally left to state power (regulating medical practice), is within the reach of federal interstate commerce power. This presumption of power may be rebutted only if the plaintiff convinces the Court that Congress irrationally believed the activity has a substantial effect on interstate commerce.

The net effect is a presumptive plenary federal power to regulate purely intrastate activities under the guise of regulating commerce between the states, and a concomitant evisceration of meaningful federalism, a principle which was designed provide greater protection to individual liberty. It should be apparent that, under the presumptive federal power framework, neither the principle of limited government nor the principle of residual individual sovereignty is given serious consideration.

Three dissenting Justices in *Raich*—Justices O'Connor, Thomas, and Chief Justice Rehnquist—understood the far-reaching implications of the majority's reasoning.[44] Justice Thomas, in a separate dissent, took the majority to task for being "interested more in the modern than the original understanding of the Constitution" and "rewriting" the Commerce Clause to fit its agenda.[45] He adroitly articulated the original meaning of the Commerce Clause and determined that, "[i]n the early days of the Republic, it would have been unthinkable that Congress could prohibit the local cultivation, possession, and consumption of marijuana."[46]

Justice Thomas is right. His observation that the majority's interpretation of the interstate commerce power will permit the federal government to "regulate quilting bees, clothes drives, and potluck suppers" is not an overstatement.[47] So long as there is some conceivable linkage, in the view of Congress, between local activity X and some broadly defined interstate economic activity, there is federal power to regulate or prohibit X. Potluck suppers, for example, could conceivably adversely affect the interstate restaurant business by removing those meals from the universe of potential restaurant meals served. Congress could rationally believe that local yard sales might have a substantial impact on the interstate market for retail goods and thus prohibit yard sales under the commerce power. As Justice Thomas correctly concluded, the *Raich* majority's rationale "makes a mockery of Madison's assurance to the people of New York [in *Federalist No. 45*] that the 'powers delegated to the Federal Government are 'few and defined,' while those of the States are 'numerous and indefinite.'"[48]

But beyond the *Raich* Court's disregard for the principle of limited government, there is an equally disturbing disregard for the principle of residual individual sovereignty. Because the Ninth Circuit relied upon the plaintiffs' Commerce Clause objection, neither it nor the Supreme Court addressed the plaintiffs' more intriguing objections based upon the Ninth and Tenth Amendments or the substantive liberty component of the Due Process Clause.[49] By failing to reach these liberty-based objections, the Court once again avoided articulating to the American people the nature and scope of their liberty against government.

If the courts in *Raich* had paid proper homage to the morality of American law, they would not have been reticent to address the liberty-based objections. They would have begun with a presumption of individual liberty, requiring the federal government to articulate a legitimate governmental need to apply the CSA to individuals who use medicinal marijuana pursuant to a doctor's advice. To rebut this presumption, the federal government would need to establish that application of the CSA to such individuals was needed to protect the life, liberty, or property of others. If the government could prove, for example, that marijuana was neither safe nor effective when used as directed, there could be a legitimate LLP basis for restricting individual liberty to use it. Without this sort of harm-based evidence, however, there is no legitimate basis for exercising governmental power. After all, if there is no evidence that medical marijuana harms the LLP of citizens who consume it, prohibiting its use is a shocking perversion of the very purpose of government. Instead of protecting citizens, government is harming them, using its vast power to stop citizens from ingesting a substance that improves their health and ability to function.

If the majority in *Raich* had adopted the analytical framework mandated by the morality of American law, the decision would have come out differently, for the simple reason that there is no evidence that medicinal use of marijuana is harmful to the patient or others, either in the sense of physical, life-based harms, or property-based harms based on lack of efficacy.[50] Indeed, the government never articulated any harm-based arguments in *Raich,* not even in response to the plaintiffs' liberty arguments. The only harm identified by the Supreme Court in *Raich* was harm to the federal government's "war on drugs"—a war that, in the case of medical marijuana, is being fought against vulnerable citizens, acting under the advice of their own doctors and with the blessing of their own state governments, and who are harming no one, not even themselves.

THE LIBERTY TO REFUSE TREATMENT

Inherent in the notion of patient autonomy to make informed medical decisions is the concomitant autonomy to refuse recommended medical treatment once so informed. Back in 1891, the Supreme Court, in *Union Pacific Railroad Co. v. Botsford,* declared that "no right is held more sacred, or is more carefully guarded, by the common law, than the right of every individual to the possession and control of his own person, free from all restraint or interference of others, unless by clear and unquestionable authority of law. As well said by Judge Cooley, 'The right to one's person may be said to be a right of complete immunity: to be let alone.'"[51]

The *Botsford* Court referred only to the common law right of bodily autonomy, because the *Botsford* case was a common law case alleging negligence against a railroad, not a case involving constitutional law. Specifically, the plaintiff in *Botsford* was hit on the head by an upper berth of a railroad sleeping car, and she subsequently sued the railroad for negligence, seeking recovery for her head and neck injury. The railroad sought a court order requiring the plaintiff to submit to a physical examination to confirm the nature and extent of her injuries. The trial court refused to order the examination on grounds that it lacked authority to require someone to submit involuntarily to a physical exam. The railroad appealed to the Supreme Court, which affirmed the trial court.

The parties in *Botsford* did not raise an issue of constitutional liberty, and the Supreme Court appropriately decided the case according to the common law. But the *Botsford* decision gives us a fascinating glimpse into the deep reverence given to bodily autonomy by the common law. The Court noted that under the common law, a person's body was considered so inviolable that something as small as a piece of jewelry could not be removed involuntarily to satisfy a judgment of debt or writ of replevin.[52] It then observed that "[t]he inviolability of the person is as much invaded by a compulsory stripping and exposure as by a blow. To compel anyone . . . to lay bare the body, or to submit it to the touch of a stranger, without lawful authority, is an indignity, an assault, and a trespass[.]"[53]

Given the strong rhetoric in *Botsford* about the fundamental and inviolable nature of bodily autonomy, it is rather odd that, over one hundred years later, the Supreme Court had difficulty deciding whether bodily autonomy was sufficiently important to be recognized as an aspect of individual liberty protected by the Constitution. Specifically, in *Cruzan v. Director, Missouri Department of Health*,[54] the Court was asked to determine whether a person has a constitutional right to refuse unwanted medical treatment. The case involved a young woman, Nancy Cruzan, who was injured in a car accident and subsequently diagnosed as being in a persistent vegetative state (PVS). As with many PVS patients, Cruzan's lower brain, which regulates reflexes and breathing, was still functioning, so she breathed independently and responded in various reflexive ways. But Cruzan's unconscious state left her unable to feed herself, so she was wholly dependent on tubes for nutrition and hydration.

Six years after the accident, Cruzan's parents requested that the hospital disconnect her feeding and hydration tubes, but the hospital refused. The parents filed suit, claiming that Cruzan would not want to continue receiving treatment, but the Missouri courts disagreed, concluding that there was not "clear and convincing evidence" that Cruzan would want her nutrition and hydration discontinued.[55] The parents then asked the U.S. Supreme Court to review the case, asserting that Missouri's heightened evidentiary standard violated their daughter's constitutional liberty to refuse unwanted medical treatment. The Supreme Court rejected the parents' argument, concluding that Missouri's heightened evidentiary standard did not infringe Cruzan's liberty.[56]

There are several remarkable and disconcerting aspects to the Supreme Court's decision. First, the court strangely "assumed" for purposes of deciding the case that Cruzan, when she was competent, had a constitutional right to refuse unwanted medical treatment.[57] Yet the Court refused explicitly to acknowledge the existence of this right, or more specifically decide whether the right survived an individual's subsequent incompetency.[58] The Court's demurrer on these important issues has left lawyers, health care providers, and ordinary Americans guessing as to whether such liberty exists and, if it does, what its duration and scope may be.

If there is indeed a constitutional liberty to refuse unwanted medical care, why not say so unambiguously? Why is it so hard to say that individuals have autonomy to choose whether to undergo medical treatment absent evidence of some weighty governmental need, as was said so clearly in *Botsford* nearly one hundred years before? The Court's reticence explicitly to acknowledge such a basic aspect of individual liberty illustrates how exceedingly far modern constitutional law has drifted from the foundational principles of limited government and residual individual sovereignty—and how narrow indeed is the present scope of constitutional liberty.

Second, the rationale supporting the Court's decision in *Cruzan* is disjointed in fundamentally disturbing ways. On the one hand, the majority implies that because Cruzan was incompetent, the state has a parens patriae power to safeguard her best interests.[59] This rationale, if it had been explicitly embraced and relied upon without conflicting rationales, would have provided a logical and legitimate basis for the outcome reached. Since Nancy Cruzan was incompetent at the time, undoubtedly the state of Missouri had a parens patriae power to ensure that her best interests were guarded.[60]

Missouri's evidentiary hurdle was high, but this alone does not infringe an incompetent's liberty interest, since it was enacted pursuant to a parens patriae power to protect the life of individuals who are incapable of making their own decisions. Missouri could have chosen other methods to safeguard the life of incompetents such as, for example, enacting a statute to give parents or other family members authority to make treatment decisions on their behalf. The enactment of a family consent statute may be a preferable way to safeguard incompetents' interests because it would recognize and respect the role of the family in such difficult decisions. Be that as it may, Missouri's choice, though perhaps not the ideal, was nonetheless a legitimate exercise of its parens patriae power to protect Nancy Cruzan's life and was thus consistent with the morality of American law.

If the Court had simply explained its *Cruzan* decision this way, I would not be writing further. But the Court muddied the waters considerably by relying on the states' interests in preserving and protecting human life. The *Cruzan* majority believed that Missouri had an interest in protecting life qua life, declaring, "[W]e think a State may properly decline to make judgments about the 'quality' of life that a particular individual may enjoy, and simply assert an unqualified interest in the preservation of human life to be weighed against the constitutionally protected interests of the individual."[61]

Notice that the *Cruzan* majority deems the states' interest in preserving human life to be both "unqualified" and of sufficient importance that it may be weighed against an individual's constitutional rights in all instances. This broad, unqualified power to protect life is a disturbing perversion of government's obligation to protect the life, liberty, and property of its citizens. Yes, government has a duty to protect the lives of its citizens. But this does not mean that government has an unlimited power to preserve the life of its citizens abstracted from those citizens' own preferences.

To fully understand the meaning of the *Cruzan* Court's rationale, we should stop for a moment and think. Did the Court really mean that states have a sovereign power to preserve our lives, a power that is separate and distinct from, and equally weighty to our own sovereign power to decide for ourselves? If so, where on earth does this power come from? Although the *Cruzan* majority does not say, the only possible source for such a broad power to control the lives of citizens is the so-called police power. The absurdity of this should be apparent, since, as discussed extensively in Chapter 2, the police power is a power to protect the life, liberty, and property of citizens against the actions of others, not a power to protect us from ourselves or to preserve our LLP when we do not wish to preserve it. If the police power has become this broad, it has been transmogrified from a power to protect to a power to control.

Under the morality of American law, then, does government have a legitimate power to protect life? Yes, but only in specific situations that are harmonious with the purpose of government. First, it has not only the power, but the duty, to protect citizens' lives, liberty, and property from harm inflicted or reasonably threatened by the actions of others. Second, it has a parens patriae power to safeguard the best interests of those who are incompetent to exercise sovereignty over their own lives, liberty, and property. For incompetent individuals such as Nancy Cruzan, the state legitimately may implement measures that protect their lives, liberty, and property from harm, including the adoption of heightened evidentiary standards as a prerequisite for terminating life support.

But the Supreme Court of the United States should not confuse a governmental duty to protect citizens' LLP with a paternalistic right to protect citizens' LLP when those citizens do not desire such protection. If government legitimately has an "unqualified interest in the preservation of human life" that may be given weight apart from the desires of the citizen whose life is in question, the citizen's ability to control his own body and life is not really a right at all. Instead, it is merely a privilege, granted by the beneficence of an all-powerful sovereign, and like all privileges may be taken away when the sovereign deems it desirable. It means also that the legal enforceability of advance directives such as living wills and health care powers of attorney is not grounded in recognition of and respect for individual autonomy, but merely an extension of sovereign grace that may be revoked by legislative whim at any time.

After all, if the government has an "unqualified" interest in the preservation of our lives, its interest cannot, by definition, become qualified or lessened under any circumstances. A citizen who signs an advance directive may be trying to give us some indication of her preferences, but these are merely preferences that the state may or may not honor, since the state's interest in preserving the citizen's life is unqualified. The *Cruzan* Court's rationale implies that while legislative recognition of advance directives may be desirable, it is not constitutionally required, and states could refuse to recognize them without violating any constitutional principles (such as residual individual sovereignty). As with so many issues of individual liberty under orthodox constitutional analysis, our ability to control our own bodies after incapacity by appointing a surrogate decision-maker or writing a living will hinges upon the wisdom and kindness of the legislature. If this is really the state of American constitutional law, the British Leviathan government that the Framers rebelled against—one that doled out as privileges those liberties deemed to be inalienable individual rights—has successfully resurrected itself in the New World.

THE LIBERTY TO CHOOSE DEATH: EUTHANASIA
AND PHYSICIAN-ASSISTED SUICIDE

Given the *Cruzan* Court's conception of unqualified governmental power to protect life, what does it suggest about the related issues of physician-assisted suicide (PAS) and euthanasia?

First, some terminology clarification is required. Physician-assisted suicide refers to the situation in which an individual requests the assistance of a physician with terminating his own life. The person who requests PAS may or may not be terminally ill, and the physician's assistance is essentially passive—that is, providing a medical means, such as a lethal dose of medication, which the patient then employs to end his own life. Euthanasia, by contrast, involves a more active role for the health care provider. Specifically, euthanasia occurs when the provider (usually a physician) not only provides the means for bringing about death, but actively employs them as well. As a simple illustration, a physician who injects a patient with a lethal dose of medication commits euthanasia, whereas a physician who writes a prescription for a lethal dose of medication that is subsequently taken by the patient is providing PAS.

In 1997, the U.S. Supreme Court, in *Washington v. Glucksberg*,[62] rejected a substantive liberty challenge to Washington state's law banning PAS. The *Glucksberg* majority rejected the idea of a constitutionally protected liberty to obtain assistance with suicide, invoking the orthodox substantive due process analysis which requires that a citizen convince the Court that the activity sought to be protected is objectively "deeply rooted" in the history and traditions of the nation.[63] The Court concluded that "for over 700 years, the Anglo-American common-law tradition has punished or otherwise disapproved of both suicide and assisting suicide."[64] This history accordingly precluded recognition of a liberty to commit suicide or obtain assistance with suicide.

The *Glucksberg* Court's conclusion about the history of suicide and assisted suicide is essentially correct, but its invocation of the history-driven substantive due process analytical framework illustrates the deep deficiencies of that framework and its inherent disregard for the principles of limited government and residual individual sovereignty. To fully assess the weaknesses of the orthodox analytical approach to substantive liberty claims such as assisted suicide, we should begin where the *Glucksberg* Court began—with an overview of the history of suicide and assisted suicide.

English common law condemned suicide as a type of "self-murder" and punished the family of the deceased by imposing forfeiture of property.[65] Early

American colonies adopted their English ancestors' approach, but by the time of the ratification of the Constitution, most American states had departed from English common law and eliminated punishment for suicide, intimating that the American political philosophy was more respectful of individual autonomy, at least with regard to the suicide's surviving family.[66] But elimination of punishment for suicide did not mean that suicide itself was considered acceptable—it simply meant that American society no longer deemed it just to punish the innocent survivors through the imposition of property forfeiture and ignominious burial.[67]

Even if suicide itself was no longer considered a crime in America, what about assistance with suicide? English common law considered assistance with suicide to be a felony, and the American colonies followed suit. But after the ratification of the Constitution and Bill of Rights, there are no reported cases of prosecution for assisted suicide until the appearance of specific statutes that identified assisted suicide as a crime, the first of which appeared in 1828, over forty years after the ratification of the Constitution.[68]

Does this jurisprudential silence indicate early American acquiescence to assistance with suicide? No. The absence of case law or statutes addressing assistance with suicide is most likely due to the American adoption of the common law doctrine relating to accessories before the fact. Specifically, the common law did not permit an individual to be convicted for aiding the commission of a crime—i.e., as an accessory—unless and until the person who actually committed the crime—the principal—was convicted.[69] If X assisted Y with committing suicide, the death of Y obviously made conviction of the Y impossible, and this, in turn, made conviction of X as an accessory impossible.

The common law requirement of prior principal conviction was not abolished until the mid-to-late 1800s.[70] The fall of the common law requirement of conviction of the principal opened the door, for the first time, for conviction of assisting a suicide. Indeed, by the time of the ratification of the Fourteenth Amendment in 1868, most states had criminalized assisted suicide, usually through the enactment of specific assisted suicide statutes.[71]

The demise of the common law's principal conviction requirement was likely due to many factors. There was a growing sense that accessories, both before and after the fact, had culpability equal to that of the principal actor. There were also many situations under common law wherein a principal could escape conviction, frustrating the government's ability to secure convictions for guilty accessories.[72] American states accordingly began abolishing the distinction between accessories and principals, enacting statutes that allowed accessories to be charged as principals and tried before or after the principal, and imposing equal punishment upon both.[73] But even under this revised criminal law, there was still an important prerequisite to conviction of one who aids the principal actor—the commission of a criminal act. If A helps B prepare for a robbery which B subsequently commits, the revised statutes would allow both A and B to be convicted independently for the substantive crime of robbery, or allow A to be tried as an accessory before B. But it would not allow A to be convicted of and sentenced for the accessory charge if B committed no crime.[74]

The common law's principal conviction requirement's basic premise—that a person should not be convicted for assisting with the commission of a crime if there has been no antecedent conviction for the alleged underlying crime—is still alive and well in American law, and understanding its logic is essential to analyzing the validity of criminalizing assisted suicide. Although American law historically has not considered suicide to be a criminal act punishable by law, it was (and is) still considered by many Americans to be a "grievous . . . wrong."[75] But despite continued moral condemnation of suicide, the fact remains that suicide is not currently a crime in any American state and, in fact, has not been a crime in most American states since 1798.[76] As such, we must be prepared to ask ourselves: Is it appropriate to criminalize assistance with an act that itself is not criminal?

If suicide itself is not a crime, why should assisting someone with suicide be considered criminal? If you steal Susan's car and I assist you by loaning you my tools, knowing that you will use them to steal Susan's car, I may of course be convicted of aiding and abetting the theft. But if you water Susan's flowers and I assist you beforehand by loaning you my watering can, knowing that you will use it to water Susan's flowers, I may not be convicted of anything, because although I have aided and abetted your watering of Susan's flowers, watering Susan's flowers is not a crime. If an act is not criminal, it cannot and should not be criminal to assist someone with that act.[77]

Think about it this way: Abortion is no longer a crime in any American state though, much like suicide, it was considered a crime by the common law. Since abortion is not a crime, would it be legitimate for a legislature to enact a statute making assistance with abortion a crime? Abortion is of course now a recognized constitutional right, but this should not alter the fundamental question as to whether an assisting an act, not itself a crime, can be criminalized. To use an example not involving a constitutional right, consider whether a state could criminalize assistance with rock climbing, stock car racing, rollerblading, or any other legal activity. If a majority of Americans found such activities to be grievous, morally reprehensible activities, yet did not criminalize the acts themselves, would it be legitimate to condemn those who assist such acts as criminals? Of course not.

So why should we consider assisting suicide to be criminal, when committing suicide is not? One possibility is public morality. We might cling to religious beliefs that condemn suicide as sinful, or even a superstitious belief that suicide creates lost souls who wander the earth. Another reason why American states have chosen to criminalize assisted suicide has nothing to do with public morality or concerns about victimization, but instead a more generalized concern about the slippery slope to euthanasia. This concern was evident in the Supreme Court's decision in *Glucksberg,* "[T]he State may fear that permitting assisted suicide will start it down the path to voluntary and perhaps even involuntary euthanasia. . . . Thus, it turns out that what is couched as a limited right to 'physician-assisted suicide' is likely, in effect a much broader license, which could prove extremely difficult to police and contain."[78] But again, we should dissect this rationale carefully before jumping to any conclusions.

First, there is an important distinction between voluntary and involuntary euthanasia, although the *Glucksberg* majority did not acknowledge it. Voluntary euthanasia is when an individual voluntarily asks another to take an affirmative act to end his life—for example, by shooting him or injecting him with poison. Involuntary euthanasia is when a person, perhaps out of a sense of mercy, takes an affirmative act to end the life of another, without any antecedent voluntary request by the victim. In the case of voluntary euthanasia, the act that causes death is initiated at the request of the victim; the victim consents to the act. In the case of involuntary euthanasia, there is no victim consent.

Why does the consent distinction matter? It matters because the inescapable, core legal question presented by either assisted suicide or voluntary euthanasia is to what extent, if any, an individual's consent to the receipt of lethal force or medication should be honored by the state. After all, the whole purpose of advance directives—living wills or durable health care powers of attorney—is to document the wishes of the patient. Advance directives are inherently designed to document and implement the patient's advance consent to the withdrawal of life-sustaining medical treatment. They are "advance consent" directives, and they are routinely honored in modern America and widely praised as an important tool for ensuring patient autonomy. If we support an individual's right to grant advance consent to an act that will cause death, why should we not similarly support the right to grant contemporaneous consent to an act that will cause death?

Yet the law maintains this artificial temporal distinction, even though logic suggests that in many cases prior consent will not reflect a person's wishes as accurately as contemporaneous consent. Under current law, if Bill gives Mary a health care power of attorney and tells her that he would never want to be kept alive by a respirator or a feeding tube, Mary is free to order the discontinuation of such life-sustaining treatment even though it will result in Bill's death. By contrast, if Bill knowingly and voluntarily asks Mary to kill him and she accedes, Mary can be charged with homicide, and she cannot defend herself on the basis that Bill consented to be killed.[79] But why not? Bill has consented to an act by Mary that will result in his death—just as if he had given Mary a health care power of attorney and she had ordered removal of his feeding tube.

Indeed, homicide and statutory rape stand alone as the only crimes that are not vitiated by consent. All other crimes can be defended on the basis that the victim consented, so that, for example, a woman's consent to sex will vitiate a charge of rape and a property owner's consent to relinquish control of property will vitiate a charge of theft. But are statutory rape and homicide analogous? No. Statutory rape is a crime, created by statute, that punishes any act of intercourse with a person under a specified age, even if the person consents. Statutory rape laws deem certain individuals insufficiently mature—i.e., incompetent—to decide for themselves whether to consent to sex. As discussed more extensively in Chapter 5, statutory rape laws are an exercise of the state's parens patriae power to protect incompetent individuals against harm, either from themselves or from others. A thirteen-year-old's consent to sex is irrelevant to the charge of statutory rape simply because the thirteen-year-old has been deemed incapable of granting legally valid consent to sex. So long as the age of consent for sex is reasonable, statutory rape laws, as an exercise of the parens patriae power to protect vulnerable citizens' best interests, would be a classic, legitimate exercise of governmental power to protect citizens' LLP.

But can the same analysis hold true for homicide laws? Laws against homicide are undoubtedly enacted to protect citizens' LLP by punishing and deterring acts that deprive citizens of their lives. But if an adult competent citizen consents to the deprivation of her life, why should the law disregard her consent? Unlike statutory rape, consent to homicide cannot be disregarded on the justification that the citizen is incompetent to grant consent. A competent adult, after all, is a competent adult, and her consent is presumptively valid in all other contexts, including other potentially violent crimes such as theft, burglary, battery, and rape.[80] Although courts have occasionally waxed philosophic and declared that "private persons can not license crime" by consenting thereto, these broad declarations prove meaningless when scrutinized care-fully.[81] Consent does indeed vitiate most crimes—in fact all crimes other than statutory rape and homicide—and thus the notion that individuals are inca-pable of "licensing" crime by consenting thereto is pragmatically untenable. The exceptions have swallowed this rule.

Courts have alternatively attempted to justify the homicide consent excep-tion on grounds that "the right to life and personal security . . . is inalien-able."[82] But this is a gross perversion of the concept of inalienable rights. Granted, the rights to life and personal security are inalienable rights. But the entire concept of inalienable rights refers to their inviolability vis-à-vis govern-ment power. To say that a right is "inalienable" is to say that the government has no power to alienate it. It does not mean that individuals, who by nature pos-sess these rights, are not free to knowingly and voluntarily relinquish them to other private individuals.

If inalienable rights belong exclusively to individual citizens—which by def-inition is what they are supposed to be—we must acknowledge that individu-als may do with them what they please, provided their choices are voluntary, competent, and not harmful to the LLP of others. We may bemoan, morally condemn, or disagree with a fellow citizen's relinquishment of his own life, but this does not give us the right to transmogrify his inalienable right to sover-eignty over his own body and life into one that may, indeed, be alienated by a legislative majority.

Another possible reason why Americans generally have chosen to criminalize assisted suicide is pragmatic concern about the availability of evidence and the fear of coercion. Since there are generally only two people who can tell us what actually happened at the moment of death—the individual requesting assis-tance with suicide and the person who assists—the death of the former often leaves only one witness. If there was anything involuntary about the death, it may prove difficult to obtain such evidence. Moreover, if we permitted assisted suicide, we might render certain individuals vulnerable to coercion, and they might end their lives for inappropriate reasons, such as to spare others inconve-nience or hardship.[83] Perhaps because of these pragmatic concerns, assisted sui-cide is presently considered criminal in all American states except Oregon.[84]

As an initial matter, we should pause to consider the source and basis of these pragmatic concerns. We are worried about the inherently private nature of PAS and the resulting risk of coercion or unprovable aggression. But these concerns are omnipresent in the present realm of PAS prohibition. The practice of ter-minal sedation is ubiquitous. A health care provider—usually a nurse—administers an intravenous drug (commonly benzodiazepenes or barbituates) that induces a pharmacologic coma. During the coma, the patient is not given food or water, and this hastens his death. The practice of terminal sedation rarely, if ever, triggers any prosecutorial scrutiny, and it occurs in nursing homes, hospices, hospitals, and private residences all across America every single day. My own father, who died in a nursing home while I was writing this book, died because a nurse administered to him a lethal dose of morphine. While the administration of the morphine was intended to be humane—a "mercy killing," if you will—it was an act undertaken sua sponte by the nurse, without informing the family of its ultimate effect, and certainly without the consent of my father.

But there is nothing unusual in what happened to my father. Terminal sedation is widely accepted and considered humane, a human version of putting the dog to sleep. And though it may be both ethical and well-intentioned, it is completely unregulated. Patients or their families may or may not be consulted prior to administration. They may or may not be fully informed as to the purpose and effect of the drug's administration. The health care provider holds the power over life and death and essentially decides whether or when to administer the lethal dose.

Would it not be better, more humane, and more respectful of both patient autonomy and patients' families to explicitly acknowledge and regulate the practice of terminal sedation? Terminal sedation is assisted suicide, and it should be regulated to minimize the high potential for abuse, coercion, and lack of patient or family knowledge. The Supreme Court in *Vacco v. Quill*—an equal protection companion case to *Glucksberg*—steadfastly clung to the belief that assisted suicide meaningfully differed from what it termed "aggressive palliative care" by asserting that "painkilling drugs may hasten a patient's death, but the physician's purpose and intent is, or may be, only to ease his patient's pain."[85] The importance of intent in drawing legal distinctions among possible criminal acts is undoubtedly important. But in the case of terminal sedation, the intent is not only to ease the patient's pain, but to ease it by ending the patient's life. The patient's pain cannot be eased adequately without a lethal dose (otherwise, presumably a non-lethal dose would be administered), and the provision of the lethal dose is intended to hasten death, the only possible way to ease the pain. There is no principled way, in other words, to disentangle the health care provider's intent to ease pain from the intent to hasten death. The intent to accomplish both goals ineluctably is present in all instances of terminal sedation.

Since we legalize many acts that are designed to cause death—terminal sedation and advance directives, for example—is it reasonable to single out physician-assisted suicide as a distinct criminal act? It should be obvious by now that
the morality of American law espoused in this book does not recognize the legitimacy of public morality as a legitimate basis for law. Moral, religious, or superstitious beliefs about suicide provide no legitimate authority for restricting
assisted suicide. But the pragmatic concerns about evidentiary problems and
coercion are concededly real and legitimate governmental concerns. After all, if
the purpose of government is to protect the LLP of citizens, it would seem reasonable for government to enact laws that protect citizens' lives by safeguarding
them from coercion or aggression.

But while these pragmatic concerns are both real and legitimate, they are insufficient to justify a total prohibition on assisted suicide. There are many alternative approaches, short of total prohibition, that would alleviate these concerns and permit individuals to exercise sovereignty over their lives, while
simultaneously respecting the principle of limited government. If we are really
concerned about these issues, the Oregon assisted suicide law provides several
examples of legitimate means to address them. For example, under Oregon law,
the person who wishes to obtain a physician's assistance with suicide must make
two oral requests separated by at least fifteen days; execute a separate written request signed by two witnesses; obtain two different physicians' confirmation of
the diagnosis of terminal illness and patient capacity; be informed of alterna-
tives such as hospice care and pain management; and must be referred for a psychological examination if either of the two physicians believes the patient's
judgment is impaired by a psychological or psychiatric disorder.[86]

Data from seven years of experience with the Oregon PAS law indicates that
these procedural safeguards are working well. Approximately sixty Oregonians
per year successfully overcome the procedural hurdles and obtain a lethal prescription, but only about two-thirds of them subsequently ingest the drug and
die.[87] Demographic characteristics of the terminally ill patients who do obtain
lethal prescriptions reveal that they are younger, unmarried, and with a high
level of education.[88] There have been no reported cases of coercion or other im-
proper influence.

Despite Oregon's apparent success at implementing PAS, in 2001 the U.S.
Department of Justice issued the so-called Ashcroft Directive, in which then—
Attorney General John Ashcroft announced that physicians who prescribe a
lethal dose of medication pursuant to the Oregon law are in violation of the
federal Controlled Substances Act (CSA).[89] Specifically, the Ashcroft Directive

asserted that prescribing drugs for PAS does not constitute a "legitimate medical purpose" under the CSA, as required by existing federal regulations.[90] A few years earlier, in 1998, the Clinton administration's attorney general, Janet Reno, had reached the opposite determination, concluding that the CSA was not "intended to displace the states as the primary regulators of the medical profession, or to override a state's determination as to what constitutes legitimate medical practice."[91]

The Ashcroft Directive was challenged in court by a group of Oregon physicians, pharmacists, and the State of Oregon. In January 2006, the Supreme Court agreed with the plaintiffs, ruling in *Gonzales v. Oregon* that Attorney General Ashcroft's directive exceeded his authority under the CSA.[92] The Court concluded that "the structure of the CSA . . . conveys unwillingness to cede medical judgments to an Executive official who lacks medical expertise."[93] The Court noted that a contrary interpretation of the CSA would give the attorney general authority to make medical judgments that are "not limited to physician-assisted suicide. . . . [H]e could decide whether any particular drug may be used for any particular purpose, or indeed whether a physician who administers any controversial treatment could be deregistered. This would occur, under the Government's view, despite the statute's express limitation of the Attorney General's authority to registration and control, with attendant restrictions on each of those functions, and despite the statutory purposes to combat drug abuse and prevent illicit drug trafficking."[94] The Supreme Court's analytical framework employed in the *Gonzales v. Oregon* case was undoubtedly correct. The CSA was designed to combat drug abuse and addiction, not to interfere with a state's power to restrict (or not restrict, as was the case in Oregon) individual bodily autonomy. Although the Court's opinion was solely based on a statutory rather than a constitutional interpretation, it nonetheless intimated that its statutory interpretation was consistent with the constitutional allocation of powers between the federal and state governments. Specifically, the Court acknowledged that the CSA "presume[s] and rel[ies] upon a functioning medical profession regulated under the States' police powers."[95] Because the regulation of medical care is an area of power reserved to the states under the Tenth Amendment, the attorney general lacks authority to second-guess a state's determination of how best to protect the lives of its citizens. If the State of Oregon believes that its law will adequately protect the lives of vulnerable citizens and ensure that those who obtain lethal prescriptions are doing so knowingly and voluntarily, what business does the federal government have in second-guessing this judgment?

The Supreme Court's clear understanding post-*Glucksberg* was that although there was no constitutionally protected liberty to engage in PAS, the individual states would be permitted to determine for themselves whether to permit or prohibit PAS: "Throughout the Nation, Americans are engaged in an earnest and profound debate about the morality, legality, and practicality of physician-assisted suicide. Our holding permits this debate to continue, as it should in a democratic society."[96] As the Court in *Gonzales v. Oregon* intimated, this "earnest and profound debate" could not have continued if the Ashcroft Directive was upheld.[97]

Perhaps more important, Oregon's long struggle to implement its PAS law illustrates the incredible resistance that can be faced by a state wishing to blaze a trail in a direction contrary to the ardently held moral beliefs of some citizens. Despite the fact that Oregon's PAS law was repeatedly approved by a majority of its own citizens, some citizens in other states simply could not accept Oregonians' sovereignty to make their own choice on this contentious issue. Oregonians' unique approach allows the state to fulfill its police power obligation to protect its potentially vulnerable citizens, while simultaneously honoring its citizens' residual individual sovereignty. It is a rare example of governmental restraint of power which implicitly implements the morality of American law by recognizing that reasonable regulations aimed at protecting citizens from coercion and aggression are legitimate exercises of governmental power, while complete restrictions on individual liberty are not. The State of Oregon struck a logical and careful balance that should have been praised, not fought and delayed by citizens who disagreed with the law solely on moral grounds.

COMPULSORY TREATMENT

As this chapter has demonstrated, there are many facets to the liberty to refuse unwanted medical treatment, a liberty that implicitly recognizes some degree of bodily autonomy. Yet we have also seen that the liberty to refuse medical treatment is not absolute. There are times when countervailing interests may effectively trump an individual's liberty to forgo treatment. The Supreme Court, for example, has allowed a state's "unqualified" interest in life to trump a citizen's own desire to end his life. Although I think the Court's reasoning is untenable and contrary to the morality of American law, it nonetheless illustrates that bodily autonomy is not viewed as absolute.

I agree that bodily autonomy is not absolute, not because the state has an unqualified interest in life abstracted from a competent adult citizen's own preferences, but because the purpose of government, as discussed in Chapter 2, is to protect the life, liberty, and property of its citizens. A citizen's bodily autonomy, therefore, must give way if exercising such autonomy would harm or reasonably threaten harm to the LLP of others. For example, the government legitimately may restrict bodily autonomy by effectuating mandatory quarantines and vaccinations if there is reasonable evidence that an illness could spread to others. Indeed, President George W. Bush recently said that he is considering the possibility of using the military to enforce a mandatory quarantine in the event of a bird flu pandemic.[98] Putting aside the issue of the propriety of using the military, it is undoubtedly legitimate for government to invoke a mandatory quarantine if it is needed to prevent harm to other citizens. When government restrains the liberty of citizens in order to prevent harm to the LLP of other citizens, it acts consistently with the morality of American law.

The crucial questions with such exercises of governmental power are: What interests are sufficient to overcome a competent individual's objection to medical treatment? And as with all questions of individual liberty, who should bear the burden of proof—government or individual? The seminal case in the area is *Jacobsen v. Massachusetts,* in which the Supreme Court upheld the use of mandatory vaccinations as a legitimate exercise of state police power to protect public health.[99] The Court in *Jacobsen* reasoned that, "[a]ccording to settled principles, the police power must be held to embrace, at least, such reasonable regulations established directly by legislative enactment as will protect the public health and the public safety."[100]

Intriguingly, the *Jacobsen* Court invoked the harm principle, asserting that "[r]eal liberty for all could not exist under the operation of a principle which recognizes the right of each individual person to use his own, whether in respect of his person or his property, regardless of the injury that may be done to others."[101] The fair implication of this statement is that citizens do not have a liberty to harm the LLP of others. Jacobsen's refusal to submit to an efficacious smallpox vaccination in a time of epidemic posed a reasonable threat of harm to the lives of his fellow citizens, and was therefore an exercise of liberty that was properly restrained under the police power.

The Court's rationale in *Jacobsen* is a classic invocation of the harm principle and consistent with the morality of American law. Indeed, the Court even went so far as to recognize a presumption of individual liberty, which the government must overcome, stating throughout the decision that the government had established that the mandatory vaccination was "necessary" for public health and safety and based on a principle of "paramount necessity."[102] It further clarified that a law designed to protect public health and safety must have a "real or substantial relation" to those goals, which would necessarily require the government to offer proof of harm.[103]

The *Jacobsen* analytical approach was far removed from modern constitutional analysis. Modern constitutional analysis, as discussed extensively in previous chapters, begins with a presumption that legislative restrictions on individual liberty are constitutional, the only exceptions being for a handful of rights deemed "fundamental"—a label that is supported neither by constitutional text nor by history. In modern American law, the liberty of individual citizens may therefore be restricted at the whim of legislative majorities, and the Court will uphold such restrictions so long as there is some arguably rational basis for them, including something as flimsy as majoritarian morality.

Jacobsen, by contrast, employed a radically different analytical framework that is consistent with the morality of American law espoused in this book. The *Jacobsen* Court appropriately recognized that states have a police power to protect the LLP of citizens and that this power may be exercised if the government can establish the necessity of doing so. The Court began with a presumption of individual liberty, but permitted the presumption to be overcome with evidence of harm-based need, a framework that is respectful of the twin principles of limited government and residual individual sovereignty.

It is doubtful that the modern Supreme Court would invoke the same presumption of liberty invoked by the Court in *Jacobsen*. Cases such as *Cruzan, Glucksberg* and *Raich* have signaled a retreat from the early common law reverence of bodily autonomy and a simultaneous expansion of governmental power to interfere with it. The net result in the context of compulsory treatment is that the government now has greater power to compel citizens to undergo treatment, enjoying a presumptive power to do so without offering specific proof of need. Some may deem such broad governmental power to be expedient in a time of feared biological terror and bird flu. But the morality of American law would grant government the power to restrain individual liberty to protect against these threats, without granting government a virtually plenary power over citizens' lives. Indeed, the morality of American law is built upon recognition of governmental power to protect its citizens from actual or reasonably threatened harm, and there is no need, in the name of convenience or otherwise, to depart from its foundational principles of limited government and residual individual sovereignty.

Chapter 8 Food, Drugs, and Alcohol

[T]he right of liberty and pursuing happiness secured by the constitution, embraces the right, in each compos mentis individual, of selecting what he will eat and drink, in short, his beverages, so far as he may be capable of producing them, or they may be within his reach, and that the legislature cannot take away. . . . If the constitution does not secure this right to the people, it secures nothing of value. If the people are subject to be controlled by the legislature in the matter of their beverages, so they are as to their articles of dress, and in their hours of sleeping and waking. And if the people are incompetent to select their own beverages, they are also incompetent to determine anything in relation to their living, and should be placed at once in a state of pupilage to a set of government sumptuary officers; eulogies upon the dignity of human nature should cease; and the doctrine of the competency of the people for self government be declared a deluding rhetorical flourish. If the government can prohibit any practice it pleases, it can prohibit the drinking of cold water. Can it do that? If not, why not?
—*Indiana Supreme Court, declaring an early prohibition law unconstitutional in* Herman v. State *(1855)*

INTRODUCTION

American law has become increasingly intolerant of individual sovereignty to make choices regarding which substances to consume. This intolerance would come as a surprise to the Framers, who lived in an era in which governmental restrictions on ingested substances were rare indeed. The modern governmental power to prohibit ingestion of certain substances is essentially unlimited, and most Americans simply take it for granted. But as this chapter will show, the vast bulk of this power is exercised illegitimately, in a way that is antithetical to the limited purpose of government and the principle of residual individual sovereignty. The monolithic "war on drugs," for example, is of modern vintage, begun only in the 1970s.

The purported purpose behind drug, alcohol, and other sumptuary laws is unabashed paternalism: these substances can hurt you, so we will protect you from yourself by prohibiting their use entirely. This paternalism, however, is woefully incomplete, prohibiting individuals from consuming some potentially harmful substances, while allowing them to consume others without limitation. The inconsistency from substance to substance shows that the real purpose behind sumptuary laws is not paternalistic protection, but public morality—a sense of moral danger associated with certain substances and the people who use them.

Tobacco products, for example, are consumed regularly by over seventy million Americans, yet kill approximately 400,000 each year, often via painful, debilitating conditions such as emphysema or cancer of the lungs, throat, or mouth.[1] The addictive ingredient in tobacco—nicotine—is both stimulating and tranquilizing. Its powerful effects prompted the Catholic Church to issue formal prohibitions against its consumption in the mid-seventeenth century.[2] Many European nations followed suit by enacting laws prohibiting tobacco consumption entirely, sometimes on pain of death.[3] Fourteen American states banned tobacco at the turn of the twentieth century, though these laws fell into disfavor after World War I, when many soldiers began smoking.[4] Despite all that is known about the extreme hazard associated with tobacco products, they remain legally sold and consumed by anyone over the age of eighteen.[5]

Likewise caffeine, a central nervous system stimulant, is downed daily by millions of Americans jittery for their coffee, tea, or soda fix. Individuals addicted to caffeine experience physical dependence and withdrawal symptoms when regular consumption is interrupted.[6] Its stimulating effect engendered emotional opposition and strict legal prohibition upon its introduction in the Middle East, and its effects have been analogized by Western medical practitioners to morphine and alcohol.[7] An early-twentieth-century medical school textbook widely adopted in America and Britain described caffeine addiction in a manner familiar to anyone who has ever used too much No-Doz in college or tried to swear off coffee: "The sufferer is tremulous, and loses his self-command; he is subject to fits of agitation and depression; he loses color and has a haggard appearance. The appetite falls off, and symptoms of gastric catarrh may be manifested. The heart also suffers; it palpitates, or it intermits. As with other such agents, a renewed dose of the poison gives temporary relief, but at the cost of future misery."[8] It has been known for many years that excessive caffeine consumption can lead to physical aggression.[9] If consumed in great quantities—approximately ten grams (the equivalent of 70–100 cups of coffee)—caffeine can even be fatal.[10]

Besides products containing caffeine, numerous foods and beverages contain substances that are potentially quite harmful. Salt and sugar, for example, are well known to contribute to high blood pressure and tooth decay. Saccharin, a low-calorie sugar substitute, was blessed by Congress in 1977, with the condition that products containing it carry a warning that proclaimed, "Use of this product may be hazardous to your health. This product contains saccharin which has been determined to cause cancer in laboratory animals."[11] Many people disregarded the warnings, believing that the risk to humans was very remote because the rats were fed enormous quantities of saccharin. But a joint study conducted by the FDA and the National Cancer Institute in 1980 revealed that what the study called "heavy" users—defined as those who consumed two or more eight-ounce diet drinks per day—had a 50–60 percent higher risk of bladder cancer, a type of cancer with a latency period of thirty to fifty years.[12] In 1997, an advisory panel to the National Toxicology Program voted to keep saccharin on its list of suspected human carcinogens, but a year later reversed this decision based on new criteria for carcinogen classification.[13] As a result of the de-listing, Congress repealed the mandatory saccharin warning in 2000.

A similar conundrum was recently posed by Olestra, a fat substitute that alters the sugar molecule in a way that allows fat to pass out of the digestive tract unabsorbed. Research conducted by Olestra's manufacturer revealed that its consumption could lead to loose stools, diarrhea, and loss of important vitamins. The FDA eventually approved Olestra for use in food, but required a warning label that read, "This product contains Olestra. Olestra may cause abdominal cramping and loose stools. Olestra inhibits the absorption of some vitamins and other nutrients. Vitamins A, D, E and K have been added."[14] Subsequent research has revealed that the problems identified in the Olestra warning label are mild, and that other problems exist that are not revealed by the label. For example, a study conducted in 1998 by researchers at the Harvard School of Public Health concluded that Olestra interfered with the body's absorption of carotenoids, a substance that gives fruits and vegetables an orange, red, or yellow color, and that has been associated with reduced incidence of certain diseases.[15] The Harvard study surmised that consumption of Olestra would result in a declined absorption of carotenoids, which in turn could produce many additional cases of heart disease, cancer, and macular degeneration.[16] In 2003 the FDA rescinded its warning label requirement based on the lack of convincing evidence that carotenoid loss would result in disease, its belief that consumers were aware of the risks of Olestra, evidence that digestive problems were mild, and confusion by consumers who thought that eating Olestra products would harm their ability to digest vitamins and minerals generally.[17] Olestra products may now be sold without the provision of any warnings.

Why does American law allow carte blanche consumption of tobacco, caffeine, sugar, salt, saccharin, and Olestra, yet completely prohibit the consumption of other harmful substances? The answer lies not in any difference in the potential for harm posed by these products, but merely in the perceived morality—or more precisely, immorality—of their consumption. Some products have become domesticated, accepted, tolerated. No one associates consumption of caffeine, Olestra potato chips, or saccharin with poor morals. We have no trouble envisioning a caffeine user as a hard-working, family-loving, upright neighbor, even though he may be addicted to his morning coffee and persists in consuming a product that both makes him high and poses a risk of self-harm. By contrast, there is beginning to be a hint of moral disapproval of smoking based on a perceived link between smokers and negative character traits such as lack of discipline, lack of intelligence, and lower economic status. Ultimately these negative assumptions about a smoker's character may culminate in a moral crusade to prohibit smoking entirely, similar to the history of alcohol prohibition. Indeed, the public morality roots of sumptuary laws are deep and undeniable, and we will begin exploring these roots by discussing the regulation of alcohol.

ALCOHOL

America's intoxicant of choice is alcohol, a depressant that induces physiological effects remarkably similar to short-acting barbiturates such as secobarbital.[18] Each American age fifteen and older consumes an average of 2.2 gallons of alcohol per year—a consumption level that, other than in the years during and shortly after prohibition, has remained remarkably consistent since 1850.[19] The social and moral acceptance of alcohol is widespread, despite the fact that an estimated eighteen million Americans have alcohol problems, and over 100,000 Americans die due to alcohol each year.[20]

There was a time, of course, when America temporarily lost its tolerance for alcohol. Opponents of alcohol consumption enjoyed early success in state legislatures, though there were occasional rebellions by political leaders and judges schooled in the foundational principles of limited government and residual individual sovereignty. Abraham Lincoln, for example, sagely observed that "[p]rohibition will work great injury to the cause of temperance. It is a species of intemperance . . . [and] attempts to control a man's appetite by legislation, and makes a crime out of things that are not crimes. A prohibition law strikes at the very principles upon which our government was founded."[21] Lincoln thus understood that sumptuary laws were contrary to the morality of American law—they were antithetical to the "principles upon which our government was founded"—because they criminalized an act that harmed no one but the user.

Likewise, in 1855 the Indiana Supreme Court declared a state prohibition law invalid, declaring, "Counsel say the maxim that you shall so use your own as not to injure another, justifies such a law by the legislature. But the maxim is misapplied; for it contemplates the free use, by the owner, of his property, but with such care as not to trespass upon his neighbor; while this prohibitory law forbids the owner to use his own in any manner, as a beverage. It is based on the principle that a man shall not use at all for enjoyment what his neighbor may abuse, a doctrine that would, if enforced by law in general practice, annihilate society, make eunuchs of all men, or drive them into the cells of the monks, and bring the human race to an end, or continue it under the direction of licensed county agents."[22] Notice that the court employs the sic utere tuo maxim discussed in Chapter 3—that is, individuals are at liberty to use their own LLP, so long as it does not injure others. The Indiana Supreme Court also grapples with a common perversion of the harm principle that is still evident today—the argument that an act results in legally cognizable harm if it harms the actor. The court correctly dismisses this argument, recognizing that one man's abuse of a substance harms only himself and cannot deprive other men of their liberty if liberty has any substantive meaning.

Eventually, however, the prohibitionists had their way, and in 1919 the Eighteenth Amendment was ratified, prohibiting the manufacture and sale of all intoxicating beverages within the United States.[23] The Prohibition Amendment represented the culmination of several decades of work by the so-called temperance movement which, despite its name, evolved to advocate not temperance but abstinence and eventually, legal prohibition. Prohibitionist groups such as the Woman's Christian Temperance Union and the Anti-Saloon League were founded and funded by Protestant denominations who asserted that the negative effects associated with alcohol, particularly its impact on family life, were immoral.[24] Leaders of the temperance movement concluded that although liquor did not always produce drunkenness or its ill effects, it was a dangerously addictive substance for which no safe level of consumption could be established or tolerated—an argument commonly used today in the context of the war on drugs.[25]

On a deeper level, as Jacob Sullum has pointed out, the Protestant condemnation of alcohol was not really based on any theological disagreement—after all, the Bible, both Old Testament and New, is replete with numerous references to the joys of temperate alcohol consumption. Instead, the drive for prohibition was fueled, at least in part, by a cultural divide between Protestants and non-Protestants, and between Protestants and non-Christians. Recent immigrant groups from Germany, Ireland, and Italy, who were primarily Catholic and Jewish, were perceived with hostility and distrust by American Protestants. The unabashed acceptance and use of alcohol by these immigrant groups highlighted the perceived cultural differences and intensified the desire of Protestants to impose prohibition.[26]

The Prohibition Amendment remained in effect for twenty-four violent, turbulent years, finally ended by ratification of the Twenty-First Amendment in 1933.[27] Much like the modern war on drugs, the Prohibition era glamorized alcohol in the eyes of many, encouraged disrespect for the rule of law, created a black-market trade dominated by organized crime, necessitated significantly expanded governmental expenditures, resulted in an unparalleled invasion of citizens' privacy, and put many Americans behinds bars.[28]

The only thing good about Prohibition is that it was enacted and repealed by legitimate means. The processes used to ban alcohol were those provided by the Framers in Article V of the Constitution—approval by two-thirds of both houses of Congress and ratification by three-fourths of the states.[29] Although the Prohibition Amendment altered the fundamental principle of residual individual sovereignty as it related to alcohol, it was validly enacted pursuant to constitutional procedures, and was therefore a legitimate exercise of governmental power.

Fortunately, the American people saw the error of their ways, mobilized themselves, and ratified a subsequent repeal amendment. The use of Article V amendment to both enact and repeal a prohibition against alcohol illustrates that, contrary to popular perception, Article V is not an insurmountable hurdle, but an appropriately high hurdle that the American people both can and will overcome when fundamental changes in government are necessary. Article V gives Americans the luxury of altering the principles of limited government or residual individual sovereignty when they desire, yet purposefully makes these alterations in fundamental principles difficult—no mere legislative majority will do. And as the Prohibition experience shows, Article V gives Americans the power to recognize and remedy their own mistakes.

LEGAL DRUGS

Other than America's brief failed experiment with alcohol prohibition, there was no federal law prohibiting recreational drug use until 1970, when President Nixon declared a national "war on drugs" and Congress enacted the Controlled Substances Act (CSA).[30] The CSA created five schedules of drugs, only one of which (Schedule I) cannot be lawfully possessed or sold. Drugs placed in Schedules II–V, by contrast, may be prescribed by a physician for medical treatment under certain circumstances. The characterization of a drug as illegal (Schedule I) or legal (Schedules II–V) turns on only one factor—whether the drug has a "currently accepted medical use in treatment in the United States."[31] Illegal drugs, by definition, have no currently accepted medical use. Legal drugs, by contrast, are drugs that are currently accepted as a medical treatment for a specific disease or condition, and thus may be sold to consumers.

Legal controlled substances—that is, those drugs in Schedules II–V—include many very intoxicating and potentially addictive substances, including many opiates, amphetamines, anabolic steroids, barbitals, and even methamphetamine.[32] The degree of regulation imposed on a legal drug decreases with each succeeding schedule, so Schedule II drugs are more tightly controlled than Schedule III and so on. The authority to determine a drug's scheduling rests with the attorney general, who may alter scheduling or even remove a drug from the list of controlled substances.[33] A drug's placement in a specific schedule hinges on its potential for abuse and its potential for physical or psycholog-ical dependence. A drug placed on Schedule II has a "high" potential for abuse, and its abuse may lead to "severe" physical or psychological dependence.[34] Schedule III drugs have a potential for abuse "less than the drugs or other sub-stances in schedules I or II" and abuse of them may lead to "moderate or low physical dependence or high psychological dependence."[35] Schedule IV drugs concomitantly pose a lower risk of abuse and dependence, and Schedule V lower still.[36]

There are literally thousands of drugs sold legally in the United States, both over the counter and by prescription, that may accurately be described as in-toxicating or mind-altering. Indeed, the most popular category of illicit drugs, after marijuana, is drugs that are lawfully used for medical purposes, including pain relievers, tranquilizers, stimulants, and sedatives.[37] Although they are manufactured lawfully only for medical treatment, drugs such as Codeine, Vi-codin, OxyContin, and Valium are popular recreational drugs, particularly with young persons, because they can often be obtained simply by raiding a parent's medicine cabinet. Yet nothing of real importance separates these legal psychotherapeutic drugs from their illegal counterparts, other than an implicit and hypocritical condemnation of getting high—or more precisely, getting high in certain ways.

ILLEGAL DRUGS

America now spends approximately thirty-five billion dollars each year to en-force its drug prohibitions, and has prisons and jails that are literally overflow-ing with drug offenders.[38] There are over 1.5 million arrests each year in Amer-ica for drug law violations, more than 80 percent of which are for simple possession.[39] Many of those arrested will serve time, and their incarceration is increasingly long, due to the enactment of uniform sentencing guidelines and "three strikes, you're out" laws. In 1983, only 9.3 percent of state prisoners were incarcerated for drug-related offenses; by 2002, this figure had soared to 24.7 percent.[40] In federal prisons the percentage of drug-related offenders is even higher; 55 percent of federal prisoners now serve time for drug offenses, more than double the rate in 1980.[41]

One of the most obvious inequities that has emerged from the drug war has been its impact on racial minorities, particularly African-Americans. African-Americans comprise only 12.9 percent of the American population, yet they comprise 32.5 percent of all drug arrests.[42] As discussed in Chapter 1, the disproportionate impact of the drug war on minority groups has exacerbated their sense of estrangement from community, contributed to an overall decline in participation and respect for government, and heightened racial tension.

There is a stereotype in America that African-Americans use drugs at a significantly higher rate than whites, but the data reveals this to be false: 49 percent of white Americans will try illicit drugs in their lifetime, whereas only 43 percent of African-Americans will.[43] If African-Americans use drugs less often than whites and comprise less than 13 percent of the population, why do they comprise almost one-third of all drug arrests? The most likely answer is that law enforcement focuses its drug enforcement efforts on communities populated predominantly by minorities, sweeping more minorities into the drug war net than whites. Little wonder that the war on drugs is often perceived by minorities to be a war on minorities.

Despite the incredible amounts of money and human resources devoted to the war on drugs, the rate of illicit drug usage has remained relatively constant from the mid-1970s until today.[44] This apparent futility of drug prohibition should eventually cause Americans to conduct some serious soul searching. The current legal framework permits many dangerous, mind-altering, and addictive drugs to be sold legally. We allow them to be sold simply because they have an accepted medical use. This is fine, as far as it goes, since it is undoubtedly the duty of government to protect the lives of its citizens by allowing them to use therapeutically beneficial drugs.

But implicit in the CSA's condemnation of drugs that lack a currently accepted medical use is a moral condemnation of drugs that are manufactured and used simply for fun, or a pretext for discrimination against the people who use them. After all, is there really anything wrong with consuming a substance because you like the way it makes you feel? Presumably not, since just about everything we ingest that is non-therapeutic (e.g., food) is ingested because we find its ingestion to be pleasurable. Or perhaps our legal condemnation of recreational drugs is based on a belief that there something inherently immoral about getting high? Unlikely, since most Americans, as witnessed by the widespread use and acceptance of alcohol and tobacco, enjoy ingesting substances for the purpose of inducing a recreational high. If it is not considered immoral per se to get high, why are some drugs legal while others are illegal?

Some have suggested that the difference between legal and illegal intoxicants is based on a belief that some intoxicants (the illegal ones) are more dangerous than others—that they induce a more intense or dangerous high that competent adults cannot handle. This argument is of course little more than paternalism, though many unabashedly believe that paternalism is a legitimate justification for laws prohibiting drug use. H. L. A. Hart, for example, argues that application of a harm principle to drug use is too quixotic, since it requires an assumption that adults are rational, intelligent, and self-aware, when in fact this is not the case.[45] The ineluctable intellectual demarcation is thus between those who believe that competent adults should be respected as capable of making their own decisions (even bad ones), and those who believe that competent adults are not always so competent, and therefore should be paternalistically protected from their own bad decisions.

The morality of American law espoused in this book takes the former view, not because it denies the possibility of competent adults making bad and self-harmful choices, but because respect for the equality of citizens, grounded in the twin principles of limited government and residual individual sovereignty, demands it. To recognize that some competent adults need to be protected from themselves is to disrespect them, treat them as children, and open the door to plenary governmental power that disregards individual autonomy against government. Paternalism is an instinctive and potentially constructive force, but its proper place lies in private compassion, education, and guidance, not public condemnation and punishment.

Invoking paternalism to restrict the liberty of competent adults is a destructive, demeaning, ultimately futile effort. It can be used to mask discriminatory animus against those individuals viewed as less intelligent, rational, or disciplined. The enactment of drug prohibitions during the 1970s came on the heels of great social upheaval, in which a majority of Americans felt threatened by long-haired hippies and minorities who appeared to reject traditional values. The publicly flaunted use of drugs during this period created a deep-seated, albeit inaccurate, stereotype that "bad," "dangerous," or "radical" people consume certain kinds of drugs.

But drugs do not make people bad, dangerous, or radical. Despite the government's insistence to the contrary, consuming drugs or getting high, alone, does not result in danger, either to one's self or others. Nineteen million Americans consume illicit drugs on a regular basis, and only a tiny subset of them commit crimes while high.[46] If an individual consumes a substance that induces intoxication and subsequently harms the life, liberty, or property of others, only one thing is clear: he must be held responsible for his harmful actions, and there is ample authority to impose punishment for the harm inflicted, without the need to restrict the liberty of law-abiding Americans who wish consume the intoxicating substance.

Since the morality of American law recognizes the legitimacy of external harm as a basis for restricting liberty, we will proceed to explore whether, or to what extent, there is any evidence suggesting that the most popular recreational drugs harm or reasonably threaten harm to the LLP of others.

Marijuana

Over 40 percent of Americans have tried marijuana.[47] Over fourteen million use it at least once a month.[48] Over three million use it every day.[49] Given these statistics, it should come as no surprise that almost 40 percent of all drug possession arrests in the United States are for possession of marijuana.[50]

The justifications proffered for spending the tremendous resources to find, arrest, prosecute, and incarcerate marijuana users include its potential to be a gateway drug, its potential to decrease cognitive function, and its association with violent or other anti-social behaviors. While there is some data regarding all of these points, the data is often significantly overstated and its deficiencies rarely revealed.

MARIJUANA AS A "GATEWAY" DRUG

Marijuana's potential as an entree to perceived "harder" illicit drugs—the so-called gateway hypothesis—is repeatedly touted as a justification for its continued prohibition. Yet evidence of a causal link between marijuana use and the use of other drugs is surprisingly sparse. There is reliable evidence that young adults who use marijuana by age seventeen are two to five times more likely to use, abuse, or become dependent on other drugs or alcohol.[51] At first blush, this sort of evidence seems to prove that marijuana usage causes the use or abuse of other drugs or alcohol. But an association between marijuana use and the use of other drugs is just that: an association, not a causal link. An association between A and B, no matter how strong, does not establish that A causes B. There are many possible reasons why young marijuana users are more likely to use or abuse other drugs or alcohol, and the authors of studies that establish association caution that "it is not possible to draw strong causal conclusions solely on the basis of the associations shown."[52]

Young persons who decide to experiment with drugs, for whatever reason, will generally begin with readily available, cheap, and mild intoxicants. This does not mean, however, that these mild intoxicants wrap themselves around users' minds and bodies and effectively force them to use harder drugs. Instead, those who experiment with these drugs, particularly at a young age, are likely to exhibit personal, social, psychological, or attitudinal attributes that predispose them to experiment, take risks, enjoy the physical or social aspects of intoxication, or rebel against authority. In addition, an individual who tries marijuana may conclude that it is pleasurable and relatively safe, which may encourage future experimentation with other intoxicants.[53] Drug use at an early age, moreover, presumably opens access to drug dealers who then may push harder and more lucrative drugs.[54] Indeed, a desire to stop access to harder drugs was one motivation behind the Netherlands' decriminalization of marijuana, which appears to have been successful, at least with regard to reducing the number of marijuana users who subsequently use cocaine.[55]

Moreover, if a mere association between marijuana use and the use of other drugs is a sufficient basis to criminalize marijuana, we will need to criminalize cigarettes and alcohol as well. There is a strong association between cigarettes and illicit drug use. According to the National Survey on Drug Use and Health, young persons age twelve to seventeen who smoked cigarettes were eight times more likely to use illicit drugs than non-smokers.[56] Similarly, young persons who were heavy drinkers were thirteen times more likely to use illicit drugs than non-drinkers.[57] Yet even in the face of strong associational data such as this, we must understand that association is not causation. There are many reasons why people decide to try drugs, and it makes common sense that marijuana, cigarettes, and alcohol—all readily available and relatively cheap—are often the first drugs of choice. Of the millions of Americans who try these first-choice drugs, many of them will enjoy the experience, and consequently may be emboldened to try other drugs in the future. But arbitrary legal prohibitions aside, there is nothing inherently wrong with trying a recreational drug in the first place, and nothing inherently wrong with liking it and trying another recreational drug later on.

SELF-HARMS ASSOCIATED WITH MARIJUANA

Another reason often cited as a basis for retaining legal prohibition is that marijuana is harmful to the user, that it is highly addictive and dangerous to the mind. We know that the prevalence of marijuana abuse and dependence behavior[58] is very low—1.1 and 0.4 percent of the U.S. population, respectively.[59] This population of problem users declines markedly with age, suggesting that marijuana dependence and abuse is significantly age-related, and something that the vast majority of users, even heavy users, tend to outgrow.[60] Moreover, there is substantial evidence that marijuana dependence symptoms are mild and short-lived compared to drugs such as heroin, cocaine, alcohol, or tobacco.[61]

So what are the harmful effects potentially posed by marijuana? Studies have shown that heavy use of cannabis can result in a short-term decrease in memory, psychomotor functioning, and manual dexterity.[62] One recent study suggested that these deficits continue and are compounded by long-term cannabis use,[63] but this study suffered from numerous important shortcomings. First, study participants consisted of individuals who were seeking treatment for cannabis dependence and who likely suffered from greater cognitive defects generally, either because they exhibited antisocial behavior and consequently were ordered by a court to seek drug treatment, or because they suffered from other disorders such as depression, anxiety, or attention deficit/hyperactivity disorder (ADHD) that contributes to their dependency.[64] Furthermore, because the study did not exclude individuals suffering from psychiatric conditions such as depression or anxiety, those receiving psychiatric drugs that may negatively impact cognitive function, or those with a history of regular use of or dependence on alcohol or other drugs, the ability to draw a causal link between reduced cognition and long-term cannabis usage is substantially weakened.[65] Finally, and perhaps most important, the study measured cognitive functioning only at a single snapshot of seventeen hours after last cannabis usage, making it impossible to determine whether the decreased function continued beyond this short time frame.[66]

Other studies, including a meta-analysis of available data, indicate that marijuana use does not cause long-term cognitive impairment.[67] More significantly, a recent longitudinal study conducted by Canadian researchers concluded that "marijuana does not have a long-term negative impact on global intelligence."[68] The study did conclude, not surprisingly, that marijuana produces cognitive changes during the period of active high, but they do not extend beyond short-term intoxication. The only negative effect discovered was a 4.1 point average decrease in IQ for heavy, current users of marijuana—defined as greater than five joints per week.[69] Notably, these IQ losses disappeared with cessation of marijuana use, and former heavy users experienced no observable IQ deficit compared to non-users.[70] Those who smoked fewer than five joints per week experienced no demonstrable IQ effect at all.[71]

Even assuming that marijuana imposes some risks upon its users, we should query whether these risks, which are by definition voluntarily self-imposed, are relevant considerations in determining its legality. Under the morality of American law, activities that may result in self-harm are not legitimately proscribable. If self-harm may provide a legitimate basis for governmental restriction of liberty, the sphere of individual liberty is essentially non-existent and the realm of governmental power is correspondingly unlimited. Citizens could be thrown in jail for eating fast food, having sex without a condom, hang-gliding, riding a bike without a helmet, swimming without a life preserver, and other potentially dangerous activities. Granting the government a power to prevent citizens from harming themselves is diametrically opposed to the foundational principles of limited government and residual individual sovereignty. Unless there is some reasonable evidence that suggests that marijuana use threatens harm to others, prohibiting it is an illegitimate exercise of governmental power. We will now proceed to explore whether evidence of such external harm exists.

EXTERNAL HARMS ASSOCIATED WITH MARIJUANA

Some might contend that marijuana legitimately may be banned because its users, like users of other drugs, are prone to steal the property of others—a cognizable property deprivation—to support their habit. Even assuming that this is true—a big assumption given the low cost of marijuana—we should not accept it as a valid harm-based argument. If a marijuana user steals another person's property to support his marijuana habit, there is indeed an external harm that the government legitimately may punish—the theft. Once the theft qua theft has been punished, there is no legitimate basis for further governmental action. The property harm has been remedied, and the thief's use of marijuana (or any other drug, for that matter) is simply irrelevant. If Susan steals Robert's computer and pawns it because she needs to pay off her credit cards, she legitimately may be prosecuted for stealing the computer, not because she has failed to use her credit cards in a responsible manner. We may find her irresponsible use of credit to be immature, stupid, or immoral, but it harms only herself. But when Susan harms Robert's property interests, Susan has crossed the line drawn by the morality of American law.

Indeed, we should think long and hard about giving any further credence to the "drugs made me do it" hypothesis that links drug use and crime. Although many arrestees admit using drugs at the time they committed the crime, do we really believe that the drug qua drug caused the crime to be committed? In the broadest conceivable sense, anything can be said to cause anything. But for Richard's decision to drop out of school in the ninth grade, he would not have been unemployed, and if he had not been unemployed he would not have resorted to robbing the liquor store. But the robbery Richard committed was not caused by his dropping out of school or being unemployed; it was caused by Richard. As a society we should be firm about the proper locus of responsibility for crimes that harm the LLP of others—the person who committed the crime, not the unfortunate circumstances of his life or the drug he consumed. We live in an age in which acceptance of personal responsibility for our actions is at its nadir, and allowing citizens to shift the burden of responsibility for their crimes to drugs only exacerbates this societal decline. To paraphrase a slogan often employed in the context of gun control, drugs do not make people commit crimes—people commit crimes.

Heroin and Other Opiates

The opiate family of drugs—commonly referred to as narcotics—are all made from the opium poppy and include opium, morphine, heroin, and codeine. There are also synthetic opiates, such as Demerol and Dolophine, and semi-synthetic opiates, such as oxycodone (OxyContin, Percodan, Percocet) and hydrocodone (Vicodin, Lortab), which mimic the effects of opiates, but are not solely derived from the opium poppy.[72] Narcotics relieve pain and produce sedation and relaxation.

Morphine, opium, and heroin were readily available and widely consumed in nineteenth-century America, sold over the counter in pharmacies and grocery stores and by mail.[73] They were sold as laudanum (a morphine-alcohol mixture), teething remedies for infants, "soothing syrups," diarrhea remedies, and treatments for "women's trouble."[74] Morphine became so popular during the Civil War that morphine addiction was referred to as the "soldier's disease."[75]

Perhaps the most remarkable characteristic about opiate usage in the 1800s is that, although many users were undeniably addicted, the addiction did not interfere with the addict's family, work, or social life so long as the opiate could be obtained on a regular basis. Indeed, opiates, particularly morphine, were often recommended by physicians as a substitute for alcohol. Although physicians knew morphine to be addictive, many concluded that the negative effects of morphine addiction were much to be preferred to those of alcohol addiction. For example, a physician writing in 1889 concluded, "I would urge the substitution of morphine instead of alcohol for all to whom such a craving is an incurable propensity. In this way I have been able to bring peacefulness and quiet to many disturbed and distracted homes. . . . I might, had I time and space, enlarge by statistics to prove the law-abiding qualities of opium-eating peoples, but of this anyone can perceive for himself, if he carefully watches and reflects on the quiet, introspective gaze of the morphine habitué and compares it with the riotous devil-may-care leer of the drunkard."[76] A British physician, writing in 1873, similarly observed that opiate users "are not uproarious, and don't swear. There are none of the deeds of brutal violence that are inspired by beer, and none of the foul language."[77] The ability of opiate addicts to maintain jobs, support families, and live a normal life if provided access to their opiate of choice is, in fact, the basis for successful efforts to treat heroin addicts by providing them with the synthetic narcotic methadone.[78]

Of all the opiates, heroin is perhaps the most feared and reviled. Mention of the word conjures up images of anorexic drug addicts in tattered clothes, lying on a floor amid dirty needles. But as the success of methadone treatment clinics has proved, many of the negative side effects of heroin addiction are due to heroin's illegal status. Individuals addicted to heroin are forced to buy it from pushers, and the street heroin obtained is subject to great variability in both purity and potency. Before it reaches the street, heroin is diluted many times by various white substances, including quinine, powdered milk, baking soda, laxatives, and sugar.[79] As with other opiates, the active ingredient in heroin is morphine and, once consumed, heroin is converted back into morphine, leading Consumers Union to conclude that "it is difficult to distinguish an addict who takes a grain of heroin a day from one who takes a grain of morphine a day[.]"[80] Heroin is several times stronger than morphine, however, so injecting it produces an instantaneous but short-lived ecstatic reaction, followed by a deep relaxation that lasts for several hours.[81] Despite its appealing high, and contrary to the popular belief that heroin use is an epidemic, there are only 166,000 Americans who have used heroin in the last 30 days.[82]

The bottom line is that heroin, like other opiates, is highly addictive, but it is not a particularly dangerous drug, nor does its use lead to any outwardly violent behavior. It is actually very difficult to overdose on heroin, particularly for a user who has developed tolerance. Many of the deaths labeled as overdoses are in fact not overdoses, but likely the result of quinine poisoning or a fatal mixing of heroin with alcohol or barbiturates.[83] And to the extent that heroin addicts commit crimes, responsibility for their crimes must rest with themselves, not heroin. The use of heroin itself does not result in aggression toward others—to the contrary, heroin users, like morphine users, are sedated and tranquil. The risks posed by heroin, to the extent that they exist at all, are purely self-harms, which are not a legitimate basis for the restriction of individual liberty.

Hallucinogens

There are many different types of hallucinogens—sometimes called psychedelics—and some continuing debate regarding what exactly a "hallucinogen" is, but for present purposes suffice it to say that the CSA classifies marijuana (which has already been discussed), PCP, Ecstasy, LSD, mescaline, and peyote as hallucinogens. There other substances that induce a hallucinogenic effect that are not classified by the CSA, including certain types of mushrooms, nutmeg, and some types of morning glory seeds, yet their recreational use is limited and they are correspondingly unregulated.[84] At present, there are only 929,000 Americans who have used hallucinogens in the last thirty days—a significant number, but far from an epidemic.[85] The most likely reason for this low rate of current use is that unlike many other drugs, hallucinogens do not cause physical dependence. Users of hallucinogens, even long-term users, will not suffer from physical withdrawal symptoms if they stop usage.

PCP ("angel dust") is perhaps the most widely feared hallucinogen and, partially as a result of this fear, it has been tried by only 2.8 percent of Americans, zero percent of whom are regular users.[86] The lack of regular users among those who have tried PCP is likely attributable to its unpleasant high and ease of overdose, leading the National Institute on Drug Abuse to concede that "[a]fter using PCP once, many people will not knowingly use it again."[87] Unlike other hallucinogens, PCP causes users to feel disassociated or detached from their surroundings and to experience a sense of strength and invulnerability. There are anecdotal reports of PCP-induced aggression, but it would be a large and unsupported leap to conclude that PCP use, rather than the individual involved, should bear responsibility for such aggression. In those instances in which a person high on PCP harms another, the morality of American law permits punishment of the harmful act, without the need for restricting the liberty of other competent adults.

Another hallucinogen in vogue today is Ecstasy or MDMA (3–4 methylenedioxymethamphetamine), a synthetic "club drug" with both hallucinogenic and stimulant characteristics. Despite its limited availability as a Schedule I drug, almost 5 percent of Americans have tried Ecstasy at least once—mostly young adults—but only 0.2 percent of Americans are regular users.[88] Ecstasy affects serotonin in the brain, causing users to experience a sense of euphoria, well-being, and affection toward others—the genesis of its nicknames "hug" and the "love drug." Ecstasy use has been associated with elevated body temperature and dehydration, yet it is unclear whether these effects are caused by Ecstasy or the hot, crowded conditions of nightclubs and raves at which the drug is commonly consumed.

The most popular hallucinogen in the 1960s and '70s was undoubtedly LSD, and although its popularity has waned, it is still the most widely sampled hallucinogen besides marijuana. Almost 10 percent of Americans have tried LSD, yet only 0.1 percent of the population has used it in the last 30 days.[89] Despite its reputation as a hard drug, the overwhelming majority of people who try LSD does not become regular users, much less lose control over their lives, most likely because, as with other hallucinogens, LSD use results in tolerance, but not physical addiction, so even heavy users will experience no withdrawal symptoms.[90]

The use of LSD, peyote, mescaline, and to a lesser extent Ecstasy, creates altered consciousness, surreal visions, a sense of trust and affection, intensification of sound, and a kaleidoscope of colors. Because of these effects, hallucinogens historically have been associated with spiritual and religious ceremonies. Native Americans, for example, used peyote in specific ceremonies for hundreds of years until the CSA and state laws banned them.[91] Prominent intellectuals such as Timothy Leary and Aldous Huxley believed that LSD raised consciousness and provided the means by which Buddha, Mohammed, Krishna, Jesus, and other religious leaders achieved their spiritual insight.[92] In the mid-twentieth century, before passage of the CSA, psychiatrists and psychologists tried LSD themselves in an attempt to better understand the psychotic state and even prescribed it as an adjunct treatment to psychotherapy.[93]

There is no evidence that hallucinogenic drugs harm either their users or anyone else. An occasional "bad trip" is experienced, but most users find their experience with hallucinogens to be positive, allowing them to experience feelings of tolerance, self-awareness, reduced materialism and egocentricity, and a heightened appreciation for art and music.[94] There is no notable self-harm caused by the use of hallucinogens, nor is there any external harm. In short, the only thing hallucinogens seem to do is cause users to be temporarily euphoric and spiritual, effects that are hardly sufficient to justify restricting the liberty of competent adults to use them.

Cocaine, Crack, and Other Amphetamines

Cocaine, crack, Benzedrine, and methamphetamine are amphetamines, central nervous system stimulants. Cocaine and crack (a crystalline form of cocaine that is smoked) are natural substances derived from coca leaves, whereas most other amphetamines are synthetically derived. Because amphetamines have accepted therapeutic uses as appetite suppressants, antidepressants, hyperactivity treatments, and anesthesia, they are legal, albeit controlled, substances under the CSA. Amphetamines, particularly if injected, are potentially addictive and high doses may induce agitation, sleeplessness, paranoia, hyperactivity, and occasional aggressive behavior.[95] A little over 8 percent of Americans have used such stimulants, and fewer than one percent use them on a regular basis.[96]

Cocaine and crack remain the most popular amphetamines in America, though as with all other drugs, the incidence of regular use is much smaller than many believe.[97] Cocaine historically was viewed as a positive stimulant, much as caffeine is today, and was used for hundreds of years by natives of the Andes Mountains, who still chew coca leaves on a regular basis with no apparent problems or addiction.[98] Europeans learned of the salutary effects of cocaine and preferred to mix cocaine with beverages, most notably a beverage called "Mariani's Wine," a mixture of red wine and coca popular with fasting Christian ascetics, including Pope Leo XIII.[99] Americans, too, enjoyed cocaine-laced beverages, as evidenced by the name of the now-reformulated Coca-Cola, which originally contained a mixture of cocaine and caffeine derived from the kola nut.[100] The widespread use of these cocaine-laced beverages does not appear to have created any adverse effects, suggesting that "the imbibing of beverages containing small amounts of coca is [no] more damaging to the mind or body than the drinking of coffee or tea."[101]

The epidemic drug du jour, methamphetamine—"speed," "meth," or "ice," —is a potent amphetamine, though fewer than 5 percent of Americans have ever tried it and only 0.6 percent are current users.[102] Congress in recent years has responded to the perceived meth crisis by enacting laws that enhance the penalties associated with meth possession or use.[103] The fear associated with meth is so strong that some lawmakers have begun to call for tighter controls on the availability of pseudoephedrine (PSE), a component used to make methamphetamine that is available over the counter in many cough and cold medications. Proposed restrictions have included limiting the amount of PSE consumers can purchase in a thirty-day period and limiting the sale of PSE cold and cough products to behind a pharmacy counter.[104] Amphetamines, like all other drugs (and indeed most ingested substances), can be abused, and their abuse can result in harm to the user.

But as this book has asserted, the mere potential of an activity to harm the actor is an illegitimate basis for restricting the actor's liberty. Virtually any activity, if conducted irresponsibly, can pose a risk of harm to the actor. If a mere risk of self-harm is a legitimate basis for restricting individual autonomy, our nation, founded on a philosophy of limited government and residual individual autonomy, is neither the nation it was intended to be nor the one it should be.

America's drug laws are a stark illustration of how far we have drifted from the original philosophy that animated the founding generation and their memorial to us, the Constitution. They join a long list of other laws with this dubious distinction, including laws regulating whether and whom we can marry, whether, with whom, and how we can have sex, how we can procreate or avoid procreation, and what kind of medical providers and treatment we can use.

America started with a concept of limited government, designed to protect and improve the life, liberty, and property of citizens, and has ended with a concept of unlimited government, capable of restricting our life, liberty, and property in the name of protecting us from ourselves. America started with a concept of residual individual sovereignty, designed to respect the autonomy and equality of citizens, and has ended with a concept of limited liberty, presumptively unavailable and parsed out reluctantly by an all-powerful sovereign. America started with a concept of federalism, designed to better protect individual liberty, and has ended with a concept of nationalism, exercised vigorously to stifle controversial liberties recognized by the state. We have done all of this, experienced these foundational changes, without the benefit of a constitutional amendment. We have allowed mere legislative majorities, often motivated by morality, passion, and prejudice, to take away our most precious liberties. We should be ashamed.

Notes

CHAPTER 1. INTRODUCTION

1. I will offer a specific definition of legally cognizable harm in Chapter 2.
2. This is the message of the Supremacy Clause, which declares that the Constitution "shall be the supreme Law of the Land; and the Judges in every State shall be bound thereby, any Thing in the Constitution or Laws of any state to the Contrary notwithstanding." U.S. Const. art. VI.
3. Much of this amnesia is attributable to pragmatic considerations that arose during the Great Depression, which necessitated a broad interpretation of national powers in order to validate federal laws aimed at ameliorating deplorable economic conditions. For a concise statement of the constitutional revolution that occurred during the New Deal era, see Michael Les Benedict, The Blessings of Liberty: A Concise History of the Constitution of the United States 284–98 (1996). See also Bruce Ackerman, We the People: Foundations 105–30 (1991).
4. The norm in constitutional adjudication is for the court to apply so-called "rationality review," by which the law is presumed constitutional unless the plaintiff can convince the court that the law lacks any conceivable "rational basis." See Washington v. Glucksberg, 521 U.S. 702, 728 (1997). The only time the modern Court will shift the burden onto the government to justify the necessity of a law is when the Court concludes that the law interferes with a "fundamental" right, which has been narrowly defined to encompass only

those that the Court considers to be "deeply rooted" in the nation's history and tradition, *see id.* at 720–21, or if the law singles out a "suspect" class for different legal treatment. *See* Vacco v. Quill, 521 U.S. 793, 799 (1997); Romer v. Evans, 517 U.S. 620, 631 (1996).

5. A recent book by Randy Barnett makes a powerful case that misinterpretation of various constitutional provisions has resulted in a "lost Constitution" that disregards the importance of individual liberty. RANDY E. BARNETT, RESTORING THE LOST CONSTITUTION: THE PRESUMPTION OF LIBERTY (Princeton Univ. Press 2004). Though I agree with Professor Barnett's thesis, my aim here is different. I will demonstrate that there is a morality underlying American law itself—both federal and state—that defines the legitimate reach of governmental power. The loss of this morality has created a ubiquitous and intractable tension between public morality and individual privacy. I will then offer a specific analytical framework, consistent with the morality of American law, that can significantly reduce this tension.

6. Griswold v. Connecticut, 381 U.S. 479 (1965).

7. For an excellent discussion of the "overcriminalization" phenomenon in America, see Erik Luna, *The Overcriminalization Phenomenon,* 54 AM. U.L. REV. 703 (2005).

8. *See, e.g.,* MONT. CODE ANN. § 7-5-4104 (hats); W.VA. CODE § 61-6-16 (same); Okla. R. N.C. Admin. Dist. Ct. R. 1.8 (no hats in courtroom); Tex. Dist. Ct. McLennan Cty. L.R. 3(h) (same); Tex. Dist. Ct. Coryell Cty. Ct. Personnel (same); IND. CODE § 14-22-9-1(a) (fishing); Abilene, Tx. Ordinances § 20-6(a)–(b) (fishing); Fort Smith, Ark. Ordinances § 14-29 (slingshot); KY. REV. STAT. § 436.600 (colored baby chicks); Sulpher, La. Ordinances § 8-136(a)(1) (indecent language); Cumberland, Md. Ordinances § 15-52 (same); Rockville, Md. Ordinances § 13-53(a) (same); FLA. STAT. § 877.16 (displaying deformed animal); ARIZ. REV. STAT. § 36-601(A)(13) (spitting); LA. REV. STAT. ANN. § 40:1121 (same); MASS. GEN. LAWS ch. 270, § 14 (same); N.H. REV. STAT. ANN. § 147:18 (same); N.M. STAT. ANN. § 30-8-12(D) (same); VA. CODE ANN. § 18.2-322 (same); MISS. CODE ANN. § 97-29-43 (teaching polygamy); Peabody, Ma. Ordinances § 24-18 (garage sales); Darien, Ct. Ordinances § 30-4 (same); Narragansett, R.I. Ordinances § 14-197(a) (same); Holyoke, Ma. Ordinances § 66-91(a) (same); CALIF. PENAL CODE § 332(a) (fortune telling); MINN. STAT. § 609.725(4) (same); N.Y. PENAL LAW § 165.35 (same); N.C. GEN. STAT. § 14-401.5 (same); OKLA. STAT. tit. 21 § 931 (same); 18 PA. CONS. STAT. ANN. § 7104(a) (same); S.C. CODE ANN. § 16-17-690 (same); WIS. STAT. § 947.02(4) (same); Bartlesville, Okla. Ordinances § 3-25(A) (cats in yard); East Lansing, Mich. Ordinances § 4-4 (same); NEV. REV. STAT. ANN. § 201.280 (liquor near religious camp meeting); Mount Laurel, N.J. Ordinances § 109-1(A) (annoying drunk in house); S.C. CODE ANN. § 53-1-40 (Sunday law); ALA. CODE § 13A-12-1 (same); MICH. COMP. LAWS § 435.251 (same); N.J. STAT. ANN. § 2C:33-26 (same). State laws limiting liquor sales on Sunday are ubiquitous, though they vary significantly from state to state and often allow individual localities to decide whether to be wet or dry. *See, e.g.,* IDAHO CODE §§ 23-303, 23-307, 23-312, 23-614, 23-615, 23-927; NEB. REV. STAT. § 53-179; FLA. STAT. ANN. §§ 562.11, 567.01, 568.02; TENN. CODE ANN. §§ 57-3-106, 57-3-406, 57-4-204.

9. I am alluding to the famous statement that the United States was designed to be "a nation of laws, not men." *See* JOHN ADAMS, 4 THE WORKS OF JOHN ADAMS 106 (Charles Francis Adams ed., Little Brown 1850) (1774). Adams likely borrowed the phrase from

British political philosopher James Harrington, whose *Oceana* quixotically refers to the British Commonwealth as "an Empire of Laws and not of Men." JAMES HARRINGTON, THE COMMONWEALTH OF OCEANA, *reprinted in* THE OCEANA & OTHER WORKS OF JAMES HARRINGTON 45 (John Toland ed., A. Millar Pub. 1737) (1656). Harrington attributes the formation of this idea to Aristotle and Livy. *Id.*

10. James Harrington, whose work was influential at the time of the American Revolution, said, "Laws that are perplexed, intricate, tedious and voluminous, leave the greatest arbitrary power to the judge or judicatory; and, raining snares on the people, make the most corrupt government." JAMES HARRINGTON, A SYSTEM OF POLITICS, *reprinted in* JAMES HARRINGTON: THE COMMONWEALTH OF OCEANA & A SYSTEM OF POLITICS 289 (J.G.A. Pocock ed., 1992) (1700).

11. CNN 2004 Presidential Election Exit Poll, *available at* http://www.cnn.com/ELECTION/2004/pages/results/states/US/P/00/epolls.0.html.

12. Americans may feel powerless to alter the path of pop culture, but they are in fact not. Individuals who disapprove of unnecessarily violent or sexually explicit media should not watch or purchase it. Individuals are free to opt instead to read a good book. And it is still possible for parents to limit their children's exposure to offensive media. Abiding by and educating one's children about personal values are the essence of maturity and private morality.

13. The two most likely culprits are abortion and same-sex marriage. The 2004 presidential election exit polls revealed deep division among Americans on these two issues. For abortion, 55% of Americans believe it should be "mostly legal" (34%) or "always legal" (21%) whereas 42% think it should be "mostly illegal" (26%) or "always illegal" (16%). *Id.* Americans are similarly divided on same-sex marriage, with 37% stating that there should be "no legal recognition" for same-sex couples, 35% stating that same-sex couples should be allowed to enter into "civil unions," and only 25% stating that same-sex couples should be permitted to "legally marry." *Id.*

14. This is based on a poll conducted in September 2005 by the American Bar Association. The poll asked respondents whether they strongly agreed, somewhat agreed, neither agreed nor disagreed, somewhat disagreed, strongly disagreed, or did not know how they felt about recent public statements critical of the judiciary. The statement quoted in the text was a statement from U.S. Congressman Lamar Smith, a Republican from Texas. Of the poll respondents, 29% strongly agreed with Representative Smith's statement and an additional 27% somewhat agreed. *See* Martha Neil, *Half of U.S. Sees "Judicial Activism Crisis": ABA Journal Survey Results Surprise Some Legal Experts,* ABA J. e-Rep., Sept. 30, 2005, *available at* http://www.abanet.org/journal/ereport/s30survey.html.

15. Justice Scalia is one of the most forceful proponents of this view: "Let me be clear that I have nothing against homosexuals, or any other group, promoting their agenda through normal democratic means. Social perceptions of sexual and other morality change over time, and every group has the right to persuade its fellow citizens that its view of such matters is the best. . . . But persuading one's fellow citizens is one thing, and imposing one's views in absence of democratic majority will is something else. . . . What Texas has chosen to do [criminalizing homosexual sodomy] is well within the range of traditional democratic action, and its hand should not be stayed through the invention of a brand-

new 'constitutional right' by a Court that is impatient of democratic change." Lawrence v. Texas, 539 U.S. 558, 603 (2003) (Scalia, J., dissenting). It is not just the conservative wing of the Court that employs the orthodox response, however; a majority of the current Court—including its most liberal members—employed it to deny an asserted liberty, explicitly granted by state law, to grow and consume marijuana for medicinal use. *See* Gonzales v. Raich, 125 S. Ct. 2195, 2215 (2005) ("As the Solicitor General confirmed during oral argument, the [federal controlled substances] statute authorizes procedures for the reclassification of Schedule I drugs. But perhaps even more important than these legal avenues is the democratic process, in which the voices of voters allied with these respondents may one day be heard in the halls of Congress.").

16. *See* City of New Orleans v. Dukes, 427 U.S. 297, 303 (1976) ("[T]he judiciary may not sit as a superlegislature to judge the wisdom or desirability of legislative policy determinations made in areas that neither affect fundamental rights nor proceed along suspect lines"); *see also* Washington v. Glucksberg, 521 U.S. 702, 720 (1997) ("[B]y extending constitutional protection to an asserted right or liberty interest we, to a great extent, place the matter outside the arena of public debate and legislative action. We must therefore 'exercise the utmost care whenever we are asked to break new ground in this field,' lest the liberty protected by the Due Process Clause be subtly transformed into the policy preferences of the members of the Court.").

17. F.A. HAYEK, THE CONSTITUTION OF LIBERTY 117 (1960).

18. As Penn Kimball concluded, "If casting a vote is the most elemental form of political participation, and if one collects data on who does and does not vote in America, those most often outside the system are the poor, the non-White, the young, and the uneducated. . . . As long as great segments of the population do not take part in the formal expression of popular participation, their sense of involvement will be minimal." PENN KIMBALL, THE DISCONNECTED 61 (1972). A majority of individuals age 18 to 24 are not registered to vote. U.S. CENSUS BUREAU, CURRENT POPULATION SURVEY tbl. 2 (Nov. 2000). Non-registration is highest for Hispanic (76.8%) and African-American (51.3%) youths. *Id.* By comparison, a majority of white 18-to-24-year-olds (51.7%) are registered to vote. *Id.*

19. In 1958, the American National Election Study revealed that 73% of Americans trusted the government to do the right thing "just about always or most of the time." *See* Robert J. Blendon, et al., *Changing Attitudes in America, in* WHY PEOPLE DON'T TRUST GOVERNMENT 206 (Joseph S. Nye et al. eds., 1997). By 1996, this figure had dropped to 25%—a precipitous decline. *Id.* Between 1964 and 1994, the number of Americans who believed that the "government is run by a few big interests looking out for themselves" jumped from 29% to 76%. *Id.* at 207. During the same period, the percentage of Americans who believed that "public officials don't care about what people like me think" soared from 36% to 66%. *Id.*

20. LANI GUINIER, THE TYRANNY OF THE MAJORITY 10 (1994). One of the solutions offered by Professor Guinier is the use of cumulative voting, whereby each voter is assigned an equal number of multiple votes which can be used strategically and collectively to express the relative intensity of voting preferences. *See id.* at 14–15, 149. The cumulative voting theory is designed to enable substantive legal change through a procedural change

in voting. *Id.* at 14. The theory set forth in this book likewise seeks to enable substantive change, not through procedural changes, but through returning to a constitutional theory embraced by the Framers that would likely reduce the sense of disenfranchisement of minority groups.

21. As Michael Lawrence has observed, "It is *OUR individual freedom*—and we must reclaim it from government. If we continue to accept this status quo, we are just timid sheep, as Tocqueville predicted." Michael Anthony Lawrence, *Reviving a Natural Right: The Freedom of Autonomy,* 42 WILLAMETTE L. REV. 123, 147 (2006) (emphasis in original). Lawrence's reference is to Tocqueville's *Democracy in America,* in which Tocqueville described the threat of democratic sovereignty thus: "The [democratic] sovereign . . . spreads a fine mesh of uniform, minute, and complex rules, through which not even the most original minds and most vigorous souls can poke their heads above the crowd. . . . Rather than tyrannize, he inhibits, represses, saps, stifles, and stultifies, and in the end he reduces each nation to nothing but a flock of timid and industrious animals, with the government as its shepherd." ALEXIS DE TOCQUEVILLE, DEMOCRACY IN AMERICA 819 (Arthur Goldhammer trans., Library of Am. 2004) (1835).

22. In this respect I agree with Roger Pilon's insightful conclusion that "[T]he issue, in the end, is one of right and wrong—of what it is, in particular, we may do to another by right. And that issue will be finally resolved . . . by going behind the Constitution to the rigorous, analytical theory of rights that alone can legitimately form its broad texture, that alone can justify our resort to force, which is what government, in the end, is all about." Roger Pilon, *Legislative Activism, Judicial Activism, & the Decline of Private Sovereignty,* 4 CATO J. 813, 832 (1985).

CHAPTER 2. THE MORALITY OF AMERICAN LAW

1. *See generally* THOMAS HOBBES, LEVIATHAN (C.B. MacPherson ed., 1968) (1651). There is no such thing, in a Leviathan government, of rights retained by the people, since subjects cede all of their liberty to the sovereign in return for its protection and retain nothing. Hobbes's view of absolute sovereignty was the norm on the European continent. *See also* JEREMY BENTHAM, A FRAGMENT ON GOVERNMENT 218 (F.C. Montague ed., Oxford Univ. Press 1951) (emphasis in original) ("[T]he authority of the supreme body [i.e., the sovereign] cannot, *unless limited by express convention,* be said to have any assignable, any certain bounds. That to say there is any act they *cannot* do, to speak of any thing of their's as being *illegal,* as being *void;* to speak of their exceeding their *authority* (whatever be the phrase)—their *power,* their *right,* is, however common, an abuse of language.").

2. U.S. CONST. pmbl.

3. The Declaration of Independence makes this clear: "We hold these Truths to be self-evident, that all Men are created equal, that they are endowed by their Creator with certain inalienable Rights, that among these are Life, Liberty, and the Pursuit of Happiness—That to secure these Rights, Governments are instituted among Men, deriving their just Powers from the Consent of the Governed. . . ." THE DECLARATION OF INDEPENDENCE para. 2.

4. MD. CONST. art. I (1776).

5. DEL. DECLARATION OF RIGHTS § 5 (1776) ("[P]ersons intrusted with the Legislative and Executive Powers are the Trustees and Servants of the public"); GA. CONST. pmbl. (1777) ("We, therefore, the representatives of the people, from whom all power originates, and for whose benefit all government is intended, by virtue of the power delegated to us, do ordain and declare"); MASS. CONST. art. V (1780) ("All power residing originally in the people, and being derived from them"); N.J. CONST. pmbl. (1776) ("Whereas all the constitutional authority ever possessed by the kings of Great Britain over these colonies . . . was, by compact, derived from the people, and held of them, for the common interest of the whole society"); N.Y. CONST. art. I (1777) ("This convention, therefore, in the name and by the authority of the good people of this State, doth ordain, determine, and declare that no authority shall, on any presence whatever, be exercised over the people or members of this State but such as shall be derived from and granted by them."); N.C. CONST. art. I (1776) ("That all political power is vested in and derived from the people only"); PA. CONST. art. IV (1776) ("That all power being originally inherent in, and consequently derived from, the people"); VT. CONST. art. V. (1777) ("That all power being originally inherent in, and consequently, derived from, the people"); VA. CONST. § 2 (1776) ("That all power is vested in, and consequently derived from, the people").

6. At the time not all citizens were permitted to cast votes (e.g., women and African-Americans). The "People of the several States" directly elected members to the U.S. House and indirectly (through their state legislatures) elected members to the U.S. Senate. U.S. CONST. art. I, §§ 2, 3. The Seventeenth Amendment, ratified in 1913, permitted direct election of U.S. senators. U.S. CONST. amend. XVII.

7. *See* THE FEDERALIST NO. 46 (James Madison) ("The federal and state governments are in fact but different agents and trustees of the people. . . . The adversaries of the Constitution seem to have lost sight of the people altogether in their reasonings on this subject; and to have viewed these different establishments not only as mutual rivals and enemies, but as uncontrolled by any common superior in their efforts to usurp the authorities of each other. These gentlemen must here be reminded of their error. They must be told that the ultimate authority, wherever the derivative may be found, resides in the people alone. . . .").

8. For example, Michael Kammen's thought-provoking book *Sovereignty and Liberty* assumes that there is a tension between sovereignty and liberty: "During the years from about 1765 until 1785, popular sovereignty appeared utterly compatible with individual liberty because the power of the people as a *collective force* would shield free individuals from government tyranny. Gradually, however, Americans came to recognize that an overbearing majority of the people might pose just as great a threat to liberty as tyrannical officials. When the shock of recognition took hold, the meanings ascribed to sovereignty, to liberty, and to republicanism all required adjustment." MICHAEL KAMMEN, SOVEREIGNTY & LIBERTY: CONSTITUTIONAL DISCOURSE IN AMERICAN CULTURE 14 (1988) (emphasis supplied). As this passage reveals, the founding generation recognized that majoritarian tyranny was a substantial threat to individual liberty. On this much Kammen and I agree. But unlike Kammen, I believe that the founding generation's conception of popular sovereignty did *not* stop with collective majoritarian action, but in-

stead purposefully incorporated individual sovereignty. In this sense, there is no tension between popular sovereignty and individual liberty because the former includes the latter.

9. Letter from James Madison to Thomas Jefferson (Oct. 17, 1788), 25 LETTERS OF DELEGATES TO CONGRESS, 1774–1789 (Paul H. Smith et al. eds., Library of Congress, 1976–2000). Madison similarly remarked to Jefferson in 1787, "The great desideratum in Government is so to modify the sovereignty as that it may be sufficiently neutral between different parts of the society to controul one part from invading the rights of another, and at the same time sufficiently controuled itself from setting up an interest adverse to that of the entire society." Letter from James Madison to Thomas Jefferson (Oct. 24, 1787), *in* 1 THE FOUNDERS' CONSTITUTION 647 (Philip B. Kurland & Ralph Lerner eds., 1987).

10. Letter from Thomas Jefferson to Isaac H. Tiffany (Apr. 4, 1819), *in* THE POLITICAL WRITINGS OF THOMAS JEFFERSON: REPRESENTATIVE SELECTIONS 55 (Edward Dumbauld ed., 1955).

11. *See, e.g.,* AN OLD WHIG, No. 2 (1787), *in* 3 THE FOUNDERS' CONSTITUTION, at 239 ("Under [the Necessary and Proper Clause] can any thing be said to be reserved and kept from Congress? Can it be said that Congress have no power but what *is expressed*? 'To make all laws which shall be necessary and proper' is in other words to make all such laws which *the Congress shall think necessary and proper*—for who shall judge for the legislature what is necessary and proper? . . . . To me it appears that no other power on earth can dictate to them or controul them, unless by force. . . .") (emphasis in original); BRUTUS No. 1 (Oct. 18, 1787), *in* 3 THE FOUNDERS' CONSTITUTION, at 240 ("The powers given by [the Necessary and Proper Clause] are very general and comprehensive, and it may receive a construction to justify the passing almost any law. . . . And if they may do it, it is pretty certain they will; . . . Besides, it is a truth confirmed by the unerring experience of ages, that every man, and every body of men, invested with power, are ever disposed to increase it, and to acquire a superiority over every thing that stands in their way."); AN OLD WHIG, No. 6 (1787), *in* 2 THE FOUNDERS' CONSTITUTION, at 413–14 ("[I]n establishing a government which is to last for ages, and which, if it be suffered to depart from the principles of liberty in the beginning, will in all probability, never return to them, that we consider carefully what sort of government we are about to form. Power is very easily encreased [sic]; indeed, it naturally grows in every government; but it hardly ever lessens. . . . [W]e are told that . . . 'direct taxation will be unnecessary'; that 'it is probable the principal branch of revenue will be duties on imports.' Some of those who have used such language in public and private, I believe to be very honest men; and I would therefore ask of them, what security they can give us, that the future government on the continent will in any measure confine themselves [sic] to the duties on imports, or that the utmost penny will not be exacted which can possibly be collected either by direct or indirect taxation? How can they answer for the conduct of our future rulers?").

12. *See* THE FEDERALIST No. 84 (Alexander Hamilton) ("It is evident . . . that [a bill of rights has] no application to constitutions, professedly founded upon the power of the people and executed by their immediate representatives and servants. Here, in strictness, the people surrender nothing; and as they retain everything they have no need of particular

reservations [of rights]. . . . I go further and affirm that bills of rights . . . are not only unnecessary in the proposed Constitution but would even be dangerous. They would contain various exceptions to powers which are not granted; and, on this very account,
would afford a colorable pretext to claim more than were granted. For why declare that
things shall not be done which there is no power to do?").

13. *See id.*; *see also* Speech of James Wilson before the Pennsylvania Ratifying Convention
(Nov. 28, 1787), *in* 1 THE FOUNDERS' CONSTITUTION, at 454 ("In a government possessed
of enumerated powers, such a [bill of rights] would be not only unnecessary, but prepos-
terous and dangerous. . . . If we attempt an enumeration [of rights], every thing that is
not enumerated is presumed given. The consequence is, that an imperfect enumeration
would throw all implied power into the scale of the government, and the rights of the
people would be rendered incomplete.").

14. *See, e.g.,* Speech of John Smilie before the Pennsylvania Ratifying Convention (Nov. 28,
1787), *in* 1 THE FOUNDERS' CONSTITUTION, at 456 ("So loosely, so inaccurately are the
powers which are enumerated in this constitution defined, that it will be impossible,
without a [bill of rights], to ascertain the limits of authority, and to declare when government has degenerated into oppression. In that event the contest will arise between the
people and the rulers: 'You have exceeded the powers of your office, you have oppressed
us,' will be the language of the suffering citizen. The answer of the government will be
short—'We have not exceeded our power; you have no test by which you can prove it.'
Hence, sir, it will be impracticable to stop the progress of tyranny"). *See also* Letter from
Richard Henry Lee to Samuel Adams (Oct. 5, 1787), *in* 1 THE FOUNDERS' CONSTITU-
TION, at 448 ("The corrupting nature of power, and its insatiable appetite for increase,
hath proved the necessity, and procured the adoption of the strongest and most express
declarations of that *Residuum* of natural rights, which is not intended to be given up to
Society; and which indeed is not necessary to be given up for any good social purpose. In
a government therefore, when the power of judging what shall be for the *general welfare,*
which goes to every object of human legislation; and where the laws of such Judges shall
be the *supreme Law of the Land:* it seems to be of the last consequence to declare in most
explicit terms the reservations above alluded to.") (emphasis in original).

15. *See* THE FEDERALIST No. 78 (Alexander Hamilton). Madison began to recognize the
need for constitutional checks against majoritarian tyranny in 1788, as revealed by his
comments to Thomas Jefferson: "Wherever the real power in a Government lies, there is
the danger of oppression. In our Governments the real power lies in the majority of the
Community, and the invasion of private rights is chiefly to be apprehended, not from
acts of Government contrary to the sense of its constituents, but from acts in which the
Government is the mere instrument of the major number of the constituents. This is a
truth of great importance, but not yet sufficiently attended to. . . ." Letter from James
Madison to Thomas Jefferson (Oct. 17, 1788), *in* 1 THE FOUNDERS' CONSTITUTION, at
477.

16. A [MARYLAND] FARMER No. 1 (1788), *reprinted in* 1 THE FOUNDERS' CONSTITUTION, at
464–65.

17. *See, e.g.,* N.H. CONST. pmbl. (1776) ("We the members of the Congress of New Hampshire . . . [h]ave taken into our serious consideration the unhappy circumstances, into

which this colony is involved by means of many grievous and oppressive acts of the British Parliament, depriving us of our natural and constitutional rights and privileges. . . ."); N.Y. CONST. pmbl. (1777) ("Whereas the many tyrannical and oppressive usurpations of the King and Parliament of Great Britain on the rights and liberties of the people of the American colonies. . . .").

18. Letter from Richard Henry Lee to Samuel Adams (Oct. 5, 1787), *in* 5 THE FOUNDERS' CONSTITUTION, at 448 (emphasis in original).

19. Indeed, the fundamental change wrought by the Reconstruction era was the shift in confidence from state to federal government regarding which level of government was trusted to be the protector of individual liberty.

20. U.S. CONST. art. VI.

21. U.S. CONST. amend. IX.

22. *Id.* at amend. X.

23. Joseph Story acknowledged this unavoidable conclusion: "Being an instrument of limited and enumerated powers, it follows irresistibly, that what is not conferred, is withheld, and belongs to the state authorities, if invested by their constitutions of government respectively in them; and if not so invested, it is retained BY THE PEOPLE, as part of their residuary sovereignty." JOSEPH STORY, 3 COMMENTARIES ON THE CONSTITUTION OF THE UNITED STATES 752 (1833) (capitals in original). Indeed, one state constitution of the founding era, Georgia's, was amended in 1795 to include similar language to the Ninth Amendment, declaring: "All powers not delegated by the constitution as amended, are retained by the people." GA. CONST. art. VIII (1789) (as amended May 16, 1795).

24. EDWARD INGERSOLL, PERSONAL LIBERTY & MARTIAL LAW: A REVIEW OF SOME PAMPHLETS OF THE DAY 24 (1862)

25. This notion was articulated most forcefully by John Locke: "But though men when they enter into society give up the equality, liberty, and executive power they had in the state of nature into the hands of the society, to be so far disposed of by the legislative as the good of society shall require, yet it being only with an intention in everyone the better to preserve himself, his liberty and property (for no rational creature can be supposed to change his condition with an intention to be worse). . . . And all this [government] to be directed to no other end but the peace, safety, and public good of the people." JOHN LOCKE, THE SECOND TREATISE OF GOVERNMENT 59 (Dover Publications 2002) (1690). *See also* JEAN-JACQUES ROUSSEAU, DISCOURSE ON POLITICAL ECONOMY 10 (Christopher Betts trans., Oxford Univ. Press 1994) (1755) ("Seek out the motives by which men, in the greater society united by need have been led to unite themselves more closely in civil societies: the only one you will find is to guarantee each member's property, life, and liberty by putting them under the protection of all."); JAMES OTIS, THE RIGHTS OF THE BRITISH COLONIES ASSERTED & PROVED (1764), *reprinted in* 1 PAMPHLETS OF THE AMERICAN REVOLUTION 1750–1765, at 425 (Bernard Bailyn ed., 1965) ("The *end* of government being the *good* of mankind points out its great duties: it is above all things to provide for the security, the quiet, and happy enjoyment of life, liberty and property. There is no one act which a government can have a *right* to make that does not tend to the advancement of the security, tranquility, and prosperity of the people.") (emphasis in original).

26. *See* SAMUEL ADAMS, THE RIGHTS OF THE COLONISTS (1772), *reprinted* in 5 THE FOUNDERS' CONSTITUTION, at 60 (emphasis added) ("[I]t is the greatest absurdity to suppose it in the power of one or any number of men at the entering into society, to renounce their natural rights, or the means of preserving those rights *when the great end of civil government from the very nature of its institution is for the support, protection and defence [sic] of those very rights: the principal of which as is before observed, are life liberty and property.*"). Along similar lines, Adams, in an address to the Massachusetts Legislature in 1794, declared, "I think it appears, that the Constitutions referred to [of Massachusetts and the United States], different as they may be in forms, agree altogether in the most essential principles upon which legitimate governments are founded. I have said essential principles, because I conceive that without Liberty and Equality, there cannot exist that tranquility of mind, which results from the assurance of every citizen, that his own personal safety and rights are secure: This, I think is a sentiment of the celebrated Montesquieu; and it is the end and design of all free and lawful Governments." Samuel Adams, *Speech to the Massachusetts Legislature* (Jan. 17, 1794), *in* 4 THE WRITINGS OF SAMUEL ADAMS 358 (Harry Alonzo Cushing ed., 1968); JAMES WILSON, LECTURES ON LAW (1790–91), *reprinted in* 2 THE WORKS OF JAMES WILSON, at 592 (Robert Green McCloskey ed., Belknap Press 1967) ("Government, in my humble opinion, should be formed to secure and to enlarge the exercise of the natural rights of its members; and every government, which has not this in view, as its principal object, is not a government of the legitimate kind. . . . [M]an has a natural right to his property, to his character, to his liberty, and to his safety."); Fisher Ames, *Speech in Congress* (Feb. 9, 1790), *in* 1 WORKS OF FISHER AMES 759 (W.B. Allen ed., Liberty Classics 1983) ("What is the object for which men enter into society, but to secure their lives and property?"); LETTER FROM CATO TO THE CITIZENS OF THE STATE OF NEW YORK (No. III) (1787), *reprinted in* 2 THE COMPLETE ANTI-FEDERALIST, at 110 (Herbert J. Storing ed., Univ. of Chicago Press 1981) ("It is acknowleged that there are defects in this [proposed Constitution] . . . ; the great question then . . . is whether it will answer the ends for which it is said to be offered to you, and for which all men engage in political society, to wit, the mutual preservation of their lives, liberties, and estates."); ESSAYS OF REPUBLICUS (1788), *reprinted in* 5 THE COMPLETE ANTI-FEDERALIST, at 162 ("[M]ankind find it necessary to enter into solemn compacts of mutual defence [sic], and security . . . [Civil government] instead of infringing the rightful liberties of mankind, tends to secure them; and by this criterion may every government be tried: that government which tends not to secure the lives, liberties and properties of every individual of the community . . . is unjust and iniquitious [sic] and merits not the name of civil government."); ESSAY No. III OF PHILADELPHIENSIS (1787), *reprinted in* 3 THE COMPLETE ANTI-FEDERALIST, at 110 ("The only thing in which a government should be efficient, is to protect the liberties, lives and property of the people governed, from foreign and domestic violence. This, and this only is, what every government should do effectually. For any government to do more than this, is impossible, and every one that falls short of it is defective."); *id.* at 119 (Essay VI) ("[T]he nature of a free government is to protect the lives, liberties, and property of the people, that each may enjoy what he hath by honest industry acquired. . . ."). John Adams, who authored the 1779 document entitled *The Report of a Constitution or Form of Government*

for the Commonwealth of Massachusetts, declared in its preamble: "The end of the institution, maintenance, and administration of government is to secure the existence of the body politic; to protect it, and to furnish the individuals who compose it with the power of enjoying, in safety and tranquillity, their natural rights and blessings of life . . . ." THE REPORT OF A CONSTITUTION, OR A FORM OF GOVERNMENT, FOR THE COMMONWEALTH OF MASSACHUSETTS (1779), *reprinted in* 4 THE WORKS OF JOHN ADAMS, SECOND PRESIDENT OF THE UNITED STATES, at 219 (Charles Francis Adams ed., Little & Brown 1851). And of course the Declaration of Independence reveals this philosophy quite clearly: "We hold these Truths to be self-evident, that all Men are created equal, that they are endowed by their Creator with certain inalienable rights, that among these are Life, Liberty and the Pursuit of Happiness—that to secure these Rights, Governments are instituted among Men . . . ." THE DECLARATION OF INDEPENDENCE para. 2 (1776). Much has been made of Jefferson's substitution of the phrase "pursuit of happiness" for the word "property"—but for present purposes, suffice it to say that Jefferson, in authoring the 1776 Virginia Declaration of Rights, explicitly acknowledged property as an inalienable right of the people. *See* VIRGINIA DECLARATION OF RIGHTS § 1 (1776).

27. THE FEDERALIST NO. 45 (James Madison) (emphasis added). Intriguingly, in 1842 the Supreme Judicial Court of Massachusetts cited *Federalist No. 45* or the proposition that "[t]he powers reserved to the States are considered to extend to all the objects which, in the ordinary course of affairs, affect the lives, liberties and property of the people, and the internal order, improvement and prosperity of a State." Norris v. City of Boston, 45 Mass. 282, 288 (1842).

28. James Madison, *Property,* NAT'L GAZETTE, Mar. 29, 1792, *available at* The Constitution Society, Selected Works of James Madison (Jon Rowland ed.), http://www.constitution. org/jm/17920329_property.txt (emphasis added).

29. This broad conceptualization of property as including individual liberty as well as tangible items was common during the revolutionary era. *See* JOHN LOCKE, THE SECOND TREATISE OF GOVERNMENT 38 (Dover Publications 2002) (1690).

30. VT. CONST. pmbl. (1777).

31. *Id.* at art. I.

32. DEL. DECLARATION OF RIGHTS § 10 (1776) ("That every member of society hath a right to be protected in the enjoyment of life, liberty and property"); *id.* at § 12 ("That every freeman for every injury done him in his goods, lands or person, by any other person, ought to have remedy by the course of the law of the land"); MA. CONST. art. I (1780) ("All men are born free and equal, and have certain natural, essential, and unalienable rights; among which may be reckoned the right of enjoying and defending their lives and liberties; that of acquiring, possessing, and protecting property; in fine, that of seeking and obtaining their safety and happiness."); *id.* at art. X ("Each individual of the society has a right to be protected by it in the enjoyment of his life, liberty and property, according to standing laws."); *id.* at art. XI ("Every subject of the Commonwealth ought to find a certain remedy, by having recourse to the laws, for all injuries or wrongs which he may receive in his person, property, or character."); *id.* at art. XXIX ("It is essential to the preservation of the rights of every individual, his life, liberty, property and character, that there be an impartial interpretation of the laws, and administration of justice."); N.Y.

Const. pmbl. (1777) (incorporating and reciting in toto the words of the Declaration of Independence, including "We hold these truths to be self-evident, that all men are created equal; that they are endowed by their Creator with certain unalienable rights; that among these are life, liberty, and the pursuit of happiness; that to secure these rights, governments are instituted among men."); Pa. Const. § 1 (1776) ("That all men are born equally free and independent, and have certain natural, inherent and inalienable rights, amongst which are, the enjoying and defending life and liberty, acquiring, possessing and protecting property, and pursuing and obtaining happiness and safety."); *id.* at § 5 ("That government is, or ought to be, instituted for the common benefit, protection and security of the people, nation or community"); *id.* at § 8 ("That every member of society hath a right to be protected in the enjoyment of life, liberty and property"); Va. Const. § 1 (1776) ("That all men are by nature equally free and independent, and have certain inherent rights, of which, when they enter into a state of society, they cannot, by any compact, deprive or divest their posterity, namely, the enjoyment of life and liberty, with the means of acquiring and possessing property, and pursuing and obtaining happiness and safety."); *id.* at § 3 ("That government is, or ought to be, instituted for the common benefit, protection, and security of the people, nation, or community").

33. The New York ratifying convention, for example, declared, "That all power is originally vested in and consequently derived from the people, and that *government is instituted by them for their common interest, protection, and security.* That the enjoyment of life, liberty and the pursuit of happiness are essential rights which every government ought to respect and preserve." 5 The Founders' Constitution, at 12. Similarly, the ratifying conventions of Virginia and North Carolina asked the First Congress to consider the following amendatory language to the Constitution:

> 1ˢᵗ. That there are certain natural rights, of which men, when they form a social compact, cannot deprive or divest their posterity; among which are the enjoyment of life and liberty, with the means of acquiring, possessing, and protecting property, and pursuing and obtaining happiness and safety.
>
> 2d. That all power is naturally invested in, and consequently derived from, the people. . . .
>
> 3d. That government ought to be instituted for the common benefit, protection, and security of the people. . . .

5 The Founders' Constitution, at 15 (Virginia); *id.* at 17 (North Carolina).

34. *See, e.g.,* Richard Henry Lee, *Letters from the Federal Farmer (Letter III)* (Oct. 10, 1787), *reprinted in* Pamphlets on the History of the Constitution of the United States Published During its Discussion by the People 1787–1788 302 (Paul Leicester Ford ed., 1888) [hereinafter Pamphlets] ("Should the general [i.e., federal] government think it politic, as some administration (if not all) probably will, to look for a support in a system of influence, the government will take every occasion to multiply laws, and officers to execute them, considering these as so many necessary props for its own support."); Brutus No. 1 (1787), *reprinted in* 1 The Founders' Constitution, at 261 ("[I]t is a truth confirmed by the unerring experience of ages, that every man, and every body of men, invested with power, are ever disposed to increase it, and to acquire a superiority

over every thing that stands in their way."); ELBRIDGE GERRY, *Observations on the New Constitution, & on the Federal and State Conventions* (1788), *reprinted in* PAMPHLETS, at 16 ("[L]et the best informed historian produce an instance when bodies of men were entrusted with power, and the proper checks relinquished, if they were ever found destitute of ingenuity sufficient to furnish pretences [sic] to abuse it.").

35. *See* W.G. Hastings, *The Development of Law as Illustrated by the Decisions Relating to the Police Power of the States,* 39 PROC. AM. PHIL. SOC'Y 359, 359–60 (1900) ("The 1898 edition of Bouvier's *Law Dictionary* says that the law on this subject [the police power] is all of recent growth, and most of it in the last half of the nineteenth century. It could not consistently say otherwise."). Hastings credits Chief Justice John Marshall with coining the phrase initially in the *Brown v. Maryland* case of 1827 and states that "[a] somewhat careful search for the phrase fails to find it in legal or political writings of this country prior to that time." *Id.* at 360.

36. For an interesting discussion of the evolution of the police power, see Glenn H. Reynolds and David B. Kopel, *The Evolving Police Power: Some Observations for a New Century,* 27 HASTINGS CON. L.Q. 511 (2000). Reynolds and Kopel assert:

> The conventional wisdom about the scope of state police powers goes like this: in the early days of the Republic, state regulation was limited by the common law principle of *sic utere tuo ut alienum non laedas* (you should use what is yours so as not to harm what is others'), implying that legitimate regulation existed only to prevent concrete harm to specified interests. Sometime around the (previous) turn of the century, the story continues, the principle changed from the old *sic utere* to the new principle of *salus populi est suprema lex* (the good of the public is the supreme law), suggesting that states could regulate as they chose so long as they claimed to be working to promote the public safety, welfare, or morality.
>
> Like all such conventional wisdom, this approach is somewhat simplistic. But it captures a large grain of truth. The range of activity that courts, and legal scholars, view as within the scope of legitimate regulation is considerably larger than it was previously.

Id. at 511. Alfred Russell noted and explained the expansion of the police power at the turn of the twentieth century:

> Before the last half of the present [nineteenth] century, neither the legislatures nor the courts were much occupied with considering the police power. But the spirit of what we call individualism, which pervaded the early history of our States, has given way before the increasing desire to look to government for aid, and the police power has been seized upon by our newly-composed legislatures, elected from the working classes, and statutes have been passed interfering with many of the ordinary concerns of life, hitherto not meddled with by legislation. At the same time constitutional guaranties have either been enlarged or newly created. It has therefore followed that judicial decisions touching the exercise of police power have increased in number enormously. . . .

ALFRED RUSSELL, THE POLICE POWER OF THE STATE & DECISIONS THEREON AS ILLUSTRATING THE DEVELOPMENT & VALUE OF CASE LAW 25 (1900). *See also* WILLIS REED BIERLY, POLICE POWER, STATE & FEDERAL, DEFINITIONS & DISTINCTIONS 8 (Rees

Welsh and Co. 1907) ("The scope of the police power has been much broadened in American jurisprudence, and by some noted writers, until it is as comprehensive as sovereignty itself, whereas it originally was, and now ought to be only a distinct power of the sovereign, as applied to specific objects.").

37. For a recent thorough analysis of the founding generation's concept of police power and its relation to the preservation of natural rights, see Randy E. Barnett, *The Proper Scope of the Police Power*, 79 NOTRE DAME L. REV. 429 (2004).

38. "Use what is yours so as not to harm what is others'."

39. 4 WILLIAM BLACKSTONE, COMMENTARIES ON THE LAWS OF ENGLAND 162 (William S. Hein & Co. 1992) (1769).

40. JOHN BOUVIER, 2 INSTITUTES OF AMERICAN LAW 491, 491–586 (Robert E. Peterson Publisher 1851).

41. THOMAS MCINTYRE COOLEY, A TREATISE ON THE CONSTITUTIONAL LIMITATIONS WHICH REST UPON THE LEGISLATIVE POWER OF THE STATES OF THE AMERICAN UNION 572 (1868).

42. CHRISTOPHER G. TIEDEMAN, A TREATISE ON THE LIMITATIONS OF THE POLICE POWER 4–5 (1886). Tiedeman asserts: "As presently developed, the doctrine of natural rights may be tersely stated to be a freedom from all legal restraint that is not needed to prevent injury to others; a right to do any thing that does not involve a trespass or injury to others; or, to employ the language of Herbert Spencer: 'Every man has freedom to do aught as he wills, provided he infringes not the equal freedom of any other man.' The prohibitory operation of the law must be confined to the enforcement of the legal maxim, *sic utere tuo, ut alienum non laedas.*" CHRISTOPHER G. TIEDEMAN, THE UNWRITTEN CONSTITUTION OF THE UNITED STATES 76 (1890).

43. *See* W.P. PRENTICE, POLICE POWERS ARISING UNDER THE LAW OF OVERRULING NECESSITY 4 (1894).

44. WILLIS REID BIERLY, POLICE POWER, STATE & FEDERAL, DEFINITIONS & DISTINCTIONS 9 (Rees Welsh & Co. 1907). Bierly lamented that the police power had "been much broadened in American jurisprudence" and asserted that "it originally was, and now ought to be only a distinct power of the sovereign, as applied to specific objects." *Id.* at 8.

45. Commonwealth v. Alger, 61 Mass. 53, 84–85 (1851) (emphasis added). The Court went on to say:

This principle of legislation is of great importance and extensive use, and lies at the foundation of most enactments of positive law, which define and punish mala prohibita. Things done may or may not be wrong in themselves, or necessarily injurious and punishable as such at common law; *but laws are passed declaring them offences, and making them punishable, because they tend to injurious consequences;* but more especially for the sake of having a definite, known and authoritative rule which all can understand and obey. In the case already put, of erecting a powder magazine or slaughterhouse, it would be indictable at common law, and punishable as a nuisance, if in fact erected so near an inhabited village as to be actually dangerous or noxious to life or health. . . . The tradesman needs to know, before incurring expense, how near he may build his works without violating the law or committing a nuisance; builders of houses need to know, to what distance they must keep from the obnoxious works already erected, in order to be sure of the protection of the law for their habitations. This requisite certainty and precision can only be obtained by a positive enactment, fixing the distance, within which the use shall be prohibited as noxious, and beyond which it will be allowed, and enforcing the rule thus fixed, by penalties.

Id. at 96–97 (emphasis added).

46. Thorpe v. Rutland and Burlington R.R. Co., 27 Vt. 140, 149 (1854).

47. State v. Noyes, 47 Me. 189, 211–12 (1859) (emphasis added).

48. Munn v. Illinois, 94 U.S. 113, 124–25 (1876) (internal citation omitted).

49. R.R. v. Husen, 95 U.S. 465, 471 (1877) (emphasis added).

50. The First Amendment's language expressly indicates that it is to be applied only against the federal Congress. U.S. Const. amend. I ("Congress shall make no law. . . ."). The Seventh Amendment—at least the Reexamination Clause—similarly contains express language limiting its applicability to the federal judiciary. U.S. Const. amend. VII ("In Suits at common law, where the value in controversy shall exceed twenty dollars, the right of trial by jury shall be preserved, and no fact tried by a jury shall be otherwise re-examined in any Court of the United States, than according to the rules of the common law.").

51. "This Constitution, and the laws of the United States which shall be made in Pursuance thereof; and all Treaties made, or which shall be made, under the Authority of the United States, shall be the supreme Law of the Land; and the Judges in every State shall be bound thereby, any Thing in the constitution or Laws of any State to the Contrary notwith-standing." U.S. Const. art. VI.

52. People v. Goodwin, 18 Johns. 187, 200–01 (N.Y. Sup. Ct. 1820).

53. State v. Moor, 1 Miss. 134, 138 (1823).

54. State v. Ledford, 3 Mo. 102, 105–06, 110 (1832).

55. State v. Powell, 7 N.J.L. 244 (1823).

56. *See* William Winslow Crosskey, *Charles Fairman, "Legislative History," and the Constitutional Limitations on State Authority,* 22 U. Chi. L. Rev. 1, 125–31 (1954).

57. 17 U.S. (4 Wheat.) 235 (1819).

58. 17 U.S. at 242 ("But we cannot admit, that the section which gives effect to those laws amounts to a re-enactment of them, so as to sustain them, under the powers of exclusive legislation, given to Congress over this district.").

59. *Id.* ("Was this act void, as a law of Maryland? If it was, it must have become so under the restrictions of the constitution of the State [of Maryland], or of the United States.").

60. *Id.* at 244 (emphasis in original).

61. *Id.*

62. *See* Cong. Globe, 39th Cong., 1st Sess. 1088 (remarks of Mr. Bingham) ("What is the object of the proposed amendment? . . . It is intended to enable Congress by its enactments when necessary to give to a citizen of the United States in whatever State he may be, those privileges and immunities which are guarantied to him under the Constitution of the United States."); *id.* at 1089 ("Why are gentlemen opposed to the enforcement of the bill of rights, as proposed? Because they aver it would interfere with the rights of the States! Who ever before heard that any State had reserved to itself the right, under the Constitution of the United States, to withhold from any citizen of the United States . . .

any of the privileges of a citizen of the United States, or to impose upon him . . . any burden contrary to that provision of the Constitution which declares that the citizen shall be entitled in the several States to all the immunities of a citizen of the United States?").

63. The original draft proposed by Representative Bingham read, "The Congress shall have power to make all laws which shall be necessary and proper to secure to the citizens of each State all privileges and immunities of citizens in the several States; and to all persons in the several States equal protection in the rights of life, liberty, and property." Cong. Globe, 39th Cong., 1st Sess. 1082 (1866).

64. Hale asserted: "[R]eading the language [of the proposed Fourteenth Amendment] in its grammatical and legal construction it is a grant of the fullest and most ample power to Congress to make all laws 'necessary and proper to secure to all persons in the several States protection in the rights of life, liberty, and property,' with the simple proviso that such protection shall be equal. It is not a mere provision that when States undertake to give protection which is unequal Congress may equalize it: it is a grant of power in general terms—a grant of the right to legislate for the protection of life, liberty, and property, simply qualified with the condition that it shall be equal legislation." Cong. Globe, 39th Cong., 1st Sess. 1063 (1866). *See also id.* at 1065 ("[I]f at a single stride we take such a step as this, if we confer upon the Federal Congress powers, in such vague and general language as this amendment contains, to legislate upon all matters pertaining to life, liberty and property of all the inhabitants of the several States, I put it to the gentleman [Rep. Bingham] . . . to state where he apprehends that congress and the courts will stop in the powers they may arrogate to themselves under this proposed amendment. . . . I believe that this is, of all times, the last when we should undertake a radical amendment of the Constitution, so immensely extending the power of the Federal Government, and derogating from the power of the States.").

65. *Id.* at 1064 (emphasis added).

66. *Id.*

67. *Id.*

68. *Id.* (emphasis added).

69. *Id.* at 1089–90.

70. 32 U.S. (7 Peters) 243 (1833).

71. U.S. Const. amend. V ("nor shall private property be taken for public use without just compensation.").

72. *Barron,* 32 U.S. (7 Peters) at 250.

73. Nunn v. State, 1 Ga. 243, 250–51 (1846).

74. 11 Ga. 353 (1852).

75. *Id.* at 365.

76. *Id.*

77. *Id.* at 366.

78. *Id.* at 366–67.

79. *Id.* at 368.

80. *Id.* at 369.

81. *Id.* at 371–72 (emphasis added).

82. For example, the Illinois Supreme Court concluded that the Fifth Amendment's Due Process Clause was binding in Illinois courts:

> The fifth article of the amendments to the constitution of the United States contains this clause: "No person shall be deprived of life, liberty, or property, without due process of law;" and the words "due process of law" have been shown to correspond in meaning, to the words, "law of the land," in the eighth section of the eighth article of our own State constitution. *Now, as the constitution of the United States, in this respect is obligatory upon all the States of the Union,* is it not strange, if the construction contended for by the counsel for the plaintiff in error be correct, that "due process of law" means trial, judgment and execution, that of all these States, from the foundation of the government up to the present time, Tennessee and Illinois alone should have made the discovery, that they were *violating the constitution of the United States,* which is everywhere admitted to be the supreme law of the land, by depriving the freehold citizen of an important right, which was secured by his Anglo-Saxon forefathers by magna charta, and divesting him of his property without the judgment of his peers, or the law of the land?

Rhinehart v. Schuyler, 7 Ill. 473, 523 (1846) (emphasis added). *See also* State v. Buzzard, 4 Ark. 18, 28 (1842) ("I am therefore, after a careful and deliberate consideration of the question, of the opinion that the enactment of the legislature [prohibiting the carrying of a concealed weapon] . . . is in no wise repugnant either to the Constitution of the United States or the Constitution of this State"); State v. Smith, 11 La. Ann. 633, 633–34 (1856) (assuming that the Second Amendment applied to the states, but did not prohibit the enactment of police regulations necessary for public safety); Merriam v. Mitchell, 13 Me. 439 (1836) (assuming that Fourth Amendment's probable cause requirement was applicable and violated); McDaniel v. State, 16 Miss. 401, 416 (1847) (assuming applicability of Confrontation Clause of Sixth Amendment and finding the Clause not violated by introduction of dying declaration).

83. *Barron,* 32 U.S. (7 Peters) at 250.

84. U.S. CONST. art. VI ("The . . . members of the several State Legislatures, and all executive and judicial Officers, both of the United States and of the several States, shall be bound by Oath or Affirmation, to support this Constitution.").

85. Scott v. Sandford, 60 U.S. 393, 404 (1856) ("The question before us is, whether the class of persons described in the plea in abatement compose a portion of this people, and are constituent members of this sovereignty? We think they are not, and that they are not included, and were not intended to be included, under the word 'citizens' in the Constitution, and can therefore claim none of the rights and privileges which that instrument provides for and secures to citizens of the United States."). The *Dred Scott* decision was effectively overruled by the ratification of the Fourteenth Amendment. *See* U.S. CONST. amend. XIV, § 1 ("All persons born or naturalized in the United States and subject to the jurisdiction thereof, are citizens of the United States and of the State wherein they reside.").

86. Federal courts inherited this reluctance as well, but there was relatively little opportunity for them to manifest this reluctance in the context of federal civil rights claims because

federal courts were not generally empowered by Congress to adjudicate federal question claims until 1875. *See* Idaho v. Coeur D'Alene Tribe, 521 U.S. 261, 275 (1997).

87. *See* J.C. HOLT, MAGNA CARTA 43–62 (1965). A similar tradition was mimicked in the American colonies. For example, the governor of Pennsylvania, William Penn, granted to his citizens a "Charter of Privileges" in 1701. *See* CHARTER OF PRIVILEGES GRANTED BY WILLIAM PENN, ESQ. TO THE INHABITANTS OF PENNSYLVANIA & TERRITORIES (Oct. 28, 1701), *available at* http://www.yale.edu/lawweb/avalon/states/pa07.htm.

88. *See* HOLT, at 38–42, 105–74 (1965); GEORGE BURTON ADAMS, CONSTITUTIONAL HISTORY OF ENGLAND 125–28 (1934).

89. *See* HOLT, at 70 ("[T]he king enjoyed an ill-defined capacity to direct, suspend, or withhold justice. Behind the keen interest of Henry II and John in the operations of the courts of justice there lay a ready instinct to ensure that judgment inclined favourably towards the king's friends and ministers and away from those who were out of favour or distrusted.").

90. The House of Commons evolved over time to be the branch of British government that protected the interests of "commoners" and hence checked monarchical usurpations of citizens' privileges. *See* JAMES WILSON, CONSIDERATIONS ON THE NATURE & EXTENT OF THE LEGISLATIVE AUTHORITY OF THE BRITISH PARLIAMENT (1774), *reprinted in* 2 THE WORKS OF JAMES WILSON, at 730–31 (Robert Green McCloskey ed., 1967). *See generally also* D. PASQUET, AN ESSAY ON THE ORIGINS OF THE HOUSE OF COMMONS (1925).

91. *See* 1 WILLIAM BLACKSTONE, COMMENTARIES ON THE LAWS OF ENGLAND 119–20 (Wayne Morrison ed., 2001) (1793).

92. *See, e.g.,* VA. DECLARATION OF RIGHTS art. I (1776).

93. *See, e.g.,* N.C. Const. art. VIII (1776) ("That no freeman shall be put to answer any criminal charge, but by indictment"); *id.* at art. IX ("That no freeman shall be convicted of any crime, but by the unanimous verdict of jury"); *id.* at art. XII ("That no freeman ought to be taken, imprisoned, or disseized of his freehold liberties or privileges . . . or in any manner destroyed, or deprived of his life, liberty, or property, but by the law of the land."). *See id.* at art. VII ("That, in all criminal prosecutions, every man has a right to be informed of the accusation against him, and to confront the accusers and witnesses with other testimony, and shall not be compelled to give evidence against himself."); *id.* at art. XVII ("That the people have a right to bear arms"); *id.* at art. XIX ("That all men have a natural and inalienable right to worship Almighty God according to the dictates of their own consciences.").

94. *Compare* GA. CONST. art. LVI (1777) ("All persons whatever shall have the free exercise of their religion"); *id.* at art. LXI ("Freedom of the press and trial by jury to remain inviolate forever."); *with id.* at art. IX ("All male white inhabitants, of the age of twenty-one years, and possessed in his own right of ten pounds value, and liable to pay tax in this State, or being of any mechanic trade, and shall have been resident six months in this State, shall have a right to vote at all elections for representatives"). *See, e.g.,* MD. CONST. art. III (1776) ("That all the inhabitants of Maryland are entitled to the common law of England and the trial by Jury"); *id.* at art. V ("every man, having property in, a common interest with, and an attachment to the community, ought to have a right of suffrage."); *id.* at art. XIX ("That, in all criminal prosecutions, every man hath a right to be informed

of the accusation against him; to have a copy of the indictment or charge . . . to be allowed counsel; to be confronted with the witnesses against him; to have process for his witnesses; to examine the witnesses . . . and to a speedy trial by an impartial jury"); *id.* at art. XX ("That no man ought to be compelled to give evidence against himself"); *id.* at art. XXI ("That no freeman ought to be taken, or imprisoned, or disseized of his freehold, liberties, or privileges . . . or deprived of his life, liberty, or property, but by the judgment of his peers, or by the law of the land.").

95. The original Constitution contained three references to slavery which permitted it to continue in existing states until at least 1808, at which time Congress was explicitly given the power to prohibit it. U.S. Const. art. I, § 9, cl. 1 ("The Migration or Importation of such Persons as the States now existing shall think proper to admit, shall not be prohibited by the Congress prior to the Year one thousand eight hundred and eight"). *See also id.* at art. I, § 2, cl. 3 (apportioning Representatives according to the number of free persons and "three-fifths of all other Persons"); *id.* at art. IV, § 2, cl. 3 (requiring delivery upon demand of any escaped slave).

96. U.S. Const. amend. XIV, § 1.

97. *See generally* Michael Kent Curtis, No State Shall Abridge: The Fourteenth Amendment & the Bill of Rights (Duke Univ. Press 1986); Randy Barnett, Restoring the Lost Constitution: The Presumption of Liberty 191–208 (Princeton Univ. Press 2004); William Winslow Crosskey, *Charles Fairman, "Legislative History," and the Constitutional Limitations on State Authority,* 22 U. Chi. L. Rev. 1 (1954).

98. 83 U.S. (16 Wall.) 36 (1873).

99. *Id.* at 79.

100. *Id.* at 79–80.

101. Twenty-three years after *Slaughterhouse,* the Supreme Court in *Plessy v. Ferguson* concluded that such Jim Crow laws were constitutional. Plessy v. Ferguson, 163 U.S. 537, 548 (1896) ("[W]e think the enforced separation of the races, as applied to the internal commerce of the State, neither abridges the privileges or immunities of the colored man, deprives him of his property without due process of law, nor denies him the equal protection of the laws, within the meaning of the Fourteenth Amendment."). *Plessy* was finally overruled in 1954. Brown v. Board of Educ., 347 U.S. 483 (1954).

102. The selective incorporation approach has been rightly criticized on many grounds. Perhaps one of the most eloquent criticisms was voiced by Justice Black (joined by Justice Douglas):

My study of the historical events that culminated in the Fourteenth Amendment, and the expressions of those who sponsored and favored, as well as those who opposed its submission and passage, persuades me that one of the chief objects that the provisions of the Amendment's first section, separately, and as a whole, were intended to accomplish was to make the Bill of Rights, applicable to the states. With full knowledge of the import of the *Barron [v. Baltimore]* decision, the framers and backers of the Fourteenth Amendment proclaimed its purpose to be to overturn the constitutional rule that case had announced. This historical purpose has never received full consideration or exposition in any opinion of this Court interpreting the Amendment. . . .

> If the choice must be between the selective [incorporation] process of *the Palko [v. Connecticut]* decision applying some of the Bill of Rights to the States, or the *Twining [v. New Jersey]* rule applying none of them, I would choose the *Palko* selective process. But rather than accept either of these choices, I would follow what I believe was the original purpose of the Fourteenth Amendment—to extend to all the people of the nation the complete protection of the Bill of Rights. To hold that this Court can determine what, if any, provisions of the Bill of Rights will be enforced, and if so to what degree, is to frustrate the great design of a written Constitution.

Adamson v. California, 332 U.S. 46, 71–72,89 (1946) (Black, J., dissenting).

103. *See. e.g., Adamson,* 332 U.S. at 62, 64, 67 (Frankfurter, J., concurring) (referring to incorporation of "the first eight Amendments"); Wolf v. Colorado, 338 U.S. 25, 26 (1949) (referring to the Bill of Rights as "Amendments I to VIII"); Malloy v. Hogan, 378 U.S. 1, 4 (1964) (discussing incorporation of the "first eight Amendments").

104. U.S. CONST. amend. X.

105. This is the infamous characterization given to the Ninth Amendment by Judge Bork during his U.S. Senate confirmation hearings: "I do not think you can use the Ninth Amendment unless you know something of what it means. For example, if you had an amendment that says 'Congress shall make no' and then there is an inkblot, and you cannot read the rest of it, and that is the only copy you have, I do not think the court can make up what might be under the inkblot." WALL ST. J., Oct. 5, 1987, at A-22. Bork's view is the commonly accepted view today. *See* John Hart Ely, *The Ninth Amendment, in* 1 THE RIGHTS RETAINED BY THE PEOPLE: THE HISTORY & MEANING OF THE NINTH AMENDMENT 179 (Randy E. Barnett ed., 1989) ("Occasionally a commentator will express a willingness to read [the Ninth Amendment] for what it seems to say, but this has been, and remains, a distinctly minority impulse. In sophisticated legal circles mentioning the Ninth Amendment is a surefire way to get a laugh ('What are you planning to rely on to support that argument, Lester, the Ninth Amendment?')." Akhil Amar takes another approach, insisting that interpreting the Ninth Amendment as "a palladium of individual rights—like privacy—is to engage in an anachronism." AKHIL REED AMAR, THE BILL OF RIGHTS 120 (1998). He asserts that the phrase "the people," as it appears throughout the Constitution (including the Ninth Amendment), refers only to the collective interests of popular sovereignty, not individual interests. *Id.* at 120–21. Amar later concedes, however, that interpreting the Ninth Amendment as protecting individual rights may "make sense today—but only . . . after and because of the Reconstruction of the Bill of Rights" that occurred after the adoption of the Fourteenth Amendment. *Id.* at 124.

106. U.S. CONST. amend. IX.

107. Justice Goldberg realized this in his concurrence in *Griswold:*
> [T]he Ninth Amendment shows a belief of the Constitution's authors that fundamental rights exist that are not expressly enumerated in the first eight amendments and an intent that the list of rights included there not be deemed exhaustive. As any student of this Court's opinions knows, this Court has held, often unanimously, that the [Due Process Clauses of the] Fifth and Fourteenth Amendments protect certain fundamental personal liberties from abridgment by the Federal Government or the States. The

Ninth Amendment simply shows the intent of the Constitution's authors that other fundamental personal rights should not be denied such protection or disparaged in any other way simply because they are not specifically listed in the first eight constitutional amendments. I do not see how this broadens the authority of the Court; rather it serves to support what this Court has been doing in protecting fundamental rights.

Griswold v. Connecticut, 381 U.S. 479, 492–93 (1965) (Goldberg, J., concurring).

108. Washington v. Glucksberg, 520 U.S. 702, 720–21 (1997).

109. Early Court decisions recognized the importance of a presumption in favor of individual sovereignty. In the 1819 decision *Bank of Columbia v. Okely,* for example, the Supreme Court affirmed the use of summary procedures to collect on an unpaid bank note, prefacing its analysis with the statement, "We readily admit, that *the provisions of this law are in derogation of the ordinary principles of private rights and, as such, must be subjected to a strict construction,* and under the influence of this admission, will proceed to consider the several questions which the case presents." 17 U.S. (4 Wheat.) 235, 241–42 (1819) (emphasis added).

110. As Randy Barnett has observed, "[U]ntil the Fourteenth Amendment, [the police power] was simply that power contained in state constitutions, which did not conflict with the powers delegated to the United States or prohibited by it to the states. . . . Therefore, until the passage of the Fourteenth Amendment, there simply was no reason to develop what might be called a 'positive theory' of the police power that could trump even state constitutions. Such a theory immediately became necessary, however, once the Constitution was amended to give the national government the power to protect the privileges or immunities of citizens from infringements by their own state governments." Randy E. Barnett, *The Proper Scope of the Police Power,* 79 NOTRE DAME L. REV. 429, 478 (2004).

CHAPTER 3. BEING SOVEREIGN

1. JAMES WILSON, LECTURES ON LAW (1790–91), *reprinted in* 1 THE WORKS OF JAMES WILSON, at 136 (James DeWitt Andrews ed., Callaghan & Co. 1896) [hereinafter WORKS OF JAMES WILSON].

2. Grotius, for example, defined a sovereign as a person "whose actions are not subject to the controul [sic] of any other power, so as to be annulled at the pleasure of any other human will." HUGO GROTIUS, THE RIGHTS OF WAR & PEACE 62 (A.C. Campbell trans., M. Walter Dunne Publisher 1901) (1625). *See also* EMMERICH DE VATTEL, THE LAW OF NATIONS OR THE PRINCIPLES OF NATURAL LAW 5 (Charles G. Fenwick trans., 1916) (1758) [hereinafter VATTEL] ("Owing to the freedom and independence of Nations, the conduct of one Nation may be unlawful and censurable according to the laws of conscience, and yet other Nations must put up with it so long as it does not infringe upon their perfect rights. The liberty of a Nation would not remain complete if other Nations presumed to inspect and control its conduct"); *id.* at 6 ("Since Nations are free and independent of one another as men are in nature . . . each Nation should be left to the peaceable enjoyment of that liberty which belongs to it by nature. . . . In consequence of that liberty and independence it follows that it is for each Nation to decide

what its conscience demands of it, what it can or can not do; what it thinks well or does not think well to do"); SAMUEL VON PUFENDORF, 2 DE JURE NATURAE ET GENTIUM LIBRI OCTO 1055 (C.H. Oldfather & W.A. Oldfather eds., Clarendon Press 1934) (1688) (saying of sovereignty that "no greater liberty, setting aside the sovereignty of God, can be understood as belonging to individual men, than the ability to dispose of their actions, strength, and faculties at their own judgment . . . . 'To do with impunity what one fancies is to be a king.'"); *id.* at 1063–64 ("Just as it is understood to be the highest and absolute liberty of individual men, when they can decide upon their own affairs and acts in accordance with their own wish and judgement and not those of another . . . and that liberty belongs by nature to all men who are not subject to the sovereignty of another man").

3. JAMES WILSON, LECTURES ON LAW (1790–91), *reprinted in* 1 WORKS OF JAMES WILSON, at 147 ("The first and necessary duty of nations, as well as of men, is to do no wrong or injury."). *See also* John Jay, *Charge to the Grand Jury* (1793), *in* 3 THE CORRESPONDENCE & PUBLIC PAPERS OF JOHN JAY, at 481–82 (Henry P. Johnston ed., G.P. Putnam's Sons 1890) [hereinafter CORRESPONDENCE & PUBLIC PAPERS OF JOHN JAY] ("[Nations] have a perfect right to establish such governments and build such houses as they prefer, and their neighbors have no right to pull down either because not fashioned according to their ideas of perfection; in a word, one has no right to interfere in the affairs of another, but all are bound to behave to each other with respect, with justice, with benevolence, and with good faith."); VATTEL, at 119 ("[Sovereigns] can not qualify the prohibition not to do wrong to others or to cause them any harm; in a word, to *injure* them") (emphasis in original); *id.* at 243 ("The right to use force, or to make war, is given to [sovereign] Nations only for their defense and for the maintenance of their rights."); *id.* at 244 ("[T]he purpose or lawful object of every war, [] is *to avenge or to prevent an injury.*") (emphasis in original); J.J. BURLAMAQUI, THE PRINCIPLES OF NATURAL LAW 196–97 (Lawbook Exchange 2003) (1748) ("[L]et us observe that the natural state of [sovereign] nations in respect to each other, is that of society and peace. This society is likewise a state of equality and independence, which establishes a parity of right between them; and engages them to have the same regard and respect for one another. . . . Polity considered with regards to states, is that ability and address by which a sovereign provides for the preservation, safety, prosperity and glory of the nation he governs, by respecting the laws of justice and humanity; that is, without doing any injury to other states").

4. *See, e.g.,* Steven D. Smith, *The Hollowness of the Harm Principle,* Legal Studies Research Paper Series, Research Paper No. 05–07 (Sept. 2004), *available at* http://ssrn.com/abstract=591327 ("My argument will be . . . that, upon closer examination the harm principle turns out to be not mistaken, exactly, but hollow—and hence mischievous. It is an empty vessel, alluring and even irresistible but without any inherent legal or political content, into which advocates can pour whatever substantive views and values they happen to favor.").

5. Patrick Devlin is the most ardent proponent of this criticism: "I think there can be no theoretical limits to legislation against immorality. You may argue that if a man's sins affect only himself it cannot be the concern of society. If he chooses to get drunk every night in the privacy of his own home, is anyone except himself the worse for it? But sup-

pose a quarter or a half of the population got drunk every night, what sort of society would it be? You cannot set a theoretical limit to the number of people who can get drunk before society is entitled to legislate against drunkenness." PATRICK DEVLIN, THE ENFORCEMENT OF MORALS 14 (1965) [hereinafter DEVLIN].

6. JOEL FEINBERG, HARM TO OTHERS 12 (1984) (emphasis in original). Feinberg was preceded in this criticism by others, including Wordsworth Donisthorpe, who wrote of Mill's thesis in 1895, "[W]e might plausibly maintain that every act performed by a citizen from his birth to his death injures his neighbors more or less indirectly. If he eats dinner he diminishes the supply of food and raises the price. His very existence causes an enhanced demand for the necessaries of life . . . . One who marries a girl loved by another injures that other . . . . One who wins a game pains the loser." WORDSWORTH DONISTHORPE, LAW IN A FREE STATE 68 (1895).

7. DEVLIN, at 121. Another eloquent articulation of this societal harm thesis is James Fitzjames Stephens. See JAMES FITZJAMES STEPHENS, LIBERTY, EQUALITY, FRATERNITY & THREE BRIEF ESSAYS 150 (Univ. of Chicago Press 1991) (1873) ("In England at the present day many theories about morality are current, and speculative men differ about them widely. . . . The result is that the object of promoting virtue and preventing vice must be admitted to be both a good one and one sufficiently intelligible for legislative purposes.").

8. Mill acknowledged that his thesis was "anything but new," but had been historically rejected by societies due to the "disposition of mankind, whether as rulers or fellow-citizens, to impose their own opinions and inclinations as a rule of conduct on others. . . . " JOHN STUART MILL, ON LIBERTY 72 (Gertrude Himmelfarb ed., Penguin Books 1974) (1859) [hereinafter MILL].

9. *Id.* at 68.

10. Locke asserted that, prior to the formation of government, an individual had a "power not only to preserve his property—that is, his life, liberty and estate—against the injuries and attempts of other men, but to judge and punish the breaches of that law . . . ." JOHN LOCKE, THE SECOND TREATISE OF GOVERNMENT 38–39 (Dover Publications 2002) (1690) [hereinafter LOCKE'S SECOND TREATISE]. Upon forming government, however, individuals "hath quitted this natural power, resigned it up into the hands of the community . . . . And thus all private judgment of every particular member being excluded, the community comes to be umpire, by settled, standing rules, indifferent, and the same to all parties." *Id.* at 39. *See also id.* at 57 (individuals form government "for the mutual preservation of their lives, liberties, and estates, which I call by the general name, property. The great and chief end, therefore, of men's uniting into commonwealths, and putting themselves under government, is the preservation of their property").

11. ALGERNON SIDNEY, DISCOURSES CONCERNING GOVERNMENT 397–98 (2d ed. 1704) (emphasis added).

12. JEREMY BENTHAM, THEORY OF LEGISLATION 63 (C.K. Ogden ed., Harcourt, Brace & Co. 1931). *See also id.* at 95 ("The care of his enjoyments ought to be left almost entirely to the individual. The principal function of government is to guard against pains."); *id.* at 144–45 ("Individual interests are the only real interests. Take care of the individuals; never molest them, never suffer any one to molest them, and you will have done enough

for the public."). *See also* Jeremy Bentham, An Introduction to the Principles of Morals & Legislation 158 (J.H. Burns & H.L.A. Hart eds., Univ. of London Press 1970) ("The general object which all laws have, or ought to have, in common, is to augment the total happiness of the community; and therefore, in the first place, to exclude, as far as may be, every thing that tends to subtract from that happiness: in other words, to exclude mischief.").

13. Richard Price, Observations on the Nature of Civil Liberty, the Principles of Government & the Justice & Policy of the War with America 12–13 (1776) (emphasis added).

14. Thomas Paine, The Rights of Man (1791), *reprinted in* 2 A Treasury of Philosophy 887 (Dagobert D. Runes ed., 1955) ("Natural rights are those which appertain to man in right of his existence. Of this kind are intellectual rights, or rights of the mind, and also all those rights of acting as an individual for his own comfort and happiness which are not injurious to the natural rights of others. Civil rights are those which appertain to man in his right of being a member of society. Every civil right has for its foundation some natural right pre-existing in the individual, but to the enjoyment of which his individual power is not, in all cases, sufficiently competent. Of this kind are all those which relate to security and protection."). Mimicking the language of the Ninth Amendment, Paine asserted that civil power "cannot be applied to invade the natural rights which are retained by the individual . . . ." *Id.* at 888.

15. Edmund Burke was a prominent philosopher and Whig member of the British House of Commons who urged toleration toward American colonists. He once asserted that "[w]hatever each man can separately do, without trespassing upon others, he has a right to do for himself . . . ." Edmund Burke, Reflections on the Revolution in France (1790), *reprinted in* The Philosophy of Edmund Burke 46 (Louis I. Bredvold & Ralph G. Ross eds., 1960).

16. Lord John Somers, The Judgment of Whole Kingdoms & Nations, at 28 (David S. Berkowitz & Samuel E. Thorne eds., 1979) (1709) ("It is therefore called Common Right, and is a greater Inheritance to every Man, than that which descends to him . . . [b]ecause thereby his Goods, Lands, Wife, Children, his Body, Life, Honour, and Estimation, *are protected from Injury and Wrong.*") (emphasis added).

17. According to Burlamaqui, "[w]e should do no wrong to any one, either in word or action; and we ought to repair all damages by us committed; for society could not subsist, were injustices tolerated." J.J. Burlamaqui, Principles of Natural Law 171 (M. Nugent trans., 1748); *see also id.* at 189 ("the principal and last end of punishment is therefore the safety and tranquility of society").

18. Hume asserted that individuals have a natural liberty which may, when exercised, harm others; individuals thus form government for which "the sole foundation of the duty of allegiance is the *advantage,* which it procures to society, by preserving peace and order among mankind." David Hume, 2 Essays: Moral, Political & Literary (1742), *reprinted in* 4 David Hume: The Philosophical Works, at 197 (Thomas Hill Green & Thomas Hodge Grose eds., Scientia Verlag Aalen 1964) (emphasis in original).

19. In his 1761 *Historical Law-Tracts,* Lord Kames observed that "[t]he perfection of human society, consists in that just degree of union among individuals, which to each reserves

freedom and independency, *so far as is consistent with peace and good order*." Henry Home, Lord Kames, Historical Law-Tracts 80 (Legal Classics Library Special ed. 1988) (2d ed. 1761) (emphasis added).

20. DeLolme tersely observed, "What then is Liberty? Liberty, I would answer, as far as it is possible to exist in a Society of Beings whose interests are almost perpetually opposed to each other, consists in this, that every Man, while he respects the persons of others, and allows them quietly to enjoy the produce of their industry, be certain himself likewise to enjoy the produce of his own industry; and that his person be also secure." J.L. De Lolme, The Constitution of England 225 (1775).

21. *See* Cesare Beccaria-Bonesana, An Essay on Crimes & Punishments 17 (Edward D. Ingraham trans., Academic Reprints 1953) (1764) ("[E]very act of authority of one man over another, for which there is not absolute necessity, is tyrannical."); *id.* at 18 ("[I]t was necessity that forced men to give up a part of their liberty. It is certain, then, that every individual would choose to put into the public stock the smallest portion possible, as much only as was sufficient to engage others to defend it. The aggregate of these, the smallest portions possible, forms the right of punishing; all that extends beyond this, is abuse, not justice.").

22. Grotius reasoned, "Now right reason and the nature of society . . . prohibit not all force, but only that which is repugnant to society, by depriving another of his right. For the end of society is to form a common and united aid to preserve to every one his own. . . . It is not therefore contrary to the nature of society to provide and consult for ourselves, if another's right is not injured; the force therefore, which inviolably abstains from touching the rights of others, is not unjust." Hugo Grotius, The Rights of War & Peace 33–34 (A.C. Campbell ed., M. Walter Dunne 1901) (1625).

23. "The political liberty of the subject is a tranquility of mind arising from the opinion each person has of his safety. In order to have this liberty, it is requisite that government be so constituted as one man need not be afraid of another." M. De Secondat, Baron De Montesquieu, 1 The Spirit of Laws 218–19 (Thomas Nugent trans., 4th ed. 1766).

24. Samuel Von Pufendorf, 2 De Officio Hominis et Civil Juxta Legem Naturalem Libri Duo 37 (Frank Gardner Moore trans., 1927) (1673) ("Among the absolute duties, i.e., of anybody to anybody, the first place belongs to this one: let no one injure another."); *id.* at 110 ("[I]t is the chief end of states, that by mutual agreement and help men should be safe from the losses and injuries which their fellow-men can, and often do, inflict."); Samuel Von Pufendorf, 2 De Jure Naturae Et Gentium Libro Octo 313 (C.H. Oldfather & W.A. Oldfather trans., 1934) (1688) ("Thus far we have shown what duties the law of nature enjoins upon a man toward himself, and how much freedom or indulgence it allows him in the preservation of his person and his property. . . . Under absolute duties, which obligate men even before the formation of any human institution, we allow, with all confidence, first place to these two: *I. No one should hurt another; and II. If he has caused another loss, he should make it good.*") (emphasis in original).

25. John Warr, The Corruption & Deficiency of the Laws of England, Soberly Discovered: Or, Liberty Working Up to its Just Height, *reprinted in* 6 The Harleian Miscellany, at 213–15 (1810) (1649) ("That the pure and genuine intent of laws was to bridle princes, not the people, and to keep rulers within the bounds of just

and righteous government . . . . So that here is the proper fountain of good and righteous laws, a spirit of understanding big with freedom, and having a single respect to people's rights . . . . But how can such laws be good, which swerve from their end? *The end of just laws is the safety and freedom of a people.*") (emphasis added).

26. JAMES WILSON, LECTURES ON LAW (1790–91), *reprinted in* 1 WORKS OF JAMES WILSON, at 276 (emphasis added).

27. *Id.* at 2 WORKS OF JAMES WILSON, at 612–13.

28. *Id.* at 612 ("Every crime includes an injury: every offence is also a private wrong: it affects the publick [sic] but it affects the individual likewise. . . . Violence against the person of an individual is a disturbance of the public peace. On this disturbance punishment may be inflicted. But in the crime and punishment, the injury is not sunk, nor is the reparation lost. The party who has suffered the violence may bring his action against the party who has committed it: and recover in damages a satisfaction for the loss, which has been sustained.").

29. JOHN DICKINSON, THE LETTERS OF FABIUS ON THE FEDERAL CONSTITUTION (1788), *reprinted in* PAMPHLETS, at 176.

30. John Jay, *Charge to the Grand Jury* (May 22, 1793), *in* 3 CORRESPONDENCE & PUBLIC PAPERS OF JOHN JAY, at 484 (emphasis added).

31. THE FEDERALIST NO. 54 (James Madison).

32. James Madison, *Property,* NAT'L GAZETTE, Mar. 29, 1792, *available at* The Constitution Society, Selected Works of James Madison (Jon Rowland ed.), http://www.constitution. org/jm/17920329_property.txt (emphasis added). Madison's article also stated that a "larger and juster meaning [of property] . . . embraces . . . everything to which a man may attach a value and have a right . . . . [A] man has property in his opinions and the free communication of them. He has a property of peculiar value in his religious opinions, and in the profession and practices dictated by them. He has property very dear to him in the safety and liberty of his person. He has an equal property in the free use of his faculties and free choice of the objects on which to employ them. In a word, as a man is said to have a right in his property, he may be equally said to have a property in his rights." *Id.* Madison's broad conception of "property" is very similar to that of John Locke. *See* LOCKE'S SECOND TREATISE, at 12 ("Though the earth and all inferior creatures be common to all men, yet every man has a property in his own person: this nobody has any right to but himself."); *id.* at 57 (Individuals unite to form a government "for the mutual preservation of their lives, liberties, and estates, which I call by the general name, property.").

33. John Hancock declared that "[t]he institution of Civil Government is intended to promote the happiness, and to *ensure the safety* of the People. . . ." John Hancock, *Speech to the Massachusetts House of Representatives* (May 26, 1791), *in* PAUL D. BRANDES, JOHN HANCOCK'S LIFE & SPEECHES 389 (1996) (emphasis added).

34. See James Iredell, *Speech Before the North Carolina Ratifying Convention* (July 31, 1788), *in* 4 ELLIOT'S DEBATES 227 (2d ed. 1836) ("The great principle is, [t]he safety of the people is the supreme law. Government was originally instituted for their welfare, and whatever may be its form, this ought to be its object.").

35. Fisher Ames, *Speech in Congress* (Feb. 9, 1790), *in* 1 WORKS OF FISHER AMES 759 (W.B.

Allen ed., Liberty Classics 1983) ("What is the object for which men enter into society, but to secure their lives and property?").

36. Hamilton concluded that the American colonies needed to break their ties with Great Britain because the British Parliament had "divest[ed] [colonists] of that *moral security for our lives and properties, which we are entitled to, and which is the primary end of society to bestow.*" ALEXANDER HAMILTON, THE FARMER REFUTED (1775), *reprinted in* 1 THE WORKS OF ALEXANDER HAMILTON, at 61 (Henry Cabot Lodge ed., 1885) (emphasis added).

37. ELBRIDGE GERRY, OBSERVATIONS ON THE NEW CONSTITUTION & ON THE FEDERAL & STATE CONVENTIONS BY A COLUMBIAN PATRIOT (1788), *reprinted in* PAMPHLETS, at 6 ("All writers on government agree, and the feelings of the human mind witness the truth of these political axioms, that man is born free and possessed of certain unalienable rights—that government is instituted for the protection, safety and happiness of the people").

38. THOMAS JEFFERSON, NOTES ON THE STATE OF VIRGINIA 235–36 (1801) (emphasis added). Joseph Story likewise viewed the First Amendment as implicitly embracing a harm principle. *See* JOSEPH STORY, 3 COMMENTARIES ON THE CONSTITUTION OF THE UNITED STATES 732 (Hilliard Gray & Co. 1833) ("It is plain, then, that the language of this [First] amendment imports no more, than that every man shall have a right to speak, write and print his opinions upon any subject whatsoever, without any prior restraint, so always, that he does not injure any other person in his rights, person, property, or reputation").

39. Thomas Jefferson, *First Inaugural Address* (1801), *reprinted in* THE POLITICAL WRITINGS OF THOMAS JEFFERSON: REPRESENTATIVE SELECTIONS 43–44 (Edward Dumbauld ed., 1955) (emphasis added) [hereinafter WRITINGS OF JEFFERSON]. Jefferson also helped Lafayette draft the French Revolution's primary document, the *Declaration of the Rights of Man and Citizen,* which proclaimed in Article IV, "Liberty consists in the freedom to do everything which injures no one else; hence the exercise of the natural rights of each man has no limits except those which assure to the other members of the society the enjoyment of the same rights." DECLARATION OF THE RIGHTS OF MAN & CITIZEN art. IV (1789).

40. Letter from Thomas Jefferson to Francis W. Gilmer (June 7, 1816), *in* WRITINGS OF JEFFERSON, at 55 (emphasis added).

41. Centinel stated that "*the great end of civil government is to protect the weak from the oppression of the powerful,* to put every man upon the level of equal liberty." LETTER FROM CENTINEL TO THE PEOPLE OF PENNSYLVANIA (No. IV) (1787), *reprinted in* 2 THE COMPLETE ANTI-FEDERALIST, at 172–73 (Herbert J. Storing ed., Univ. of Chicago Press 1981) (emphasis added) [hereinafter COMPLETE ANTI-FEDERALIST].

42. LETTER FROM THE IMPARTIAL EXAMINER TO THE FREE PEOPLE OF VIRGINIA (No. I) (1788), *reprinted in* 5 COMPLETE ANTI-FEDERALIST, at 176 ("[T]he advantages derived from a government are to be estimated by the *strength* of the *security,* which is attended at once with the *least sacrifice* and the *greatest acquired benefits.* The government, therefore, which is best adapted to these three *great ends,* must certainly be the best constituted scheme of *civil policy.*") (emphasis in original).

43. Brutus asserted:

> In a state of nature every individual pursues his own interest. . . . In this state of things, every individual was insecure; common interest therefore directed, that government should be established . . . to *protect and defend every one who composed it. The common good, therefore, is the end of civil government . . . .* To effect this end, it was necessary that a certain portion of natural liberty should be surrendered, in order, that what remained should be preserved . . . . *So much, however, must be given up, as will be sufficient to enable those, to whom the administration of the government is committed, to establish laws for the promoting the happiness of the community, and to carry these laws into effect. But it is not necessary, for this purpose, that individuals should relinquish all their natural rights. Some are of such a nature that they cannot be surrendered. Of this kind are the rights of conscience, the right of enjoying and defending life, etc.*

ESSAYS OF BRUTUS (NO. II) (1787), *reprinted in* 2 COMPLETE ANTI-FEDERALIST, at 373 (emphasis added). Brutus makes this point again in a later letter when he asserts, "The design of civil government is to protect the rights and promote the happiness of the people. For this end, rulers are invested with powers. But we cannot from hence justly infer that these powers should be unlimited. There are certain rights which mankind possess, over which government ought not to have any controul [sic], because it is not necessary they should, in order to attain the end of its institution." ESSAYS OF BRUTUS (NO. IX) (1788), *reprinted in* 2 COMPLETE ANTI-FEDERALIST, at 408. *Accord id.* at 400–01 (discussing how the "protection and defence" of the community is the proper exercise of governmental authority).

44. James Winthrop, a Harvard librarian writing under the pseudonym of "Agrippa," stated it succinctly: "It is universally agreed, that the object of every just government is to render the people happy, *by securing their persons and possessions from wrong.*" JAMES WINTHROP, LETTERS OF AGRIPPA (NO. XII) (1788), *reprinted in* 4 COMPLETE ANTI-FEDERALIST, at 93 (emphasis added).

45. Writing as the "Republican Federalist," Massachusetts Speaker of the House James Warren asserted that "Of all compacts, a Constitution or Frame of government is the most solemn and important, and should be strictly adhered to. The *object of it is the preservation of that property, which every individual of the community has, in his life, liberty, and estate.*" LETTERS OF A REPUBLICAN FEDERALIST (NO. III) (1788), *reprinted in* 4 COMPLETE ANTI-FEDERALIST, at 172 (emphasis added).

46. Mercy Otis Warren (the wife of James Warren), writing as the "Columbian Patriot" in 1788, stated, "All writers on government agree, and the feelings of the human mind witness the truth of these political axioms, that man is born free and possessed of certain inalienable rights—*that government is instituted for the protection, safety, and happiness of the people.*" OBSERVATIONS ON THE NEW CONSTITUTION & ON THE FEDERAL & STATE CONVENTIONS BY A COLUMBIAN PATRIOT (1788), *reprinted in* 4 COMPLETE ANTI-FEDERALIST, at 274 (emphasis added).

47. George Clinton, writing as Cato, asked his readers to consider "whether [the proposed Constitution] will answer the ends for which it was offered to you, and *for which all men engage in political society, to wit, the preservation of their lives, liberties, and estates.*" CATO,

III (Oct. 25, 1787), *reprinted* in Essays on the Constitution of the United States Published During its Discussion by the People, 1787–1788 255 (Paul Leicester Ford ed., Historical Printing Club 1892).

48. 1 William Blackstone, Commentaries on the Laws of England 125–130 (William S. Hein & Co. 1992) (1765) [hereinafter Blackstone's Commentaries].

49. Thomas Jefferson, *Legal Argument* (1770), *in* 1 The Writings of Thomas Jefferson 376 (Paul Leicester Ford ed., 1892).

50. 1 Blackstone's Commentaries, at 130.

51. U.S. Const. art. I, § 9. *See also* 1 Blackstone's Commentaries, at 131–34 (discussing the importance of the writ of habeas corpus to the protection of the right of personal liberty).

52. *See* Saenz v. Roe, 526 U.S. 489, 498 (1999); U.S. v. Guest, 383 U.S. 745, 757 (1966); Crandall v. Nevada, 73 U.S. (6 Wall.) 35 (1868). Justice Stewart asserted that the right to travel was protected by the Constitution against either governmental or private interference. Shapiro v. Thompson, 394 U.S. 618, 643 (1969) (Stewart, J., concurring) ("[The right to travel] is a right broadly assertable against private interference as well as governmental action. Like the right of association, it is a virtually unconditional personal right, guaranteed by the Constitution to us all.") (internal citations omitted). Justice Stewart's conception of the right to travel was approvingly cited by a majority of the Court in *Saenz*. 526 U.S. at 498. The right to travel is of course an unenumerated right, mentioned nowhere in the text of the Constitution. The Supreme Court still has not explicitly decided the constitutional source of the right to travel. If the Court would simply honor the substantive meaning of the Ninth Amendment, the proper source of this and other unenumerated rights would be immediately clear.

53. An individual's reputation was clearly regarded, at the time of the founding, to be one of the essential rights of mankind. Blackstone, for example, considered it to be included within the "absolute rights of individuals." *See* 1 Blackstone's Commentaries, at 125, 130; 3 Blackstone's Commentaries, at 123–27. *See also* 2 Works of James Wilson, at 594 ("Well may character, then, be considered as one of the natural rights of man: well may it be classed among those rights, the enjoyment of which it is the design of good government and laws to secure and enlarge: well does it deserve their encouragement and protection").

54. U.S. Const. amend. V ("nor shall private property be taken for public use without just compensation."); *id.* at amend. IV ("The right of the people to be secure in their persons, houses, papers, and effects, against unreasonable searches and seizures, shall not be violated"); *id.* at art. I, § 10 ("No State shall . . . pass any . . . Law impairing the Obligation of Contracts"); *id.* at amend. V ("No person shall . . . be deprived of life, liberty or property, without due process of law"); *id.* at amend. XIV, § 1 ("No State shall . . . deprive any person of life, liberty, or property, without due process of law").

55. *See generally* 2 Blackstone's Commentaries. It should be noted that the definitional framework I offer here for the three categories of harms differs with Blackstone in one minor respect. Blackstone conceptualized reputational harm as a "life" harm, whereas I conceptualize it as a type of "property" harm. *See* 1 Blackstone's Commentaries, at 125, 130. I choose to conceptualize reputational harms as a type of intangible personal

property, similar to intellectual property, simply because I think it offers a better intellectual fit. Harm to one's reputation, after all, may hurt one's standing with neighbors or business associates—a valuable type of intangible property—but it will not harm one's body. *Accord* 2 Works of James Wilson, at 595 ("[T]he honour of character is a property, which is, indeed, precious.").

56. My definition of harm is similar to that proffered by Randy Barnett, who limits cognizable legal harm to physical interference with another's resources. *See* Randy E. Barnett, The Structure of Liberty 74 (1998) ("Persons should be free to do whatever they wish with their own justly acquired resources provided that this use does not (a) *physically interfere* with (b) another person's *use and enjoyment* of his or her resources.") (emphasis in original). As Barnett rightly points out, employing external, physical interference as the demarcation line between legitimate and illegitimate exercises of government authority may not easily decide all hypothetical cases, "[y]et no rule or principle is entirely without difficulties. The fact that a legal rule produces many hard cases does not mean that it does not also handle most cases with relative ease: cases of murder, rape, robbery, and theft, for example." *Id.* at 75.

57. Reputational damage, to the extent it results from an act of adultery, reasonably can be expected to flow to the cheating spouse, not the non-cheater.

58. Reputational harm, after all, is a specific type of property harm, since one's reputation surely has a value that can be harmed by defamatory remarks. Of course, in order to recover for damage to one's reputation, one bears the burden of proving, by a preponderance of the evidence, that one has suffered a demonstrable reputational loss.

59. For an incisive article arguing for the elimination of recovery for noneconomic damages relating to pain and suffering, see Joseph H. King, Jr., *Pain & Suffering, Noneconomic Damages & the Goals of Tort Law,* 57 SMU L. Rev. 163 (2004).

60. Joel Feinberg posed this interesting hypothetical. *See* Joel Feinberg, Harm to Others: The Moral Limits of the Criminal Law 49 (1984).

61. William Prosser was the primary advocate for the recognition of the tort of intentional infliction of emotional distress, beginning in the late 1930s. *See generally* William L. Prosser, *Intentional Infliction of Mental Suffering: A New Tort,* 37 Mich. L. Rev. 874 (1939). The tort of negligent infliction of emotional distress is of even more recent origin.

62. See Paul T. Hayden, *Religiously Motivated "Outrageous" Conduct: Intentional Infliction of Emotional Distress as a Weapon Against "Other People's Faiths,"* 34 Wm. & Mary L. Rev. 580 (1993); Dennis P. Duffy, *Intentional Infliction of Emotional Distress & Employment at Will: The Case Against "Tortification" of Labor & Employment Law,* 74 B.U. L. Rev. 387 (1994); Susan Kirkpatrick, *Note, Falwell v. Flynt: Intentional Infliction of Emotional Distress as a Threat to Free Speech,* 81 Nw. U. L. Rev. 993 (1987); Robert J. Rhee, *A Principled Solution for Negligent Infliction of Emotional Distress Claims,* 36 Ariz. St. L.J. 805, 806 (2004) ("Although mental injuries can be as real and severe as physical ones, the law dealing with this interest is anything but principled or uniform. . . . The criticism has been legion, and even courts at the highest levels have candidly conceded the arbitrary nature of these rules.").

63. This hypothetical was posed by Patrick Devlin. *See* Devlin, at 106.

64. *Id.*

65. *Id.* at 110.

66. *Cf.* Friends of the Earth, Inc. v. Laidlaw Envtl. Services, 528 U.S. 167, 183–84 (2000) (recognizing that group of nearby residents had suffered injury in fact, and hence had standing to sue company charged with violating the Clean Water Act, based on allegations of harmed economic, recreational, and aesthetic interests).

67. The Indiana Supreme Court delivered a classic exposition of the law of nuisance in 1855:

> [T]he legislature cannot declare the path from my house to my barn, nor any obstruction I may place in it, a nuisance, and order it discontinued; nor can it declare my storeroom and stock of goods a nuisance, prohibit my selling them, and order them destroyed; because such acts would invade private property which the constitution protects. Still, the fact may be that the path and the store-room are nuisances which I have no right to maintain; for while I have the right to use my own property, still I must not so use it as to injure others. So all trades, practices and property, may, by the manner, time, or place or use, become nuisances in fact, in quality; and subject, consequently, to forfeiture and abatement: for example, slaughter-houses in cities, or some descriptions of retailing houses; and this the legislature may have inquired into, and, if the fact of nuisance be found, may have the forfeiture and abatement adjudged and executed. And it is the province of the judiciary to conduct the inquiry, and declare the fact, or deny it, as the truth may turn out to be.

Herman v. State, 8 Ind. 490, 498 (1855).

68. *See* H.G. WOOD, A PRACTICAL TREATISE ON THE LAW OF NUISANCES 1–10 (1883); *accord* E. HOLROYD PEARCE & DOUGALL MESTON, LAW RELATING TO NUISANCES 49–76 (1926).

69. *See, e.g.,* Village of Euclid v. Ambler Realty Co., 272 U.S. 365 (1926); Camfield v. U.S., 167 U.S. 518, 522 (1897). *See also* 3 BLACKSTONE'S COMMENTARIES, at 217.

70. *See, e.g.,* NYC C.L.A.S.H., Inc. v. City of New York, 315 F. Supp.2d 461, 494–95 (S.D.N.Y. 2004) ("[T]he evidence in the record before the Court makes clear that the smoking prohibition . . . [is] but the latest development of what has been an evolution of smoking regulation prompted by scientific research confirming over the past 20 years or so that ETS [environmental tobacco smoke] poses potential health risks to non-smokers.").

71. *See, e.g.,* Hill v. Colorado, 530 U.S. 703 (2000); Ward v. Rock Against Racism, 491 U.S. 781 (1989); City Council of the City of Los Angeles v. Taxpayers for Vincent, 466 U.S. 789 (1984).

72. James Wilson, for example, seems to assume, by his definition of injury, that legally cognizable injury cannot be self-inflicted. *See* 2 WORKS OF JAMES WILSON, at 611 ("An injury is a loss arising to an individual, from the violation or infringement of his right."). It would be difficult to see how, under Wilson's definition, an individual could be considered to have violated or infringed his own rights. John Stuart Mill likewise did not believe that purely self-regarding conduct could be properly cognizable under the law, though indulgence in self-regarding conduct could ultimately cause injury to others that would be cognizable, such as a drunkard who fails to pay his debts or a parent who fails to support his child. *See* MILL, at 148–49.

73. For example, although Locke clearly condemned suicide as beyond the realm of individual liberty, he does not address other, less severe forms of self-harm. *See* LOCKE'S SECOND TREATISE, at 3 ("But though this be a state of liberty, yet it is not a state of license; though man in that state may have an uncontrollable liberty to dispose of his person or possessions, yet he has not liberty to destroy himself"); *id.* ("Every one, as he is bound to preserve himself, and not to quit his station willfully . . . ."); *id.* at 62 ("nobody has an absolute arbitrary power over himself, or over any other, to destroy his own life, or take away the life or property of another."). *See also* BECCARIA, ON CRIMES & PUNISHMENTS & OTHER WRITINGS 83–86 (Richard Bellamy ed. & Richard Davies trans., 1995) (1765) (concluding about suicide "because only he [God] can punish after death, it [suicide] is not a crime among men, since the punishment, instead of falling on the malefactor, falls on his family. If it should be urged . . . that such a punishment may nevertheless draw a man back from killing himself, I reply that one who calmly gives up the benefits of life, who so hates life here below to prefer an eternity of sorrow, could hardly be prevailed upon by the less powerful and more distant thought of his children or relatives.").

74. Thomas Jefferson, *Notes on Locke and Shaftesbury, in* 1 PAPERS OF THOMAS JEFFERSON, 1760–1776, at 546 (Julian P. Boyd ed., 1950).

75. 17 U.S. (4 Wheat.) 235 (1819).

76. *Id.* at 242.

77. *Id.* at 242–43.

78. *Id.* at 243–44.

79. *Id.* at 242.

80. *Id.*

81. *Id.* at 242–43.

82. *See, e.g.,* Elk Grove Unified Sch. Dist. v. Newdow, 542 U.S. 1 (2004) (noncustodial father lacked prudential standing to challenge Pledge of Allegiance on behalf of daughter); Allen v. Wright, 468 U.S. 737 (1984) (parents of black school children lacked standing to challenge IRS standards regarding tax-exempt status of racially discriminatory private schools).

83. I am grateful to Randy Barnett for coining this phrase and articulating this powerful conception of the purpose of the Ninth Amendment. *See* Randy E. Barnett, *Introduction: Implementing the Ninth Amendment, in* 2 THE RIGHTS RETAINED BY THE PEOPLE: THE HISTORY & MEANING OF THE NINTH AMENDMENT 23–27 (Randy E. Barnett ed., 1993).

84. At what age or level of incapacitation the government may presume an individual to be a minor or non compos mentis is not the subject of this work. Suffice it to say that such line-drawing should be based on reasonable evidence and should, in order to effectuate fully the morality of American law, be rebuttable upon evidence to the contrary.

85. Section 71 of the Restatement (Second) of Contracts defines consideration thus:

   (1) To constitute consideration, a performance or a return promise must be bargained for.
   (2) A performance or return promise is bargained for if it is sought by the promisor in exchange for his promise and is given by the promisee in exchange for that promise.
   (3) The performance may consist of

(a) an act other than a promise, or

(b) a forbearance, or

(c) the creation, modification, or destruction of a legal relation.

RESTATEMENT (SECOND) OF CONTRACTS § 71.

86. For an interesting recent article on the complexities of consideration (and recent trends indicating its relaxation), see Peter Linzer, *Teaching Important Contracts Concepts: Consider Consideration,* 44 St. LOUIS L.J. 1317 (2000).

87. Some courts have, on occasion, dispensed with consideration and enforced contracts based on the provision of past services, reasoning that there is a "moral obligation" to enforce the promise. *See, e.g.,* Webb v. McGowin, 168 So. 196 (Ala. Ct. App. 1935); Estate of Hatten, 288 N.W. 278 (Wis. 1940). *See also* RESTATEMENT (SECOND) OF CONTRACTS § 86(1) ("A promise made in recognition of a benefit previously received by the promisor from the promisee is binding to the extent necessary to prevent injustice."). Perhaps needless to say, I find the notion of enforcing promises based solely on moral obligation to be contrary to the morality of American law.

88. 123 S. Ct. 2472 (2003).

89. 478 U.S. 186 (1986).

90. The majority stated, "The petitioners are entitled to respect for their private lives. The State cannot demean their existence or control their destiny by making their private sexual conduct a crime. Their right to liberty under the Due Process Clause gives them the full right to engage in their conduct without intervention of the government." 123 S. Ct. at 2484.

91. *See id.* (O'Connor, J., concurring) ("I agree with the Court that Texas' statute banning same-sex sodomy is unconstitutional. Rather than relying on the substantive component of the Fourteenth Amendment's Due Process Clause, as the Court does, I base my conclusion on the Fourteenth Amendment's Equal Protection Clause.").

92. *See id.* (O'Connor, J., concurring). Justice O'Connor asserted, "Texas attempts to justify its law, and the effects of the law, by arguing that the statute satisfies rational basis review because it furthers the legitimate governmental interest of the promotion of morality. In *Bowers* we held that a state law criminalizing sodomy as applied to homosexual couples did not violate substantive due process. We rejected the argument that no rational basis existed to justify the law, pointing to the government's interest in promoting morality. . . . This case raises a different issue than *Bowers:* whether, under the Equal Protection Clause, moral disapproval is a legitimate state interest to justify by itself a statute that bans homosexual sodomy, but not heterosexual sodomy. It is not." *Id.* at 2486 (O'Connor, J., concurring).

93. *Id.* at 2486–87 (O'Connor, J., concurring).

94. *Id.* at 2487 (O'Connor, J., concurring).

95. *Id.* at 2490 (Scalia, J., dissenting).

96. *Id.* at 2491 (Scalia, J., dissenting).

97. *Id.* at 2490 (Scalia, J., dissenting).

98. *Id.* at 2491 (Scalia, J., dissenting). This last reference—60 hours per week in a bakery—refers to *Lochner v. New York,* a 1905 decision of the Supreme Court which invalidated, under substantive due process, a New York law limiting the number of hours per week a

baker could work. 198 U.S. 45 (1905). *Lochner* is routinely condemned by modern jurists as the height of subjective, anti-majoritarian judicial activism.

99. Specifically, the *Lawrence* majority concluded that laws prohibiting sodomy were historically directed at stopping non-procreative (not homosexual) sex, were not enforced against private activity between consenting adults, and were out of step with national and international trends toward toleration toward homosexuals. Lawrence, 123 S. Ct. at 2478–81.

100. *Id.* at 2483 ("In the United States criticism of *Bowers* has been substantial and continuing, disapproving of its reasoning in all respects, not just its historical assumptions.").

101. *Id.* ("The holding in *Bowers* . . . has not induced detrimental reliance comparable to some instances where recognized individual rights are involved. Indeed, there has been no individual or societal reliance on *Bowers* of the sort that could counsel against overturning its holding once there are compelling reasons for doing so.").

102. *Id.* at 2481 ("Two principal cases [*Casey* and *Romer*] decided after *Bowers* cast its holding into even more doubt.").

103. *Id.* at 2483 (quoting from Bowers v. Hardwick, 478 U.S. at 216 (Stevens, J., dissenting)) (emphasis added).

104. *Id.* at 2484.

105. This may appear to be a rather strange hypothetical, but it is based upon an English law passed during the reign of King Edward IV, which "forbad the fine gentlemen of those times . . . to wear pikes upon their shoes or boots of more than two inches in length[,]" a law that Blackstone characterized as "a law that favoured of opression." 1 BLACKSTONE'S COMMENTARIES, at 122.

106. Again, this hypothetical is based upon an early law in the Massachusetts colony that proclaimed that "no person shall henceforth use the . . . game of Shuffle-board" in a "house of common entertainment" because "much pretious [sic] time is spent unfruitfully and much wast [sic] of wine and beer occasioned." *See* LAWRENCE M. FRIEDMAN, CRIME & PUNISHMENT IN AMERICAN HISTORY 36 (1993).

CHAPTER 4. MARRIAGE

1. *See* LAWRENCE STONE, THE FAMILY, SEX & MARRIAGE IN ENGLAND 1500–1800 30 (Weidenfeld & Nicholson 1977). Blackstone described marriage this way: "Our law considers marriage in no other light than as a civil contract. The holiness of the matrimonial state is left entirely to the ecclesiastical law. . . . The punishment therefore, or annulling, of incestuous or other unscriptural marriages, is the province of the spiritual courts; which acts *pro salute animae*. And, taking it in this civil light, the law treats it as it does all other contracts; allowing it to be good and valid in all cases, where the parties at the time of making it were, in the first place, *willing* to contract; secondly, *able* to contract; and lastly, actually *did* contract, in the proper forms and solemnities required by law." 1 WILLIAM BLACKSTONE, COMMENTARIES ON THE LAWS OF ENGLAND 421 (1765) (emphasis in original). Jewish tradition still considers marriage to be a contract between the betrothed, requiring married couples to sign a contract (the ketuba), which, though primarily symbolic, sets forth the basic expectations of marriage. *See*

Note, *Enforceability of Religious Law in Secular Courts—It's Kosher, But is it Constitutional?*, 71 MICH. L. REV. 1641 (1972).

2. STONE, at 35. English ecclesiastical courts acquired jurisdiction over the basic accouterments of marriage after King Henry VIII broke with the Catholic Church in an effort to obtain a divorce from Catherine of Aragon and marry his mistress Anne Boleyn.

3. *See* Skinner v. Oklahoma, 316 U.S. 535, 541 (1942) (describing marriage as one of the "basic civil rights of man"); Loving v. Virginia, 388 U.S. 1, 12 (1967) (marriage is "one of the vital personal rights essential to the orderly pursuit of happiness by free men"); Zablocki v. Redhail, 434 U.S. 374, 384 (1978) ("the decision to marry [i]s among the personal decisions protected by the right of privacy").

4. 388 U.S. 1 (1967).

5. *Id.* at 12.

6. *Id.* ("There can be no doubt that restricting the freedom to marry solely because of racial classifications violates the central meaning of the Equal Protection Clause."); *id.* ("The Fourteenth Amendment [Due Process Clause] requires that the freedom of choice to marry not be restricted by invidious racial discriminations.").

7. 434 U.S. 374, 375 (1978).

8. *Id.* at 384.

9. *Id.* at 386.

10. *Id.* at 389.

11. *See id.* at 388 ("When a statutory classification significantly interferes with the exercise of a fundamental right, it cannot be upheld unless it is supported by sufficiently important state interests and is closely tailored to effectuate only those interests.").

12. *Id.* at 396–97 (Powell, J., concurring) ("The Court does not present, however, any principled means for distinguishing between the two types of regulations. Since state regulation in this area typically takes the form of a prerequisite or barrier to marriage or divorce, the degree of 'direct' interference with the decision to marry or to divorce is unlikely to provide either guidance for state legislatures or a basis for judicial oversight.").

13. Erie R.R. v. Tompkins, 304 U.S. 64 (1938). *See also* Guaranty Trust Co. v. York, 326 U.S. 99, 108 (1945) ("Matters of 'substance' and matters of 'procedure' are much talked about in books as though they defined a great divide cutting across the whole domain of law. But, of course, 'substance' and 'procedure' are the same key-words to very different problems.").

14. *Zablocki*, 434 U.S. at 392 (Stewart, J., concurring).

15. *Id.* (Stewart, J., concurring).

16. Justice Stewart explained, "[T]he State's legitimate concern with the financial soundness of prospective marriages must stop short of telling people they may not marry because they are too poor or because they might persist in their financial irresponsibility. The invasion of constitutionally protected liberty and the chance of erroneous prediction are simply too great." *Id.* at 395 (Stewart, J., concurring).

17. In Massachusetts, Representative Paul Losocco introduced legislation to abolish all civil marriages, rendering marriage a religious ceremony, much like a baptism or bar mitzvah. *See Weekend All Things Considered* (Nat'l Public Radio broadcast, Apr. 25, 2004), *avail-*

able at LEXIS, News Library, Curnws File (interview with Rep. Losocco). I have also previously argued that civil marriage should be abolished, not because I am opposed to same-sex marriage, but because I am not convinced that regulating marriage is a legitimate exercise of governmental power. *See* Elizabeth Price Foley, *Promote Families,* Nat'l L.J., Sept. 20, 2004, at 27.

18. Seven American states still have cohabitation statutes: Florida, Fla. Stat. Ann. 6 798.02 (West 2003); Massachusetts, Mass. Gen. Laws ch. 272, § 16 (2004); Michigan, Mich. Comp. Laws § 750.335 (2004); Mississippi, Miss. Code Ann. § 97-29-1 (2004); North Carolina, N.C. Gen. Stat. § 14-184 (2004); North Dakota, N.D. Cent. Code § 12.1-20-10 (2003); Virginia, Va. Code Ann. § 18.2-345 (2004); and West Virginia, W. Va. Code § 61-8-4 (2004).

19. Cohabitation statutes sometimes are broadly worded to prohibit any "lewd and lascivious" (i.e., sexual) cohabitation, regardless of the gender of the parties. *See, e.g.,* Mich. Comp. Laws § 750.335; Va. Code Ann. § 18.2-345; W. Va. Code § 61-8-4. Other cohabitation statutes are more narrowly worded to prohibit only sexual cohabitation by opposite-sex couples. *See, e.g.,* Fla. Stat. Ann. § 798.02; N.D. Cent. Code § 12.1-20-10.

20. *See* Mass. Gen. Laws ch. 208, § 40; Mich. Comp. Laws § 750.32; Miss. Code Ann. § 93-5-29.

21. *See* U.S. Census Bureau, Census 2000 Summary File 3 (over 5.2 million adults lived in unmarried-partner households in 2000, 87.4% of which were male-female, and 12.6% of which were same-sex).

22. Tom W. Smith, Nat'l Opinion Research Ctr., Univ. of Chicago, GSS Topical Rep. No. 25, *American Sexual Behavior: Trends, Socio-Demographic Differences, & Risk Behavior* tbl. 3(A) (45% of adults age 30–34 and 42% of adults age 25–29 have cohabited at some point).

23. *See, e.g.,* Erwin v. Erwin, 773 P.2d 847, 849 (Utah Ct. App. 1989) (trial court did not abuse discretion in considering mother's open cohabitation as a factor in awarding custody to father).

24. A recent case of housing discrimination occurred in North Dakota, in which a landlord refused to rent an apartment to an engaged couple. The North Dakota Supreme Court ruled that such discrimination was lawful. North Dakota Fair Housing Council, Inc. v. Peterson, 625 N.W.2d 551 (N.D. 2001). The furor surrounding the decision resulted in the introduction of legislation to repeal the law. *See* Dale Wetzel, *Lawmaker Asks for Repeal of Cohabitation Law,* Bismark Tribune, Jan. 14, 2003, at 4D, *available at* LEXIS, Nexis Library, Curnws File. In April 2003 the North Dakota Senate voted to retain cohabitation as a crime, with one Republican senator explaining that the law "stands as a reminder that there is right and there is wrong." *See Cohabiting Ban Stays,* The Press (Christchurch), Apr. 7, 2003, at B7, *available at* LEXIS, Nexis Library, Curnws File (quoting Senator John Andrist). Other states have reached the same conclusion. *See, e.g.,* Minnesota v. French, 460 N.W.2d 2 (Minn. 1990); Mister v. A.R.K. Partnership, 553 N.E.2d 1152 (Ill. Ct. App. 1990); Maryland Comm'n on Human Relations v. Greenbelt Homes, 475 A.2d 1192 (Md. Ct. App. 1984). *Contra* Foreman v. Anchorage Equal Rights Comm'n, 779 P.2d 1199 (Alaska 1989) (landlord's policy against renting to unmarried

couples violated laws prohibiting discrimination based on marital status); Zahorian v. Russell Fitt Real Estate Agency, 301 A.2d 754 (N.J. 1973) (same).

25. *See, e.g.,* Waggoner. v. Ace Hardware Corp., 953 P.2d 88 (Wash. 1998) (state statute prohibiting discrimination based on "marital status" does not prohibit employer from terminating cohabiting employees).

26. *See, e.g.,* McFadden v. Elma Country Club, 613 P.2d 146 (Wash. Ct. App. 1980) (country club may deny membership to cohabiting applicant); Prince George's County v. Greenbelt Homes, 431 A.2d 745 (Md. Ct. App. 1981) (same).

27. *See* Bettie Fennell, STAR NEWS (WILMINGTON, N.C.), Mar. 24, 2004, at 1A, *available at* LEXIS, News Library, Curnws File.

28. *Id.*

29. This is the language of the Uniform Marriage and Divorce Act. *See* UNIF. MARRIAGE & DIVORCE ACT § 201, 9 U.L.A. 101 (1979) ("Marriage is a personal relationship between a man and a woman arising out of a civil contract to which the consent of the parties is essential.").

30. *Leviticus* 18:22.

31. Baehr v. Lewin, 852 P.2d 44 (Hawaii 1993).

32. HAWAII CONST. art. I, § 23 ("The legislature shall have the power to reserve marriage to opposite-sex couples.").

33. HAWAII REV. STAT. § 572-1 ("[T]he marriage contract . . . shall be only between a man and a woman.").

34. 28 U.S.C. § 1738C, Pub. L. No. 104–199, § 2(a), 110 Stat. 2419 (1996).

35. *See* David Morris, *Political Trump Card: Poll: Voters Side with Bush in Same-Sex Marriage Debate, available at* http://more.abcnews.go.com/sections/us/Relationships/same_sex_marriage_poll_040310.html (Mar. 10, 2004) (March 2004 poll conducted by ABC News and the *Washington Post* found 59% of Americans opposed to legalizing gay marriage). Interestingly, this same poll revealed that a slight majority (51%) of Americans support civil unions for same-sex couples. *Id.*

36. At present, 3 American states have enacted DOMA-inspired state constitutional bans on same-sex marriage. *See* ALASKA CONST. art. I, § 25; NEB. CONST. art. I, § 29; NEV. CONST. art I., § 21. In addition, 35 states have enacted DOMA-inspired statutory bans on same-sex marriage. Three American states also have statutes limiting marriage to opposite-sex couples that were enacted prior to DOMA. *See* MD. CODE ANN. FAMILY LAW § 2-201; N.H. REV. STAT. ANN. § 457:1; *id.* at § 457:2; WYO. STAT. ANN. § 20-1-101.

37. 123 S. Ct. 2472 (2003).

38. *See id.* at 2478 ("The statutes [involved in this case] seek to control a personal relationship that, whether or not entitled to formal recognition in the law, is within the liberty of persons to choose without being punished as criminals."); *id.* ("This, as a general rule, should counsel against attempts by the State, or a court, to define the meaning of the relationship or to set its boundaries absent injury to a person or abuse of an institution the law protects."); *id.* at 2484 ("The present case does not involve . . . whether the government must give formal recognition to any relationship that homosexual persons seek to enter.").

39. Justice Scalia's dissent in *Lawrence* acknowledged that the majority's opinion opened the

door to new constitutional arguments in favor of same-sex marriage: "The Court today pretends that . . . we need not fear judicial imposition of homosexual marriage . . . . Do not believe it. . . . Today's opinion dismantles the structure of constitutional law that has permitted a distinction to be made between heterosexual and homosexual unions, insofar as formal recognition in marriage is concerned. . . . This case 'does not involve' the issue of homosexual marriage only if one entertains the belief that principle and logic have nothing to do with the decisions of this Court. Many will hope that, as the Court comfortingly assures us, this is not so." *Id.* at 2497–98 (Scalia, J., dissenting).

40. Several lower courts have upheld state prohibitions against same-sex marriage against federal constitutional challenges, reasoning that there is a "rational basis" for distinguishing between opposite-sex and same-sex couples. *See, e.g.,* Seymour v. Holcomb, No. 2004-0458, 2005 WL 440509 (N.Y. Sup. Ct. Feb. 23, 2005); Standhardt v. Superior Court, 77 P.3d 451 (Ariz. Ct. App. 2003). A recent decision of a federal trial court, by contrast, concluded that Nebraska's prohibition against same-sex marriage constituted an impermissible bill of attainder and violated the First and Fourteenth Amendments of the U.S. Constitution. *See* Citizens for Equal Protection, Inc. v. Bruning, 368 F. Supp.2d 980 (D. Neb. 2005).

41. The courts relying on state constitutional provisions are split in their conclusions regarding the constitutionality of prohibitions on same-sex marriage. *See, e.g.,* Marriage Cases, No. 4365, 2005 WL 583129 (Cal. Superior Ct. Mar. 14, 2005) (statutes limiting marriage to opposite-sex couples violate California constitutional equal protection guarantee); Andersen v. King County, No. 04-2-04964-4-SEA, 2004 WL 1738447 (Wash. Super. Ct. Aug. 4, 2004) (state law banning same-sex marriage violates substantive due process and privileges and immunities clause of Washington constitution); Lewis v. Harris, 875 A.2d 259 (N.J. Super. Ct. 2005) (no due process or equal protection violations under New Jersey constitution); Li v. State, 110 P.3d 91 (Or. 2005) (county officials lacked authority under Oregon law to issue marriage licenses to same-sex couples); Morrison v. Sadler, 821 N.E.2d 15 (Ind. Ct. App. 2005) (no equal protection, due process, or privacy violations under Indiana constitution). Within New York, the lower courts have disagreed with each other as to whether the New York constitution's guarantees of equality and due process are violated. *Compare* Shields v. Madigan, 783 N.Y.S.2d 270 (Sup. Ct. 2004) (no violation of state equal protection or due process rights) *with* Hernandez v. Robles, 2005 WL 363778 (N.Y. Sup. Ct. Feb. 4, 2005) (denial of marriage licenses to same-sex couples violates their state constitutional rights to due process and equal protection); *and* People v. Greenleaf, 780 N.Y.S.2d 899 (Justice Ct. 2004) (no rational basis for ban on same-sex marriage).

42. Unlike the situation in Vermont, the Massachusetts high court explicitly advised the Massachusetts legislature that a proposed "civil union" law granting equal benefits but not the label "marriage," would not satisfy state constitutional requirements. *See* 802 N.E.2d 565 (Mass. 2004).

43. The Full Faith and Credit Clause of the U.S. Constitution requires states to give "full faith and credit" to the "public Acts, Records, and judicial Proceedings of every other State. And the Congress may by general Laws prescribe the Manner in which such Acts, Records and Proceedings shall be proved, and the Effect thereof." U.S. CONST. art. IV, § 1.

44. A handful of lower courts have directly addressed constitutional challenges to DOMA. Most of them have failed. *See, e.g.,* Smelt v. County of Orange, 2005 LEXIS U.S. Dist. 12195 (C.D. Calif., June 16, 2005) (rejecting equal protection and due process challenges to DOMA); Wilson v. Ake, 354 F. Supp.2d 1298 (M.D. Fla. 2005) (rejecting Full Faith & Credit, due process, and equal protection challenges); In re Kandu, 2004 Bankr. LEXIS 1233 (W.D. Wa. 2004) (mem.) (rejecting Fourth, Fifth, and Tenth Amendment challenges). One recent decision of the Superior Court of Washington did, however, invalidate DOMA based on the Privileges or Immunities Clause of the Washington constitution. Castle v. State, 2004 WL 1985215 (Wash. Super. Ct. 2004). For a succinct statement of the alleged constitutional infirmities of DOMA, see MARK S. STRASSER, THE CHALLENGE OF SAME-SEX MARRIAGE: FEDERALIST PRINCIPLES & CONSTITUTIONAL PROTECTIONS 185–213 (Praeger 1999). *See also* Andrew Koppelman, *Dumb & DOMA: Why the Defense of Marriage Act is Unconstitutional,* 83 IOWA L. REV. 1 (1997). For a defense of the constitutionality of DOMA, see *Gay Marriage & the Courts, Hearing Before the Senate Judiciary Comm.,* 108th Cong., 2d Sess. (Mar. 3, 2004) (statement of Leah Brilmayer, Howard M. Holtzmann Professor of International Law, Yale Law School); *see also* Leonard G. Brown, III, *Constitutionally Defending Marriage: The Defense of Marriage Act, Romer v. Evans, & the Cultural Battle They Represent,* 19 CAMPBELL L. REV. 159 (1996).

45. The proposed Federal Marriage Amendment reads: "Marriage in the United States shall consist only of the union of a man and a woman. Neither this Constitution, nor the constitution of any State, shall be construed to require that marriage or the legal incidents thereof be conferred upon a union other than the union of a man and a woman." S.J. Res. 1, 109th Cong. (2005).

46. As I stated in the Preface, the judiciary's willingness to effectively "amend" the Constitution through judicial interpretation undoubtedly has contributed to Americans' laissez-faire attitude toward constitutional amendment.

47. Supporters of a federal constitutional amendment banning same-sex marriage believe an amendment is needed in order to prevent an activist judiciary from changing the traditional one man, one woman definition of marriage. *See, e.g.,* 150 CONG. REC. H5951 (2004) (statement of Rep. Osborne) ("Do we allow a small number of members of the judiciary to alter an institution which has been the backbone of this Nation? Do we allow these same jurists to do so with the great majority of our citizens . . . firmly opposed to a change?"); *id.* at S7888 (statement of Sen. Sessions) ("Marriage has been defined by every legislature . . . the same way, but now we have unelected judges altering and changing that fundamental institution. . . . This cannot be won at the ballot box. It can only be imposed on the people of America through a judicial ruling under the guise of interpreting the Constitution. That is what activism is. It is judges allowing personal views to infect their decision-making process, where they override the actions of the legislature."); *id.* at S5893 (statement of Sen. Brownback) ("This attempt by an imperious judiciary to radically redefine marriage by a few people is both a grave threat to our central social institution and a serious affront to democratic rule in our Nation. . . . The actions of the Massachusetts Supreme Court . . . is [sic] simply the latest instance of arrogant judges riding roughshod over the democratic process and constitutional law alike, in a quest to impose a radical social agenda on America."); *id.* at S5489 (statement of Sen.

Cornyn) ("The fundamental question we are going to have to address, sooner or later, is who will define marriage in the United States? Will it be the American people, or will it be the activist judges . . . .?"); *id.* at S1414 (statement of Sen. Frist) ("We will not let activist judges redefine marriage for our entire society.").

48. *Lawrence,* 123 S. Ct. at 2481.

49. *Id.* at 2482.

50. *Id.* at 2484.

51. *Id.* at 2478.

52. *Id.* (emphasis added).

53. *See, e.g.,* Morrison v. Sadler, 821 N.E.2d 15, 24–25 (Ind. Ct. App. 2005); People v. Greenleaf, 780 N.Y.S.2d 899, 901, 903 (Justice Ct. 2004).

54. Saint Augustine, for example, asserted that every marriage contract should have "an express clause . . . that [the betrothed couple] marry 'for the procreation of children.'" *See* John Witte, Jr., From Sacrament to Contract: Marriage, Religion & the Law in the Western Tradition 21 (1997) [hereinafter Witte] (*citing* Augustine, City of God, XIV, *Sermons on New Testament Lessons,* Sermon I.22, *in* Fathers' Library, 6:253).

55. *Id.* at 25; *see also* R.H. Helmholz, 1 The Oxford History of the Laws of England 547 (2004). Protestant reformers such as Calvin likewise embraced the notion that procreative sexual relations were a necessary part of marriage. Witte, at 105–07. The necessity of sexual relations between spouses as a component of valid marriage is reflected in various papal decrees and canons that declared that impotency, frigidity, or sterility was a valid basis for divorce. *See* John Fulton, The Laws of Marriage 115–18 (1883).

56. *See e.g.,* Alaska Stat. § 25.05.031; Cal. Fam. Code § 2210(f); 750 Ill. Comp. Stat. 5/301; Ky. Rev. Stat. § 403.120 ; Minn. Stat. § 518.02(b); Mont. Code Ann. § 40-1-402(b).

57. Mirizio v. Mirizio, 150 N.E. 605, 607 (N.Y. 1926). *See also* Height v. Height, 187 N.Y.S.2d 260, 262 (N.Y. Sup. Ct. 1959) ("[I]t is a matter of public policy that marriage exists primarily for begetting offspring, and the right to normal and proper sex relations is implicit in the marital contract.").

58. Canon law considers the use of contraception to be sinful. *See* Witte, at 40 (noting that after the Decree of Tametsi of 1563, the Council of Trent issued various canons relating to marriage, including a definition of marriage that required that married couples "bring up children in the truth faith and service of God," which Professor Witte observes "automatically renders contraception and abortion 'a most heinous crime—nothing less than wicked conspiracy to commit murder.'").

59. The use of "no child" clauses in prenuptial and antenuptial contracts is increasingly common, though their enforceability has yet to be litigated. *See generally* Joline F. Sikaitis, Comment, *A New Focus of Family Planning? The Enforceability of No-Child Provisions in Prenuptial Agreements,* 54 Cath. U. L. Rev. 335 (2004). *See also* Height v. Height, 187 N.Y.S.2d 260, 262 (N.Y. Sup. Ct. 1959) (invalidating antenuptial agreement to forgo children on public policy grounds).

60. This was, for example, the argument put forth by the State of Vermont in Baker v. State,

744 A.2d 864, 881 (Vt. 1999) ("The principal purpose the State advances in support of the excluding same-sex couples from the legal benefits of marriage is the government's interest in 'furthering the link between procreation and child rearing.' The State has a strong interest, it argues, in promoting a permanent commitment between couples who have children to ensure that their offspring are considered legitimate and receive ongoing parental support.").

61. Lisa Bennett & Gary J. Gates, Human Rts. Campaign Found. Rpt, The Cost of Marriage Inequality to Children & Their Same-Sex Parents 3 (2004) [hereinafter Human Rts. Campaign Found. Rpt.].

62. The statistics on same-sex households with children and those in which the custodial parent is a homosexual are difficult to obtain. Some data indicates that households headed by lesbian mothers number between 1.5 and 5 million. See Baker v. State, 744 A.2d 864, 881 (Vt. 1999) (citing D. Flaks, et al., *Lesbians Choosing Motherhood: A Comparative Study of Lesbian & Heterosexual Parents & their Children*, 31 Dev. Psychol. 105, 105 (1995)). Other studies suggest that the number of children whose parents are homosexual ranges between 6 and 14 million. *Id.* (citing C. Patterson, *Children of the Lesbian Baby Boom: Behavioral Adjustment, Self-Concepts, & Sex Role Identity*, in Lesbian & Gay Psychology (B. Green et al. eds., 1994)).

63. Human Rts. Campaign Found. Rpt., at 6 (stating that, according to 2000 Census data, 6% of same-sex couples are raising adopted children versus 5.1% of married opposite-sex couples); *id.* (8% of the children of same-sex couples have disabilities versus 5.8% for married opposite-sex couples).

64. Smelt v. County of Orange, 2005 U.S. Dist. 12195 (C.D. Calif., June 16, 2005).

65. Tom W. Smith, Nat'l Opinion Research Ctr., Univ. of Chicago, *American Sexual Behavior: Trends, Socio-Demographic Differences & Risk Behavior* 7 (Apr. 2003) (reporting that recent studies reveal that only 2–3% of sexually active males and 1–2% of sexually active females engage in sexual activity with a member of the same gender).

66. Human Rts. Campaign Found. Rpt., at 5.

67. *Id.*

68. *Id.* at 6 (citing Sondra E. Solomon et al., *Pioneers in Partnership: Lesbian & Gay Male Couples in Civil Unions Compared With Those Not in Civil Unions & Married Heterosexual Siblings*, J. Fam. L & Psych. (forthcoming)) (on file with author).

69. 388 U.S. at 12 n.11.

70. *Id.* ("Appellants contend that this distinction renders Virginia's anti-miscegenation statutes arbitrary and unreasonable even assuming the constitutional validity of an official purpose to preserve 'racial integrity.' We need not reach this contention because we find the racial classifications in these statutes repugnant to the Fourteenth Amendment, even assuming an even-handed state purpose to protect the 'integrity' of all races.").

71. This point is well made by Mark Strasser. *See* Mark Strasser, Legally Wed: Same-Sex Marriage & the Constitution 11 (1997) ("[O]ne might imagine not only that someone's claiming interreligious or interracial marriages should be precluded but that people of a particular race or religion should not be allowed to marry at all because unions involving such people cheapen the institution of marriage. Although such a view might be

sincerely held, that is hardly the test for whether individuals should be allowed to marry. Bigoted views should not be allowed to circumscribe the rights of others, regardless of the sincerity with which such views are held.").

72. *Exodus* 20:14.

73. *Leviticus* 20:10. ("And the man that committeth adultery with another man's wife, even he that committeth adultery with his neighbour's wife, the adulterer and the adulteress shall surely be put to death."). In the New Testament, an adulterous woman was brought before Jesus, who was asked whether she should be stoned to death. Jesus replied, "He that is without sin among you, let him first cast a stone at her." *John* 8:7. All of the people thereafter disbursed, leaving Jesus alone with the adulteress, whom Jesus told to "go, and sin no more." *Id.* at 8:11.

74. For example, Jacob's two wives, Rachel and Leah, allowed Jacob to sleep with their maids, Bilhah and Zilpan, who together bore Jacob four sons. *Genesis* 30:1–13. Jacob's son (by Leah), named Reuben, later slept with his father's concubine, Bilhah. *Id.* at 35:22 ("And it came to pass, when Israel dwelt in that land, that Reuben went and lay with Bilhah his father's concubine: and Israel heard it."). Sarah similarly allows her husband Abraham to sleep with her maid, Hagar, so that Abraham may have heirs. *Id.* at 16:1–16.

75. *Matthew* 5:28.

76. *Id.* at 5:32 ("But I say unto you, that whosoever shall put away his wife, saving for the cause of fornication, causeth her to commit adultery: and whosoever shall marry her that is divorced, committeth adultery."). Jesus later expands the definition of adultery even further, to include married men who divorce their wives and marry again. *Id.* at 19:9 ("And I say unto you, whosoever shall put away his wife, except it be for fornication, and shall marry another, committeth adultery: and whoso marrieth her which is put away, doth commit adultery.").

77. A passage in the New Testament echoes the view of a wife as the husband's property: "For the woman which hath an husband is bound by the law to her husband so long as he liveth; but if the husband be dead, she is loosed from the law of her husband. So then if, while her husband liveth, she be married to another man, she shall be called an adulteress; but if her husband is dead, she is free from that law; so that she is no adulteress, though she be married to another man." *Romans* 7:2–3.

78. *See generally* 2 AM. JUR. 2D *Adultery & Fornication* §§ 1-2. *Accord* Kline v. Ansell, 414 A.2d 929, 930 (Md. 1980) (Under common law, the "husband was regarded as having a property right in the body of his wife and an exclusive right to the personal enjoyment of her. The wife's adultery was therefore considered to be an invasion of the husband's property rights.").

79. 3 WILLIAM BLACKSTONE, COMMENTARIES ON THE LAWS OF ENGLAND 139 (John H. Langbein ed., Univ. of Chicago Press 2002) (1768).

80. *See* THE COLONIAL LAWS OF MASSACHUSETTS 14–15 (William Henry Whitmore ed., 1887) (1672); R.R. HINMAN, THE BLUE LAWS OF NEW HAVEN COLONY 103 (1838).

81. *See* LENORE J. WEITZMAN, THE MARRIAGE CONTRACT: SPOUSES, LOVERS, & THE LAW 213 (Free Press 1981). In those states that recognize fault-based divorce actions, adultery by either husband or wife is considered a basis for divorce.

82. MICH. COMP. LAWS § 750.30 ("Any person who shall commit adultery shall be guilty of

a felony; and when the crime is committed between a married woman and a man who is unmarried, the man shall be guilty of adultery, and liable to the same punishment").

83. MINN. STAT. § 609.36 ("When a married woman has sexual intercourse with a man other than her husband, whether married or not, both are guilty of adultery").

84. The 24 states that consider adultery to be a crime are Alabama, Arizona, Colorado, Florida, Georgia, Idaho, Illinois, Kansas, Maryland, Massachusetts, Michigan, Minnesota, Mississippi, New Hampshire, New York, North Carolina, North Dakota, Oklahoma, Rhode Island, South Carolina, Utah, Virginia, West Virginia, and Wisconsin.

85. The four felonious adultery states are Massachusetts, Michigan, Oklahoma, and Wisconsin.

86. See ALA. CODE § 13A-13-2(a); ARIZ. REV. STAT. § 13-1408; FLA. STAT. ANN. § 798.01; IDAHO CODE § 18-6601; 720 ILL. COMP. STAT. 5/11–7; KAN. STAT. ANN. § 21-3507; MD. CODE ANN., Crim. Law § 10-501 MASS. GEN. LAWS ch. 272, § 14; MISS. CODE ANN. § 97-29-1; N.H. REV. STAT. ANN. § 645:3; N.Y. PENAL LAW § 255.17; N.C. GEN. STAT. § 14-184; OKLA. STAT. tit. 21, § 871; R.I. GEN. LAWS § 11-6-2; S.C. CODE ANN. § 16-15-70; WIS. STAT. § 944.16.

87. See COLO. REV. STAT. § 18-6-501; GA. CODE. ANN. § 16-6-19; N.D. CENT. CODE § 12.1-20-09; UTAH CODE ANN. § 76-7-103; VA. CODE ANN. § 18.2-365; W. VA. CODE §§ 61-8-3 (providing penalty for adultery) , 48-5-204 (defining adultery). Some of these states do not consider the unmarried person's acts to constitute adultery, though they may be punishable as some other crime, such as fornication. See, e.g., UTAH CODE ANN. § 76-7-104 ("Any unmarried person who shall voluntarily engage in sexual intercourse with another is guilty of fornication.").

88. See Tom W. Smith, Nat'l Opinion Research Ctr., Univ. of Chicago, American Sexual Behavior: Trends, Socio-Demographic Differences & Risk Behavior 6 (Apr. 2003).

89. The case, Virginia v. Bushey, is unreported. The ACLU of Virginia has agreed to represent the defendant in his appeal, which asserts that private sexual conduct between adults is a liberty protected by the Constitution. See ACLU of Virginia Asking Judge to Rule that State Law Criminalizing Adultery is Unconstitutional, ACLU of Va. Press Release, Feb. 25, 2004, available at http://www.acluva.org/pressreleases2004/feb25adultery.doc.

90. The charges were dismissed by the trial court because the special prosecutor admitted that his authority as special prosecutor did not include bringing such charges. See Decision of Interest, Southern District, Thomas v. County of Putnam, 229 N.Y. L.J. 23 (May 6, 2003).

91. The charges were filed after the trial judge, a Methodist minister, heard testimony in which the couple admitted to living together and having sexual relations. Hannah Mitchell, Man Convicted on Rare Adultery Charge, CHARLOTTE OBSERVER, Oct. 9, 2001, at 4B; Don Hudson, Verdict Could Set Sex Back 200 Years, CHARLOTTE OBSERVER, Oct. 11, 2001, at 1B.

92. Hannah Mitchell, Adultery Charges Raise Eyebrows, CHARLOTTE OBSERVER, Aug. 18, 2001, at 4B.

93. See For the Record: Legal News Briefs, 12 NAT'L L.J. 6 (May 21, 1990).

94. ALA. CONST. art. VIII, § 182 ("The following persons shall be disqualified both from reg-

istering, and from voting, namely . . . those who shall be convicted of . . . living in adultery, sodomy . . . or crime involving moral turpitude; also, any person who shall be convicted as a vagrant or tramp . . . .").

95. Recent examples include Major General David Hale, who admitted having affairs with the wives of four subordinates, General Joseph Ralston, who withdrew his nomination to serve as Chairman of the Joint Chiefs of Staff after revelation of an affair while a student at the National War College, and Kelly Flinn, the first female B-52 bomber pilot, who was forced to resign from the Air Force after she admitted lying about an adulterous affair with a married man. *See* David Stout, *Retired General is Penalized, Not Jailed, in Adultery Case,* N.Y. TIMES, Mar. 18, 1999, at A20 (discussing Hale case); Philip Shenon, *General Gives Up Attempt to Head the Joint Chiefs,* N.Y. TIMES, June 10, 1997, at A1 (discussing Ralston and Flinn cases).

96. *See, e.g.,* Marcum v. McWhorter, 308 F.3d 635 (6th Cir. 2002); Suddarth v. Slane, 539 F. Supp. 612 (W.D. Va. 1982); Wilson v. Swing, 463 F. Supp. 555 (M.D. N.C. 1978). *See also* Hollenbaugh v. Carnegie Free Library, 439 U.S. 1052, 1053 (1978) (Brennan, J., dissenting from denial of writ of certiorari) (discussing case in which a librarian and custodian were fired for having an adulterous affair and cohabiting after learning of pregnancy).

97. *See, e.g.,* City of Sherman v. Henry, 928 S.W.2d 464 (Tex. 1996) (failure to promote police officer due to affair with coworker permissible).

98. *See, e.g.,* In re Flanagan, 690 A.2d 865 (Conn. 1997); In re Snyder, 336 N.W.2d 533 (Minn. 1983); In re Inquiry Concerning a Judge, 336 So.2d 1175 (Fla. 1976).

99. *See, e.g.,* Griffith v. Griffith, 506 S.E.2d 526 (S.C. Ct. App. 1998); Kirtley v. Kirtley, 1997 WL 1070481 (Va. Cir. Ct. 1997).

100. *See, e.g.,* Jarrett v. Jarrett, 400 N.E.2d 421, 425 (Ill. 1979) ("[T]he moral values which [the mother] currently represents to her children [by cohabiting], and those which she may be expected to portray to them in the future, contravene statutorily declared standards of conduct and endanger the children's moral development."); Bower v. Bower, 758 So.2d 405 (Miss. 2000) ("While it is true that an adulterous relationship is not to be used as a sanction against a guilty parent in awarding custody of children, it is a factor to consider when that conduct manifests itself into the moral fitness of a parent to raise a child."); Commonwealth v. Holland-Moritz, 292 A.2d 380, 385 (Pa. 1972) (ordering reconsideration of whether custody should be restored to mother since cohabiting boyfriend had departed and "home environment had been corrected in good faith.").

101. *See* In re Cienfuegos, 17 I. & N. Dec. 184 (1979); Brea-Garcia v. I.N.S., 531 F.2d 693 (3d Cir. 1976); In re Johnson, 292 F. Supp. 381 (E.D.N.Y. 1968).

102. The commentary to Alabama's adultery law explicitly confesses this "useful" aspect to retaining criminal sanctions: "The number of liaisons which are illegal under Alabama law is, undoubtedly, very high. On the other hand, arrests and prosecutions are rare. . . . While sympathizing with the argument that continuation of a 'dead letter' statute may tend to bring the criminal law into disrespect, the committee felt that formal repudiation of the adultery offense was premature. Moreover, it may prove useful on occasions, as for example in plea bargaining." ALA. CODE § 13A-13-2, commentary.

103. Commonwealth v. Stowell, 449 N.E. 2d 357, 359 (Mass. 1983).

104. *Id.* at 360 ("[T]here is no fundamental personal privacy right implicit in the concept of

ordered liberty barring the prosecution of consenting adults committing adultery in private."). *Accord* City of Sherman v. Henry, 928 S.W.2d 464, 470 (Tex. 1996) ("sexual relations with the spouse of another is not a right that is 'deeply rooted in this Nation's history and tradition.'"); Oliverson v. West Valley City, 875 F. Supp. 1465, 1480 (D. Utah 1995) ("Extramarital sexual relationships are not within the penumbra of the various constitutional provisions or the articulated privacy interests protected by the Constitution.").

105. Stowell, 449 N.E.2d at 360.

106. The eight states are Alaska, Arizona, Hawaii, Kansas, Louisiana, Maine, New Mexico, and West Virginia.

107. *See* Norton v. MacFarlane, 818 P.2d 8, 16 (Utah 1991) (criminal conversation "is not designed to indemnify the aggrieved spouse for any loss to the marriage relationship. Indeed, a damage award may well be a complete windfall to the plaintiff."). Similarly, the Iowa Supreme Court noted that "recovery may be allowed where stability of the marriage survives unimpaired." Bearbower v. Merry, 266 N.W.2d 128 (Iowa 1978).

108. *See* Kline v. Ansell, 414 A.2d 929, 931 (Md. Ct. App. 1980) (criminal conversation is "notorious for affording a fertile field for blackmail and extortion" and is often brought "for purely mercenary or vindictive motives.").

109. *See* Norton, 818 P.2d at 16 (criminal conversation "may impose large punitive damages on one of two parties to a mutual act, even though the one liable under the law was not the aggressor and was less culpable.").

110. *See* Hunt v. Hunt, 309 N.W.2d 818, 821–22 (S.D. 1981) (describing criminal conversation as an "outmoded archaic holdover" that must be abolished due to "overriding considerations of reality."); Fadgen v. Lenkner, 365 A.2d 147, 152 (Pa. 1976) (abolishing criminal conversation because it "is no longer in accord with modern realities"); Saunders v. Alford, 607 So.2d 1214, 1218–19 (Miss. 1992) (presumptions upon which criminal conversation is based "have no vitality in today's society.").

111. *See, e.g.,* ARIZ. REV. STAT. § 13-1408(B) ("No prosecution for adultery shall be commenced except upon complaint of the husband or wife."); OKLA. STAT. tit. 21, § 871 ("Prosecution for adultery can be commenced and carried on against either of the parties to the crime only by his or her own husband or wife as the case may be, or by the husband or wife of the other party to the crime.").

112. *See* Wilson v. Koppy, 653 N.W.2d 68 (N.D. 2002) (prisoner seeking writ of mandamus to compel county attorney to prosecute his wife and her paramour for adultery and unlawful cohabitation).

113. *Lawrence,* 123 S. Ct. at 2478.

114. It should be noted that if the law recognizes business entities as artificial persons for certain purposes—for example, contract law or criminal law—it would be consistent with the morality of American law to recognize harms to the property of these artificial persons.

115. *See, e.g.,* Pankey v. Pankey, 848 So.2d 958, 962 (Ala. Civ. App. 2002).

116. *Mark* 10:11 ("Whosoever shall put away his wife, and marry another, committeth adultery against her."); *id.* at 10:12 ("And if a woman shall put away her husband, and be married to another, she committeth adultery.").

117. 1 WILLIAM BLACKSTONE, COMMENTARIES ON THE LAWS OF ENGLAND 424 (1765).

118. Although Hawaii does not criminalize polygamy, it does state that second or subsequent marriages are void ab initio if a prior spouse is alive and no valid divorce or annulment has been obtained. HAW. REV. STAT. § 572-1(3) (2003). Several states have gone so far as to prohibit polygamy in their state constitutions. *See* ARIZ. CONST. art. XX; IDAHO CONST. art. I, § 4; N.M. CONST. art. XXI, § 1; OKLA. CONST. art. I, § 2; UTAH CONST. art. III.

119. The felony states are Alabama, Arizona, Colorado, Connecticut, Delaware, Florida, Georgia, Idaho, Illinois, Indiana, Kansas, Kentucky, Louisiana, Maryland, Massachusetts, Michigan, Minnesota, Mississippi, Nevada, New Hampshire, New Mexico, New York, North Carolina, North Dakota, Oklahoma, Oregon, South Carolina, South Dakota, Utah, Vermont, Virginia, Washington, West Virginia, Wisconsin, and Wyoming.

120. The 14 misdemeanor states are Alaska, Arkansas, California, Iowa, Maine, Missouri, Montana, Nebraska, New Jersey, Ohio, Pennsylvania, Rhode Island, Tennessee, and Texas.

121. *See* LAWRENCE FOSTER, RELIGION & SEXUALITY: THREE AMERICAN COMMUNAL EXPERIMENTS OF THE NINETEENTH CENTURY 74 (Oxford Univ. Press 1981) [hereinafter FOSTER]; MAREN LOCKWOOD CARDEN, ONEIDA: UTOPIAN COMMUNITY TO MODERN CORPORATION 49 (Johns Hopkins Press 1969) [hereinafter CARDEN]. For an excellent criticism of the Oneida community, see LOUIS J. KERN, AN ORDERED LOVE: SEX ROLES & SEXUALITY IN VICTORIAN UTOPIAS—THE SHAKERS, THE MORMONS & THE ONEIDA COMMUNITY 207–79 (Univ. of N.C. Press 1981) [hereinafter KERN].

122. *Luke* 20:34–36.

123. FOSTER, at 16.

124. *Id.* at 92. Noyes asserted that "[t]he law of marriage 'worketh wrath.' It provokes to secret adultery, actual or of the heart. . . . It gives to sexual appetite only a scanty and monotonous allowance, and so produces the natural vices of poverty, contraction of taste and stinginess or jealousy. . . . This discrepancy between the marriage system and nature, is one of the principal sources of the peculiar diseases of women, of prostitution, masturbation, and licentiousness in general." *Id.* at 91.

125. Noyes was once threatened with prosecution for statutory rape. CARDEN, at 101–02.

126. FOSTER, at 103, 120; CARDEN, at 103–04.

127. LENORE J. WEITZMAN, THE MARRIAGE CONTRACT: SPOUSES, LOVERS, & THE LAW 209–10 (Free Press 1981).

128. 321 F. Supp. 908 (N.D. Calif. 1970), *aff'd*, 487 F.2d 883 (9th Cir. 1973), *cert. denied*, 417 U.S. 910 (1974).

129. *Id.* at 909.

130. *Id.* at 911.

131. *Id.*

132. *Id.* at 911–12.

133. *Id.* at 912.

134. 416 U.S. 1 (1974).

135. 416 U.S. at 7.

136. Some states have rejected the *Village of Belle Terre* analysis and, pursuant to their own state constitutions, invalidated similar zoning ordinances. The Michigan Supreme Court, for example, invalidated an ordinance that limited residents to "[a]n individual or a group of two or more persons related by blood, marriage, or adoption, including foster children and servants, together with not more than one additional person not related by blood, marriage, or adoption, living together as a single housekeeping unit in a dwelling unit." Charter Township of Delta v. Dinolfo, 351 N.W.2d 831, 834 n.1 (Mich. 1984). The two families targeted for ejection by the township consisted of a husband and wife, their children, and six unrelated single adults, all of whom were members of the Work of Christ Community, whose religion required such non-traditional living arrangements. *Id.* at 834. Although the Michigan Supreme Court purported to invoke rationality review, *id.* at 840, it proceeded to invalidate the ordinance because the government had failed to offer any evidence that the ordinance would, in fact, further the interests asserted. *Id.* at 841 ("[The township] attempts to have us accept its assumption that different and undesirable behavior can be expected from a functional family. Yet we have been given not a single argument in support of such an assumption, only the assumption"); *id.* at 842 ("There has been no evidence presented nor do we know of any that unrelated persons . . . have as a group behavior patterns that are more opprobrious than the population at large. In the absence of such demonstration . . . the ordinance can only be termed arbitrary and capricious under the Due Process Clause of the Michigan Constitution.").

137. For an excellent historical and legal account of the evolution of polygamy within the Mormon Church and the subsequent opposition it generated, *see* SARAH BARRINGER GORDON, THE MORMON QUESTION: POLYGAMY & CONSTITUTIONAL CONFLICT IN NINETEENTH CENTURY AMERICA (2002) [hereinafter GORDON].

138. *Id.* at 22–23 (discussing the 1843 revelation and its meaning); KERN, at 146–47.

139. GORDON, at 25.

140. *Id.* at 29–30 ("Four novels written in the mid-1850s were the nucleus of the first wave of [anti-polygamy] propaganda. Metta Victor's *Mormon Wives,* Maria Ward's *Female Life Among the Mormons,* Orvilla Belisle's *Mormonism Unveiled,* and Alreda Eva Bell's *Boadicea* were the genre's cornerstones. Almost 100 novels and many hundreds of magazine and newspaper stories (including the first Sherlock Holmes story, *A Study in Scarlet,* published in 1887) built on the market for antipolygamy fiction over the next half century.").

141. *See id.,* at 34–35.

142. *See* EDWIN BROWN FIRMAGE & RICHARD COLLIN MANGRUM, ZION IN THE COURTS: A LEGAL HISTORY OF THE CHURCH OF JESUS CHRIST OF LATTER-DAY SAINTS, 1830–1900 131–32 (1988) [hereinafter ZION IN THE COURTS].

143. The chief difficulty was that polygamous marriages were conducted in secret, with no written records kept, leaving prosecutors to seek cooperation from one of the wives. Unfortunately for prosecutors, the common law rendered spouses incapable of testifying against each other. *See* id., at 149–50. *See also* United States v. Miles, 103 U.S. 304 (1880) (dismissing Mann Act charges on grounds that spouse was incompetent to testify against husband).

144. ZION IN THE COURTS, at 151.

145. Reynolds v. Sims, 98 U.S. 145, 166 (1878).

146. Indeed, no American state criminalizes attempted suicide any longer. *See* Compassion in Dying v. Washington, 79 F.3d 790, 810 (9th Cir. 1996) (en banc) ("Today, no state has a statute prohibiting suicide . . . nor has any state had such a statute for at least 10 years.").

147. 494 U.S. 872 (1990).

148. Id. at 890 ("[A] society that believes in the negative protection accorded to religious belief can be expected to be solicitous of that value in its legislation as well. It is therefore not surprising that a number of States have made an exception to their drug laws for sacramental peyote use.").

149. *Id.*

150. *Id.* at 910–18 (Blackmun, J., dissenting).

151. 2004 Utah LEXIS 167 (Sept. 3, 2004).

152. *Id.* at *2.

153. *Id.* at *3–4.

154. *Id.*

155. *Id.* at *7. The Utah code recognizes certain marriages as valid under the common law when the individuals are consenting adults who are cohabiting, mutually assuming marital rights and duties, and hold themselves out to the public as husband and wife. *See* UTAH CODE ANN. § 30-1-4.5(1). *See also* Green, 2004 Utah LEXIS, at *7 n.5.

156. Green, 2004 Utah LEXIS, at *18–19.

157. *Id.* at *33–40.

158. *See* RICHARD A. POSNER, SEX & REASON 253 (1992) ("Polygamy increases the effective demand for women, resulting in an lower average age of marriage for women and a higher percentage of women who are married.").

159. *Id.* at 258 (polygamy "reduces a father's per-child investment of time and other resources in the raising of his children, because more children are competing for those resources.").

160. Information on this group is available on their Web site, located at http://www.polygamy.org.

161. *See* http://www.polygamy.org/faq.shtml ("We have seen through history that [police raids are] not effective. We do believe, however, that an additional charge of bigamy should be added when polygamists are charged with other crimes . . . such as tax evasion, welfare fraud, medical neglect, incest, etc. . . . We feel that it may act as a deterrent, urging a man to think twice about marrying his 13 year-old niece.").

162. UTAH CODE ANN. §§ 30-1-2, 30-1-9.

163. In this sense, one is reminded of the argument invoked by gun rights advocates, who cogently argue that it is not guns, but people, who harm people.

164. *Lawrence,* 123 S. Ct. at 2478 ("[The far-reaching impact on private sexual behavior], as a general rule, should counsel against attempts by the State, or a court, to define the meaning of the relationship or to set its boundaries absent injury to a person or abuse of an institution the law protects.").

165. *Id.* ("To say that the issue in *Bowers* was simply the right to engage in certain sexual conduct demeans the claim the individual put forward, just as it would demean a married couple were it to be said marriage is simply about the right to have sexual intercourse."); *id.* ("When sexuality finds overt expression in intimate conduct with another person, the conduct can be but one element in a personal bond that is more enduring. The liberty protected by the Constitution allows homosexual persons the right to make this choice.").

166. *Id.*

167. *Id.*

168. Studies have indicated that father-child incest is rare, with most instances involving step-fathers who were not present during the child's early years. *See* Bruce Bower, *Oedipus Wrecked: Freud's Theory of Frustrated Incest Goes on the Defensive*, SCIENCE NEWS, Oct. 19, 1991, at 248. Ninety-five percent of child sex abusers are male, and evidence of mother-son incest is anecdotal, though some researchers suggest that sex abuse by females is under-reported for various sociological reasons. *See generally* Myriam S. Denov, *The Myth of Innocence: Sexual Scripts & the Recognition of Child Sexual Abuse by Female Perpetrators*, 40 J. SEX RESEARCH 303 (2003); Robert Wilkins, *Women Who Sexually Abuse Children*, 300 BRITISH MED. J. 1153(2) (1990).

169. *Leviticus* 18:6.

170. *Id.* at 18:7–16.

171. *Id.* at 18:17 ("Thou shalt not uncover the nakedness of a woman and her daughter, neither shall thou take her son's daughter, or her daughter's daughter, to uncover her nakedness; for they are her near kinswomen: it is wickedness.").

172. *Id.* at 18:18 ("Neither shalt thou take a wife to her sister, to vex her, to uncover her nakedness, beside the other in her life time.").

173. *See* 1 WILLIAM BLACKSTONE, COMMENTARIES ON THE LAWS OF ENGLAND 333–34 (Wayne Morrison ed., 2001).

174. *Id.* at 334.

175. J. C. ARNOLD, THE MARRIAGE LAW OF ENGLAND 17 (1951). For an interesting table of the degrees of consanguinity and affinity prohibited in the early twentieth century, see MARRIAGE & DIVORCE LAWS OF THE WORLD 22 (Hyacinthe Ringrose ed., 1911).

176. Of these 33 states, 24 prohibit all marriages between first cousins; the remaining 9 states allow first cousins to marry, but only if certain prerequisites are met. The most common requirement is that one or both of the first cousins be over a certain age (usually 65) or be completely sterile. *See, e.g.,* ARIZ. REV. STAT. § 25-101(B); WIS. STAT. § 765.03.

177. The 18 states that allow first cousins to marry are: Alabama, Alaska, California, Colorado, Connecticut, Georgia, Hawaii, Maryland, Massachusetts, New Jersey, New Mexico, New York, Rhode Island, South Carolina, Tennessee, Texas, Vermont, and Virginia. The missing state is North Carolina, which prohibits marriage between so-called "double" first cousins—i.e., those whose parents are also first cousins. *See* N.C. GEN. STAT. § 51-3.

178. *See, e.g.,* ME. REV. STAT. ANN. § 701(2)(B) (first cousins may marry "as long as . . . the man or woman provides the physician's certificate of genetic counseling.").

179. *See* MARGARET MEAD, MALE & FEMALE: A STUDY OF THE SEXES IN A CHANGING WORLD 198–200 (William Morrow & Co. 1970).

180. *See* CLAUDE LEVI-STRAUSS, THE SAVAGE MIND 109–33 (Univ. of Chicago Press 1962). A similar point was made by Saint Augustine, who hypothesized that incest bans furthered social harmony by forcing individuals to seek intimate relationships outside narrow family circles. *See* R.H. HELMHOLZ, 1 THE OXFORD HISTORY OF THE LAWS OF ENGLAND 541 (Oxford Univ. Press 2004).

181. Robin L. Bennett, et al., *Genetic Counseling & Screening of Consanguineous Couples & Their Offspring: Recommendations of the Nat'l Soc'y of Genetic Counselors,* 11 J. GENETIC COUNSELING 97, 105, 115 (2002). [hereinafter *Nat'l Soc'y of Genetic Counselors*].

182. The chance of having a child with chromosomal abnormalities increases with age. *See* Gary A. Dildy, et al., *Very Advanced Maternal Age: Pregnancy After Age 45,* 175 AM. J. OF OBSTETRICS & GYNECOLOGY 668 (1996). On the other hand, other types of birth defects do not seem to increase with maternal age. *See* Patricia A. Baird, et al., *Maternal Age & Birth Defects: A Population Study,* LANCET, Mar. 2, 1991, at 527.

183. *See* UNIF. MARRIAGE & DIVORCE ACT § 207(a)(2).

184. Similar cases have been reported, with mixed outcomes. A Pennsylvania trial court upheld the denial of a marriage license to a man and his sister by adoption, even though they were both adults who had not been raised in the same household. *See* Marriage of M.E.W. and M.L.B., 4 Pa. D & C.3d 51 (1977). By contrast, the Colorado Supreme Court, the following year, concluded that there was no rational basis for denying a marriage license to adults who were siblings by adoption. *See* Israel v. Allen, 577 P.2d 762 (Colo. 1978).

185. *See, e.g., Israel,* 577 P.2d at 764 ("[D]efendant argues that this marriage prohibition provision [prohibiting adoptive siblings from marrying] furthers a legitimate state interest in family harmony.").

186. This was the case, for example, in the *Israel* case. *Id.* at 764 n.2 ("Plaintiff's parents filed affidavits indicating that they had no objection to the proposed marriage and, in fact, were in favor of the marriage. In addition, Bishop Evans of the Roman Catholic Archdiocese of Denver filed an affidavit stating that the Church had no objection to the proposed marriage.").

187. See generally Mark T. Erickson, *Rethinking Oedipus: An Evolutionary Perspective of Incest Avoidance,* 150 AM. J. PSYCHIATRY 411 (1993).

188. *See* Jean-Pierre Vernant, *Oedipus Without the Complex, in* MYTH & TRAGEDY IN ANCIENT GREECE 85, 107–09 (Jean-Pierre Vernant ed., 1988).

189. See generally Joseph Shepher, *Mate Selection Among Second Generation Kibbutz Adolescents & Adults: Incest Avoidance & Negative Imprinting,* 1 ARCHIVES OF SEXUAL BEHAVIOR 293 (1971). See also Yonina Talmon, *Mate Selection in/on Collective Settlements,* 29 AM. SOCIOLOGICAL REV. 491 (1964).

190. *See generally* ARTHUR WOLF & CHIEH-SHAN HUANG, MARRIAGE & ADOPTION IN CHINA, 1845–1945 (Stanford Univ. Press 1980); Arthur Wolf, *Childhood Ass'n & Sexual Attraction: A Further Test of the Westermarck Hypothesis,* 72 AM. ANTHROPOLOGIST 503 (1970).

191. *Nat'l Soc'y of Genetic Counselors,* at 99.
192. *Id.* at 98.

CHAPTER 5. SEX

1. 381 U.S. 479 (1965).
2. Stanley v. Georgia, 394 U.S. 557 (1969).
3. 405 U.S. 438 (1972).
4. *See id.* at 450 ("The Supreme Judicial Court in *Commonwealth v. Baird* [ ] held that the purpose of the amendment was to serve the health needs of the community by regulating the distribution of potentially harmful articles.").
5. *See id.* at 447–52.
6. *Id.* at 454–55.
7. *Id.* at 450 ("If there is a need to have a physician prescribe (and a pharmacist dispense) contraceptives, that need is as great for unmarried persons as for married persons.").
8. *See id.* at 449.
9. *Id.*
10. *Griswold,* 381 U.S. at 485–86.
11. 431 U.S. 678 (1977).
12. The statute in question made it a misdemeanor for "[a]ny person to sell or distribute any instrument or article . . . for the prevention of contraception . . . to a person other than a minor under the age of sixteen years . . . [except] by a licensed pharmacist." *Carey,* 431 U.S. at 681 n.1. It also prohibited the sale or distribution of any contraceptives to minors under age 16 as well as any advertisement of contraceptives. *Id.*
13. *Id.* at 686–87.
14. *Id.* at 687.
15. *Id.* at 688–89.
16. *Id.* at 688 ("The significance of these cases is that they establish that the same test must be applied to state regulations that burden an individual's right to decide to prevent conception or terminate pregnancy by substantially limiting access to the means of effectuating that decision as is applied to state statutes that prohibit the decisions entirely. Both types of regulation may be justified only by a compelling state interest . . . and . . . must be narrowly drawn to express only the legitimate state interests at stake.") (internal quotations omitted).
17. The Court endorsed the analytical framework espoused by Justice Stevens in his *Bowers* dissent, in which Stevens asserted:

> Our prior cases make two propositions abundantly clear. First, the fact that the governing majority in a State has traditionally viewed a particular practice as immoral is not a sufficient reason for upholding a law prohibiting the practice; neither history nor tradition could save a law prohibiting miscegenation from constitutional attack. Second, individual decisions by married persons, concerning the intimacies of their physical relationship, even when not intended to produce offspring, are a form of "liberty"

protected by the Due Process Clause of the Fourteenth Amendment. Moreover, this protection extends to intimate choices by unmarried as well as married persons.

Lawrence, 123 S. Ct. at 2483. The Court concluded that "Justice Stevens' analysis, in our view, should have been controlling in *Bowers* and should control here." *Id.* at 2484.

18. *Id.* at 2478 ("The statutes [prohibiting sodomy] do seek to control a personal relationship that, whether or not entitled to formal recognition in the law, is within the liberty of persons to choose without being punished as criminals. This, as a general rule, should counsel against attempts by the State, or a court, to define the meaning of the relationship or to set its boundaries absent injury to a person or abuse of an institution the law protects.").

19. *See id.* at 2488 (Scalia, J., dissenting).

20. *See, e.g., id.* at 2481–82 ("At the heart of liberty is the right to define one's own concept of existence, of meaning, of the universe, and of the mystery of human life. . . . Persons in a homosexual relationship may seek autonomy for these purposes, just as heterosexual persons do.") (internal quotation marks omitted).

21. *Id.* at 2482.

22. *Id.* ("Were we to hold the statute invalid under the Equal Protection Clause some might question whether a prohibition would be valid if drawn differently, say, to prohibit the conduct both between same-sex and different-sex participants.").

23. A book written in the 1950s echoes this morality:

Promiscuity, fornication, adultery and all irregular sexuality are evil because they constitute a perverse use of a right impulse for wrong ends; namely, the gratification of desire divorced from its legitimate purpose. The intense pleasure associated with the sex act is lawful and right in its proper context, notwithstanding the strictures placed upon it by some Christian writers. To isolate it from procreation and the sacramental character and significance of the marriage relationship is an abuse of the sex instinct, and in the case of adultery it has disastrous consequences, inflicting serious injury on the other partner and the family. Furthermore, by bringing discord into the domestic group and making family life insecure it has a harmful effect on society.

E.O. JAMES, MARRIAGE & SOCIETY 151–52 (1955).

24. As Jeremy Bentham observed:

The operation [i.e., sex] has for its *effect* the preservation of the species, but has it for its *object* the production of that effect? No. On the part of the inferior animal it never has any such object; if on the part of the human animal it is directed to any such object, it is only in a highly cultivated state of the species, and in that state only in a comparatively small number of instances and, as it were, by accident. The titled aristocrat of Europe, yes—but the savage of Asia, of Africa, of America; what cares he about the continuance of his race?

JEREMY BENTHAM, OFFENCES AGAINST TASTE, *reprinted in* JEREMY BENTHAM, THE THEORY OF LEGISLATION, at 477 (C.K. Ogden ed., Harcourt, Brace & Co. 1931) (emphasis in original). This is not to suggest, however, that procreation is never the primary goal of sex. Anyone who has ever known a couple that is having difficulty conceiving a child is well aware of this phenomenon.

25. For an interesting and thorough discussion of the prevalence of homosexual behavior in animals, see BRUCE BAGEMIHL, BIOLOGICAL EXUBERANCE: ANIMAL HOMOSEXUALITY & NATURAL DIVERSITY (1999).

26. 123 S. Ct. at 2478.

27. *See* Laurence H. Tribe, *Lawrence v. Texas: The Fundamental Right that Dare Not Speak its Name,* 117 HARV. L. REV. 1893, 1904 (2004) [hereinafter Tribe] ("And what kind of relationship was it? Apparently, it was quite fleeting, lasting only one night and lacking any semblance of permanence or exclusivity.").

28. The relationship between happiness and marital status is murky, with several studies suggesting a positive correlation. There does not appear to be any evidence that marriage decreases happiness, though it may increase it, and there are well-documented positive effects from marriage, including improved health. *See* Joel Stein, *Is there a Hitch? Does Marriage Make You Happy? Or do Happy People Tend to be the Marrying Kind? The Facts About Wedded Bliss,* TIME, Jan. 17, 2005, at A37. Similarly, although some studies indicate that caring for children is not an activity that induces happiness, a recent poll revealed that 77% of respondents, when asked, "What are your major sources of happiness?" answered that it was "your relationship with your children." Claudia Wallis, *The New Science of Happiness: What Makes the Human Heart Sing?,* TIME, Jan. 17, 2005, at A2.

29. *See generally* David G. Blanchflower & Andrew J. Oswald, *Money, Sex & Happiness: An Empirical Study,* 106 SCANDINAVIAN J. ECON. 393 (2004).

30. THE DECLARATION OF INDEPENDENCE, para. 2 (U.S. 1776) ("We hold these truths to be self-evident, that all men are created equal, that they are endowed by their Creator with certain inalienable Rights, that among these are Life, Liberty, and the Pursuit of Happiness").

31. Laurence Tribe makes a strong case for viewing *Lawrence* as a statement about associational freedom, which may be protected under either the First Amendment as "expressive" association, or substantive liberty as "intimate" association. *See* Tribe, 117 HARV. L. REV., at 1934–44.

32. H.L.A. HART, LAW, LIBERTY & MORALITY 15 (1963) (citing ALI Model Penal Code, Tentative Draft No. 4, p. 277–78).

33. Some states had concluded, prior to *Lawrence,* that fornication statutes, as applied to adults, were unconstitutional. *See, e.g.,* State v. Saunders, 381 A.2d 333, 339–343 (N.J. 1977). The ability to declare fornication laws unconstitutional post-*Lawrence,* however, will likely be hindered by procedural barriers such as standing and ripeness. *See, e.g.,* Berg v. State, 100 P.3d 261 (Utah Ct. App. 2004) (plaintiff lacked standing to challenge constitutionality of fornication law as applied to consensual adult sex because there was no realistic threat of prosecution); Doe v. Duling, 782 F.2d 1202 (4th Cir. 1986) (same).

34. *See* GA. CODE ANN. § 16-6-18 ; IDAHO CODE § 18-6603; 720 ILL. COMP. STAT. 5/11–8; MASS. ANN. LAWS ch. 272, § 18; MINN. STAT. § 609.34; S.C. CODE ANN. § 16-15-80; UTAH CODE ANN. § 76-7-104; VA. CODE ANN. § 18.2-344; W. VA. CODE § 61-8-3.

35. 607 S.E.2d 367 (Va. 2005).

36. *Id.* at 370.

37. *Id.*

38. *Lawrence,* 123 S. Ct. at 2484; *see also Ziherl,* 607 S.E.2d at 370.

39. *Ziherl,* 607 S.E.2d at 370.

40. *Ziherl's* analytical approach thus implicitly conceptualizes *Lawrence* as adopting a balancing approach to substantive liberty, placing the government's justification on one side of the analytical scale and the burden on liberty on the other side. This interpretation of *Lawrence* would be in accord with the Court's abortion precedents, which will deem unconstitutional those laws that are viewed as placing an "undue burden" on a woman's right to choose. *See, e.g.,* Stenberg v. Carhart, 530 U.S. 914, 921 (2000).

41. The *Lawrence* Court intimated as much. 123 S. Ct. at 2484 ("The present case . . . does not involve public conduct or prostitution.").

42. *See, e.g.,* Doe v. Duling, 603 F. Supp. 960, 967 (E.D. Va. 1985) (defending fornication statute on grounds that it "is designed to protect the State's citizens from sexual diseases and to minimize illegitimate births"). The federal trial court in *Doe* ruled that the fornication statute violated the plaintiffs' right to privacy, but this decision was vacated by the Fourth Circuit because it concluded that the plaintiffs lacked standing. *See* Doe v. Duling, 782 F.2d 1202, 1206 (4th Cir. 1986) ("The record in this case establishes that the Does face only the most theoretical threat of prosecution.").

43. *Lawrence,* 123 S. Ct. at 2484. *See also* Carey v. Population Services Int'l, 431 U.S. 678, 713 (1977) (Stevens, J., concurring) ("I would not leave open the question whether there is a significant state interest in discouraging sexual activity among unmarried persons under age 16 years of age. Indeed, I would describe as 'frivolous' appellees' argument that a minor has the constitutional right to put contraceptives to their intended use, notwithstanding the combined objection of both parents and the State"); *id.* at 702–03 (White, J., concurring) (explicitly agreeing with Stevens); *id.* at 709 (Powell, J., concurring) ("The State justifiably may take note of the psychological pressures that might influence children at a time in their lives when they generally do not possess the maturity necessary to understand and control their responses. Participation in sexual intercourse at an early age may have both physical and psychological consequences."); *id.* at 718 (Rehnquist, J., dissenting) ("New York has simply decided that it wishes to discourage unmarried minors under 16 from having promiscuous sex with one another. Even the Court would scarcely go so far as to say that this is not a subject with which the New York Legislature may properly concern itself.").

44. *Ziherl,* 607 S.E.2d at 371.

45. RICHARD A. POSNER & KATHERINE B. SILBAUGH, A GUIDE TO AMERICA'S SEX LAWS 44 (1996).

46. *See* ASAPH GLOSSER, ET AL., THE LEWIN GROUP, STATUTORY RAPE: A GUIDE TO STATE LAWS & REPORTING REQUIREMENTS 5 (2004) (reporting that 34 states establish 16 as the age of consent); *see also id.* at 6–7 tbl. 1.

47. *See id.* at 5 (age of consent is 17 in six states and 18 in eleven states); *see also id.* at 6–7 tbl. 1.

48. HAWAII REV. STAT. §§ 707-30.

49. *See* Tom W. Smith, Nat'l Opinion Research Ctr., Univ. of Chicago, *Am. Sexual Behavior: Trends, Socio-Demographic Differences & Risk Behavior* 31 tbl. 1 (Apr. 2003) [hereinafter *Am. Sexual Behavior*]. *See also* Dawn M. Upchurch, et al., *Gender & Ethnic Differences in*

the Timing of First Sexual Intercourse, 30 FAMILY PLANNING PERSPECTIVES 121, 124 tbl. 2 (1998) (median age at first sex, in descending order of age, is 17.3 years for Hispanic females; 16.6 years for White males and White females; 16.5 years for Hispanic males; 16.3 years for Black females; and 15.0 years for Black males).

50. The U.S. Supreme Court has, however, ruled that statutory rape laws that punish only males who have sex with underage females (and not vice versa) do not violate the Equal Protection Clause. Michael M. v. Superior Court, 450 U.S. 464 (1981).

51. *See, e.g.,* CAL. PENAL CODE § 261.5; GA. CODE ANN. § 16-6-3; OHIO REV. CODE ANN. § 2907.04; WASH. REV. CODE §§ 9A.44.073, 9A.44.076, 9A.44.079.

52. *See* CAL. PENAL CODE § 261.5(a); IDAHO CODE § 18-6101; 720 ILL. COMP. STAT. § 5/12-15(2)(c); LA. REV. STAT. ANN. §§ 14:80.1, 14:81; MO. REV. STAT. § 566.068; N.Y. PENAL LAW §§ 130.05(2)(b), 130.03(3)(a), 130.20; N.D. CENT. CODE § 12.1-20-07(1)(f); VA. CODE ANN. § 18.2-371; WIS. STAT. § 948.09.

53. 575 S.E.2d 441 (Ga. 2003). The opinion was unanimous regarding the outcome; however, Justice Sears mysteriously decided to concur only in the judgment, yet provided no separate concurrence explaining why he differed with the majority's rationale.

54. *Id.* at 443 (citing GA. CODE ANN. 6 16-6-3(a)).

55. *Id.* at 444.

56. Commonwealth v. Holmes, 17 Mass. 336 (1821). "Fanny Hill" is the colloquial title for a novel written by John Cleland, *Memoirs of a Woman of Pleasure,* that tells the story of a young orphan who comes of age in the London bordellos. The book was uniformly banned in England, where it was published, and occasionally banned in the United States. In 1966, however, the U.S. Supreme Court ruled that the novel was not obscene because it had redeeming literary value. Memoirs v. Massachusetts, 383 U.S. 413 (1966).

57. THE REPORT OF THE COMM'N ON OBSCENITY & PORNOGRAPHY 348–49 (Bantam Books 1970) [hereinafter OBSCENITY COMM'N].

58. Miller v. California, 413 U.S. 15, 24 (1973).

59. A plurality of the Court has stated that sexually explicit activities or material that are not technically "obscene," such as nude dancing, are "marginally" within the parameters of the First Amendment. Barnes v. Glen Theatre, Inc., 501 U.S. 560, 566 (1991) (plurality opinion).

60. 394 U.S. 557 (1969).

61. *See Barnes,* 501 U.S. at 566 (plurality opinion); *id.* at 581 (Souter, J., concurring) (agreeing with plurality that nude dancing "is subject to a degree of First Amendment protection.").

62. *See* United States v. Reidel, 402 U.S. 351 (1971); United States v. Thirty-Seven Photographs, 402 U.S. 363 (1971); United States v. Orito, 413 U.S. 139 (1973).

63. The *Stanley* Court explained:

Appellant is asserting the right to read or observe what he pleases—the right to satisfy his intellectual and emotional needs in the privacy of his own home. . . . Georgia contends that appellant does not have these rights, that there are certain types of materials that the individual may not read or even possess. Georgia justifies this assertion by arguing that the films in the present case are obscene. But we think that mere categorization of these films as 'obscene' is insufficient justification for such a drastic invasion of personal liberties guaranteed by the First and Fourteenth Amendments. Whatever may be the justifications for other statutes regulating obscenity, we do not think they reach into the privacy of one's own home. If the First Amendment means anything, it means that a State has no business telling a man, sitting alone in his own house, what books he may read or what films he may watch.

Stanley, 394 U.S. at 565.

64. *Id.* at 566.

65. *Id.* at 566, 567.

66. *See, e.g.,* Kimberly A. Davies, *Voluntary Exposure to Pornography & Men's Attitudes Toward Feminism & Rape,* 34 J. Sex Research 131 (1997) (concluding that "[n]o correlations were found between the number of [sexually explicit] videos a man had rented and his attitudes toward feminism and rape. These findings suggest that calloused attitudes towards women may not be generated by sexually explicit videos but are more deeply ingrained in our society."); Edward Donnerstein, *Pornography: Its Effect on Violence Against Women, in* Pornography & Sexual Aggression 78 (Neil M. Malamuth & Edward Donnerstein eds., 1984) ("While it seems that certain types of pornography can influence aggression and other asocial attitudes and behaviors towards women, this is not the case for other forms of pornography, especially nonaggressive pornography."). *See also id.* at 54 (defining "nonaggressive" pornography as that in which "no overt depictions of physical force are displayed."); Edna F. Einsiedel, *The Experimental Research Evidence: Effects of Pornography on the 'Average Individual,' in* Pornography: Women, Violence & Civil Liberties 267 (Catherine Itzin ed., 1992) (surveying research literature and concluding that "[b]ecause specific attributes that may characterize these films (other than the fact that they contain no violence) and explain their effects either are confounded . . . or not clearly explicated, it is more difficult to say definitively that this particular class of materials has a particular pattern of effects."). *But see* Dolf Zillman & Jennings Bryant, *Effects of Massive Exposure to Pornography, in* Pornography & Sexual Aggression 135 (Neil M. Malamuth & Edward Donnerstein eds., 1984) (concluding that "massive exposure" to pornography "appears to contribute to beliefs about sexual desire and sexual conduct that are not conducive to respect for the opposite (or the same) sex.").

67. *See id.* at 130 ("Initial massive and moderate exposure to explicit erotica produced a significant trend toward decreased motivated aggression following exposure to equally explicit erotic materials. . . . A close correspondence is evident between decreased excitatory reactions to erotica, decreased repulsion (or increased enjoyment, respectively), and reduced aggressiveness.").

68. *See, e.g.,* Edward Donnerstein, et al., The Question of Pornography: Research Findings & Policy Implications 133–36 (1987); Edward I. Donnerstein & Daniel G. Linz, *The Question of Pornography: It is Not Sex, but Violence, that is an Obscenity in our Society,* Psych. Today, Dec. 1986, at 56 ("[I]t must be concluded that violent images, rather than sexual ones, are most responsible for people's attitudes about women and rape."). *See also* Kevin W. Saunders, Violence as Obscenity: Limiting the Media's First Amendment Protection 29–44 (1996).

69. A sampling of the names of rap songs is illustrative: Poetic Hustla'z, "Don't Trust a Bitch"; Dove Shack's "Slap a 'Ho"; Coolio, "Ugly Bitches"; DMX, "What These Bitches Want"; Ghetto Boys, "Bitches and Hoes"; Snoop Doggy Dog, "Break a Bitch 'Til I Die." I do not mean to suggest that rap music is the only genre of music with misogynist themes. Marilyn Manson, for example, has recorded songs such as "F——d with a Knife" and the Rolling Stones hit the charts with "Under My Thumb."

70. OBSCENITY COMM'N, at 57.

71. *Id.* at 58.

72. *See id.* at 63–64 (recommending some legislative restrictions on distribution or sale of obscenity to prevent exposure to minors, but acknowledging that the legislation recommended "applies only to distribution to children made without parental consent.").

73. *See id. See also* FCC v. Pacifica Found., 438 U.S. 726 (1978) (upholding FCC's authority to restrict broadcast of obscene language to times when minors are unlikely to hear it).

74. *See* U.S. v. Extreme Associates, Inc., 352 F. Supp.2d 578 (W.D. Pa. 2005) (government's interest in protecting unwitting adults from exposure to obscenity was "not advanced at all, let alone by the least restrictive means possible" by a total ban on obscenity when defendant limited Web site access to individuals who became members of the Web site).

75. *See, e.g.,* Renton v. Playtime Theatres, Inc., 475 U.S. 41 (1986).

76. *Extreme Associates,* 352 F. Supp.2d at 592 ("It cannot be seriously disputed that, historically, the government's purpose in completely banning the distribution of sexually explicit obscene material, including to consenting adults, was to uphold the community sense of morality.").

77. *Id.* at 578.

78. *Id.* at 586–87.

79. *Id.* at 591 ("[I]t is reasonable to find that the [*Lawrence*] court itself did not consider it was addressing a fundamental right. However, that lack of clarity in *Lawrence* need not be resolved here because we are analyzing the burden that the obscenity laws place on fundamental rights of privacy and speech of the viewer, which have already been explicitly established in *Stanley v. Georgia.*").

80. *Stanley,* 394 U.S. at 568.

81. *Extreme Associates,* 352 F. Supp.2d at 592.

82. *Id.* at 587 ("First, we find that after *Lawrence,* the government can no longer rely on the advancement of a moral code i.e., preventing consenting adults from entertaining lewd or lascivious thoughts, as a legitimate, let alone compelling, state interest."); *id.* at 589 (noting that in a prior obscenity case, United States v. Orito, the Supreme Court used rationality review and concluded that obscenity laws could be "justified as a method of protecting the public morality, a justification no longer valid after *Lawrence.*"); *id.* at 591 ("*Lawrence* . . . can be reasonably interpreted as holding that public morality is not a legitimate state interest sufficient to justify infringing on adult, private, consensual, sexual conduct even if that conduct is deemed offensive to the general public's sense of morality.").

83. *See, e.g.,* United States v. Gartman, 2005 U.S. Dist. LEXIS 1501 (N.D. Tex. Feb. 2, 2005). The *Gartman* court concluded that "no fundamental right exists to receive commercially distributed obscene materials through public channels, even when those materials are

eventually viewed in the privacy of one's home." *Id.* at *3. It also explicitly disagreed that *Lawrence* deemed public morality to be an illegitimate basis for law. *Id.* at *6 n.1 ("Defendants rely on the *Extreme Associates* ruling for the proposition that *Lawrence v. Texas* made protecting morality an illegitimate government reason. This Court does not agree with such an interpretation of *Lawrence.*") (internal citations omitted).

84. United States v. Extreme Associates, Inc., 431 F.3d 150 (3d Cir. 2005).

85. *Id.* at 155 (quoting Rodriguez de Quijas v. Shearson/American Express, Inc., 490 U.S. 477, 484 (1989)).

86. *Id.* at 159.

87. *Id.* at 161.

88. *See* Ashcroft v. ACLU, 542 U.S. 656 (2004).

89. *See, e.g.,* ALA. CODE § 13A-12-200.2(a)(1); GA. CODE ANN. § 16-12-80(c); KAN. STAT. ANN. § 21-4301(a); LA. REV. STAT. ANN. § 14:106.1; MISS. CODE ANN. § 97-29-105; TEX. PENAL CODE §43.21(a)(7); VA. CODE ANN. §§ 18.2-373(3), 18.2-376.

90. *See, e.g.,* PHE, Inc. v. State, 877 So.2d 1244 (Miss. 2004); Morrison v. State, 526 S.E.2d 336 (Ga. 2000); Red Bluff Drive-In, Inc. v. Vance, 648 F.2d 1020 (5th Cir. 1981).

91. *See* People v. Seven Thirty-five East Colfax, Inc., 697 P.2d 348, 369–70 (Colo. 1985) ("We need not decide whether the state may properly regulate the kinds of devices sought to be prohibited by this statute. [The statute], however, sweep[s] too broadly in their blanket proscription of all devices 'designed or marketed as useful primarily for the stimulation of human genital organs.' The statutory scheme, in its present form, impermissibly burdens the right of privacy of those seeking to make legitimate medical or therapeutic use of such devices."); State v. Hughes, 792 P.2d 1023, 1032 (Kan. 1990) ("We hold the dissemination and promotion of such devices for purposes of medical and psychological therapy to be a constitutionally protected activity. As the legislature made no provisions for such acts, those sections dealing with obscene devices were properly found to be overbroad and unconstitutional."); State v. Brenan, 772 So.2d 64, 75, 76 (La. 2000) ("The State's unqualified ban on sexual devices ignores the fact that, in some cases, the use of vibrators is therapeutically appropriate. . . . Given these therapeutic uses, we cannot say that the State's actions in banning all devices that are designed or marketed primarily for the stimulation of the human genitals without any review of their prurience or medical use is rationally related to the 'war on obscenity.'").

92. *See Hughes,* 792 P.2d at 1025; *Seven Thirty-Five East Colfax,* 697 P.2d at 370, n.27 (citing Federal Food and Drug Administration regulations permitting the sale of "powered vaginal muscle stimulator[s] for therapeutic use"); *see also* 21 C.F.R. § 884.5940.

93. *See* Today's News for State Medicaid Directors, Dep't of Health & Human Serv., Health Care Financing Admin., Center for Medicaid and State Operations, July 2, 1998 ("Under current law . . . Viagra is covered by Medicaid when a physician renders a diagnosis that the drug is medically necessary to treat erectile dysfunction."). Under federal Medicaid law, states are not required to pay for prescription drugs, but if they do, they must pay for all medically necessary drugs made by drug manufacturers who have given Medicaid a statutorily prescribed rebate. *See* 42 U.S.C. § 1396r-8.

94. A recent report by the respected Berman Center, a Chicago-based woman's sexual health organization, revealed that 55% of women age 18–55 who are in relationships have used

a vibrator, and 34% of single women have used them as well. *See* Laura Berman, *Study: Sex Toys Help in the Bedroom,* CHI. SUN-TIMES, Sept. 20, 2004, at 54.

95. *See* Elizabeth Querna, *Have More Sex,* U.S. NEWS & WORLD REP., Dec. 27, 2004, at 60. *See also* Clive M. Davis, et al., *Characteristics of Vibrator Use Among Women,* 33 J. SEX RESEARCH 313 (1996) [hereinafter Davis] (survey of women revealed that vibrators enhanced sexual pleasure and intensity of orgasm); E. Sandra Byers, *Relationship Satisfaction & Sexual Satisfaction: A Longitudinal Study of Individuals in Long-Term Relationships,* 42 J. SEX RESEARCH 113 (2005) (longitudinal study confirming positive correlation between sexual satisfaction and relationship satisfaction).

96. *See* RACHEL P. MAINES, THE TECHNOLOGY OF ORGASM: "HYSTERIA," THE VIBRATOR & WOMEN'S SEXUAL SATISFACTION 5 (Johns Hopkins Univ. Press 1999) ("[M]ore than half of all women, possibly more than 70 percent, do not regularly reach orgasm by means of penetration alone").

97. *Id.* at 1–20.

98. *Id.* The American Psychiatric Association did not withdraw recognition of hysteria-related disorders until 1952.

99. *Id.* at 19–20.

100. *See* Davis, 33 J. SEX RESEARCH at 313 (two-thirds of women surveyed used vibrators in partnered sex and majority of women reported orgasms triggered by vibrators to be more intense).

101. *See* Williams v. Pryor, 220 F. Supp.2d 1257, 1264–65 (N.D. Ala. 2002).

102. 378 F.3d 1232 (11th Cir. 2004), *reh'g, en banc, denied,* 2004 U.S. App. LEXIS 28061 (11th Cir. 2004), *cert. denied,* 125 S. Ct. 1335 (2005).

103. ALA. CODE § 13A-1-200.2(a)(1).

104. *Williams,* 220 F. Supp.2d at 1275.

105. 431 U.S. 678 (1977).

106. *See Carey,* 431 U.S. at 689.

107. *Williams,* 378 F.3d at 1236–37.

108. *Id.* at 1238 n.8.

109. *Gartman,* 2005 U.S. Dist. LEXIS 1501, at *6 n.1.

110. *Williams,* 378 F.3d at 1238.

111. Williams v. Pryor, 240 F.3d 944, 949 (11th Cir. 2001).

112. This is indeed the analytical framework employed by the Eleventh Circuit in *Williams* to deny the plaintiffs' claim of a liberty to distribute sex toys so that consenting adults could use them in private. *Williams,* 378 F.3d at 1239. *See also* Washington v. Glucksberg, 521 U.S. 702, 720–21 (1997).

113. *Williams,* 378 F.3d at 1244–45 (emphasis in original).

114. *Id.* at 1250.

115. *See* ROBERT J. MACCOUN & PETER REUTER, DRUG WAR HERESIES: LEARNING FROM OTHER VICES, TIMES & PLACES 145 (2001).

116. *See* NEV. REV. STAT. § 201.354 ("It is unlawful for any person to engage in prostitution or solicitation therefore, except in a licensed house of prostitution."). According to the Nevada Brothel Association, there are 29 legal brothels that employ approximately 1,000 prostitutes. *See* http://www.nvlb.com.

117. *Am. Sexual Behavior,* at 17–18. There have been several localized studies conducted in urban centers (e.g., Central Harlem, Los Angeles, and Dallas) that have revealed somewhat higher percentages of female involvement in prostitution, *id.* at 17, but "extrapolations from these few local studies to national estimates could well be wrong, especially if prostitution is heavily concentrated in urban centers."). *Id.* at 18.

118. Although there are concededly some female "Johns" who pay for sex, there are no reliable statistical data available. The data regarding men who have paid for sex includes men who have paid for sex with other men.

119. *Id.* at 18.

120. *Id.* at 19.

121. *Id.*

122. Only about 10% of prostitution-related arrests are of the clients. *See* Martin A. Monto, *Why Men Seek Out Prostitutes, in* SEX FOR SALE: PROSTITUTION, PORNOGRAPHY & THE SEX INDUSTRY 67 (Ronald Weitzer ed., 2000) [hereinafter Monto].

123. *See id.* at 69–71.

124. 381 U.S. 479 (1965).

125. *See, e.g.,* State v. Mueller, 671 P.2d 1351 (Haw. 1983).

126. *See Lawrence,* 123 S. Ct. at 2484.

127. *See id.* at 2490 (Scalia, J., dissenting) ("State laws against bigamy, same-sex marriage, adult incest, prostitution, masturbation, adultery, fornication, bestiality, and obscenity are likewise sustainable only in light of *Bowers [v. Hardwick's]* validation of laws based on moral choices. Every single one of these laws is called into question by today's decision").

128. *See* Monto, at 71 (surveying 700 men sentenced to "john school" and finding that 59% were not currently married). *Accord* Janet Lever & Deanne Dolnick, *Clients & Call Girls: Seeking Sex & Intimacy, in* SEX FOR SALE: PROSTITUTION, PORNOGRAPHY & THE SEX INDUSTRY 90 tbl. 6.1 (Ronald Weitzer ed., 2000) [hereinafter Lever & Dolnick] (survey of call girls revealed that 59% of clients were not married; survey of streetwalkers revealed that 56% of clients were not married).

129. *See* Lever & Dolnick, at 77.

130. *See* Diane Meaghan, *AIDS & Sex Workers: A Case for Patriarchy Interruptus,* 21 CANADIAN WOMAN STUD. 107 (2001) ("Studies in Denmark, Switzerland, Great Britain, Australia, New Zealand and Canada confirm that female sex workers have exceptionally high rates of prophylactic use and low seroprevalence-rates. In five out of eight studies conducted by the Centers for Disease Control and Prevention in the United States, HIV infection rates were found to be low with no evidence of HIV transmission from sex workers to clients. The U.S. Department of Health has consistently reported that only three to five percent of sexually transmitted diseases are related to prostitution. . . . A United Kingdom survey found seroprevalence HIV rates to be 5.7 percent among sex workers and 5.8 percent among non-sex workers.").

131. *See* Monto, at 75 tbl. 5.2 (reporting that the most common sexual activity with a prostitute is oral sex (47%)); Lever & Dolnick, at 95 tbl. 6.5 (reporting that most common activity reported by street prostitutes was oral sex (57%)). Interestingly, Lever and Dolnick's survey of 83 off-street call girls revealed that vaginal intercourse occurred in 66%

of recent encounters with clients, suggesting that a higher frequency of vaginal intercourse may occur with off-street than on-street prostitution. *Id.* Even with call girls, however, oral sex and manual stimulation occurred in a large percentage of encounters with clients (45% and 26%, respectively). *Id.* It is possible, of course, to transmit the herpes virus through oral sex, though this is not common. *See* Linda Bren, *Genital Herpes: A Hidden Epidemic,* FDA CONSUMER, Mar.-Apr. 2002, at 10.

132. For example, pursuant to state law, brothels are not permitted in the state's most urban county, Clark County, which contains Las Vegas. *See* Kathryn Hausbeck & Barbara G. Brents, *Inside Nevada's Brothel Industry, in* SEX FOR SALE: PROSTITUTION, PORNOGRAPHY & THE SEX INDUSTRY 223 (Ronald Weitzer ed., 2000). Several other counties, including Washoe County, home to Reno, have enacted their own county ordinances prohibiting brothels. *See id.* at 224 tbl. 13.1. In addition, brothels are subject to stringent place regulations that prohibit them from being in close proximity to schools, principal business streets, or religious buildings. *Id.* at 228–29.

133. *Id.* at 229.

134. *Id.*

135. *Leviticus* 18:23 ("Neither shalt thou lie with any beast to defile thyself therewith: neither shall any woman stand before a beast to lie down thereto: it is confusion."); *id.* at 20:15 ("And if a man lie with a beast, he shall surely be put to death: and ye shall slay the beast."); *id.* at 20:16 ("And if a woman approach unto any beast, and lie down thereto, thou shalt kill the woman and the beast; they shall surely be put to death; their blood shall be upon them.").

136. LAWRENCE M. FRIEDMAN, CRIME & PUNISHMENT IN AM. HISTORY 34–35 (1993) (cataloging several seventeenth-century cases of bestiality that resulted in sentences of death). *See also* EDWARD COKE, THE THIRD PART OF THE INSTITUTES OF THE LAWS OF ENGLAND 58 (W. Clarke & Sons 1817) (1797) ("The act [of England] hath adjudged [buggery] felony, and therefore the judgement for felony doth now belong to this offence, viz. To be hanged by the neck till he be dead.").

137. ARK. CODE ANN. § 5-14-122; CAL. PENAL CODE § 286.5; CONN. GEN. STAT. ANN. § 53a-73a; DEL. CODE ANN. § tit. 11, § 777; GA. CODE ANN. § 16-6-6; IDAHO CODE § 18-6606; 720 ILL. COMP. STAT. § 5/12-35; IOWA CODE ANN. § 717C.1; KAN. STAT. ANN. § 21-3505; LA. REV. STAT. ANN. § 14:89; ME. REV. STAT. ANN. tit. 17, § 1031; MD. CODE ANN. § 3-322; MASS. GEN. LAWS ANN. ch. 272, § 34; MICH. COMP. LAWS ANN. § 750.158; MINN. STAT. ANN. § 609.294; MISS. CODE ANN. § 97-29-59; MO. REV. STAT. § 566.111; MONT. CODE ANN. §§ 45-2-101, 54-5-505; NEB. REV. STAT. § 28-1010; N.Y. PENAL LAW § 130.20; N.C. GEN. STAT. § 14-177; N.D. CENT. CODE §§ 12.1-20-02, 12.1-20-12; OKLA. STAT. tit. 21, § 886; OR. REV. STAT. § 167.333; PA. STAT. ANN. tit. 18, § 3129; R.I. GEN. LAWS § 11-10-1; S.C. CODE ANN. § 16-15-120; S.D. CODIFIED LAWS § 22-22-42; TENN. CODE ANN. § 39-13-511; TEX. PENAL CODE ANN. § 21.07(a)(4); UTAH CODE ANN. § 76-9-301.8; VA. CODE ANN. § 18.2-361; W. VA. CODE ANN. § 944.17.

138. *See, e.g.,* N.H. REV. STAT. ANN. § 644:8(III)(b); WA. REV. CODE ANN. §§ 16.52.205, 16.52.207.

139. ALA. CODE § 13A-11-13; ARIZ. REV. STAT. § 32-1364(D); ARK. CODE ANN. § 5-60-101; CALIF. HEALTH & SAFETY CODE § 7052; COLO. REV. STAT. § 18-13-101; CONN. GEN.

STAT. § 53a-73a(a)(3); FLA. STAT. ANN. § 872.06; GA. STAT. ANN. § 16-6-7; HAW. REV. STAT. § 711-1108; IND. CODE ANN. § 35-45-11-2; IOWA CODE § 709.18; KY. REV. STAT. ANN. § 525.120; NEV. REV. STAT. § 201.450; N.Y. PENAL LAW § 130.20; OHIO REV. CODE ANN. § 2927.01; 18 PA. CONS. STAT. § 5510; R.I. GEN. LAWS § 11-20-1.2; TENN. CODE ANN. § 39-17-312; TEX. PENAL CODE § 42.08; UTAH CODE ANN. § 76-9-704(E); WASH. REV. CODE § 9A.44.105; WIS. STAT. § 940.225(7); VA. CODE ANN. § 18.2-126(B).

140. *See, e.g.,* MODEL PENAL CODE § 250.10; ALA. CODE § 13A-11-13; COLO. REV. STAT. § 18-13-101; HAW. REV. STAT. § 711-1108; ; KY. REV. STAT. ANN. § 525.120; OHIO REV. CODE ANN. § 2927.01; PA. CONS. STAT. § 5510.

141. *See, e.g.,* ARIZ. REV. STAT. § 13-3507(C)(1); ARK. CODE ANN. § 5-68-302(5); FLA. STAT. ANN. § 847.001(12)-(13); IDAHO CODE § 18-4105(C); OR. REV. STAT. § 167.087(2)(A).

142. 394 U.S. 557 (1969).

CHAPTER 6. REPRODUCTION

1. Eisenstadt v. Baird, 405 U.S. 479 (1965); Hodgson v. Minnesota, 497 U.S. 417, 434 (1990).

2. *See* Linda Timm Wagner & Charlotte A. Kenreigh, *Choosing Oral Contraceptives,* 216 AM. DRUGGIST 64 (1999); Merle S. Goldberg, *Choosing a Contraceptive,* 27 FDA CONSUMER 18 (1993).

3. *See* JOHN GUILLEBAUD, CONTRACEPTION TODAY: A POCKETBOOK FOR GENERAL PRACTITIONERS 62 (4th ed. 2003) [hereinafter CONTRACEPTION TODAY] ("Fertile ovulation is prevented [by mini-pills] in at least 60% of cycles. In the remainder there is reliance mainly on progestonic interference with mucus penetrability, backed by some anti-nidatory activity at the endometrium."). "Anti-nidatory activity" means that the fertilized egg is prevented from properly nesting or implanting into the uterine wall.

4. *See* BEVERLY WINIKOFF, THE WHOLE TRUTH ABOUT CONTRACEPTION: A GUIDE TO SAFE & EFFECTIVE CHOICES 122–23, 134 (1997).

5. *Id.* at 145–46; CONTRACEPTION TODAY, at 79–80. Copper IUDs are sometimes inserted after unprotected sex as an emergency means of preventing implantation of a fertilized egg. *Id.* at 102–03.

6. *See, e.g.,* Monica Davey & Pam Belluck, *Pharmacies Balk on After-Sex Pill & Widen Front,* N.Y. TIMES, Apr. 19, 2005, at A1; Viveca Novak & Karen Tumulty, *Morning After at the FDA,* TIME, Sept. 12, 2005, at 22.

7. *See* Helen C. Pymar & Mitchell D. Creinin, *Offering Mifepristone as an Abortion Option,* 46 CONTEMP. OB/GYN 113 (2001).

8. In 1992, a majority of the Supreme Court explicitly reaffirmed support for *Roe v. Wade*'s viability distinction. *See* Planned Parenthood of Se. Pa. v. Casey, 505 U.S. 833, 870 (1992) (plurality); *id.* at 912 (Stevens, J., concurring in part and dissenting in part); *id.* at 932–33 (Blackmun, J., concurring in part and dissenting in part).

9. *See Casey,* 505 U.S. at 860; *id.* at 933 (Blackmun, J., concurring in part and dissenting in part).

10. One of the most widely cited of the IVF frozen embryo cases, *Davis v. Davis,* refused

explicitly to label frozen embryos as "property," yet nonetheless concluded that gamete providers "have an interest in the nature of ownership, to the extent that they have decision-making authority concerning disposition of the preembryos. . . ." 842 S.W.2d 588, 597 (Tenn. 1992). Other courts have agreed that dispositional authority belongs to the progenitors, which may be defined by contract. *See* In re Marriage of Witten, 672 N.W.2d 768 (Iowa 2003); In re Marriage of Litowitz, 48 P.3d 261 (Wash. 2002); J.B. v. M.B., 783 A.2d 707 (N.J. 2001); Kass v. Kass, 696 N.E.2d 174 (N.Y. 1998).

11. *See* Lofton v. Sec'y of Dep't of Children & Family Servs., 358 F.3d 804, 811–12 (11th Cir. 2004); Mullins v. Oregon, 57 F.3d 789, 794 (9th Cir. 1995); Lindley v. Sullivan, 889 F.2d 124, 131 (7th Cir. 1989).

12. 316 U.S. 535, 541 (1941) ("We are dealing here with legislation which involves one of the basic civil rights of man. Marriage and procreation are fundamental to the very existence and survival of the race. . . . [S]trict scrutiny of the classification which a State makes in a sterilization law is essential.").

13. *Id.* at 536.

14. *Id.* at 541 ("When the law lays an unequal hand on those who have committed intrinsically the same quality of offense and sterilizes one and not the other, it has made as an invidious discrimination as if it had selected a particular race or nationality for oppressive treatment.").

15. 274 U.S. 200 (1927).

16. *See, e.g.,* ARK. CODE ANN. § 20-49-202; GA. CODE ANN. § 31-20-3; ME. REV. STAT. tit. 34-B, § 7010; MICH. COMP. LAWS § 330.1716; MINN. STAT. ANN. § 524.5-313(c)(4); MISS. CODE ANN. § 41-45-1; N.C. GEN. STAT. § 35A-1245; UTAH CODE ANN. § 62A-6-107; VT. STAT. ANN. §§ 8705, 8708; VA. CODE ANN. § 54.1-2975; WA. REV. CODE § 9.92.100; W. VA. CODE ANN. § 27-16-1. In the absence of specific sterilization statutes, courts have alternatively concluded that they possess the equitable power to order involuntary sterilization of the mentally disabled. *See, e.g.,* In re Moe, 432 N.E.2d 712 (Mass. 1982); In re Terwilliger, 450 A.2d 1376 (Pa. 1982); In re Grady, 426 A.2d 467 (N.J. 1981); In re Guardianship of Eberhardy, 307 N.W.2d 881 (Wis. 1981); In re A.W., 637 P.2d 366 (Colo. 1981); In re Guardianship of V.S.D., 660 N.E.2d 1064 (Ind. Ct. App. 1996); Estate of C.W., 640 A.2d 427 (Pa. Super. Ct. 1994).

17. *Buck,* 316 U.S. at 207.

18. *See, e.g.,* In re Guardianship of Hayes, 608 P.2d 635, 640 (Wash. 1980); In re Guardianship of V.S.D., 660 N.E.2d 1064 (Ind. Ct. App. 1996); Conservatorship of the Person & Estate of Angela D., 83 Cal. Rptr.2d 411 (Cal. Ct. App. 1999). *See also* WASH. REV. CODE § 9.92.100 (allowing involuntary sterilization of those convicted of sexual abuse of females under age 10, rape, or adjudged to be habitual criminals).

19. 221 S.E.2d 307 (N.C. 1976). *See also* In re Sallmaier, 378 N.Y.S.2d 989 (N.Y. Sup. Ct. 1976) ("The decision to exercise the power of parens patriae must reflect the welfare of society, as a whole, but mainly it must balance the individual's right to be free from interference against the individual's need to be treated, if treatment would in fact be in his best interest."). Notice how the court in *Sallmaier,* like the North Carolina Supreme Court in *Moore,* confounds two distinct legal concepts—namely, parens patriae and the police power to protect public welfare.

20. In re Sterilization of Moore, 221 S.E.2d at 311–12.

21. *See* Planned Parenthood of Se. Pa. v. Casey, 505 U.S. 833, 870 (1992) (plurality); *id.* at 912 (Stevens, J., concurring in part and dissenting in part); *id.* at 932–33 (Blackmun, J., concurring in part and dissenting in part).

22. In re Sterilization of Moore, 221 S.E.2d at 312.

23. *Id.* (quoting In re Cavitt, 157 N.E.2d 171 (Neb. 1968)).

24. *Id.*

25. Paul Gray, *Cursed by Eugenics: A Belief that Human Intelligence Could Guide Evolution Led the World to Concentration Camps,* TIME, Jan. 11, 1999, at 84.

26. This was the surprisingly bold rationale employed by the New Jersey Supreme Court in the 1913 case of *Smith v. Bd. of Examiners of Feeble-Minded,* 88 A. 963 (N.J. 1913), in which the court invalidated a sterilization order issued against epileptic Alice Smith, who was held in the State Village for Epileptics. The State of New Jersey asserted that sterilizing Smith was a valid exercise of its police power to protect public welfare, but the New Jersey Supreme Court rejected this argument, reasoning:

> [T]he feeble-minded and epileptics are not the only persons in the community whose elimination as undesirable citizens would, or might in the judgment of the Legislature, be a distinct benefit to society. . . . If in the present case, we decide that such a power exists in the case of epileptics, the doctrine we shall have enunciated cannot stop there. For epilepsy is not the only disease by which the welfare of society at large is injuriously affected . . . . So that it would seem to be a logical necessity that, if the Legislature may, under the police power, theoretically benefit the next generation by the sterilization of the epileptics of this, it both may and should pursue the like course with respect to the other diseases mentioned . . . . There are other things besides physical or mental diseases that may render persons undesirable citizens, or might do so in the opinion of a majority of the prevailing Legislature. Racial differences, for instance, might afford a basis for such an opinion . . . . Evidently a large and underlying question is, How far is government constitutionally justified in the theoretical betterment of society by means of the surgical sterilization of certain of its unoffending, but undesirable, members?

> *Id.* at 966. The court concluded that the law offended the Equal Protection Clause of the U.S. Constitution because there was no rational relation between the object sought (preventing epileptics from procreating) and the means employed (mandatory sterilization only of those epileptics who were inmates in public charitable institutions). *Id.* at 966–67.

27. *See* Wellesley v. Wellesley, (1828) 4 Eng. Rep. 1078, 1081–83 (H.L.); Beverley's Case, (1603) 76 Eng. Rep. 1118 (K.B.).

28. Some might argue that involuntary sterilization of a mentally disabled individual can never be in her best interests. The Canadian Supreme Court, for example, has reached this conclusion. *See, e.g.,* Re Eve, 31 D.L.R. (4th) 1, 32 (1986). The British House of Lords rejected this conclusion, upholding the legitimacy of involuntary sterilization pursuant to the parens patriae power when convinced that sterilization is truly in the ward's best interests. Re B. [1988] 1 A.C. 199 (H.L.).

29. 735 F. Supp. 1361 (N.D. Ill.), *aff'd without opinion, sub. nom.,* Scholberg v. Lifchez, 914 F.2d 260 (7th Cir. 1990), *cert. denied,* 498 U.S. 1069 (1991).

30. The statute in question stated, "No person shall sell or experiment upon a fetus produced by the fertilization of a human ovum by a human sperm unless such experimentation is therapeutic to the fetus thereby produced. . . . Nothing in this subsection . . . is intended to prohibit the performance of in vitro fertilization." *Id.* at 1363–64 (citing ILL. REV. STAT. ch. 38, para. 81–26, § 6(7) (1989)).

31. *Id.* at 1367–70.

32. *Id.* at 1369.

33. *Id.* at 1376.

34. *Id.* at 1377.

35. Eisenstadt v. Baird, 405 U.S. 438, 453 (1972).

36. In the Matter of Baby M, 537 A.2d 1227 (N.J. 1988).

37. *Id.* at 1235.

38. *Id.* at 1237.

39. *Id.* at 1253.

40. *Id.*

41. *Id.*

42. *Id.*

43. 702 F. Supp. 1452 (W.D. Mo. 1988), *aff'd*, 908 F.2d 1395 (8ᵗʰ Cir. 1990).

44. *Goodwin,* 702 F. Supp. at 1453.

45. *Goodwin,* 908 F.2d at 1398.

46. *See* Washington v. Harper, 494 U.S. 210, 223 (1990). The *Harper* Court made it clear that the "legitimate penological interest" standard—and not strict scrutiny—is the correct standard to apply to prison regulations, even if the constitutional right allegedly infringed is a fundamental one. *Id.*

47. 291 F.3d 617 (9ᵗʰ Cir. 2002) (en banc).

48. *Id.* at 623.

49. *Id.* at 622.

50. Parthenogenesis, or "virgin birth," is a process whereby an egg spontaneously begins the process of cell division, without the need for sperm. *See* LAURENCE E. KARP, GENETIC ENGINEERING: THREAT OR PROMISE? 185 (1976). Parthenogenesis differs from cloning because it does not require the removal of the nucleus of an egg and its replacement with a donor cell. In parthenogenesis, the egg is somehow coaxed to begin dividing as if it had been fertilized, usually by soaking in a combination of chemicals. If the mix of chemicals is right, the egg begins spontaneously dividing as though it had been fertilized with a sperm. Parthenogenesis occurs naturally in several animal species, including drone bees, poultry, mice, golden hamsters, *id.* at 189–90, aphids, turkeys, and some reptiles. *See* Rick Weiss, *'Parthenotes' Expand the Debate on Stem Cells,* WASH. POST, Dec. 10, 2001, at A-11. Scientists have successfully induced parthenogenesis in human eggs stimulated by chemicals. *See* Joseph B. Cibelli, et al., *Somatic Cell Nuclear Transfer in Humans: Pronuclear and Early Embryonic Dev.,* 2 E-BIOMED: THE J. OF REGENERATIVE MED. 25, 27–28 (2001). Androgenesis requires only the use of sperm, but research on androgenesis is much less developed than parthenogenesis. *See* Mark J. McKone and Stacey L. Halpern, *The Evolution of Androgenesis,* 161 AM. NATURALIST 641 (2003).

51. IVF involves the removal of an egg, combining it in a petri dish with sperm, and follow-

ing fertilization, implanting the embryo into a womb. *See* U.S. DEP'T OF HEALTH & HUMAN SERVICES, CENTERS FOR DISEASE CONTROL & PREVENTION, 2002 ASSISTED RE-PROD. TECH. SUCCESS RATES: NAT'L SUMMARY & FERTILITY CLINIC REP. 474 [here-inafter 2002 CDC FERTILITY CLINIC REP.]. Gamete intrafallopian transfer (GIFT) differs from IVF in that the egg and sperm are immediately injected back into the woman's fallopian tubes, and fertilization (if it occurs), occurs inside the fallopian tubes, not in a petri dish. *See id.* Zygote intrafallopian transfer (ZIFT) differs from GIFT in that fertilization takes place outside the body and the fertilized egg is then injected back into the fallopian tubes, rather than into the womb directly. *Id.* at 475.

52. See George J. Annas, *Human Cloning: A Choice or an Echo?*, 23 U. DAYTON L. REV. 247, 254 (1998); Lori B. Andrews, *Is There a Legal Right to Clone? Constitutional Challenges to Bans on Human Cloning*, 11 HARV. J.L. & TECH. 643, 666 (1998).

53. *See* Chapter 4 (analyzing same arguments in context of same-sex marriage, adultery, for-nication, incest, and polygamy); Chapter 5 (context of sex toys, prostitution, and ob-scenity). The "sanctity of human life" argument was not specifically addressed in the foregoing chapters, but it is undeniably based on a moral assumption that life begins at conception. Because this argument is based solely on morality, it cannot provide the ba-sis for legitimate governmental restrictions on individual liberty to procreate. Even as-suming arguendo that life begins at conception, I have elsewhere debunked the assump-tion that reproductive cloning would actually devalue human life. *See* Elizabeth Price Foley, *The Constitutional Implications of Human Cloning*, 42 ARIZ. L. REV. 647, 719–21 (2000).

54. See, e.g., Jeffrey Kluger, *Goodbye Dolly: Think You Might Like to Get Cloned? Think Again,* TIME, June 7, 1999, at 70.

55. NAT'L ACAD. OF SCI., SCIENTIFIC & MED. ASPECTS OF HUMAN REPROD. CLONING 48 (2002) [hereinafter NAS CLONING REP.].

56. Sonia Schaetzlein, et al., *Telomere Length is Reset During Early Mammalian Embryogene-sis,* 101 PROC. NAT'L ACAD. SCI. 8034 (2004); N. Miyashita, et al., *Natural Telomere Lengths of Spermatozoa in Somatic Cell-Cloned Bulls,* 59 THERIOGENOLOGY 1557 (2003); Dean H. Betts, et al., *Reprogramming of Telomorase Activity & Rebuilding of Telomere Length in Cloned Cattle,* 98 PROC. NAT'L ACAD. SCI. 1077 (2001).

57. See Gretchen Vogel, *In Contrast to Dolly, Cloning Resets Telomere Clock in Cattle,* 288 SCI-ENCE 586 (2000); see also Robert P. Lanza, et al., *Extension of Cell Life: Span and Telom-ere Length in Animals Cloned from Senescent Somatic Cells,* 288 SCIENCE 665 (2000).

58. NAS CLONING REP., at 47–49.

59. *Id.* at 42.

60. *Id.*

61. *Id. See also* William M. Rideout, et al., *Nuclear Cloning & Epigenetic Reprogramming of the Genome,* 293 SCIENCE 1093 (2001) ("In a cloned embryo, reprogramming has to occur in a cellular context radically different from gametogenesis and within the short interval between transfer of the donor nucleus into the egg and the time when zygotic transcrip-tion becomes necessary for further development. . . . The phenotypes observed in nu-clear clones suggest that complete reprogramming is the exception.").

62. *See, e.g.,* Cinzia Allegrucci, et al., *Stem-Cell Consequences of Embryo Epigenetic Defects,*

364 LANCET 206 (2004) ("Because the oocyte is designed to reprogramme the sperm genome . . . perhaps many of the epigenetic errors induced by somatic-cell nuclear transfer could be avoided by a more targeted approach."); Wolf Reik, et al., *Epigenetic Reprogramming in Mammalian Dev.,* 293 SCIENCE 1089 (2001) (discussing DNA methylation pattern reprogramming, but cautioning that "it is still unclear whether or not methylation is involved in the control of gene expression during normal development."); Y.K. Kang, et al., *Influence on Oocyte Nuclei on Demethylation of Donor Genome in Cloned Bovine Embryos,* 499 FEBS LETTERS 55 (2001) (suggesting that inefficient demethylation of cloned donor genomes could potentially be "rescued" by "unknown mechanisms" in oocytic nuclei); William M. Rideout, et al., *Nuclear Cloning and Epigenetic Reprogramming of the Genome,* 293 SCIENCE 1093 (2001) (surmising that "the most likely explanation for the developmental failure of NT embryos is the inability to 'reprogram' the epigenetic profile of the somatic donor nucleus to that of a fertilized zygote."); W. Shi, et al., *Epigenetic Reprogramming in Mammalian Nuclear Transfer,* 71 DIFFERENTIATION 91 (2003); Y.K. Kang, et al., *Reprogramming DNA Methylation in the Preimplantation Stage: Peeping with Dolly's Eyes,* 15 CURRENT OPINION IN CELL BIOLOGY 290 (2003) (surmising that the "fastidious nature of the [somatic] donor genome might prevent completion of epigenetic reprogramming.").

63. NAS CLONING REP., at 44.

64. *Id.*

65. *Id.*

66. *See* Emily L. Niemitz & Andrew P. Feinberg, *Epigenetics & Assisted Reprod. Tech.,* 74 AM. J. HUMAN GENETICS 599 (2004) (hereinafter Niemitz & Feinberg]. *See also* Christine Gicquel, et al., *In Vitro Fertilization May Increase the Risk of Beckwith-Wiedemann Syndrome Related to the Abnormal Imprinting of the KCNQ10T Gene,* 72 AM. J. OF HUMAN GENETICS 1338 (2003) [hereinafter Gicquel] ("In both [sheep and cattle], the [large offspring] syndrome is caused by the in vitro exposure of embryos, between fertilization and the blastocyst stage, to various unusual environments. . . . In vitro preimplantation procedures in mice are also responsible for the overgrowth owing to the abnormal expression of various imprinted genes"); S. Khosla, et al., *Culture of Preimplantation Mouse Embryos Affects Fetal Dev. & the Expression of Imprinted Genes,* 64 BIOL. REPROD. 918 (2001).

67. *See* Eamonn R. Maher, *Imprinting & Assisted Reprod. Tech.,* 14 HUMAN MOLECULAR GENETICS 1 (2005); Niemitz & Feinberg, at 599.

68. ICSI is used to overcome male infertility by injecting a single sperm directly into an egg.

69. See Gerald F. Cox, et al., *Intracytoplasmic Sperm Injection May Increase the Risk of Imprinting Defects,* 71 AM. J. HUMAN GENETICS 162 (2002); K.H. Orstavik, et al., *Another Case of Imprinting Defect in a Girl with Angelman Syndrome who was Conceived by Introcytoplasmic Sperm Injection,* 72 AM. J. HUMAN GENETICS 218 (2003).

70. See generally E.R. Maher, et al., *Beckwith-Wiedemann Syndrome & Assisted Reprod. Tech.* (ART), 40 J. MED. GENETICS 62 (2003); Michael R. DeBaun, et al., *Ass'n of In Vitro Fertilization with Beckwith-Wiedemann Syndrome & Epigenetic Alterations of LIT1 and H19,* 72 AM. J. HUMAN GENETICS 156 (2003). Gicquel, at 1338.

71. *See* Gicquel, at 1338; *accord* Cinzia Allegrucci, et al., *Stem-Cell Consequences of Embryo*

Epigenetic Defects, 364 LANCET 206 (2004) ("Loss of methylation in imprinted genes has also been associated with increased incidence, compared with natural conception, of human imprinting disorders (Beckwith-Wiedemann and Angelman syndromes) in children conceived via an assisted-reproduction technology. Because the extent to which embryo-assisted epigenetic disruptions affects early fetal loss is unknown, the incidence of affected embryos could be underestimated at present.").

72. See J. Keith Killian, et al., *Divergent Evolution in M6P/IGF2R Imprinting from the Jurassic to the Qaternary,* 10 HUMAN MOLECULAR GENETICS 1721 (2001).

73. *See* Nancy S. Green, *Risks of Birth Defects & Other Adverse Outcomes Associated with Assisted Reprod. Tech.,* 114 PEDIATRICS 256 (2004) ("Rates of ART-associated birth defects are 1.4- to 2-fold higher than the overall rate of 3% to 4% of births in general.").

74. *Ethical Considerations of Assisted Reprod. Tech.,* 62 FERTILITY & STERILITY 14S (1994) (Supp. 1) (report of the Ethics Committee of the American Fertility Society); R. Alta Charo, *The Hunting of the Snark: The Moral Status of Embryos: Right-to-Lifers & Third World Women,* 6 STAN. L. & POL'Y REV. 11, 16 (1995).

75. An even greater number of fertilized eggs are miscarried prior to a clinical diagnosis of pregnancy, perhaps 30% or more. Gillian Bentley, *Doing What Comes Naturally,* NEW SCIENTIST, Aug. 31, 1996, at 43. The miscarriages of such early embryos often goes unnoticed by the woman, who often does not even know she is pregnant. *Id.*

76. An estimated 40% of human embryos created by sexual reproduction do not successfully implant into the womb, and half of these (20% of all human pregnancies) do not successfully implant because of a genetic defect. GREGORY E. PENCE, WHO'S AFRAID OF HUMAN CLONING? 132 (1998). The incidence of serious deformities in children conceived sexually is 1–2%. *Id.* at 133.

77. Fertility Clinic Success Rate & Certification Act of 1992, Pub. L. No. 102–493, 106 Stat. 3146 (codified at 42 U.S.C. § 263a-1).

78. 2002 CDC FERTILITY CLINIC REP., at 45 fig. 33. The rates of singleton birth are even higher for frozen non-donor embryos. *See id.* at 46 fig. 34 (75.4% of births resulting from IVF using frozen non-donor eggs are singletons; 22.3% are twins; 2.3% are triplets or more).

79. *Id.*

80. *Id.* at 71. The average transfer of 3 embryos includes fresh embryos using non-donor eggs, frozen embryos using non-donor eggs, and both fresh and frozen donor eggs. For IVF using fresh, non-donor eggs or embryos—by far the most common type of IVF—the number of embryos transferred is the highest, ranging from 2.7 embryos transferred for a woman under age 35, to an average of 3.5 embryos transferred for a woman age 41 or 42. *Id.* Indeed, of all transfers involving fresh eggs or embryos, 62% involved transfer of 3 or more embryos. *Id.* at 34.

81. For IVF using fresh non-donor eggs, 64.6% of births are singletons. *Id.* at 20 fig. 8. Of the remaining births, the overwhelming number involve twins. *Id.* Only 3.8% of births result in triplets or more. *Id.*

82. These numbers are derived using the 2002 CDC statistics, which reveal that for ART cycles using fresh non-donor eggs, 64.6% of live births are singletons, 31.6% are twins, and 3.8% are triplets or more. *Id.* at 20 fig. 8. Although the CDC reports only "triplets or

more," which fails to reveal the number of, say, quadruplets, I have assumed that the 1.33 instances of "triplet or more" births would range on average from triplets to quintuplets, thus yielding approximately 4 to 7 babies.

83. *See, e.g.,* Anne Lawton, *The Frankenstein Controversy: The Constitutionality of a Federal Ban on Cloning,* 87 Ky. L.J. 277, 352 (1998) ("If Dr. Wilmut's experiment is any indication, hundreds of thousands of embryos will be created and destroyed in the process of perfecting human cloning techniques. It took Dr. Wilmut 277 tries before he successfully created the clone known as 'Dolly'."); George J. Annas, *Human Cloning, A Choice or an Echo?,* 23 U. Dayton L. Rev. 247, 267 (1998) ("Dolly's birth was a 1-in-277-embryo chance. . . . The birth of a human from cloning might be technologically possible, but we could only discover this by unethically subjecting the planned child to the risk of serious genetic or physical injury.").

84. *See* Lee M. Silver, Remaking Eden: Cloning & Beyond in a Brave New World 103 (1997). *See also* Cloning Human Beings: Rep. & Recommendations of the Nat'l Bioethics Advisory Comm'n 22 (1997) [hereinafter NBAC Rep.].

85. NBAC Rep., at 22.

86. NAS Cloning Rep., at 114–20 tbl. 1. This table also reported an even lower success rate methodology, by which live births are expressed as a percentage of the total "number of embryos produced," which includes those embryos produced in vitro that do not develop sufficiently to ever be transferred into a womb.

87. NAS Cloning Rep., at 114–17.

88. Most of the various animal embryos created by cloning have died before or soon after implantation. *See* NAS Cloning Rep., at 123 fig. 3 (revealing that of the embryos created by cloning in various animal species, the vast majority did not survive to the blastocyst stage); R. Jaenisch, et al., *Nuclear Cloning, Stem Cells & Genomic Reprogramming,* 4 Cloning & Stem Cells 389 (2002) (acknowledging that most animals created by cloning using an adult somatic cell died soon after implantation).

89. *See* Planned Parenthood of Se. Pa. v. Casey, 505 U.S. 833, 870 (1992) (plurality); *id.* at 912 (Stevens, J., concurring in part and dissenting in part); *id.* at 932–33 (Blackmun, J., concurring in part and dissenting in part).

90. *See supra* note 10.

91. *See, e.g.,* Cal. Health & Safety Code § 125315; Fla. Stat. Ann. §§ 742.17.

92. *See, e.g.,* Fla. Stat. § 782.09; Ga. Code Ann. § 16-5-80; Iowa Code § 707.7.

93. *See, e.g.,* 720 Ill. Comp. Stat. 5/9–1.2, 5/9–2.1; Ind. Code § 35-42-1-6; La. Rev. Stat. Ann. § 14:32.5.

CHAPTER 7. MEDICAL CARE

1. *See* Slater v. Baker & Stapleton, 95 Eng. Rep. 860 (K.B. 1767).

2. *See* Jessica W. Berg, et al., Informed Consent, Legal Theory & Clinical Practice 18 (2d ed. 2001) [hereinafter Berg].

3. Minors are presumptively not competent to make their own health care decisions and therefore the decision-making authority generally reverts to the parents. But parents' authority to consent to medical care on behalf of their children is generally limited to ther-

apeutic care that is in the best interests of the child. As the recent case involving the Kennedy Krieger Institute has shown, parents should not have the authority to consent to health research involving their children if the research is of no therapeutic benefit to the child; the court has a parens patriae power to negate such consent. *See* Grimes v. Kennedy Krieger Inst., Inc., 782 A.2d 807 (Md. Ct. App. 2001).

4. BERG, at 20–21.

5. Examples include the surreptitious study of syphilis in African-American men by the Tuskegee Institute and the federal government's radiation experiments that subjected hospital patients and individuals living in certain areas to radiation without their knowledge. *See generally* JAMES H. JONES, BAD BLOOD (1993); ADVISORY COMM. ON HUMAN RADIATION EXPERIMENTS REP. (1995).

6. *See* 21 U.S.C. § 355(a)–(b) (drugs); 21 U.S.C. § 360c(a) (devices).

7. *See* 21 U.S.C. § 355(i) (drugs); 21 U.S.C. § 360j(g) (devices).

8. The Food and Drug Administration's regulations specifically govern informed consent in the context of clinical trials. *See* 21 C.F.R. pt. 50, 56. There are additional comprehensive informed consent regulations governing medical research funded by federal agencies such as the National Institutes of Health, which are referred to as the "Common Rule." *See* 45 C.F.R. pt. 46.

9. See Nancy M. P. King, *The Line Between Clinical Innovation & Human Experimentation,* 32 SETON HALL L. REV. 573 (2002).

10. *See* 21 U.S.C. § 396 ("Nothing in this [Federal Food, Drug and Cosmetic] Act shall be construed to limit or interfere with the authority of a health care practitioner to prescribe or administer any legally marketed device to a patient for any condition or disease within a legitimate health care practitioner-patient relationship.").

11. *See, e.g.,* State Bd. of Registration for Healing Arts v. McDonagh, 123 S.W.3d 146 (Mo. 2003) (disciplinary action against physician for off-label use of chelation therapy); Southard v. Temple Univ. Hosp., 781 A.2d 101 (Pa. 2001) (informed consent duty does not require physician to inform patient that use of medical device was off-label); Bissett v. Renna, 710 A.2d 404 (N.H. 1998) (tort action against physician for off-label use of drug feldene).

12. A "dietary supplement" is defined by federal law as a vitamin, mineral, herb or other botanical, amino acid, dietary substance used to increase total dietary intake, or a concentrate, metabolite, constituent, extract, or combination of any of the above. 21 U.S.C. § 321(ff)(1).

13. *See* 21 U.S.C. § 342(f)(1)(A)(i)., –(f)(1)(C). As Peter Hutt has accurately pointed out, DSHEA actually subjects dietary supplements to greater regulation than food, but still significantly less regulation than drugs or food additives. *See generally* Peter Barton Hutt, *FDA Statutory Authority to Regulate the Safety of Dietary Supplements,* 31 AM. J. L. & MED. 155 (2005).

14. 21 U.S.C. § 342(f)(1)(A)(i). The statute specifically states that "the United States shall bear the burden of proof on each element to show that a dietary supplement is adulterated. The court shall decide any issue under this paragraph on a de novo basis." *Id.* at § 342(f)(1). The FDA also bears the burden of persuasion in actions to declare a food adulterated. *See* Continental Seafoods, Inc. v. Schweiker, 674 F.2d 38 (D.C. Cir. 1982).

15. 69 Fed. Reg. 6788 (Feb. 11, 2004).

16. *See* Michael Sachs, *Ephedra & the Failure of Dietary Supplement Regulation*, 54 CATH. U. L. REV. 661 (2005). Ephedra-related injuries have spawned numerous lawsuits. *See, e.g.,* In re Ephedra Products Liab. Litig., 2005 WL 2260204 (S.D.N.Y. Sept. 18, 2005). Ephedra has been banned by Major League Baseball, the National Basketball Association, and the National Football League. Gardiner Harris, *Judge's Decision Lifts Ban on Sale of Ephedra in Utah*, N.Y. TIMES, Apr. 15, 2005.

17. Nutraceutical Corp. v. Crawford, 364 F. Supp.2d 1310 (D. Utah 2005).

18. *Id.* at 1312.

19. *Id.* at 1319.

20. *Id.*

21. *Id.* at 1321.

22. Kava is a botanical extract contained in numerous supplements marketed for use in reducing stress, anxiety, insomnia, and premenstrual syndrome. The FDA has warned consumers that kava supplements may cause liver damage. *See* Consumer Advisory, Center for Food Safety & Applied Nutrition, U.S. Food & Drug. Admin., *Kava-Containing Dietary Supplements May be Associated with Severe Liver Injury*, Mar. 25, 2002. Glyburide is an ingredient used in many prescription drugs to lower blood sugar that has been marketed as a supplement to help control diabetes. *See* FDA Talk Paper, *FDA Issues Nationwide Alert for "Liqiang 4" Due to Potential Health Risk*, July 1, 2005. Comfrey is an herbal ingredient that has been shown to be toxic to the liver and potentially carcinogenic. *See* U.S. Food & Drug Admin., Center for Food Safety & Applied Nutrition, *FDA Advises Dietary Supplement Manufacturers to Remove Comfrey Products from the Market*, July 6, 2001. Aristolochic acid is a botanical ingredient that has been linked to permanent kidney damage. *See* Consumer Advisory, Center for Food Safety & Applied Nutrition, U.S. Food & Drug Admin., *FDA Warns Consumers to Discontinue Use of Botanical Products that Contain Aristolochic Acid*, Apr. 11, 2001. L-tryptophan is an amino acid associated with a U.S. outbreak in 1989 of eosinophilia-myalgia syndrome (EMS), which resulted in at least 37 deaths. The FDA has not taken statutory action under DSHEA to ban L-tryptophan, but it has warned consumers of its risk. *See* U.S. Food & Drug Admin., Center for Food Safety & Nutrition, Office of Nutritional Products, Labeling & Dietary Supplements, *Information Paper on L-tryptophan & 5-hydroxy-L-tryptophan*, Feb. 2001. St. John's wort is an herbal product marketed as a mood enhancer and depression treatment that has been identified as creating a serious drug interaction with various drugs used to treat heart disease, depression, cancers, seizures, compromised immunity, and prevent pregnancy (oral contraceptives). *See* FDA Public Health Advisory, *Risk of Drug Interactions with St. John's wort & Indinavir & Other Drugs*, Feb. 10, 2000. Tiratricol is a hormone produced by the thyroid that can cause heart attacks and strokes. *See* FDA Talk Paper, *FDA Warns Against Consuming Dietary Supplements Containing Tiratricol*, Nov. 21, 2000.

23. Recent editorials and liberal politicians have begun to call for repeal or significant modification of DSHEA. *See, e.g., Supplementary Dangers*, CHI. TRIBUNE, Jan. 26, 2005, at C18; *Change the Law, Our Position: Make Companies Prove the Safety of Food Supplements Before They are Sold*, ORLANDO SENTINEL, Apr. 18, 2005, at A14; *Ephedra Ban Lifted by*

Judge in Utah, SALT LAKE TRIB., Apr. 15, 2005 (quoting Democratic Representative Henry Waxman of California as suggesting it may be "time for Congress to revisit DSHEA and give FDA the authority it needs to protect American consumers from dangerous supplements."); Gardiner Harris, *Judge's Decision Lifts Ban on Sale of Ephedra in Utah,* N.Y. TIMES, Apr. 15, 2005 (U.S. Senator Kennedy of Massachusetts stating, "If FDA can't take a supplement as dangerous as ephedra off the market, then Congress needs to change the law to allow it to do so.").

24. *See* U.S. v. Rutherford, 442 U.S. 544 (1979) (upholding FDA determination that cancer drug Laetrile could not be sold unless established to be both safe and effective).

25. INST. OF MED., DIV. OF NEUROSCIENCE & BEHAVIORAL HEALTH, MARIJUANA & MED.: ASSESSING THE SCIENCE BASE 4, 137-92 (Janet E. Joy, et al. eds., 1999) [hereinafter IOM MARIJUANA REP.]

26. *Id.* at 203.

27. *Id.*

28. *See, e.g.,* ALASKA STAT. § 11.71.090; COLO. CONST. art. XVIII, § 14; COLO. REV. STAT. § 18-18-406.3; HAW. REV. STAT. § 329-121; ME. REV. STAT. ANN. tit. 22, § 2383-B(5); MONT. CODE ANN. §§ 50-46-101- 50-46-210; NEV. CONST. art. 4, § 38; NEV. REV. STAT. §§ 453A.010-453A.810; ORE. REV. STAT. §§ 475.300-475.346; VT. STAT. ANN., tit. 18, §§ 4472-4474d; WASH. REV. CODE §§ 69.51.010-69.51.080. The most notable localities that have decriminalized medical marijuana are Ann Arbor, Michigan, Columbia, Missouri and Detroit, Michigan. *See* Gretchen Ruethling, *Nat'l Briefing: Midwest: Michigan: Marijuana Initiative Criticized,* N.Y. TIMES, Nov. 6, 2004, at A15; Greg Jonsson, *Voter Cut Marijuana Penalties,* ST. LOUIS POST-DISPATCH, Nov. 14, 2004, at D1; Shawn D. Lewis, *Detroit Pot Law Raises Questions,* DETROIT NEWS, Aug. 5, 2004, at 2B.

29. *See* 66 Fed. Reg. 20038 (Mar. 28, 2001) (denying petition to initiate rulemaking to reschedule marijuana).

30. 125 S. Ct. 2195 (2005).

31. Plaintiff Raich suffered from an inoperable brain tumor, nausea and severe weight loss, seizures, and chronic pain. Raich v. Ashcroft, 352 F.3d 1222, 1225 (9th Cir. 2003). Plaintiff Monson was diagnosed with a degenerative spinal disease that caused chronic severe back pain and spasms. *Id.*

32. *Raich,* 125 S. Ct. at 2200.

33. *Id.* at 2199. *See also* CAL. HEALTH & SAFETY CODE ANN. § 11362.5.

34. *Raich,* 125 S. Ct. at 2200.

35. *See* Appellants' Opening Brief at 63, Raich v. Ashcroft, No. 03–15481 (9th Cir. Apr. 23, 2003). The remedy was home-grown marijuana and the various creative forms in which the plaintiffs learned to use it, including baked foods, cooking oil, massage oil, and skin balm. *Id.*

36. *Id.* at 58–60.

37. U.S. CONST. art. I, § 8, cl. 3.

38. *See* Raich v. Ashcroft, 352 F.3d 1222, 1234 (9th Cir. 2003).

39. *Raich,* 125 S. Ct. at 2215 ("Congress could have rationally concluded that the aggregate impact on the national market of all the transactions exempted from federal supervision is unquestionably substantial.").

40. 317 U.S. 111 (1942).

41. *See, e.g.,* Richard A. Epstein, *Constitutional Faith & the Commerce Clause,* 71 NOTRE DAME L. REV. 167, 173 (1996) (concluding that *Wickard* "cannot pass the 'giggle test.'"); Glenn H. Reynolds, *Is Democracy Like Sex?,* 48 VAND. L. REV. 1635, 1652 (1995) ("From James Madison's notion of a federal government whose powers are 'few and defined,' the *Wickard* case brought us to the proposition that there are few, if any, limits to congressional power."). *See also* United States v. Lopez, 514 U.S. 549, 560 (1995) (describing *Wickard* as "perhaps the most far reaching example of Commerce Clause authority over intrastate activity").

42. *Wickard,* 317 U.S. at 127–28.

43. *Raich,* 125 S. Ct. at 2208 ("We need not determine whether respondents' activities, taken in the aggregate, substantially affect interstate commerce in fact, but only whether a 'rational basis' exists for so concluding.").

44. *See id.* at 2220 (O'Connor, J., dissenting); *id.* at 2229 (Thomas, J., dissenting).

45. *Id.* at 2236 (Thomas, J., dissenting).

46. *Id.* at 2230 (Thomas, J., dissenting).

47. *Id.* at 2236 (Thomas, J., dissenting).

48. *Id.* (Thomas, J., dissenting).

49. *Id.* at 2215 ("These theories of relief were set forth in their [the plaintiffs'] complaint but were not reached by the Court of Appeals. We therefore do not address the question whether judicial relief is available to respondents on these alternative bases.").

50. I will address the harms associated with recreational use of marijuana in Chapter 8.

51. 141 U.S. 250, 251 (1891).

52. *Id.* A writ of replevin is a common law action wherein the plaintiff seeks the return of property unlawfully possessed by the defendant.

53. *Id.* at 252.

54. 497 U.S. 261 (1990).

55. Cruzan v. Harmon, 760 S.W.2d 408 (Mo. 1988).

56. Cruzan v. Dir., Missouri Dep't of Health, 497 U.S. 261, 281 (1990) ("We believe Missouri may legitimately seek to safeguard the personal element of this [medical treatment autonomy] through the imposition of heightened evidentiary requirements.").

57. *Id.* at 279 ("But for purposes of this case, we assume that the United States Constitution would grant a competent person a constitutionally protected right to refuse lifesaving hydration and nutrition.").

58. *Id.* at 279–80 ("Petitioners . . . assert that an incompetent person should possess the same right [to refuse unwanted care] as is possessed by a competent person. . . . The difficulty with petitioners' claim is that in a sense it begs the question: an incompetent person is not able to make an informed and voluntary choice to exercise a hypothetical right to refuse treatment or any other right.").

59. *Id.* at 280 ("[A]n incompetent person is not able to make an informed and voluntary choice to exercise a hypothetical right to refuse treatment or any other right. Such a 'right' must be exercised for her, if at all, by some sort of surrogate. Here, Missouri has in effect recognized that under certain circumstances a surrogate may act for the patient . . . in such a way as to cause death, but it has established a procedural safeguard to assure

that the action of the surrogate conforms as best it may to the wishes expressed by the patient while competent. The question, then is whether the United States Constitution forbids the establishment of this procedural requirement by the State. We hold that it does not.").

60. Some may argue that termination of life support is never in the best interests of an incompetent person, but this view would be antithetical to affording incompetent individuals the same degree of respect and dignity afforded to those who are competent. If competent individuals are at liberty to decide whether the continuation of life support is in their best interests, by definition incompetent individuals should have the same liberty, subject of course to whatever reasonable surrogacy requirements may be imposed by the state.

61. *Id.* at 282. The state's "unqualified interest" in preserving life was reiterated in the Court's 1997 assisted suicide decision, *Washington v. Glucksberg,* 521 U.S. 702, 728 (1997).

62. 521 U.S. 702 (1997). The Court simultaneously decided a related case, *Vacco v. Quill,* which rejected an Equal Protection Clause challenge to the New York law prohibiting PAS. 521 U.S. 793 (1997). I will not discuss *Vacco* extensively because its reasoning hinges upon the Court's conclusion that it was rational for the New York legislature to distinguish between refusing life-sustaining medical treatment and assisted suicide. Although I disagree with the *Vacco* Court's conclusion and will briefly address the basis of my disagreement, the case (unlike *Glucksberg*) did not involve a claim of substantive individual liberty, which is the subject of this book.

63. 521 U.S. at 720–21.

64. *Id.* at 711.

65. *See* WILLIAM BLACKSTONE, 4 COMMENTARIES ON THE LAWS OF ENGLAND 189–90 (William S. Hein & Co. 1992) (1769) [hereinafter BLACKSTONE'S COMMENTARIES].

66. *See* Glucksberg, 521 U.S. at 712–13.

67. *See id.* at 713–14.

68. *See id.* at 715 ("The earliest American statute explicitly to outlaw assisting suicide was enacted in New York in 1828 . . . . By the time the Fourteenth Amendment was ratified, it was a crime in most States to assist a suicide.").

69. *See, e.g.,* Bowen v. State, 6 So. 459 (Fla. 1889); Hatchett v. Commonwealth, 75 Va. 925 (1882). *See also* Nuthill v. State, 30 Tenn. 247 (1850) (accessory cannot be guilty of a greater offense than his principal). *See also* 4 BLACKSTONE'S COMMENTARIES, at 318–19.

70. *See* Neil M. Gorsuch, *The Right to Assisted Suicide & Euthanasia,* 23 HARV. J. L. & PUB. POL'Y 599, 637 (2000) (distinction between accessories before versus after the fact not abolished until 1861).

71. *Glucksberg,* 521 U.S. at 715.

72. *See* 4 BLACKSTONE'S COMMENTARIES, at 318–19 ("[B]y statute . . . if the principal be once convicted, and before attainder, (that is, before he receives judgment of death or outlawry) he is delivered by pardon, the benefit of clergy, or otherwise; or if the principal stands mute, or challenges peremptorily above the legal number of jurors, so as never to be convicted at all; in any of these cases, in which no subsequent trial can be had of the principal, the accessory may be proceeded against, as if the principal felon had been attainted; for there is no danger of future contradiction.").

73. *See, e.g.,* Smith v. State, 37 Ark. 274 (1881).

74. An illustrative early case is *McCarty v. State,* 44 Ind. 214 (1873), in which the defendant was indicted for a substantive count of assault and battery as well as a count for being an accessory before the fact. The defendant was tried first and found guilty as to the second count only—i.e., being an accessory before the fact. Before judgment was entered, however, the principal was tried and acquitted of the substantive charge of assault and battery. The defendant asserted that he could not be sentenced as an accessory because the principal had not been convicted. Indiana had adopted a revised statute that proclaimed, "Every person who shall be guilty of any crime . . . may be indicted and convicted before, or after the principal offender is indicted and convicted." The Indiana Supreme court reversed the defendant's conviction, reasoning as follows:

> Shall the statute be construed to authorize the conviction of the accessory after the acquittal of the principal? It does not, in terms . . . so provide. By its provisions, the accessory may be tried and convicted, either after the principal has been tried and convicted, or before the principal has been tried, his guilt remaining, in the mean time, undetermined. But if, at any time before the final conviction of the accessory, the principal has been tried and acquitted, there is no authority, either in the principles of the common law or under the statute quoted, for proceeding to the final conviction of the accessory.

Id. at 217.

75. *Glucksberg,* 521 U.S.

76. *See* Compassion in Dying v. Washington, 79 F.3d 790, 809 (9th Cir. 1996) (en banc) ("By 1798, six of the 13 original colonies had abolished all penalties for suicide either by statute or state constitution.").

77. A couple of early decisions by the Texas Court of Criminal Appeals explicitly embraced this rationale in the specific context of assisted suicide. *See* Sanders v. State, 112 S.W. 68, 70 (Tex. Crim. App. 1908) ("So far as our law is concerned, the suicide is innocent of any criminality. Therefore, the party who furnishes the means to the suicide is also innocent of violating the law. It may be a violation of morals and ethics and reprehensible that a party may furnish poison or pistols or guns or any other agency for the purpose of the suicide to take his own life, yet our law has not seen proper to punish such persons or such acts."); *accord* Grace v. State, 69 S.W. 529 (1902).

78. *Glucksberg,* 521 U.S. at 732–33.

79. *See, e.g.,* People v. Kevorkian, 639 N.W.2d 291, 442 (Mich. Ct. App. 2001) ("Simply put, consent and euthanasia are not recognized defenses to murder."); Gospodareck v. State, 666 So.2d 835, 842 (Ala. Crim. Ct. App. 1993) ("There is some evidence that the victim wanted to die and that he solicited [the defendant's] assistance in accomplishing this; however, as the appellant concedes, consent is not a defense to murder."); Martin v. Commonwealth, 37 S.E.2d 43, 47 (Va. 1946) ("Invitation and consent to the perpetration of a crime do not constitute defenses, adequate excuses, or provocations. If the doing of an act is a crime regardless of the consent of anyone, consent is obviously no excuse. It follows, therefore, that the consent of the deceased is not a defense in a prosecution for homicide. The right to life and to personal security is not only sacred in the estimation of the common law, but it is inalienable.").

80. See 65 Am. Jur. 2d Rape § 38; 6 Am. Jur. 2d Assault & Battery § 66; Judy E. Zelin, *Maintainability of Burglary Charge, Where Entry into Building is Made with Consent,* 58 A.L.R. 4th 335 (1987).

81. *See* State v. West, 57 S.W. 1071, 1074 (Mo. 1900); Cromeans v. State, 129 S.W. 1129, 1132 (Tex. Crim. App. 1910).

82. Martin v. Commonwealth, 37 S.E.2d 43, 47 (Va. 1946).

83. *See Glucksberg,* 521 U.S. at 730–32.

84. Ore. Rev. Stat. § 127.800 et seq.

85. Vacco v. Quill, 521 U.S. 793, 802 (1997).

86. Oregon Dep't of Human Services, Office of Disease Prevention & Epidemiology, Seventh Annual Rep. on Oregon's Death With Dignity Act 8 (Mar. 10, 2005).

87. *Id.* at 12. In 2004, for example, 60 lethal prescriptions were written, but only 37 patients actually used them. *Id.*

88. *Id.* at 13. "Oregonians with a baccalaureate degree or higher were 8.3 times more likely to use PAS than those without a high school diploma." *Id.*

89. 66 Fed. Reg. 56607 (Nov. 9, 2001).

90. The CSA itself does not require a "legitimate medical purpose," but a 1971 regulation promulgated by then–Attorney General John Mitchell requires it. *See* 21 C.F.R. § 1306.04; Oregon v. Ashcroft, 368 F.3d 1118, 1121–22 (9th Cir. 2004).

91. *See* Oregon v. Ashcroft, 368 F.3d 1118, 1123 (9th Cir. 2004). Attorney General Reno's determination was made as a result of a petition from several members of Congress, including then–U.S. Senator John Ashcroft, who asked the administration to declare that PAS violated the CSA. *Id.*

92. Gonzales v. Oregon, 126 S. Ct. 904, 916 (2006) ("The Attorney General has rulemaking power to fulfill his duties under the CSA. The specific respects in which he is authorized to make rules, however, instruct us that he is not authorized to make a rule declaring illegitimate a medical standard of care and treatment of patients that is specifically authorized under state law.").

93. *Id.* at 921.

94. *Id.* at 921–22.

95. *Id.* at 923.

96. *Glucksberg,* 521 U.S. at 735.

97. *Gonzales,* 126 S. Ct. at 921 ("The importance of the issue of physician-assisted suicide, which has been the subject of an 'earnest and profound debate' across the country, makes the oblique form of the claimed delegation [of authority to the Attorney General] all the more suspect.") (internal citations omitted).

98. David Brown, *Military's Role in a Flu Pandemic: Troops Might be Used to 'Effect a Quarantine,' Bush Says,* Wash. Post, Oct. 5, 2005, at A5.

99. 197 U.S. 11 (1905).

100. *Id.* at 25.

101. *Id.* at 26.

102. *Id.* at 27 ("[I]t is to be observed that the legislature of Massachusetts required the inhabitants of a city or town to be vaccinated only when . . . [it] was necessary for the public health or the public safety."); *id.* ("Upon the principle of self-defense, of para-

mount necessity, a community has a right to protect itself against an epidemic of disease which threatens the safety of its members."); *id.* at 28 ("We say necessities of the case, because it might be that an acknowledged power of a local community to protect itself against an epidemic . . . might be exercised in particular circumstances and in such an arbitrary, unreasonable manner, or might go so far beyond what was reasonably required for the safety of the public, as to authorize or compel the courts to interfere for the protection of such persons.").

103. *Id.* at 31.

CHAPTER 8. FOOD, DRUGS, AND ALCOHOL

1. Centers for Disease Control & Prevention, *Smoking-attributable Mortality & Years of Potential Life Lost—United States, 1990,* 42 MORBIDITY & MORTALITY WEEKLY REP. 645 (1993); *see also* U.S. DEP'T OF HEALTH & HUMAN SERVICES, SUBSTANCE ABUSE & MENTAL HEALTH SERVICES ADMIN., OFFICE OF APPLIED STUDIES, 2004 NAT'L SURVEY ON DRUG USE & HEALTH: NAT'L FINDINGS 3 (2005) [hereinafter NAT'L SURVEY].

2. EDWARD M. BRECHER, LICIT AND ILLICIT DRUGS: THE CONSUMERS UNION REP. ON NARCOTICS, STIMULANTS, DEPRESSANTS, INHALANTS, HALLUCINOGENS, & MARIJUANA—INCLUDING CAFFEINE, NICOTINE & ALCOHOL 211 (1972) [hereinafter CONSUMERS UNION REP.].

3. *Id.* at 212.

4. ROBERT J. MACCOUN & PETER REUTER, DRUG WAR HERESIES: LEARNING FROM OTHER VICES, TIMES, & PLACES 169–70 (2001) [hereinafter DRUG WAR HERESIES].

5. Age restrictions for tobacco products are notoriously difficult to enforce given the ubiquity of the products in virtually all retail establishments. *See id.* at 175–76.

6. *Id.* at 201–03. There is a federal law that encourages states to enact a minimum age of 18 for tobacco products by denying substance abuse block grants to noncompliant states. *See* 42 U.S.C. § 300x-26. All states now have enacted a minimum age of 18 for the purchase of tobacco products, though a few have raised it to 19. *See, e.g.,* ALA. CODE §§ 28-11-2(3), 28-11-3; ALASKA STAT. § 11.76.100; UTAH CODE ANN. § 26-42-103.

7. CONSUMERS UNION REP., at 197.

8. *Id.* at 198 (citing 2 A SYSTEM OF MEDICINE 986–87 (T. Clifford Allbutt & Humphrey Davy Rolleston eds., Macmillan 1909)).

9. *Id.* at 204–05. *See also* J.M. Peters, *Caffeine-Induced Hemorrhagic Automutilation,* 169 ARCHIVES OF INT'L PHARMACODYNAMICS 141 (1969); Margaret C. McManamy & Purcell G. Schube, *Caffeine Intoxication,* 215 NEW ENGLAND J. MED. 616 (1936).

10. CONSUMERS UNION REP., at 203.

11. 21 U.S.C. § 343(o)(1).

12. *See Saccharin & Bladder Cancer,* U.S. NEWS & WORLD REP., Feb. 4, 1980.

13. *See* Sheryl Gay Stolberg, *Panel of Experts Rebuffs Effort to Absolve Saccharin,* N.Y. TIMES, Nov. 1, 1997, at A13; Denise Grady, *Sweetener Gets Approval, a Scientist Says,* N.Y. TIMES, Dec. 19, 1998, at A10. The new criteria allowed the NTP to consider dose and other factors, whereas the old criteria required listing as a suspected carcinogen if laboratory studies revealed that the substance caused cancer in animals, regardless of

the dose. *See Saccharin Warning Disappears, But Does the Concern?*, 11 ENVTL. NUTRITION 7 (2001). Consumer groups have attacked the de-listing decision on grounds that the study relied upon by the NTP involved only 20 monkeys who received moderate doses of saccharin, and was conducted by scientists who were paid consultants to the artificial sweetener industry. *See Results of Saccharin Study Called "Worthless" by Consumer Watch-Dog Group*, FOOD & DRINK WKLY, Feb. 2, 1998.

14. *See* 61 Fed. Reg. 3118 (Jan. 30, 1996).

15. *See* Marian Burros, *Fat Substitute May Cause Disease, a Top Researcher Says*, N.Y. TIMES, June 11, 1998, at A22.

16. *Id.*

17. 68 Fed. Reg. 46364 (Aug. 5, 2003).

18. CONSUMERS UNION REP., at 249–53.

19. NAT'L INSTITUTES OF HEALTH, NAT'L INST. ON ALCOHOL ABUSE & ALCOHOLISM, *Apparent Per Capita Ethanol Consumption for the United States, 1850–2002*, updated Jan. 2005.

20. *See* Nat'l Council on Alcoholism & Drug Dependence, *Alcohol and Drug Dependence Are America's Number One Health Problem*, June 2002; DRUG WAR HERESIES, at 23.

21. Abraham Lincoln, Speech to the Ill. House of Representatives (Dec. 18, 1840), *reprinted in* THE COLUMBIA WORLD OF QUOTATIONS (1996), *available at* http://www.bartleby.com/66/23/36123.html.

22. Herman v. State, 8 Ind. 490, 503–04 (1855).

23. U.S. CONST. amend. XVIII, § 1 ("After one year from the ratification of this article the manufacture, sale, or transportation of intoxicating liquors within, the importation thereof into, or the exportation thereof from the United States and all territory subject to the jurisdiction thereof for beverage purposes is hereby prohibited.").

24. JACOB SULLUM, SAYING YES: IN DEFENSE OF DRUG USE 80 (2003) [hereinafter SULLUM].

25. *See id.* at 74–78.

26. *Id.* at 80–81.

27. The Twenty-First Amendment gave the states exclusive authority to regulate intoxicating liquor. *See* U.S. CONST. amend. XXI, § 2 ("The transportation or importation into any State, Territory, or possession of the United States for delivery or use therein of intoxicating liquors, in violation of the laws thereof, is hereby prohibited.").

28. SULLUM, at 83.

29. *See* U.S. CONST. art. V.

30. Gonzales v. Raich, 125 S. Ct. 2195, 2201 (2005). The CSA has been codified at 21 U.S.C. § 801 et seq.

31. 21 U.S.C. § 812(b).

32. *Id.* at § 812 sched. II(b)-(c).

33. *Id.* at § 811(a).

34. *Id.* at § 812(b)(2).

35. *Id.* at § 812(b)(3).

36. The CSA specifically defines (in addition to the "currently accepted medical use" requirement, which is common to Schedules II–V) Schedule IV drugs as having a "low potential for abuse relative to the drugs or other substances in Schedule III" and their abuse "may lead to limited physical dependence or psychological dependence relative to

other substances in schedule III." *Id.* at § 812(b)(4). Schedule V drugs—the least regulated of the controlled substances—are defined in the CSA as having a "low potential for abuse relative to the drugs or other substances in schedule IV" and their abuse "may lead to limited physical dependence or psychological dependence relative to the drugs or other substances in schedule IV." *Id.* at § 812(b)(5).

37. Nat'l Survey, at 12. Six million Americans (2.5% of the population) use prescription medications to achieve a recreational high. *Id.*

38. *See* Drug War Heresies, at 24.

39. U.S. Dep't of Justice, Bureau of Justice Stat., The Sourcebook of Criminal Justice Stat. 344 tbl. 4.1, 385 tbl. 4.29 (2003) [hereinafter Sourcebook].

40. *Id.* at 494 tbl. 6.19.

41. *Id.* at 519 tbl. 6.57. The percentage of federal prisoners sentenced for drug offenses was 24.9% in 1980. *Id.*

42. Jesse McKinnon, U.S. Dep't of Commerce, Econ. & Stat. Admin., U.S. Census Bureau, The Black Population: 2000 1 (2001); Sourcebook, at 538 tbl. 4.10.

43. Nat'l Survey, at 238 tbl. H.7.

44. There was a noticeable dip in illicit drug use in the early 1990s, but subsequent rises have brought it back to mid-1970s levels. *See* Drug War Heresies, at 16 fig. 2.1.

45. H.L.A. Hart, Law, Liberty & Morality 33 (1963). Specifically, Hart asserts:

> Underlying Mill's extreme fear of paternalism there is perhaps a conception of what a normal human being is like which now seems not to correspond to the facts. Mill . . . endows [the normal human being] with too much of the psychology of a middle-aged man whose desires are relatively fixed, not liable to be artificially stimulated by external influences; who knows what he wants and what gives him satisfaction or happiness; and who pursues these things when he can. . . . [H]arming others is something we may still seek to prevent by the use of the criminal law, even when the victims consent to or assist in the acts which are harmful to them.
>
> *Id.*

46. Nat'l Survey, at 7 (19 million Americans have used an illicit drug within the last 30 days).

47. *Id.* at 233 tbl. H.2.

48. *Id.* at 232 tbl. H.1.

49. *Id.* at 21.

50. Sourcebook, at 385 tbl. 4.29.

51. See Michael T. Lynskey, et al., *Escalation of Drug Use in Early-Onset Cannabis Users vs. Co-Twin Controls,* 289 J. Am. Med. Ass'n 427 (2003).

52. *Id.* at 432.

53. *Id.*

54. *Id.*

55. *Id.*

56. Nat'l Survey, at 21 (47.5% of young persons age 12–17 who smoked cigarettes were also current illicit drug users, whereas only 5.6% of non-smokers were current illicit drug users).

57. *Id.* Heavy drinkers were defined as those who had 5 or more drinks on 5 or more occasions in the past 30 days. 65.6% of heavy drinkers were also current users of illicit drugs, while only 5.0% of non-drinkers were current users of illicit drugs. *Id.*

58. Substance "abuse" is broadly defined by the American Psychiatric Association as "a pattern of substance use leading to significant impairment in functioning. One of the following must be present in a 12month period: (1) recurrent use resulting in a failure to fulfill major obligations at work, school, or home; (2) recurrent use resulting in situations which are physically hazardous (e.g., driving while intoxicated); (3) legal problems from recurrent use; or (4) continued use despite significant social or interpersonal problems caused by the substance use." DIAGNOSTIC & STAT. MANUAL OF MENTAL DISORDERS, FOURTH EDITION, DSM-IV (1994). The DSM similarly defines substance "dependence" broadly as "substance use history which includes the following: (1) substance abuse []; (2) continuation of use despite related problems; (3) intolerance (more of the drug is needed to achieve the same effect); and (4) withdrawal symptoms." *Id.*

59. See Wilson M. Compton, et al., *Prevalence of Marijuana Use Disorders in the U.S., 1991–1992 & 2001–2002,* 291 J. AM. MED. ASS'N 2114, 2116 (2004).

60. *Id.* at 2118 tbl. 2 (prevalence in 2001–02 for marijuana dependence and abuse was 4.4% in 18 to 29 year-old age group; 1.2% in 30 to 44 year-old age group; and 0.4% in 45 to 64 year-old age group). *See also* DRUG WAR HERESIES, at 342; Nadia Solowij, et al., *Cognitive Functioning of Long-Term Heavy Cannabis Users Seeking Treatment,* 287 J. AM. MED. ASS'N 1123, 1130 (2002) (reporting that only 20% of cannabis users continue through their 30s and beyond).

61. DRUG WAR HERESIES, at 355–56.

62. *See* K.I. Bolla, et al., *Dose-related Neurocognitive Effects of Marijuana Use,* 59 NEUROLOGY 1337 (2002) (tests given to heavy marijuana users who had been abstinent for 28 days indicated that heavier users had lower performance); H.G. Pope & D. Yurgelun-Todd, *Residual Cognitive Effects of Heavy Marijuana Use in College Students,* 275 J. AM. MED. ASS'N 521 (1996) (heavy users performed more poorly on tests than light users).

63. See Nadia Solowij, et al., *Cognitive Functioning of Long-Term Heavy Cannabis Users Seeking Treatment,* 287 J. AM. MED. ASS'N 1123 (2002).

64. Harrison G. Pope, *Cannabis, Cognition & Residual Confounding,* 287 J. AM. MED. ASS'N 1172, 1173 (2002).

65. *Id.* at 1173–74.

66. *Id.* at 1173.

67. See H.G. Pope, et al., *Neuropsychological Performance in Long-Term Cannabis Users,* 58 ARCHIVES GEN. PSYCHIATRY 909 (2001); Igor Grant, et al., *Long-Term Neurocognitive Consequences of Marijuana: A Meta-Analytic Study,* in NAT'L INSTITUTES OF HEALTH, NAT'L INST. ON DRUG ABUSE, WORKSHOP ON CLINICAL CONSEQUENCES OF MARIJUANA (2001), available at http://www.nida.nih.gov/MeetSum/MarijuanaIntro.html.

68. Peter Fried, et al., *Current & Former Marijuana Use: Preliminary Findings of Longitudinal Study of Effects on IQ in Young Adults,* 166 CANADIAN MED. ASS'N J. 887 (2002), available at http://www.cmaj.ca/cgi/content/full/166/8/887.

69. *Id.*

70. *Id.*

71. *Id.*

72. Consumers Union Rep., at 1.

73. *Id.* at 3; *see also* Peter McWilliams, Ain't Nobody's Business If You Do: The Absurdity of Consensual Crimes in Our Free Country 289–90 (1996) [hereinafter McWilliams].

74. Consumers Union Rep., at 3, 5; McWilliams, at 289.

75. McWilliams, at 290.

76. Consumers Union Rep., at 8–9.

77. *Id.* at 9.

78. *Id.* at 33–39 (documenting cases of successful people who were opiate addicts); *id.* at 140–52, 176–82 (detailing history and success of methadone treatment clinics). *See also* Jacob Sullum, *H: The Surprising Truth About Heroin & Addiction,* 35 Reason 32 (2003) (discussing cases of long-term moderate heroin use by successful people).

79. McWilliams, at 292; Consumers Union Rep., at 107–08.

80. Consumers Union Rep., at 1.

81. McWilliams, at 291 (quoting the *Encyclopedia Britannica* description of heroin).

82. Nat'l Survey, at 1, 12.

83. Consumers Union Rep., at 101–14.

84. *See id.* at 343–45.

85. Nat'l Survey, at 12.

86. *Id.* at 233 tbl H.2.

87. U.S. Dep't of Health & Human Services, Nat'l Institutes of Health, Nat'l Inst. on Drug Abuse, *NIDA InfoFacts: PCP, available at* http://www.nida.nih.gov/Infofax/pcp.html.

88. Nat'l Survey, at 233 tbl. H.2.

89. *Id.*

90. Consumers Union Rep., at 335, 382.

91. Native Americans challenged peyote bans on First Amendment free exercise grounds, but these claims were unfortunately rejected by a closely divided Supreme Court. *See* Employment Div. v. Smith, 494 U.S. 872 (1990). I discuss the implications of the *Smith* decision in detail in Chapter 4.

92. McWilliams, at 318. LSD was not discovered until 1938, but several hallucinogenic cousins, such as peyote, provide a similar effect and have been used for hundreds of years. Consumers Union Rep., at 337, 346.

93. Consumers Union Rep., at 349–56.

94. *Id.* at 384–85.

95. *Id.* at 267.

96. Nat'l Survey, at 233 tbl H.2.

97. *See id.* (14.2% of Americans have tried cocaine; 3.3% have tried crack; 0.8% of Americans have used cocaine in the last 30 days; 0.2% of Americans have used crack in the last 30 days).

98. Consumers Union Rep., at 269.

99. *Id.* at 270; McWilliams, at 293.

100. Consumers Union Rep., at 270; McWilliams, at 293. Coca-Cola was eventually reformulated, primarily due to pressure from the federal government after enactment of

the Pure Food and Drug Act of 1906. For a more thorough history of Coca-Cola, see E.J. KAHN, THE BIG DRINK: THE STORY OF COCA-COLA (1960).

101. CONSUMERS UNION REP., at 271.

102. NAT'L SURVEY, at 233 tbl. H.2.

103. Comprehensive Methamphetamine Control Act, P.L. 104–237, 110 Stat. 3099 (1996).

104. *See, e.g.,* S. 103, 109th Cong., 1st Sess. (2005). S. 103, known as the Combat Meth Act of 2005, was reported out by the Senate Judiciary Committee in July 2005 and subsequently incorporated into the FY 2006 Commerce/Justice Appropriations bill, which was approved by the Senate in September 2005.

Index